TALKING TO MYSELF

Other Books by Studs Terkel

WORKING: People Talk About What They Do All Day
and How They Feel About What They Do

HARD TIMES: An Oral History of the Great Depression

DIVISION STREET: AMERICA

GIANTS OF JAZZ

AMERICAN DREAMS: LOST AND FOUND

"THE GOOD WAR": An Oral History of World War Two

STUDS TERKEL

·

TALKING TO MYSELF

A Memoir of My Times

PANTHEON BOOKS

New York

Part of this book, in slightly different form and under the titles given below, first appeared in the following publications: "You Know Who I Seen?" in *The Nation;* "Frank," "The Polling Place Memory," "Glasses," "Soap Opera Memories," and "Xmas Memory" in *Chicago* magazine; "View From the 2nd Story: Two Pros on the Break-In" in *Rolling Stone* magazine; "The Ultimate Fantasy" in *Harper's.*

Grateful acknowledgment is made to Porter, Gould & Dierks (authors' agents) for permission to reprint excerpts from *The Madhouse on Madison Avenue* by George Murray. Copyright © 1965 by George Murray. Also to Harcourt Brace Jovanovich, Inc., for permission to reprint six lines from "Gone" from *The Complete Poems of Carl Sandburg* and six lines from Richard Wilbur's translation of *Tartuffe* by Molière.

Library of Congress Cataloging in Publication Data
Terkel, Louis, 1912–
Talking to Myself.
1. Terkel, Louis. 2. Broadcasters—United States—
Biography. 3. Authors, American—20th century—Biography.
I. Title.
PN1990.72.T4A37 070'.92'4 [B] 76-54308
0-394-72724-X

Remembering the hall room boys

Acknowledgments

It is my fourth time around with André Schriffrin, my editor and publisher, who is considerably more than that. So, too, with Cathy Zmuda, empress of transcribers. To Tom Engelhardt, for his perceptive comments, a low bow. To Dian Smith, who edited copy, Myriam Portnoy, who kept track, and Jeanne Morton, a salute. To my wife and my son, for their gentle, good humor, hats off. To my memory, a blessing and a curse.

I believe we are lost here in America, but I believe we shall be found. . . . I think the life we have fashioned in America, and which has fashioned us—the forms we made, the cells that grew, the honeycomb that was created—was self-destructive in nature and must be destroyed. I think these forms are dying and must die, just as I know that America and the people in it are deathless, undiscovered and immortal and must live.

—*Thomas Wolfe*

I can look back and say, "I helped put out a fire. I helped save somebody." It shows something I did on this earth.
—*Tom Gates, a fireman*

A CAVEAT

This is not quite a memoir in the literary tradition. It has little to do with chronology and even less with family. In talking to myself, words have sprung to tongue as thoughts have come to mind. As, in other circumstances, I have tried to capture the voices of others, so, in this instance, have I sought out my own. Memory has undoubtedly played tricks, especially in the recounting of early years; yet, paradoxically, these are the most keenly remembered. A tape recorder, as companion in later years, has, I hope, kept me fairly honest. Though I have undoubtedly concealed much—there is a private domain on which I'll not trespass, nor does it, I feel, matter very much to others—I have revealed, I hope, enough that may matter. For better or for worse, it is, higgledy-piggledy, an oral memoir.

CONTENTS

BOOK FOUR

BOOK FIVE

BOOK
ONE

1

The Visit

I am standing outside the door. Flat Number Five. Braemar Mansions.

It is an old high-gated stone building in Cornwall Gardens. A quiet Edwardian neighborhood in London. The green grass grows all around. Ivy Compton-Burnett lives here. It is late in October 1962.

The titmouse of a housekeeper lets me in. She whispers. Aside from the glow of the fireplace, there is no light. It is dusk. I am in some other place, some other century. Is that Jane Eyre appearing from off the wall?

Ivy Compton-Burnett insists it is time for tea, before anything else may happen. There is a magnificent plum cake. Also biscuits, bread and butter, preserves, and ginger cake. She insists that I am a growing boy and must not deprive myself. "It is better than whiskey, don't you think so?" I laugh. She insists. "Don't you think so?" Yes, yes, yes, of course.

Her nimbleness is mouselike. Here, there, elsewhere. She seats me in an armchair facing the fireplace. Her eyes, quick and darting, don't miss a bet. She is a natural observer. It is easy to understand why her novels seem so unique. "There is no need to describe people. They do it themselves. Don't you think so?" I'm plugging the extension cord of my Uher into the wall. "Don't you think so?" Yes, yes, yes, of course.

"What is that machine?"

I tell her. She asks how much it costs. I tell her. She asks about the cost of living "in the States." I try to tell her. She asks about "the servant problem." I don't know much about it, I tell her.

"Why not?"

Hers is not an accusatory tone. It never is. She simply wants to know.

Her curiosity encompasses more than life. It's something else she seeks. "I think actual life supplies characters much less than art. Life is too flat for that. You must make a clever person cleverer, a stupid person more stupid, and an amusing person more amusing. You must meet them keyed up. In unforeseen encounters. Life is merely the mounting block. Don't you think so?"

She looks directly at me in the manner of a small, obstinately curious child. How old is Ivy Compton-Burnett? Seventy-five? Seven?

"A book should do that, don't you think so?"

"I get a kick out of the way you ask these questions."

"Answer it. Don't you think so?"

"Yes, of course." And how.

In *The Mighty and Their Fall* the girl says to her grandmother, "You have no high opinion of people." The grandmother replies, "Why should I have? What are the examples before me?" Is that Ivy Compton-Burnett herself speaking?

"We might all say that, mightn't we?"

"Uh huh."

"I think people are mixed. Don't you think they are?"

I am casting a quick glance at the revolving spool. There have been times when the tape recorder has doublecrossed me. It bears watching.

"Don't you think they're mixed?"

"Yes."

"I don't know how many people stand the test or resist a real temptation. We've had so few on the whole, haven't we?"

That damn machine. It's working all right, but it seems a bit sluggish.

"Haven't we?"

"Yes."

"People who lead ordinary sorts of lives."

"You, Miss Compton-Burnett—you always put them to a real test. And the outcome isn't always pretty."

"We're all sinners up to a point, don't you think so?"

"You tellin' me."

"I'm asking you."

"Sure." I laugh.

"Both people must talk a little, mustn't they?" Do I detect a twinkle?

"You never pass judgment, do you?"

"No. Some people say I'm amoral. In one of my books, I made a nasty woman do nasty things and I didn't have her punished at all. Some critics are disturbed: I don't make evil meet retribution. Why should I? It doesn't seem to meet it in life. I think crime pays on the whole, don't you?"

Imagine a banty image of Whistler's mother seated before the fireplace, in a thin, reedy voice, whispering a confidence: "I think crime pays, don't you?"

"Yes."

Softly, a coda: "Yes."

My laughter appears to encourage her. We're both taken with the glow in the fireplace.

"What do you see in there, Miss Compton-Burnett?"

"Sometimes a face comes in the fire. It will suggest something. I don't think it really does. You're disguising from yourself the effort you're making. It just gives you a little jerk."

"Unexpected things come from your people, don't they?"

"Oh, is that so?"

"I'm asking you."

"No, I don't think so. I should have thought they did things that were natural for them to do."

"Unexpected to the reader."

"That may be. That may be. They don't surprise me."

"Nothing much surprises you, does it?"

"No. No, nothing much."

"Does it ever surprise you when a character alters under your hand?"

"A little, not very much. I write in pencil and I rub it out when I want to."

"You look at your people coolly, detached, don't you?"

"Do you really think so?"

"Don't you?"

"I feel as if I am looking at them, outside me. But you must get behind their eyes, if you're to look at things as they do. We think we know what they're thinking, but we think wrong. I daresay we do."

"How do you get inside them?"

"I'm outside them."

"The observer . . ."

"Yes. At home, when I was a small child and my family did charades, I was always in the audience. I used to sit with my mother and watch. I never wanted to be on the stage."

"You never participated?"

"Never."

"You couldn't possibly act, could you?"

"I don't think I could. Don't you think people should be themselves?"

"Yes, but I myself am such a ham . . ."

"Oh, really?" As her gimlet eyes study me, I have the crazy feeling that the eyes of the world, nonjudging, are on me.

"Yes, I'm constantly play-acting. Here, with you, I begin to talk like you. When I'm with a Chicago hoodlum, I talk like him. I'm a chameleon."

"Oh, that *is* interesting."

I *knew* it. Damn it. I had come here to interview *her*. She looks into the fire.

"I think it should be so difficult to act. You might do it for a few minutes and you'll find yourself wavering. Your real self will come through."

Oh boy, that's what I'm afraid of. I'd better get on to something else.

"You, then, are never in your books?" I ask.

"I don't think I'd find myself very useful. One doesn't quite know oneself as one thinks he knows other people. Do you think one knows oneself?"

"That's a tough one."

"Perhaps one does really know oneself."

"Do you have a pretty good idea of yourself?"

"No one knows how he'll respond to an unforeseen condition."

"Not even you?"

"Oh, I have never been tested."

As I leave, Ivy Compton-Burnett asks if I'm sure I've had enough to eat. Yes, and a lot to chew over. Yet, why does something gnaw at me? Is life no more than a mounting block for art? Is it really all that flat?

Shanta Gandhi saw it in a somewhat different light.

It is after a performance of William Saroyan's *The Cave Dwellers*. Mme. Eugenie Leontovitch is directing this Chicago production. She had played queen of the tramps during its Broadway run. Barry Jones, the British actor, was king. It is the role I'm taking a whack at, with Madame once more the elegantly tattered queen. It is a delightful and exhilarating experience.

The diminutive Leontovitch, whom years ago I loved as Grushinskaya, the dancer, in *Grand Hotel* by Vicki Baum, is astonishingly young. Though her face, a cameo, reveals all her wrinkles ("credentials of humanity," Shaw called them, on seeing Duse), her body is a girl's. At one point, I carry her across the stage; she is the lovely Gru, and I, for Christ's sake, feel like the romantic jewel thief of a baron. Imagine that! (Is Ivy Compton-Burnett right, after all? About life being flat; no more than a mounting block for art.) What was the year of this fantasy? Nineteen sixty.

Shanta Gandhi enters the dressing room. She is an Indian actress-dancer. A mutual friend had told her to look me up during her visit to Chicago. My Dickensian costume laid aside, I am dressed as my usual square self. It is a quiet, casual conversation. At first. Her reflections on the Bengal famine change all that.

What is the Bengal famine—or any famine—to us? A newsreel; a piece of footage on the six o'clock news; a Sunday magazine piece; a cluck of the tongue; an occasional mite of a contribution . . .

Shanta Gandhi had been a member of a traveling troupe of actors, dancers, and singers. During this harshest of times, they were devoting their energy and talents to raise money for the starving. Up to that moment, we had been discussing, after a fashion, art. She shifted the conversation to the province of life.

"In one village, we had an experience that I'll never, never forget. It used to be our practice that after the show we would come out and just appeal for whatever people could give.

"On one such day, in a very small village it was, after the show, when we came out of the auditorium, we found a tremendous commotion. An old woman, she must have been fifty-five or sixty, was bent, and she was dragging a cow into the auditorium. Before I could

recover out of my surprise, there she came and said, 'Take this.'
What could I say?

"I said, 'Well . . .' That's about all I could say. All the speech,
all the fine words—gone, forgotten. It was the old woman who said,
'My child, I have nothing else to give. Take this cow. It still gives
milk, you know. And as you say, the children are without milk.
Please take this cow. I'm an old woman. I don't need very much
milk. I'll live. The village will see that I don't quite starve. Take this
cow with you.'

"She insisted on giving the cow to us. What could we say? We
didn't want to depart the old woman from her cow. More than
that, it would have been very difficult indeed to take the cow to
Bengal. Luckily, I hit on an idea. I said to her, 'Grandma, please
look after the cow for us till we are able to make some arrangement
to take this cow to Bengal. It *is* our cow, we know. But you are here
and who can look after the cow better than you?' That alone persuaded the old woman to keep the cow.

"That was the India of that time. We wanted to show, as artists,
the tragedy and the slender hope." Shanta Gandhi pauses. A sigh.
"Would you like more coffee?" I say. What could I say? She continues, "I'm afraid that art is very, very pale compared to real life
sometimes. Very pale indeed."

Conversation in a dressing room. No, it is at an open-all-night
restaurant. Always, on these occasions, an air of unreality pervades.
Of course, I am moved by Ms. Gandhi's account. I am detached,
too. I am listening and recording. And there is no tape recorder
around.

The Uher or Sony, spool or cassette, is constantly with me now.
Where do I leave off and the machine takes over? Would it be
different had I used a pencil or a ballpoint pen? Would this in any
way diminish my sense of being outside? I think not. It is something
beyond Ivy Compton-Burnett's detachment. I am, despite what
appears to be a passion for life, attached to a mechanical device.
Perhaps, as Jacques Ellul maintains, the machine has a life of its own.
That isn't the point. I am the point.

Do I become most alive and imaginative when I press down the
ON lever of my mute companion? I have a theory. I am a neo-
Cartesian: I tape therefore I am. I am aware of one other: Richard
Nixon. Our purposes may differ. But we are kindred spirits in this
respect.

That may explain why I have been profoundly interested in a certain autistic child: Joey The Mechanical Boy. When Bruno Bettelheim talked of the children at the University of Chicago's Orthogenic School, it was Joey who most fascinated me. True, he was a step beyond Nixon and me. He invented his wires and plugs. He imagined them into existence. They became real to him. I have since, thanks to Dr. Bettelheim, met the real Joey. He is out in our world, getting along. He, if the weather is right, has much to teach us.

I don't, for a moment, think that I'm autistic. I can't speak for Richard Nixon. It is that feeling of something beyond detachment. Being there and not there, simultaneously.

I think it has been so with me from the very beginning.

2

Dreamland

It is nighttime. I am standing outside Dreamland. I am waiting for my brother. It is a ballroom on the West Side of Chicago. Here, black jazz bands play: Lottie Hightower and her men, one night; Charlie Cooke and his friends, another. I am impatiently shuffling my feet, though I do like the sounds I hear wafting through the open windows.

It is not to be confused with the Dreamland Café. That's on the city's South Side. Joe Oliver, up from New Orleans, played there a few years ago. He has since moved to Lincoln Gardens, where Johnny Dodds, his brother Baby, and a feisty little woman of a piano player, Lil Hardin, have joined him. His young disciple, Louis Armstrong, has been outblowing Joe and has just been called out East by Fletcher Henderson. A girl who picked up my brother took him to this place a few months ago. He said it was really something.

Here at the ballroom young men and young women come to dance rather than to listen. Preferably on a dime. To sock. In short, to rub bellies together and, thus, excite one another. Always, toward the end of the night, comes the slow blues for which everybody is waiting.

> My daddy rocks me in a steady jelly roll
> My daddy rocks me and he never lets go
> I look at the clock and the clock strikes eight
> Oh, daddy, take it out before it gets too late. . . .

It is a place where young people who work all week as shoe dogs, secretaries, shipping clerks, and telephone operators—even nurses—come to dance, make dates, and, hopefully, make love. My brother, a popular shoe dog at the Boston Store, usually does very well here. He is a natural born dancer, tells funny stories, and has a way with the girls. He is seventeen.

It is 1924. I remember the year quite well. Fighting Bob La Follette ran for President. There were two other candidates, one of whom won. It made no difference which. It might have made a considerable difference had Bob won. That's why he didn't have a ghost of a chance. He did poll five million votes and that was something—he being neither a Republican nor a Democrat. Nineteen twenty-four. And where have all the flowers gone?

Oh, I shocked and grievously disappointed Miss Henrietta Boone. She was my seventh-grade teacher at McLaren. I was her favorite. I sat in the front row, not merely because I was short. "Louis," she purred (not Louis as in the Sun King; she pronounced it as in Lewis Stone, the Prisoner of Zenda), "are you for Calvin Coolidge or John W. Davis?" Innocently—or was I damnably perverse even then?—I piped, "Fightin' Bob La Follette." She was startled, poor dear. Her wig went slightly askew. I could see the terrible hurt in her eyes. Why have I always upset such gentle hearts? Why couldn't I have been my cute little button self and said the right thing: "Keep Cool with Coolidge." It didn't take much to make her day. I failed her.

In the autumn of 1960, at the reunion of the University of Chicago Law School, class of '34, a straw vote was taken. Kennedy versus Nixon. The luncheon at the Loop Club wasn't bad. The drinks were okay. A nice fat feeling of self-satisfaction all around. Those attending were lawyers who, from appearances, had done not too badly. Slight paunches and jowls closely shaven. The vote was something like: Nixon, 45; Kennedy, 41; Fighting Bob La Follette, 1. A few uncertain laughs. That was all. Several of my fellow alumni looked toward me. They smiled benignly. He's a card, that one. I smiled, too. Charlie Chaplin.

I realize Bob has been dead many years. And yet it is a vote I was too young to cast in 1924. I did tell one luncheon companion, of raised eyebrows, that Bob La Follette, dead, had more blood to him than the two young make-out artists, who were more machine than human. His eyebrows shot up even higher. He turned to another to discuss real estate. I went for another drink. The bar was closed. Oh, the Midway, the Midway, where burning Veblen loved and sang . . .

Miss Boone did forgive me. On Inaugural morning, the following March, she allowed me to listen on the school's crystal set as President Coolidge took the oath of office on the front porch of his Vermont home. It was difficult to make out what he said. Perhaps it was because I had only one earphone; the other was being used by Dorothy, another favorite of Miss Boone. Perhaps he had nothing to say.

I could easily make out what Burton K. Wheeler said. During the previous fall, the Montana senator, Fighting Bob's running mate, spoke at Ashland Auditorium. It was only two blocks from my mother's rooming house. (Two years later she sold it and leased a men's hotel near the Loop.) And one block from Dreamland. My father arose from his sickbed and took me there. He liked Bob La Follette. My mother sniffed. She liked only sure winners. Wheeler was damning the malefactors of great wealth, loud and raspy and clear.

The vigor of his voice forty-five years later astonished me. I had visited his Washington law office in 1969. I was interested in his memories of the Great Depression. The rasp was still there; and the bite. He told of a trembling little senator from Missouri, who considered resigning because "they've indicted the old man. He made me everything I am." Tom Pendergast, political boss of Kansas City, was Harry's boss too. Wheeler had talked Truman out of it. I hadn't the heart to ask whether he thought, in retrospect, he had done the right thing. Harry grew in the presidency, it is said. The impertinent question is hardly asked: Didn't we, in a generation, diminish to his size? At eighty, Wheeler was booming out indignation. As I listened, transfixed, I was back at Ashland Auditorium. And only one block away from Dreamland.

In 1912, the year I was born, the *Titanic* sank. I have never, until now, attached any significance to it. Why is it that one of man's most astounding achievements, the ship that will not sink, did in fact do just that while arrogantly ramming an iceberg? And why is it that I, who have made it a point never to drive a car, depend so much on technology, i.e., the arrogant Uher. Will I, one day, encounter my own iceberg?

The dance is over. My brother will soon be coming out. I am hanging around for two reasons. My brother, if alone, might treat me to a chocolate malted at Leggett's, and slip me one of those song sheets they pass out at Dreamland: "Yearning," "I Wonder Who's Kissing Her Now," "Louise," "All Alone." I delight as he sings them to me in his light baritone, while I'm sipping a malted through a straw. On Friday evening, he'll take me to the Palace, where the headliners, Van and Schenck, the Pennant Winning Team of Songland, will do wonders with these tunes. Nobody in the world can sing "All Alone" the way Joe Schenck does, in his high tenor, as he sits on the apron close to the audience.

As for the other reason: I am much taken with the music I hear. I had never heard such exciting sounds before. So this is jazz. I am hooked, now and forever.

I see him. He is not alone. There goes my chocolate malted. Oh well. She's a very pretty girl. Flashy. The others he'd come out with were pretty, too, each in her own fashion, but mousey. This one is quite mature, about twenty. He's probably told her he's twenty-one. He does that often, with girls he takes to one of the vacant rooms of Dixieland. (My mother's rooming house had no such name, but I've since read *Look Homeward, Angel.*) My brother's name is Ben.

I make it a point never to crab his act. He is, in fact, pleased to see me. We have an understanding. He calls on me to see that the coast is clear; that our mother is asleep; that the key to the vacant room is still on the hallway ring and not around her waist.

On several such occasions, after he and his companion had been at it, and she, suddenly guilt-possessed, is anxious to get home at once, he gently raps at my door. He's taking her home; she lives to hell and gone; you know the crazy schedule of streetcars at this hour; the bed is badly rumpled. If, in the meantime, our mother were to awaken before his return and make the rounds, as she often does, there would be hell to pay. Will I be a good kid and do the usual? I shut the pages of *The Three Musketeers* at the moment Planchet is spitting into the Seine.

The usual: hurried bare feet to the linen closet; clean sheets, clean pillowcases, a clean Turkish towel; and I'm on my way to Canaan Land. On reaching Canaan Land, it's off with the old and on with the new. The vacant room is now free from signs of sin and is ready for any paying guest, God-fearing or not.

A thought occurs to me. Had my luck been better, I might have become a first-rate pimp. Or a candidate for public office. Or even an adviser to Presidents.

Ben and his friend reach the curb. Uh oh. There are three guys on the corner. They approach. The girl appears alarmed and touches Ben's arm. One calls out to her. She doesn't move. Neither does Ben. The guy is really angry. He calls out again. She walks toward him, uncertainly, as though her high heels are giving her trouble. He slaps her hard. Her hand goes to her cheek. She whimpers. He grabs her by the arm and pulls her away. Ben moves toward them. The other two block his way. Each takes him by the arm. Ben resists as they force him toward an automobile parked nearby. Another guy sits at the wheel. I am against the wall, watching. Ben calls out to me.

I know the guy who slapped the girl. His name is Barney. He has been bragging a great deal about how tough he is. And how when it comes to women, he's Rudolph Valentino. How he buys them Pink Ladys and Pousse Cafés at the blind pig and then takes them to bed. Ben laughs at him. I know why. I have seen my brother, arm in arm, with any number of Barney's girls, on his way to Dixieland. I have seen Barney, turning around and around, bewildered and furious. And alone. On these occasions, as I lean against the wall, I always cross my fingers. I'm afraid Barney may do something desperate.

Barney says he's a member of the Forty Two's; and Ben is gonna get it. Ben finds this brag and threat amusing. He tells me Barney is just a loud-mouthed fake. Ben laughs; the Forty Two's aren't that desperate; they haven't scraped the bottom of the barrel yet.

The Forty Two's are junior members of the Syndicate. It's a farm club. What the Toledo Mud Hens are to the New York Giants. They graduate, if they prove their worth, into the big league. I have no actuarial table at hand, but I've a hunch Forty Two alumni seldom reach the Biblical age of three score and ten. Ben may not have been scared a moment ago, but he is now. So am I.

Two of my classmates at McLaren, Jimmy One and Jimmy Two, talk of one day achieving recognition in this society. They dream of the Forty Two's as North Shore matrons dream of the

Social Register. An older brother of one and a young uncle of the other, Forty Two alumni, are in the employ of Al Capone, one of our city's most highly regarded citizens. The uncle, a few years later, was seen floating down the drainage canal. And no water wings. It was a strange place for him to have gone swimming. The waters were polluted even then.

My companions chatter incessantly. They confide in me all their Horatio Alger dreams: hard and faithful work, with its concomitant, the rise to the top. Virtue rewarded.

I have no idea why they have chosen me as their confidant. Why not the parish priest? Perhaps it is because, during examinations, I shove my paper slightly to my right as I move in my seat slightly to my left. Jimmy One, who is seated behind me, moves slightly to his right and leans forward, brow furrowed. He is properly attentive as he glances downward. When his paper is completed, he shoves it slightly to his right, as he moves in his seat slightly to his left. Seated behind him is Jimmy Two.

Miss Henrietta Boone is delighted, though somewhat surprised, that Jimmy One and Jimmy Two do so well on these occasions. They pay so little attention during the rest of the semester. She prophesizes: "In my crystal ball, I see three boys who will be successful young Americans, of whom we'll all be proud." She is Jeane Dixon.

How have her predictions come out? Jimmy One and Jimmy Two graduate from McLaren and the Forty Two's into the greater society of the Syndicate. Jimmy One, according to *Billboard*'s latest communiqué, is doing well in the jukebox industry. Occasionally, he makes the financial page of the metropolitan daily. He is the grandfather of seven, and the father-in-law of a young nuclear physicist.

Jimmy Two was doing magnificently in the field of fire and bomb insurance. His clients were, in the main, restaurants and taverns. One day, he met with an unfortunate accident. No one quite knows what happened. What is known: Jimmy Two is lying in some Chicago alley. The newspaper photograph, slightly fuzzy, shows him quite comfortable: he is staring up at the sky, though it is doubtful whether he sees much of its blue.

And I, the third of Miss Boone's favorite boys, am doing what I've done most of my life: listening to what people tell me.

Aside from moments of perversity, which I find difficult to explain, I am agreeable to most people most of the time. I find in the silent film comedian Raymond Griffith my alter ego. As a jewel thief, he fled to Mexico with his accomplice. When she felt the need to return to the United States and become respectable, he solicitously drove her back. When his two fiancées insisted on marrying him, he agreed and drove to Salt Lake City. Of course. When people talk to me of their lives, I offer the sympathetic ear. I nod understandingly as I watch the reel of tape revolving. It's tougher with a cassette; there is nothing to watch.

There was a good deal to watch during the Kefauver investigation of organized crime. It was televised. One afternoon, especially, caught my attention. And my heart. Lou Farrell, an Omaha business-man, his hair a distinguished silver-gray, was on the stand. Senator Tobey, the righteous New Englander, was trying to give the witness a hard time. I paraphrase from memory:

"Your name is Luigi Fratto, is it not?" Not Louis, not Lou, nor, for that matter, Lewis. Luigi. What Cromwell was to the Irish, this bald Cotton Mather was to Mr. Fratto's people. A sense of decorum was maintained by the witness. "Senator, you seen too many movies. My name is Lou Farrell." It was offered with the rough grace and that proper note of impertinence of a Cassius Clay telling off inquisitors: "My name is Muhammad Ali." The witness had indeed been Louis Fratto, my McKinley High School fellow alumnus. Was I perverse as, seated before the TV set, I glowed with pride?

Pride cometh before the Fall. I was to make this discovery one balmy spring night. It was a reunion of McKinley graduates. In middle age, we gathered: politicians, lawyers, a doctor, a judge or two, a funeral director, a disk jockey. It was a West Side restaurant, rococo architected. A huge fountain in the lobby below, with water flowing from out of the generous hands of a sculpted Roman goddess. Angels in stone, smiling beatifically at all the patrons from walls and ceiling. And here, amidst all this salubriousness, I experienced mortification.

As tribute was paid to teachers of the past, to honored alumni, among them Walt Disney, I was called upon. It wasn't too long after Mr. Farrell's television appearance. There was a good round of applause. I spoke of those more traditional schools, far less color-ful, who boast of bankers, generals, senators, film stars, philanthro-pists among their alumni. They are as nothing, I proclaimed. We of McKinley High have produced stars of the highest rated show in the history of TV—the Kefauver Quiz. Where I had expected appreci-ative laughter, there was a dead silence.

The toastmaster, a judge well respected by Mayor Daley,

whispered hoarsely, "For shame, Studs, for shame." From the tables, I saw only smoke rings from Upmann Fancy Tales, being thoughtfully puffed. Oh God, how I tried to recover, to win back the affection of my fellows. I talked of old glories, of our baseball teams that lost 15 to 2, of basketball teams that lost 95 to 23. (Ironically, when the school turned black, it won the city championship.) I told fast and funny stories of the olden days: of Old Powles, a nineteenth-century remainder, of Mr. Brimblecom, of scaggly gray beard and mean, nasty, nasal putdowns of "Mediterraneans," and of Mr. Potter, who favored his prize students with subscriptions to the *Dearborn Independent*, Henry Ford's anti-Semitic journal. My words tumbled out, one on top of the other.

I heard one person laugh. It was more of a nervous giggle. As I sat down, two guests clapped their hands in a slow, measured beat. About three claps. At the table, a companion murmured softly, "Kid, you went over like a lead balloon." And yet, in retrospect, it was no ethnic slur at all. I was right in expressing pride.

Consider this. Who have been more patriotic, more devoted to the service of our country in a pinch than those most often condemned by the righteous? Whom did the CIA call upon when, it was felt, our national security was endangered? When harsh measures were demanded, such as the doing in of Fidel Castro, it wasn't your Boston Brahmin or Texas cowboy whose services were requested. It was Momo Giancana, one of the jewels in our city's crown. That he failed was no fault of his disciplined upbringing. And whom does Mayor Daley most often call upon for political support on our city's West Side? Aldermen and ward committeemen, of all ethnic groups, who are faithful mourners at the funerals of some of my more distinguished fellow alumni. And who can ever forget the moving plea of Al Capone, dying in Alcatraz: "Set me free and I'll help you fight the Bolsheviks?" Ask not what your country can do for you, but what you can do for your country.

A profound sense of loyalty extends to friends as well as to country. When one is in trouble, whether with officialdom (something quite easily resolved: cash in hand, preferably brand-new bills, turneth away such wrath) or with matters of the heart (being cuckolded), he can depend on a small circle of friends.

So is it with Barney, outside Dreamland, on this night in 1924. As Ben calls out, "Kid!" I move toward him uncertainly. The back door of the automobile is open. The two strangers appear to be urging him in. "Hiya, Ben," I say, for want of anything better. "How ya doin'?" The others see me for the first time. I have a natural tendency to blend into any background.

"Who're you?" The big one is slightly puzzled.

"I'm his brother."

"Beat it."

"He's s'posed to be buyin' me a malted."

"He ain't buyin' ya nothin'."

"It's Friday night," I say apropos of nothing. I'm trembling.

"Yeah," says Ben. His voice is shaking. "A chocolate malted at Leggett's. It's the best in town, fellas."

The driver leans back against the seat. He sighs. "Are we goin' or not?"

"Let's take him too," says the short one.

"Are you nuts?" counters the big one.

"Aw, Christ," moans the chauffeur. "Make up your mind."

"Where's Barney?"

"He's gone off with his pig."

They look at one another. What's to be done? Should I suggest we all go for a malted? Always, I've been in favor of peaceful solutions.

"My mother is sick," I blurt out.

"Too bad," says the big one.

"She's callin' for Ben. That's why I came to get him."

The big one turns to my brother. "Is that your name?" Ben nods quickly. About five times.

"Okay, *Ben.* Get the fuck out of here. If we ever catch you foolin' around with our women, you're gonna wind up in the drainage canal. All wrapped in cement. Y'unnderstan'?"

Ben understands.

"Yer lucky you got a little brother."

Ben nods.

"An' yer lucky yer mother's sick."

Ben nods.

The big one reaches toward his inside pocket, smiles, and says, "Run!" Ben and I take off. We hear laughter as we run and run and run, without once looking back.

Exhausted, we lean against a fence gate. Ben touches my cheek. He pats me on the head. We walk. I reach for his hand. It is cold

and sweaty. Mine is too. It is the final scene from *The Bicycle Thief.*
He is the humiliated father and I am the small boy, Bruno
Ricci.

Rome, 1962. Vittorio De Sica is seated in his office. His classic
face betrays weariness. I observe we're within hailing distance of the
balcony from which Il Duce addressed multitudes. He smiles. He
quotes Baudelaire on Napoleon: A dictator is not as dangerous alive
as when he lives on after death. "You had your sorry period, Mc-
Carthyism. We had a bad one after the war." Closet Fascists gave
him a hard time. They were high in circles of government.

Once a matinee idol, he still acts in films, too many of which are
bad ones. Reason: he must raise much of his own money to finance
the ones he directs. It is better now, but in the beginning the government was intransigent. They abhorred his chosen themes.

Shoe Shine: homeless boys, rootless, roaming streets. *The Bicycle
Thief*: unemployment. *The Roof*: housing. *Umberto D*: indigent
old age. *Miracle in Milan*: a fable of the poor.

"I've lost all my money on these films. They are not commercial.
But I'm glad to lose it this way. To have for a souvenir of my life
pictures like *Umberto D* and *The Bicycle Thief*."

The Bicycle Thief is one of my all-time favorites, I tell him. It has
affected my life in ways I cannot quite explain. He tells how he
chose a simple workingman, a non-actor, as the father. How he
began filming without having cast the boy. He had auditioned scores.
He was looking for a kid with "human" eyes and a strange, funny
little face. As the shooting begins, a crowd gathers. "I see a boy
near me. A miracle. 'Why are you here?' I say to him. 'I'm watchin','
he says. 'What is your name?' 'Enzo Staiola.' 'How old are you?'
'Five.' 'Would you like to make a picture with me?' 'Yes.' 'Enter.
Go.'" De Sica laughs.

"Bruno Ricci," I mumble. "That kid was marvelous." De Sica looks
at me. His face softens. "You remember the name?" "Sure." "I am
so grateful. It is very emotional to me that an American can remember the name of a little boy like Bruno." "Mr. De Sica," I say, "I saw
the movie twelve times, for God's sake." And for mine, too.

As a farewell token, he offers a poem by the Neapolitan Salvatore di Giacomo. He shuts his eyes and recites. It is a letter to lost

youth and lost love. I don't understand a word. Why then do I weep?

Ben and I stumble toward Dixieland. The vacant room is not occupied that night; nor for many nights to follow. At least, not by Ben.

It is a Chicago happening. An unforeseen encounter. It may not be the kind Ivy Compton-Burnett had in mind, but it will have to do till the real thing comes along.

3

Do You Like Bruegel?

Again, Flat Number Five.

Though far from Miss Compton-Burnett's world, it is the same city. Though of another time, it is the same Christmas week. It is not Jane Eyre, gentle and wraithlike, who appears to appear. It is the shade of Mr. Micawber pointing the way. Sellworthy House on Great Titchfield Street. An important-sounding address. Something will undoubtedly turn up, my boy.

I clamber the broken wooden stairs. Intimations of dank, dark hallways. Gaunt shadows. Is this place a vestigial remainder of Dickens's day? Breathing laboriously, I knock at the door of Flat Number Five. I had always thought of three and seven as mystic numbers. The Ancient Mariner stoppeth one of three. Muddy Waters's hootchie-cootchie man was the seventh son, born on the seventh hour of the seventh day of the seventh month. Why is it five for me?

There are muffled shouts and screams of small children, a howling army. There is a banging about of furniture; sounds of a wild chase; cries and laughter. The door opens. Molly Valakis is larger than life.

Denis Mitchell had told me of the Irish Cockney waitress, who works in Soho at the Mandrake, where Dylan Thomas had, in times gone by, sung for his supper. She is married to a small-time Greek gambler. Mitchell, the most lyric of documentary filmmakers, told me not to expect plum cake.

*   *   *

Though it is several years since I've seen the film *Five Easy Pieces*, my indignation is lasting. Remember that scene, oh God, in which the waitress is the virago? She refuses to serve Jack Nicholson and his companions toast or something. "It's not on the menu," the cold bitch says. Talk about a cheap shot. Nicholson, righteous, humiliates the waitress. The audience, our eighteen-to-thirty market, applauds and cheers. The young shits.

What were we told of this nasty woman? Was it afternoon? Was it near the end of a long day for her? And how were her varicose veins? And what happened behind those swinging doors? Did she and the chef have words? And *why* was she waiting on tables? Was her old man sick? Did he run off? Was her daughter in trouble? And how many Bufferins did she just take? Perhaps she was indeed a Nogood Girlo. We'll never know. We knew more than we needed to know about Nicholson; nothing about her. Yet there she was, Medusa. Why didn't I have the guts to stand up in that darkened house and holler, "You fucking young solipsists!"?

The army turns out to be four, ages three to eleven. Their hospitality overwhelms as they scurry underfoot, onto your chair, shoulder, lap. And how did Nora get up on that mantelpiece? Flushed, rosy-cheeked, and excited, she's straight out of Gainsborough; though her dress is a flimsy piece of muslin. Catherine, seated on the floor, is out of some old print. The eldest in the manner of the grand seignior proffers tea and biscuits. "Put them on the plate, Stephen," his mother advises. The flat is cold, yet it isn't. There is no fireplace, yet it glows.

"It was always ' 'Allo Dylan, 'ow go things?' 'E'd smack you on the bottom. With a little whiskey in 'im, words, beautiful words would tumble out of his mouth. Some of those slummin' people, they couldn't understand. The ones who go collar attached. They wanted you to pay 'em due deference." Molly does an Upper-U accent. " 'Oh, my deah. It's absolutely mahvelous.' 'Ere we go, Dave. Now they got these luscious blondes at the tables, trickin' around."

How did she become a waitress? "I 'eaded for Soho after a few days doin' skippin's. This sleepin' out in the tube stations. Euston. Piccadilly. It was folly. I'd freeze up after three days. I slept in the morgue."

It's her East End childhood she best remembers. "We were a vital people. Even today, I pass on to my kids these old songs and stories, all the old tragedies. My mother was a great storyteller. She'd sit in the kitchen with the old women in shawls. There were songs even at wakes. Sure, you'd cry, but if the person 'ad a full life, you'd 'ave a song, a drink or two. Even a laugh. I remember this marvelous laugh of Mrs. Gladwin. Her belly used to go up and down. It fascinated me.

"You'd give the kids good packin'. Plenty of stews, herrings. A lot of value. My mother'd buy about sixty herrings on a Sunday mornin'. She'd feed the lot, neighbors' kids, too. She'd never turn anybody away. Now they teach you you've got to be slim, everybody a beauty queen. Ooohh! Ooohh! La de da.

"My father was a sailor. 'E could knit a jumper in one piece. 'E could make a rug. 'E could make a pudding. 'E could change a baby's napkin. 'E was a man. Forty grandchildren and 'e adopted three kids. Now you've got tailors' dummies. They couldn't wash a shirt."

Old Nielsen was forever seated in the lobby of my mother's hotel. Always in that worn black leather armchair. He was a retired Norwegian seaman. He could do just about anything. Often he was knitting, purl one, knit one, a sweater or a blanket or anything. Something for his daughter in South Dakota. One time, Hanson, the Swede, who always put his foot into it, said something about "old lady Nielsen." He was a big guy, with a nervous laugh. Nobody liked him, for reasons nobody could quite explain. Further, as our lobby Sumner let us in on folkways, there had always been some deep, dark ancestral grudge between the Norwegians and the Swedes.

Joe Cline, the carpenter, slapped his cards down hard on the table. And he'd just about played out the deck in solitaire. "He's more of a man than you'll ever be, you blowhard." The Swede was stumbling all over himself, apologizing. That was his trouble. He couldn't help getting people mad. Especially in card games. I was always afraid something terrible might happen. Years later, in reading Stephen Crane's "The Blue Hotel," I recognized the Swede. Did Crane happen to run into Hanson's father?

Nothing terrible happened to Hanson, other than a crying jag one Saturday afternoon. He had had a few. What was the trouble? I asked him.

"My father died."

There were soft, fumbled, solicitous murmurs and silence. My mother, passing by, reached in under the rolltop desk and withdrew a pint. She uncorked it, set it down by the Swede and patted his shoulder.

"When did it happen?" I asked.

"Thirty years ago," he blubbered.

My mother, without missing a beat, corked the bottle and replaced it in the rolltop desk.

"People forget these things," Molly says. "I see people clearly now, honestly. I stand off and look at 'em. It don't take you too long to judge 'em. It's a covetous world. All this keepin' up with the Joneses. *Ooo* are the Joneses? Where do they live? I think they should keep up with Valakises. It would do 'em a lot of good.

"They never think in terms of another person. They never think they hurt this person. I'm easily hurt by remarks. The smart alecks look down on you. I've got a feelin' for these simple people who just don't hit the nail on the head. They can say it in their own way, but these people don't give 'em a chance. Unless you've got this smart yackety-yack, this rapid talk. I can talk, they call me Rapid Molly. But these others, who are always put down . . ."

Frank may never have hit the nail on the head. Nor was he ever much for repartee. His jokes always went wrong. Frequently he was put down. Still, he transcended all his "betters."

He was an engineer at WFMT. He was the one I saw each day behind the glass window of the control room, fooling around with all sorts of dials, buttons, and reels of tape. The death certificate says he was forty-one. The hell with the death certificate. No damn piece of paper is going to tell me how old he was. He was no older than Huck Finn.

In Frank, the spirit of irrepressible delight was never crushed. Always, he was filled with wonder. It was as though each day he were newly born. Something terribly exciting was happening. While the others of us groused and mumbled darkly under our breaths about one stupid thing or another, he saw the sun. And it was warming. "Gee!" he said. He wasn't much for repartee.

At times, one or the other of us would get mad at him. "Frank, get with it, for God's sake! You're gonna get burned one of these days." He'd just stand there in that damn doorway, freckles and all, the country boy from Kalamazoo. Playing around with the ring of a million and a half keys that dangled from his belt, janitor-fashion. Or goofily mussing up his shock of red hair. "You really think so?" He'd look at you in the manner of a small boy, quizzically, with the intimation of a crooked grin. You'd furiously fumble with some of the junk piled high on your desk, hoping he'd get lost. No, he'd just stand there, talking about some crazy thing that had nothing to do with what we were talking about. An encounter on his way to work. There were always encounters on his way to work. Or going up the elevator. Or in the hallway. Something wondrous.

The funny thing is, his nonsequitorial anecdotes turned out to be exactly what we were talking about. There was no stopping him. Wearily, you'd lay your head against your hand and look at him. "You should've been there, Studs. It was really funny. This old lady was hollering at this poor guy, only she wasn't mad or anything like that. It just seemed that way, you know what I mean?"

You'd mumble inaudibly, get up and head for the studio where we had much work to do. He'd follow, his story continuing without pause. "For Chrissake, Frank, let's get the tape rolling or we'll be here all night!" "Wait," he'd say, "lemme finish. You ain't heard the best part."

My guests had arrived, but that didn't stop Frank. He included them in on his marvelous tale, italicizing it with a wink or a light jab. "Watch out for that Studs, know what I mean?" Hand cupped over mouth, a mumble, a conspiratorial whisper. The Swedish playwright or welfare mother or Hungarian scientist was befuddled. Of course. A sudden, astonished audience. Though these guests had no idea what the hell he was talking about, they were entranced as well as mystified. One thing I know: he made them feel more at home than I could in a million years. You see, there were no strangers in Frank's world. No one was alien to him. He was not only full of wonder, he was wonder*ful*.

Down below is the loading platform. The underground. Nobody is allowed to park his car there. Nobody but Frank. There are hotshots all over the place. Now and then, one of them tries to get cute and park his Jaguar or Toyota up against the building. It is very convenient. "Beat it, mister." The maintenance men and janitors, displaced Hungarians, Yugoslavs, Poles, and Appalachians, are adamant. They are impervious to bribery of any sort when it comes to this. But Frank's Volkswagen was something else. And the only thing he ever gave any of them was his presence. But that was more than enough. On days when he parked elsewhere for some reason or another, they showed their hurt. "Wassamatter, Frank? You don' like us no more?"

Take that cold, dark night somewhere in the West Side ghetto. There was a meeting of the Contract Buyers' League in the church basement. Frank and I pulled up in a truck, loaded with expensive and heavy recording equipment. There was a gathering of young men on the corner. Were they members of the Vice Lords or what? They appeared to be glaring at us. Or was it the stuff in the truck? As I ambled into the church to see the people in charge, I heard Frank casually call out, "Hey, will you guys give me a hand?"

The tough-seeming young blacks were busy. Each was carrying something into the church. Frank was telling them where to put the stuff. He and they were giggling. They appeared to be sharing some kind of secret to which nobody else was privy.

The meeting, an exhilarating one, was over. As I was talking to the chairman, I noticed some of the young men hurrying off with the equipment. They were whispering something to one another and laughing softly. As I said, it was very expensive stuff. I excused myself and shuffled after. "Hey, uh, guys . . ." It wasn't very loud. I doubt whether they heard me. But someone did. It was Frank, who had re-entered to pick up another piece.

"What's up, Studs?"

"Uh—nothin'. Nothing at all."

"Oh. I thought I heard you say something."

"No, I just . . . Forget it."

Frank's eyes widened. As though something quite remarkable had occurred to him. He looked at me with just the hint of a funny smile. I looked away.

"Hey, Studs, you didn't think . . . did ya?"

"Nah, nah, nah. You kiddin'?" I was staring hard at the design behind the altar. In other days, this Baptist church had been a synagogue. The six-cornered star was hardly visible, but even if it were, I'd have had a hard time making it out. Damn! Why doesn't that Frank go away. I heard a little light laugh behind me.

"Oh man, for a minute you had me goin', Studs. For a minute I thought you were scared the guys were rippin' us off. Jeez!" I kicked at the chair. More violently than I had intended. I bruised my shin. Damn that Frank!

Outside, Frank was shaking hands with the street guys. They were patting him on the back as the last piece of equipment was shoved into the truck. Frank mumbled something wholly unintelligible, at least to me, but the others thought it was terribly funny. They howled with delight. Frank nudged me. "You know what I mean?"

"I was born to be different," Molly laughs. "I was bounced on my bonnet when I was a kid. We were playing in an empty house and I fell out the window. I laid in the 'ospital for three years. That's why my family thought I was bonkers. Like my Aunt Mary. She was darlin', really, and very kind to us. But she liked to take a drink, now and then. They said, Aunt Mary isn't dead while you're alive. I didn't like that. I didn't mind being mad me. But it hurt me when they put down Aunt Mary.

"I won a scholarship when I was eleven. The school I went to was this collar-attached business. Very 'igh falutin'. We come from the East End and were always put down for anything missin'. Even if we weren't there, we were always accused.

"I can remember bein' stood up in front of the whole class. Everybody wore shoes, except me. I had boots on. I was in the hallway, where you say your prayers. I was Exhibit A. 'Look at her.' This was a Mother Superior. 'Wearin' boots. *Boots!*' An' everybody was laughin'."

Molly shakes off a cough. "I can remember this. I thought to myself, Well, the hell wi' you. I was shrinkin' inside me. I felt to myself, I'm not gonna let you see that you get me down, mate! I stood there as bold as brass, an' my chin up. I thought to myself, Well, that's that, mate. You can all get on wi' it. But I will *never* forget the humiliation. Honestly, I could've dropped through the floor, with all those people laughin' at me."

Roberto Acuna, the Chicano farmworker, was in a reflective mood. Schooldays, oh sure, he remembered them very well. Up and down California following the crops. "I'd go barefoot to school. The bad thing was they used to laugh at us, the Anglo kids. They would laugh because we would bring tortillas and frijoles to lunch. They would have their nice little compact lunch boxes with cold milk in their thermos and they'd laugh at us because all we had was dried tortillas . . ."*

"These kids 'ave a better chance now," says Molly. "Better world? I think so. But they 'aven't got this marvelous family life that we 'ad. There's no contact between parent an' child. An' this . . ." She sighs wearily.

"People used to steal in my days to eat. I've run after a baker's cart an' nicked a roll. But today they bang an old lady to death for a few pence. You could understand when times were bad, people stealin'. But these terrible crimes of violence for nothin' . . ."

We sit there, saying nothing. There is something I want to ask Molly, but I'm not sure what. I'm squinting, nearsightedly, at a picture on the wall. In the oncoming twilight, it is difficult to make out. Especially in a dingy flat where the sun never shines.

"You like Bruegel?" she asks me.

"Oh yeah."

"I always loved Bruegel. I always think of him—and us. My oldest sister came home one day very upset. She saw an accident. An old blind man was goin' across the road. Another blind man come along an' touched him an' they both walked into the road an' under a car. These poor men, the one thought the other 'ad eyesight. A little later, I saw a Bruegel print in school: *The Blind Leadin' the Blind*. It reminded me of this accident.

"In Bruegel, I saw *people*. You can only interpret art from yourself. You *know* these people. It's like Dickens. Take Mr. Pickwick. Or Pip's cousin Joe, the blacksmith. When I read about these people, I've *seen* them. I know they never died. Maybe they wear a different coat. The coat changes, but these people don't change. You constantly meet these people. You can imagine what they were doing on that day. There's life in them.

"You can't see any life in some of these pieces you see in the Tate Gallery. And some of these idiots say, 'It's mahvelous.' An' pay 35,000 dollars for it. Perhaps it's too intellectual for me, I don't know."

* Studs Terkel, *Working* (New York: Pantheon Books, 1974).

Time to go. Someone suggests a Christmas carol as a parting song. There is a lively debate as to the choice. A poll is conducted. It is "God Rest Ye Merry, Gentlemen." The Valakis Family Choir is an improvised one. Nora is on the mantelpiece, Catherine is in a chair. Michael is standing on another. Stephen is set, too. They take off.

> God rest ye merry, gentlemen
> Let nothing you dismay. . . .

No plum cake here, but sustaining enough.

4

The Greatest Story Ever Told

Was it the Christmas season of 1933 I remember best? I had become a blushing twenty-one that spring. It was a blessed year for other reasons. The Volstead Act had been repealed. Bootlegging was out. Pimping was in. Alphonse Capone, our city's most distinguished entrepreneur, aside from Samuel Insull, had switched from the craft of alky running to the fine and lively art of Pandarus. Al's was among the first conglomerates of the flesh. The Lexington, the Winchmere, and God knows how many cribs in Cicero had become a home away from home for the girl from Bloomington, Cedar Rapids, and Fond du Lac.

The Winchmere. To familiars, it was known as Da Winch. I had, by some odd circumstance, almost made it as a member of this hotel's celebrated staff. In the late thirties, as the streets were walked by more than streetwalkers, my diploma from the University of Chicago Law School was of some value, I'm certain. No one told me precisely what. A friend suggested easy money. For some reason, he saw in my face a gangster's light. The magazine *Official Detective* was paying ten dollars for properly un-American faces to illustrate the stories. He thought I was a natural.

The photographer liked my face, but not my hat. It was battered in the fashion of Heywood Broun's. "This is a special job. It requires a special hat. Pearl-gray fedora. A new one." At the haberdasher's I was fitted with a beauty. Five bucks. Half my fee, but that was fine. I had decided at that moment, it wasn't the money so much as the honor.

At the studio my new hat was carefully posed, high on my head, as I had so often seen my more successful fellow alumni sport theirs. I was handed a billy club. "Stand on the ladder, peek through the transom, and hold your billy high." I was so advised by this Cartier-Bresson.

I appeared in this menacing manner, though somewhat precariously, on the ladder's fifth step. (Five, again; my magic number.) On the other side of the prop door were two others. One was a blond young woman, *en déshabillé*. The other was a portly, middle-aged man. She, smiling, was urging him toward the door.

"Hold it!" said Walker Evans. "Closer to the door, darling," he told her. "Higher with the billy," he told me. "Great," he said, quite pleased with the whole thing. As he handed me the ten-dollar bill, I said, catching on quickly, "The old badger game, eh?" He smiled at me. "You are very believable."

Strolling down the street, my brand-new pearl-gray hat perched high on my head, I saw in my mind's eye Machine Gun Jack McGurn. The image did not at all displease me. Along came a high Chicago wind and blew off my hat. It sailed, high and wide, down the street. I took off after it. A huge Mack truck was barreling along. I jumped back onto the curb. I was unharmed. The hat was a pancake. Too flat for even Buster Keaton.

Months later, a passing acquaintance passingly told me I was the cover boy of *Official Detective*. More. He told me that Dennis Cooney liked my face. Cooney, one of Capone's most celebrated pimps, was a faithful reader of *Official Detective*. It seems he was much taken with that photograph. Of me, he said, "A perfect type for da Winch. He can have a job wid us any time he wants." As I said, it wasn't the money, it was the honor.

Small-town Madonnas were, by some grotesque alchemy, transmuted into big-town Magdalenes. Quicker than a trembling, pimply-faced boy could hand over a two-dollar bill. Eros was getting a bad name. Yet, on that Christmas Eve of 1933, Virtue triumphed.

At the time, the Swede from Galesburg was chanting plaintively:

> Nobody knows now where Chick Lorimer went.
> Nobody knows why she packed her trunk . . . a few old things
> And is gone,
>> Gone with her little chin
>> Thrust ahead of her. . . .
>
> Nobody knows where she's gone.*

I know. She was a guest at my mother's hotel. Herod led her up the golden staircase. He was otherwise known as Nick Stassiosous, proprietor of Victoria No. 2, the all-night beanery below. He laid five dollars across the desk and said the girl was his niece from Terre Haute. A music student, he further informed us. As I stared at "her soft hair blowing careless from under her wide hat," he took the key and shut the door behind them.

I had no idea Nick was a music teacher. Were they carols I was hearing? "The Bells of Paradise" perhaps? My Adam's apple was bobbing wildly, as though some piece of forbidden fruit was forever stuck in my throat.

And where was John the Baptist on this Holy Night? He was in the lobby, holding forth, roaring: "Woe unto them who call evil good and good evil; who put darkness for light and light for darkness; who put bitter for sweet and sweet for bitter. Isaiah 5:20." He reached a crescendo: "Prepare, all ye sinners, prepare!" This one was otherwise known as Myrd Llyndgyn, the Welsh scavenger. Not only was he penniless; he didn't have a vowel to his name. He was rich, though, in portents and warnings, shouting out hell-fire sermons, Gideon Bible held chest high (in the manner of Pete Seeger holding his banjo). There was room at our inn for everybody. Ours were the winking Gospels.

John the Baptist was forever prophesying the world's end. Yet his appearance was not that of your everyday nutty sidewalk Jeremiah. No glittering eye of the Ancient Mariner. Though they say he once did work in the galley of a Greek oceanliner and was fired for flinging a dish of moussaka at Aristotle Onassis's uncle. Such was the nature of his religious fervor. No long black coat nor long gray beard. His were the baggy pants of a burlesque comic and eyes that

---

* Carl Sandburg, "Gone," in "Chicago Poems," *The Complete Poems of Carl Sandburg* (New York: Harcourt Brace Jovanovich, 1969), p. 64.

popped as well as crossed. He was as cockeyed as Ben Turpin; and as wildly feverish as his fellow Welshman, the actor Hugh Griffith.

As fate would have it, John the Baptist was sweating his life away, a slavey, in the kitchen of Victoria No. 2. Nick Stassiosous was his boss, a singularly abusive and exploitive one.

John the Baptist and I had tasted little of life's forbidden, and thus delightful, fruits. He neither drank nor smoked nor, the other guests were certain, had ever known a woman. I had touched nothing stronger than Dr. Pepper. Within one hour, during this memorable eve (Eve?) our two lives were considerably altered.

As Herod and his niece from Terre Haute were engaged in a music lesson upstairs, the chimes from the Tribune Tower sounded "God Rest Ye Merry, Gentlemen," "Adeste Fideles," "Good King Wenceslas," and "Go Tell It on the Mountain."

The effect on the pinochle players in the lobby, though, was somewhat less than euphoric. Their thirst was unslaked. Some sonofabitch had killed the last pint. On this Holy Night, they were still cold, cold sober. Distemper was in the air. Cline, the journeyman carpenter, and Ed Duerr, the boomer fireman, were passing words. While the Prince of Peace was aborning. Some celebration. Go tell it on *whose* mountain?

Enter: Prince Arthur Quinn, holding high a fifth of Chapin & Gore. Placing the treasure carefully on the table, he proclaimed, "Merry Christmas, boys." It was indeed a proclamation. It was now official. Prince Arthur, son of the long deceased Hot Stove Jimmy Quinn, was our precinct captain. It was his annual show of appreciation. Aside from election day, when Chapin & Gore had the persuasive powers of ward committeemen. Though our guests numbered fifty, they counted for one hundred at the polling place.

Beatifically, Prince Arthur smiled my way. I was, this year, eligible to vote. Poor old Cermak was gone by way of a goofy assassin's bullet and is ever remembered for his martyred mumble to FDR, "I'm glad it was me instead of you." Though his grammar may have left something to be desired, his heart, unfortunately for him, was in the right place. Though his English teacher would have flunked him, he is immortal and she is dust. Anyway, there was still an X or two or three to be marked beside the Gaelic names of Big Ed Kelly, Dorsey Crowe, and Botchie Connors.

The smell of sour mash pervaded the lobby and all hearts were lifted, all spirits buoyed. All except one: John the Baptist. He cried

Damnation and predicted Apocalypse. "Woe unto them who are mighty to drink wine and men of strength to mingle strong drink." On occasion he was suspected of being in league with Mrs. Tooze of the WCTU.

Prince Arthur Quinn, his fedora a Kelly green and his face a beet red, inquired softly. "Who da fuck is dis nut? T'row 'im out." The others merely smiled. There were times past when they seriously discussed throwing him out the window. It was only a two-story drop. But propinquity has its way. Though in the beginning they had come to jeer, they remained, if not to pray, at least to nod and murmur a weary Amen. A soft word, they felt, in this instance, turneth away Wrath.

The bottle was passed around. Eventually it came my way. I hesitated. The men chuckled softly, nodding encouragement. All but John the Baptist. He howled. "No, boy! As the fire devoureth the stubble and the flame consumeth the chaff, so their root shall be as rottenness and their blossom shall go up as dust because they have cast away the law of the Lord God of Hosts. Isaiah 5:24." His breath control was wondrous. The words poured forth torrentially. Though I was uncertain as to their meaning, I had a hunch they boded no good.

Prince Arthur was indignant. "Dis guy's a fuckin' fanatic. I'll nail 'im to a cross." Toward me, Prince Arthur beamed. "Go ahead, kid, drink up. It'll put hair on your chest." Really, I wasn't *that* glabrous. As I studied the label on the bottle, I knew the moment of decision was at hand. John the Baptist was jabbing at the air, Gideon Bible held tight in his fist. Prince Arthur was imploring. "Will ya take a drink, fer Chrissake!" That did it. For *Christ's* sake. Never had I heard the Savior's name invoked so appropriately. On such a night as this, the God of Bliss . . .

I put the bottle to my lips. "No-o-o-o!" The wail of the slavey was stifled by the command of the precinct captain. "Shut up, you dirty Bolshevik!" I swallowed. My throat was on fire. I coughed. Spittle came. So did tears. I took a deep breath and once more I swallowed. Was my tongue blistered by the devil's brew as I passed the bottle to the next one? I had turned away from John the Baptist. Prince Arthur chortled. " 'Atta, kid. Dere goes your cherry. Stick wit' me, kid, and I'll take you to da Winch." In the eyes of John the Baptist, I saw a thousand hells.

I followed his look. At the door were the two of them: Herod and Chick Lorimer. "Artie! What da hell are ya doin' here?" The restaurateur was in an ebullient mood. The precinct captain was of equally blithe spirit now. A kindred soul at last. He whistled softly through his teeth as he observed the girl. "Hey, ya doin' aw right fer a Greek, huh? Huh?" A long drawn out "Yeah-h-h." Herod touched the girl's sleeve. "Oh, yeahhh. She's a good friend of mine." Turning to her, "What's yer name again, baby?" Chick Lorimer stared at the lobby's linoleum. Again, my Adam's apple was misbehaving. And a sense of some vague humiliation I couldn't get a fix on.

In the exuberance of the exchange, neither of them noticed John the Baptist. In his eyes I now saw a *million* hells. "Pi-i-imp." It was a howl. No, it was more a wail of the banshee, wholly at discord with the nearby chimes' "Silent Night."

"Wha-a-a-a?" Herod stared, mouth hung open.

"You pimp! You bully! You fat, no-good Babylonian! Woe unto them who call evil good and good evil." John the Baptist, it appeared, had a real fix on Isaiah.

Prince Arthur took a step away, toward Herod. "Dis guy's a real looney. Could be dangerous." Herod extended his thumb in the direction of his tormentor. "He's my goddamn porter! Da crazy limey!"

"I'm *Welsh*, you fool! I attended chapel, you ignorant Macedonian! Do you know the Deuteronomy? No! Do you know the Prophets? No! You don't even know Genesis!" He thumped at the Book. "No! You know nothing! Pimp! Pimp! Pimp!"

Herod, recovering his composure, held forth his pinky, the diamond of its ring shimmering in the light. "Yer fired! Did ya hear what I said? Fired! Come in my restaurant, I'll t'row you out on yer ass! Yer t'rough!" "And you're damned!" howled the slavey.

It happened so suddenly. The Gideon Bible was hurled across the lobby. It struck Nick Stassiosous just below his right eye. A direct hit. His hands flew to his face. "I'm blinded!" A long agonizing wail. "Da bastard blinded me!"

Chick Lorimer casually drew his hands away from his face. She hardly glanced at him. An angry red welt, with intimations of blueblack, was quickly puffing up. "You'll have a beaut of a shiner is all. You'll live."

"It ain't yer eye, ya whore! Jeez, it hurts! I need a doctor!" With a whimper, he turned and hurried down the golden staircase.

Prince Arthur Quinn was edging toward the doorway. He cast a wary glance at the lunatic. This was a serious matter. The green fedora disappeared as a faint mumble was heard. "I'm gettin' da cops. Dis guy is dangerous."

John the Baptist was transfixed. His crossed eyes were glazed. Glazed or not, cockeyed or not, he saw Chick Lorimer. He saw her stoop down and pick up the Book. She walked across the lobby and handed it to him. She grinned. "Good throw. Cubs could use you." John the Baptist was mute. She laughed lightly. Again, I had trouble with my Adam's apple.

She was straightening the collar of his torn coat, a World War I khaki hand-me-down. "Know the Book of Luke?" He nodded. "Cat got your tongue?" He shook his head. "Okay, then you can read me the story of Mary and Joseph and no room at the inn and all that, right?" He nodded. She took him by the hand and led him out of the lobby.

At the doorway, she turned toward me. "Sonny! Sonny!" Christ Almighty, she was no more than twenty herself. Sonny! Damn! Damn! Damn! Damn! "The Greek ran off with the key. You got a skeleton, aintcha?" I nodded. A lot of good that nod did *me*.

John the Baptist was at the window of her room, feverishly leafing through the Book. Muttering to himself, "Woe is me, for I am undone, because I am a man of unclean lips; for mine eyes have seen the King, the Lord of Hosts." He didn't seem *too* unhappy about it.

At the door, she asked softly, "How far to Cicero?" I told her. The door clicked shut.

In the lobby, I joined the others. There were still several ounces of Chapin & Gore left in the bottle. This time, it went down easier. While the journey to Bethlehem was being recounted upstairs, the Tribune Tower chimes were sounding, "Hark! The Herald Angels Sing!"

5

I Ring the Bell

A lazy afternoon, June 1975. I pass by the Wells Grand. What the hell, let's give it a whirl. The entrance to the hotel is locked. I pull at the glass door that, once upon a time, opened to the touch. Twenty-four hours a day. We Never Close. Now it is hard and fast. I put my index finger to the bell. I count to twenty. There is an answering buzz.

I ascend the staircase. Has it always been *this* narrow? The banister feels to the gliding touch as it once did. A long golden cylinder, it has, in its time, guided upward the lame, the halt, and the blind; as well as the able-bodied, after a hard payday's night.

At the top of the stairs is Bud. He clerks a few hours a day, just to keep a hand in. At seventy-three, Bud has the look of a feather-weight, long gone. Johnny Kilbane. "I seen him fight once," he says. I'll be damned. He assumes a fighting stance. "Johnny Coulon. Remember Coulon's Gym?" I'll be damned.

I explained that long, long ago I lived here. My mother ran the works. "How long ago?" he asks. His lenses are misty. "Nineteen twenty-five," I tell him. "We had the place twelve years." "I'll be damned," he says.

He invites me into the lobby. I stand there. "Sit down," he says. I look about for a torn black leather armchair. All the chairs are straight-backed. I sit in one. My God, the lobby is no bigger than a single room at the Holiday Inn. *My* lobby. Where multitudes had gathered, laughed, argued, drank, swore, made speeches, and, on occasion, swung out wildly. How could so much have happened in so circumscribed an arena? *Something* was big. What?

On the table in the middle of the room are year-old issues of *Time*, a scuffed *U.S. News & World Report*, a rent *Playboy*, and yesterday's *Tribune*. Where's the deck of cards? In the desk of the office, Bud says. A teller's cage. Is the window bulletproof? I wonder. The cribbage board? The what? Bud asks.

The guests are old-timers; on welfare, a good many of them, though several pensioners are about. "It looks well-kept, Bud." "Oh yeah," he says. "The owners are old neighborhood people, easy." "Are the rooms as clean as the lobby?"

Bud, the ring of keys in his hand, opens the door to Room Five. The one adjacent to the lobby. The occupant has gone for a medical checkup. Damn, it's much smaller than I had remembered it. Five was one of our favored showrooms. Harry Michaelson . . .

The two Harrys, Michaelson the tool and die maker and Gossweiler the baker, were feeling no pain at all that Thanksgiving afternoon in 1926. The lobby radio was on, but no one was listening to the Army-Navy game. The Pilgrim Fathers had never been so effusively toasted. Michaelson, Room Five, invited Gossweiler, Room Fourteen, into his quarters for another. Loud laughter was heard. Suddenly, the sound of something banged against the wall. A chair. A scuffle. A body hitting the floor. Loud curses. My brother Ben grabbed the skeleton and ran toward Five. I followed.

The tool and die maker had the baker in a headlock and was slapping at his face. The baker was pounding away at the tool and die maker's solar plexus. An illegal blow. Ben grabbed one. I grabbed the other. "Lemme at him," said one. "I'll kill 'im," said the other. Ben urged, pulled, hauled, shoved the baker past the lobby and across the hallway toward Fourteen. I advised the tool and die maker to enjoy his Thanksgiving holiday and quickly shut the door behind him.

A naval cadet named Hamilton kicked his third point after touchdown and the game wound up in a 21-21 tie. Nobody was listening. Ben and I looked up from the cards. Harry Michaelson had stumbled past the lobby and across the hallway toward Fourteen. Ben and I raced in pursuit.

Too late. The door of Fourteen was open. The two hostile Harrys were face to face. "How ya, Harry, ol' buddy," Gossweiler said. "Never better, pal," Michaelson replied. "How about a drink?" said the baker. "You twisted my arm," said the tool and die maker. The door closed. The spirit of Thanksgiving pervaded.

Bud remembers some of the old neighborhood people as well as a few long gone guests. Joe the Barber? He's dead. Doc Mooney? He's dead, all 350 pounds of him. Artie Quinn? Ah, Prince Arthur. Oh yeah, he's dead and gone.

Does he remember Civilization? Bud is bewildered. The crazy Serb. The one we said would live forever. We knew him only as Civilization. The one with all those books? Bud doesn't remember. No, the name doesn't ring a bell.

It does to me.

6

The Dream-possessed

Like a true apothecary slipping Romeo the potion, Civilization passes me the two-inch piece of zinc. We are newly arrived at the hotel. It is 1926 and I am a small fourteen. "Put in shoe of left foot, wear two weeks," advises the shaman. It is more than a talisman. It is, he assures me, a cure for shortness.

I dream of growing as tall as Thomas Meighan, the Admirable Crichton of silent films. Or Wendell Hall, the redheaded music maker, who let us know "It Ain't Gonna Rain No More." Or Daddy Browning, who, with the estimable help of Peaches and tabloids, let us know everything. Or, at least, as tall as one of Florenz Ziegfeld's show girls. Never mind the Little Corporal or Shorty Fernekes or Billy Rose. I want height.

Billy Rose was on the phone. "You're coming to New York tomorrow," he informed me. I must admit it did come as something of a surprise, never having met Mr. Rose.

"I am?"

"Yes. An MCA man is picking you up at the airport."

"An MCA man?"

"Yes." Billy Rose sounded a trifle impatient. "Music Corporation of America. The agents."

"Oh, sure."

"You'll be at my office around noon."

Years later, in meeting W. Clement Stone, I came to better understand PMA. Positive Mental Attitude.

Who was I to withstand such certainty? "See you tomorow," said Billy Rose. "Okay," I said, five seconds after he had hung up. Nor did I have any objections, since I wasn't doing much at the moment. It was 1952. The blacklist was picking up a full head of steam.

Billy Rose, it appeared, had seen several episodes of a television program, "Studs' Place." It was the idea of Charlie Andrews, Dave Garroway's writer. In the manner of two other Chicago telecasts, "Garroway at Large" and "Kukla, Fran, and Ollie," it had a casual, seemingly spontaneous air. John Crosby, in the *New York Herald Tribune*, called it TV, Chicago Style. Rose, I gathered, shared his enthusiasm.

Simply described: Studs' Place was a neighborhood restaurant, an arena in which dreams and realities of "ordinary people" were acted out. Four of us, Beverly Younger, Win Stracke, Chet Roble, and I— playing pretty much ourselves—called upon our memories, experiences, and felt lives. It was a strange program that paradoxically was familiar to the audience; so familiar that a great many believed there was such a place. It was, of course, El Dorado.

The response was astonishing. From every stratum of society came fervent pieces of mail: a scrawled note in pencil on lined paper; a dowager's embossed stationery; a contemplative letter from a professor in the humanities; an equally contemplative one from a truck-driver. NBC made a logical decision. It dropped the program.

Though the move was bewildering to viewers, I understood. Of course. I knew that my misbehavior in the thirties and forties had been duly noted by the FBI, the Chicago Industrial Squad, and the American Legion.

Ed Clamage, a Chicago florist, proclaimed himself head man of the Americanism Committee of the American Legion. Always, he posed with a cute little Legion cap high on his head. It gave him the appearance of a fat, cuddly baby. Ed was considerably overweight. Always, he was hunting down subversives among us. His one moment of national renown came when he pointed out the dark side of the Girl Scouts of America. They had been selling cookies on behalf of UNICEF. Ed kept himself pretty busy in these matters. He wrote more letters than Henry James or Anton Chekhov. Where he found the time to sell flowers shall remain forever a mystery to me.

The early fifties were his years of glory. His interest was not in blue-collar troublemakers or teachers or social workers. No, no, none a that. Ed was fascinated by Show Biz. Actors who had appeared on any of Ko-Ko's little lists were his pigeons. He was stage-struck. Performers of touring Broadway plays were thus honored with letters on the stationery of the American Legion. But I, being his fellow townsman, was his favorite. He was my Javert.

Though Chicago journalists found Ed funny, not so local radio and television sponsors. They regarded Ed with solemnity; and, more often than not, took his advice. And, more often than not, I was fast becoming a yo-yo. Ed kept pretty good track of me. I myself lost track of the disk jockey jobs from which I was bounced. God knows, I gave Ed plenty of reason. I talked and talked and talked before gatherings of people whom Ed, I'm sure, regarded as most subversive indeed. The more Ed showered me with attention, the more I accepted invitations from all those Nogood Boyos. I couldn't help myself; the imp of the perverse had me on the hip.

My income had become nothing to write home about. On occasion, I'd pick up fifty or a C-note, lecturing on jazz or folk music. I'd bring along phonograph records. These sponsors too—in the main, women's clubs—would hear from Ed. I remember a few trembling chairwomen, a few cancellations; most were gallant and charming.

Obviously, Ed was attracted to me. I had become his obsession. It was during one of these occasions that I hit upon the idea of acknowledging his passion. I remembered a letter that John L. Lewis, as the CIO was aborning, had sent off to Bill Green, president of the American Federation of Labor:

> Green:
> I disaffiliate.
>   Lewis.

I wrote to Ed, spelling his name in lower case:

> clamage:
> The ladies to whom you have written have, in response, decided to double my fee. Instead of paying me $100, they have given me $200. How can I show my appreciation? You have $10 due as an agent's fee. Shall I send it to your favorite charity? Please advise.
>   Terkel

I wrote him several such notes. He replied to none of them. Perhaps he was too moved. Still, he should have been courteous enough to acknowledge my gesture. Ed has since gone to the Great Legion Post Across the Sky. I'll never know what he thought. Oh well.

In honoring Ed's memory, I must confess that I had lost radio sponsors long before I had come to his attention. I attribute the loss of my very first one to a man from Aurora. A men's clothing store was my sponsor in 1940. It was a fifteen-minute news commentary.

Colonel McCormick, our *sui generis* publisher, was flailing away at the New Deal. Daily. He ate all those wild-eyed professors for breakfast: in front-page color cartoons, in editorials, in the news columns of the *Chicago Tribune*. Archibald MacLeish, the Librarian of Congress, was his favored pigeon. During one of the evening broadcasts, I read a MacLeish poem and flailed away at the Colonel. I didn't know any better.

Time passes. Two days, to be precise. Word comes that my sponsor has fired me. How come? I ask the agency man. A customer, he explains to me, came in today all the way from Aurora. To complain? I ask. No is the reply; to buy 500 dollars' worth of clothes. What's wrong with that? I ask. Wait, says the agency man. This customer, silver-haired and distinguished in appearance, asks to see the proprietor. You must remember, your sponsor doesn't listen to your program. He has no idea what the hell you're saying at six o'clock. The man says to him: I don't need any new clothes. I made this purchase merely to show my appreciation. You, sir, have had the courage to challenge Colonel McCormick. I have waited all my life for this. I congratulate you, Mr. Bloomberg. Great, I say to the agency man. Terrible, says the agency man. Bloomberg fell into a dead faint. He called me an hour ago. Get 'im off the air, he says to me. I try to dissuade him, says the agency man. No use. He was dying on the phone. Get 'im off was all he could say. Who am I, Bloomberg, to attack Colonel McCormick? Get 'im off.

Thus it was that a silver-haired, distinguished-appearing man from Aurora cost me a job as a crusading commentator.

Times being what they were in the early fifties, and business, after all, being business, what choice did NBC have? It was nothing personal. Blacklisting had become as American as the House Un-American Activities Committee. And what was more American than that?

When a network executive—word had come from New York—
suggested that I atone by disavowing my waywardness, that I "stand
up and be counted," I told him that I *was* standing up. In fact, as I
recall the moment, I was not my usual slouching self. My posture
has always been terrible. I was standing at attention, my arms stiffly
at my sides. He didn't find it very funny. "This is serious," he said.

In my obtuseness, I couldn't quite see it that way. For some unaccountable reason, I felt that a disavowal of the few exciting things
I did in a rather higgledy-piggledy, uneventful life, would amount
to a disavowal of myself. Perversely, I let the man know that I would
probably continue to be a bad boy. I can't help myself, I said to
him. I'm like an alcoholic when there's booze around. As a porker
takes to mud, so I take to disputatiousness. It was my hotel upbringing. He didn't find that very funny, either.

As I look back, my obstinacy was not due to any moral stance.
No, that had nothing to do with it. It was something else. Call it
hubris, if you wish. Though I pretend to modesty, I have an enlarged
ego. I was being asked to play the fool. "Dupe" was the word used.
True, I often play the fool, but on *my* terms. If I am to be the Clown,
I'd rather play it to King Lear than to Karl Mundt. It's a matter of
aesthetics as much as ethics. Don't you think so?

The conversation wasn't really getting anywhere. At length, after
he had suggested that I sign an oath, I suggested, gently and politely
to be sure, that he fuck off. No voices were raised. I abhor scenes.

A few years later, the drama was replayed, under somewhat
different circumstances. I had been writing scripts for Mahalia
Jackson's CBS radio program. A man from New York suggested
that I sign a piece of paper. It was a loyalty oath. Unfortunately for
him, Mahalia was passing by. It was near the Steinway. Keep Your
Hand on the Plow.

She immediately knew what it was about. Mahalia always knew
what it was about.

"He want you to sign that, baby?"

"Uh huh."

"You goin' to?"

"Uh uh."

"Okay. Let's rehearse."

"Oh, but he *must* sign it, Miss Jackson." That one didn't dig things
at all.

"If Studs don't write the show, Mahalia Jackson don't sing."

We rehearsed. The series continued. Naturally. Why is it that Mahalia Jackson's intelligence and character were of a higher order than William Paley's? He, the big panjandrum of CBS, insisted on loyalty oaths. Perhaps it was a matter of genes. Perhaps Professors Shockley and Jensen are right, after all.

To my three colleagues of "Studs' Place," I apologized. "I'm sorry for your trouble, Mrs. McPhillip," I said to Beverly Younger. In this instance, I felt as guilty as Gyppo Nolan, The Informer, though not quite for the same reason. Neither she nor Win Stracke nor Chet Roble would accept my apology. There had been some talk, among executives, that perhaps the others could carry on, without the troublesome one. The three, a lovely, obstinate Swede, an equally obstinate German, and a just as obstinate Pole, said the hell with it. The four of us or nothing. What's to be done with people like that?

It so happens that Win was as troublesome as I. A lyric bass, who was equally at home with hymns, lieder, arias, and labor songs, he often sang at rallies while I was gathering the sheaves. We subsequently called ourselves the Chicago Two.

This was the course of events at the time Billy Rose picked up the phone. My hunch is he knew nothing of these dark matters. It was all so nebulous, so unimportant out East; a Chicago happening. Naturally, I was affronted. In vain, I searched for myself in *Red Channels*. Though I didn't feel that my name, like Abou Ben Adhem's, should lead all the rest, I did feel that I, by virtue of so much voluntarism, belonged there. Again, my ego was bruised. I chalked it up to New York parochialism.

The MCA man and I approached the Ziegfeld Theatre. Billy Rose owned the building. A woman at the switchboard informed him we had arrived. As we entered his office, I was overwhelmed by its enormousness. It was the size of Dreamland. My lobby could, with ease, have been dumped into any corner.

He came to the door. His dressing gown was elegant. Wow. "What brings you to New York?" he asked. He had me there. I had no idea. I bumbled a reply. "Didn't you send for me?" He grabbed my hand. "Of course!" He remembered. I was deeply moved.

I had a difficult time seeing him across the huge desk. As he talked (it wasn't too difficult hearing him), I felt another presence in the room. Rembrandt. There, to my right, on an easel, with a soft light shining down upon it, was the master's self-portrait. It was no reproduction; it was the real thing. I didn't have to be Harold

Rosenberg to see that. What a challenge: I was facing, not one genius, but two.

Billy Rose had a proposal. His syndicated newspaper column, "Pitching Horseshoes," was being adapted for television. Jed Harris, the celebrated Broadway producer, and Rose would work together. Would I be the director? It was a mind-boggling proposition, especially since I had never directed. Dan Petrie had been our director, though all of us at "Studs' Place" contributed to the staging. It was that sort of untidy world.

I contemplated Rembrandt. He was of no help at all.

The phone rang. "Mae Murray?" Billy Rose was snappish. "Mae Murray!" I exclaimed. "She's beautiful!" I remembered some of those old-time movies. Billy Rose was unimpressed. He hung up. "Her agent. All these Johnny-Come-Suddenlies. They know Billy Rose is back in business."

Again the phone. "Director? I have a director from Chicago who'll set this town on its ear. I don't need anybody from New York." He looked at me significantly. I was impressed. Who the hell was he talking about? I looked under my chair, behind me. Only two of us were in the room, aside from Rembrandt, who didn't seem too impressed.

I thought I'd better get back to Chicago. I was homesick. There was a chance that "Studs' Place" might be saved. It did eventually appear on another network; though offered to other cities in a cursory fashion.

"Ah," murmured Billy Rose. "You can't leave your freckle-faced little boy."

"He may be homely, but he's mine," I said.

"No, he's a beautiful child."

I had no idea what either of us was talking about, though I suspect it had something to do with "Studs' Place."

I suggested Dan Petrie. On my bewildered way out, with the MCA man shaking his head forlornly, I saw Bob Banner in the wings. He had been the director of "Garroway at Large." "What brings you to New York?" I asked him.

Dan Petrie accepted the job. During his farewell party he recounted an adventure. At the Ziegfeld Theatre Building, the woman at the switchboard announced his arrival. At the door, Billy Rose asked him, "What brings you to New York?" The phone rang twice. He was snappish with the first, his prospective sponsor. "As head of

the Hudson Motor Car Company, you must know that Billy Rose
alone decides the content of the program." To the second caller he
said, "Director? I have a director from Chicago who'll set this town
on its ear." Was Rembrandt there? Yes, said Dan.

A question will remain forever unresolved: Did the woman at the
switchboard call Billy Rose on cue?

The piece of zinc Civilization gives me does nothing other
than slice up my left foot pretty bad. Bad enough for me to miss
two of Miss Olive Leekley's Latin classes at McKinley High. Amo,
amas, amat means nothing to my mother. Nor do the teachings of
Gandhi. She curses the man up and down for having maimed her
sickly child. She lets me have an outrageous tongue-lashing, too,
after wildly jabbing my injured member with iodine, peroxide, and
witch hazel. Why is she sore at me? It was *his* idea. I am nothing
but a short boy.

Nonetheless, I bleed at her public denunciation of this medicine
man. She would never dare speak in that manner to the shaman
among the Ojibways. I could, with equanimity, see her letting one
of the others at the hotel have it, but not this one. She is tweaking
the beard of Bernard Shaw, kicking the hump of Steinmetz.

Civilization is his name (his baptismal one is wholly unpro-
nounceable) and pearl diving is his game.* He is the most distinguished dishwasher in these precincts. Even Nick Stassiosous, who
hires him, fires him, hires him, fires him, is confounded. The Greek
merely winces when, as is often the case with this one, the pyramid
of blue plates topples and collapses. Civilization is forever experi-
menting with the elements. He was studying Kepler at the time of
one such catastrophe. The soup plate atop the cream pitcher did it.
Anyone else would be sacked out of hand. In this instance, the
Athenian boss is truly Spartan. Civilization, even as Casey striking
out, overawes the crowd.

The secret of his immunity is in his pockets, *all* his pockets. He
doesn't carry books, he floats on them. They are his water wings.
E. Haldemann-Julius nickel blue books swell out from all over the
man: Fabre on bees from his left coat pocket; Darrow on the

---

* For post-Depression readers and those not otherwise acquainted with Chicago's
transient life of another day, "pearl diver" is an archaic euphemism for dishwasher.

Hereafter from his right; Havelock Ellis on sex from his pants pocket; Paine's *Age of Reason* from his shirt; Voltaire on anything from his lapel pocket, a wildly impressive boutonniere.

Despite his mad scientist glasses—never before or since have I seen lenses so thick—he is as myopic as a mole. He can't see a foot in front of him. Red stop lights are green, and green, red. Yet he has never been run down by an auto, though a number have careened onto the sidewalk. His portable library stops traffic. It is his armor, too.

A. Robins is a frequent number-two vaudeville act at the Palace. He comes on with a long, incredibly voluminous overcoat. From the deeps of each pocket appears an article. Within eight silent minutes, the entire stage is overflowing with everything, including a piano. Impressive. Civilization is the A. Robins, as well as the Leonardo, of our hotel.

In the lobby, evenings, Saturdays, and Sundays, the card games stop, even pinochle, as questions of world politics, natural science, the occult arts, and human behavior are put to him. Arthur Brisbane's Sunday pieces. Mussolini's March on Rome. Darwin. Lenin. Frank Lloyd Wright. And, of course, Einstein's Theory of Relativity. His explanations, long, tortuous, and gnostic, are profoundly incomprehensible. It is a religious moment for all present. Even those under the influence of Hannah & Hogg.

With the regularity of a wound up cuckoo clock, he sends massive registered letters to Ramsey MacDonald, Henry Ford, Bertrand Russell, John D. Rockefeller, Leon Trotsky, and Mahatma Gandhi. And to Albert Einstein, of course. He is aware that John Stuart Mill is dead; no letters for him. There are no replies. Civilization is philosophical. "Idiots." Undeterred, he dashes one off to Senator William E. Borah of Idaho. For good measure, he sends an equally urgent communiqué to Al Capone, who, in 1930, is to sponsor the biggest breadline in town. Al is often cheered by the multitudes. As he and his Roman battalion take their seats at Cubs Park, Gabby Hartnett runs toward him for an exchange of autographs. Civilization squanders on stamps as other men do on booze, horses, and women.

Civilization, for all his mad quest, is not unique on the street. True, many are lost winos, lost widowers, lost sons, lost cuckolds, and lost vets, wearing khaki coats without buttons. But the street has more than its quota of autodidacts, who casually cite Shakespeare, Gibbon, Robert Burns, and Mark Twain. And Proverbs. Skilled hands are here, on the street and at our hotel. And far from lost.

There's Sprague, the old IWW organizer. And Bill Brewer, who once heard Bob Ingersoll. And McPherson, the journeyman printer, who had helped put out Oscar Ameringer's *American Guardian*. Though these men are amused by Civilization, they do not laugh at him. It is their appreciation, not so much of his heavy artillery as of the man and his wild search.

Within oratory distance is Bughouse Square. Old man Newberry, in offering a library to the city, insisted on a proviso: the square on which it stands shall be dedicated to free speech. *Any* kind of speech. On a given spring, summer, or fall evening, as many as five soapboxes feature impassioned men. And, occasionally, an impassioned woman. I am told Emma Goldman once held forth here.

Just last month, in this year 1926, I heard Lucy Parsons. She is the widow of Albert, one of the Haymarket martyrs. This feisty old lady. Forty years before, she had become a young widow, as Albert Parsons, the bonny one, walked to the gallows singing "Annie Laurie." It was an eight-hour day these troublemakers had in mind. She is shabbily dressed and yet there is something elegant about her.

Years later, at Lucy Parsons's funeral, Win Stracke sang. It was "Joe Hill" rather than "Annie Laurie."

At the end of each speech, the hat is passed around, no matter what the cause. I see nickels and dimes and occasional quarters, as well as pennies. I saw Sprague shove a dollar into the hat, after Lucy's speech. Sprague lives on practically nothing. He dines on graveyard stew every night at Victoria No. 2. No teeth. McPherson tells me that Sprague was badly beaten up some years before in Seattle, by vigilantes. And he hasn't been the same since. But I *saw* him shove that buck, surreptitiously, into Lucy's flowered hat.

Frank Midney, the Mayor of Bughouse Square, is holding forth. His appearance and manner are those of an old-time Shakespearean actor. Lank and skinny, he's a cross between Henry Irving and a decrepit Gielgud. Spotting a whelpish heckler, his bony finger circumscribes the air, as he declaims, "If brains was bedbug juice, you couldn't drown a nit." At times, he is cruel in his assault on respectable establishments. Pointing toward the nearby YMCA, he perorates, "Young Magnolias Carefully Assorted."

Dr. Ben Reitman, reputedly one of Emma Goldman's lovers, takes over. In an Aristide Bruant fedora and a flowing cape and sporting a luxuriant mustache, he is not selling Emma's anarchism. He hawks, at a dime a copy, treatises on sexual prowess. Business is always lively here. Doc is celebrated as Chicago's most eminent clap doctor.

Goodrich, the bellowing atheist, tries in vain to cow the benign Moodyite on the adjacent soapbox. They are, as a matter of course, paired off. It's a draw, despite Goodrich's occasional foul blows. He accuses Jesus of thievery. "He came into Jerusalem on an ass. Where does it say he returned it to the rightful owner? Answer that, Reverend."

In reply, he is overwhelmed by the sky pilot's freshly scrubbed young believers, who sing out "The Ninety and Nine." The implication is clear: Goodrich is a lost sheep, whom they are determined to save. The atheist has had enough for tonight. He steps down and passes the hat. Never fear, he'll be back tomorrow. So will the Moodyite.

Sister Grace, rocking on her heels, her eyes closed, ever the smile, cries out ecstatically, "I belong to Jesus. He is with me every night. He is *wonderful*!" She knows what's coming. It doesn't bother her. "How 'bout me, Grace? Won't I do?" Howls. There is a printer in the crowd, whose riposte never varies. "I'll set type for you any night, dearie." Sister Grace is undaunted. She's on her way to Canaan Land.

There is John Loughman, who subsequently puts his eloquence to use in the service of Big Bill Thompson, the Mayor. There is Jack Macbeth, dean of the Hobo College. There is old Sheridan, the wizened Cockney disciple of Keir Hardie (so he said); and his equally undernourished boys, Jack and Jim. All three are endowed with voices of bullfrogs. But their croaks easily carry across the park, as they discourse, arcanely, on *Das Kapital* and *Ulysses*. And somebody is always invoking the name of Eugene V. Debs.

In the middle of the square, a dwarfish Australian sword swallower, with the huge head of William Farnum, is excoriating a member of his audience. Somebody had just tossed a "bloomin' penny" at him. He goes at it, with a voice remarkably stentorian for one so undersized. It is the first time I have ever heard the argot of Melbourne streets, colorful and wondrously unprintable.

On the other side of the square, two small boys, one white, one black, are boxing. Sort of. They are constantly dancing around and shuffling. The blows, all of them, slash viciously at the circumambient air. An old fighter, who has taken one punch too many, is the referee. Sort of. Someone refers to him as Kansas Kid. The someone nudges me. "He coulda been world's champ."

"Yeah?" I'm impressed.

"Know what ruined 'im?"

"What?"

"Women. So if you're gonna be a fighter, lay off women." As I am thinking that one over, my informant, feeling he can really trust me, whispers, "He once fought Battlin' Nelson."

It was a seedy old hotel. In better days it had been patronized by theatrical people. By 1953 it had definitely had it. The room was barely lighted. One naked forty-watt bulb. Oscar Nelson, the Battler, one-time Lightweight Champion of the World, was crouched on the cot. His wife had let me in. "It's gonna be on the radio, huh?"

A man named Peterson called me one night and said Battling Nelson is still around. He may remember past glories. Why not get him on "Sound of the City"? As far as Peterson knew, the old fighter had never spoken into a microphone.

"Sound of the City" was a midnight radio program on which I worked nightly with Vince Garrity. The station manager, Red Quinlan, had the idea.

"What about the blacklist?" I asked.

"Piss on the blacklist."

Vince and I. Together or singly, we wandered about the city, capturing voices, with the help of an overworked sound engineer. Vince, who had been a Cubs bat boy and Mayor Kelly's office boy, knew every cop, fireman, and politician in town. As well as all the Syndicate boys worth knowing. We were at the scene of the robbery five seconds after it occurred. I swear on my mother's grave.

In one instance, the currency exchange manager saved 50,000 dollars by sounding an alarm.

"You're a hero," I said.

"I'm an ass," he replied.

"Why do you say that, sir?"

"Suppose it didn't go off? I don't know why the hell I did it. I must be nuts."

"Would you do it again?"

"Are you kiddin'? I'd give 'em the money."

I'd rush back to the station, play the dialogue on the air, and follow up with a fairly appropriate piece of music: in this instance, *Hat man nicht auch Geld beineben,* from *Fidelio.* Rough translation: Without dough, you're nothing. Always music, along with voices. On one occasion, Vince called from God knows where. I had Don Giovanni's *Deh vieni alla finestra* on, after the victim of a clothing store burglary spoke with admiration of the thieves' "excellent taste."

"Who you got on?" asked Vince.

"Mozart."

"Why him? How many precincts did he carry?"

Vince subsequently became one of Mayor Daley's most devoted disciples.

Battling Nelson had his scrapbooks laid out on the cot. There were four of them, in scuffed bindings. Huge. His wife was doing most of the remembering. The Battler was finding it difficult. Perhaps we shouldn't continue, I suggested. Nelson's battered face was scrunched up, like a baby about to cry. "I'm not gonna be on the radio?" Of course, he'd be on.

Slowly, it was coming back to him. The scrapbooks did it. A photo of him and President Theodore Roosevelt. One with the King of Sweden; a medallion around the fighter's neck. He has a strong face, this young American Swede. He has been wildly generous, too. There is one: He is being honored by the city of San Francisco. He had contributed thousands to the victims of the 1906 earthquake.

Does he remember the classic? The fight Tex Rickard had promoted for the lightweight championship of the world: Joe Gans, the Old Master, versus Battling Nelson. Goldfield, Nevada, 1908. His eyes glow. He eagerly reaches out for another scrapbook; he flips through the pages, his hands trembling. The old lady cackles. "Lookit 'im, lookit 'im."

"Millions bet on 'at one," he says.

"There wasn't millions," she says.

"Millions bet on 'at one."

He finds what he's seeking. The photograph is faded; the *San Francisco Chronicle,* yellowed. I can make out the features and certainly the stances of the two gladiators.

"Fought 'im twice. He was the best."

Ad Wolgast? Does he remember that one? He laughs and laughs and laughs. "I chase 'im all over the ring and they give 'im the title." He stands up to demonstrate: how he moves forward and the other moves back. It is tiring, clearly. Even the slight gestures. He plops back onto the cot. He reaches for another book. "I'll show ya."

"He ain't gonna find it," she says.

The man who "once fought Battlin' Nelson," the sword swallower, Goodrich, Sister Grace, Midney, the Moody Bible people, Doc Reitman, the Sheridan boys—all have their say. But it is One-Arm Cholly Wendorf whose peroration is the most memorable. Cholly eventually succeeds Frank Midney as Mayor of Bughouse Square. It is in the cards, from the beginning. Everybody knows it.

Cholly holds up the stub of his right arm. "Know where the rest of this is? Somewhere in France. Somewhere in a trench near Chatoo Teary. The French have it. Cholly Wendorf's arm is enrichin' the soil that grows the grapes that brings you da best cognac money can buy. Coovahseer. Reemy Martin. Three-Star Hennessy. I touch nothin' else.

"Know what Omar said? What is it the vintner buys one half so precious as da stuff he sells? Lemme tell you somep'n, Omar. My arm. Only he didn't buy it. I gave it to him free of charge. When my President, Woodrow Wilson, says, Cholly, I need you. You gotta defend our free way of life. You gotta kill those Huns. You gotta save poor little Belgium. Will you do me dat favor?"

"What'd you tell 'im, Cholly?" A peanut voice from the rear of the crowd, the biggest of the night.

"What do ya think I tol' 'im? I said, 'You're my President, an' if you need me, I'll go. I'm a red-blooded American and I'm gonna save da world for democracy.'" He holds high his stub. "How da hell do you think I got this? I *earned* it. Look at it. Unique. I coulda been just an ordinary run-of-da-mill clown. Wit two arms. Instead— look at me. *One*-Arm Cholly. A man of distinction."

"You tell 'em, Cholly. I stutter." Another winner in the crowd. Cholly peers out. He indicates with his stub. "Can you imagine? Savin' democracy for *him*. Ain't it awful, Mabel." Howls. The audience has come to expect call and response as much as black parishioners at a storefront church.

"I'm marchin' down Michigan Boulevard. I'm Douglas Fairbanks. You oughta see me in khaki. America, here's my boy. What a beautiful parade. It stirs my red-blooded American blood. There she is, the drum majorette leadin' the parade. Ain't she cute? Twirlin' her baton, her little fanny twitchin'. That trombone player's got a hard time keepin' his mind on his work. An' here come the open cars. Da fat boys, with the stars and da chickens. And bringin' up da rear is us, da camels. Wit' sixty-pound bags on our back. And everybody wavin' at us. We're wit'cha boys. All the way."

Cholly pauses. Someone passes him a bottle. He takes a long swig.

"What're you drinkin', Cholly?"

"Mother's milk."

An open car passes through the square. The people reluctantly part; much grumbling. An unwritten law is being violated. Only sight-seeing buses are welcome. The guides and the speakers have an arrangement.

A young soldier and two girls are in the car. The boy calls out, "Go back to Russia."

Cholly turns toward the car. It has a difficult time getting through. "Why, you pipsqueak! Look at him, ladies and gentlemen." We all look. The soldier, pale and bespectacled, grins weakly. Had he been a captain in his high school's ROTC? Give it to him, Cholly. The girls seem to have no idea what it's about. Plainly, they'd rather be elsewhere. It's no use. The soldier honks his horn. Nobody moves. Well, he asked for it.

"Why, if you ever opened your yap over there—at the Holy Name—" his stub indicates the Cathedral to the east, "—why, they'd fling the pee pot of the Virgin Mary at ya!" Cholly turns back to his audience. The car squeezes through.

"So, now we're on the ocean, on our way to prove we're da big monkey-monk. We land at Brest. Where's da parade? It's all in re-verse. *We're* at da head of it, us camels. No open car, no brass band, no drum majorette wigglin' her fanny. Across the ocean, we hear them sayin', We're wit'cha, boys, far, far away.

"So I'm walkin' down the Champ de Leesee, have a few drinks, some Frenchman bumps into me. I say to him, 'Outa my way, you frog, I'm an American.' He says, 'I beg your pardohn, monsoor. You do not own Paris.' So I haul off to sock 'im. I'm an American, by God. Next thing I know, I'm flat on my back. Knocked cold. No more Stephen Decatur.

"There I am in the trench. Chatoo Teary. Next thing I know, I'm wounded. I holler. The Red Cross comes with a canteen of water. I say, what the hell is this? I want Three-Star Hennessy. And that's what they brung me. So here I am today, saved, thanks to demon rum."

On the steps of the Newberry Library, and along the curb, bee-hives form. Here, nonfeatured performers find their own coteries. Though lacking the credentials for the big league, the soapbox, one can attract as many as thirty, forty followers. There is a mild-mannered Finnish barber who has the widest of these circles. No-body understands a word he says but, as soon as he appears, a small crowd gathers around him expectantly. He speaks softly. Could he be a guru from Helsinki? He is forever smiling, wisely. And sadly. He must know something. They look toward him for the answer.

Civilization appears in this arena. Of course. This is the evening of the big confrontation. Veterans of the beehive world tell me this has been a long time coming. I, naturally, am excited and proud. Our hotel is represented. The pearl diver and the barber. The Serb and the Finn. Never, before or since, have I heard conversation so recondite. The colloquy is as convoluted as it is profound. Editors of the *New York Review of Books* would go crazy. I, along with fifty others—there are more here than usual; the word has got around—crowd in close to the sages. We try to make out what they're saying . . .

I attended Bughouse Square as regularly as possible in the years that followed. I doubt whether I learned very much. One thing I know. I delighted in it. Perhaps none of it made any sense, save one kind: sense of life.

Today, there is the square. There are no soapboxes. There are no speeches. There are no crowds. There are, seated on benches, apart from one another, young males: the Winnebago, lost; the Appalachian, lost; the black and the Latino, lost; the sad, gay young man, lost.

The transient row, like the family slums of another day, had its terrors, its brutishness, and its meanness. But it had something else, too: the search.

Perhaps my recall is no more than the boyish fantasy of a middle-aged man. Perhaps I dreamed up the whole damn thing. One thing I know: I should have saved that two-inch piece of zinc.

7

The Man Who Shook the Hand of the Man Who Shook the Hand of Napoleon

Thirty-six years later. I am in North Wales, visiting Bertrand Russell. Ought I not remind him that, in 1926, a Serbian pearl diver, sweating it out in an open-all-night Chicago restaurant, had sent off five fat, impassioned letters? All registered. Letters never acknowledged. I decide against it. Confrontations of any sort discomfit me. I am a coward. Unlike John Fitzgerald Kennedy. It is October 1962.

After all, didn't Civilization let us in on the oncoming Apocalypse? His was a holy fire. He had wanted all of mankind to know its fate, not merely his captive audience in the hotel lobby. In his forebodings, he went beyond Spengler, whom he occasionally force-squeezed deep into his trouser pocket. The prolix German made a provocative bulge. Bandhouse Babe, on casually kneeing Civilization one evening, as he was thoughtfully spooning his Cream of Wheat, murmured, "What have you got down there, dearie?" "*Decline of the West*," he replied. "Don't look like no decline to me, cutie," riposted America's sweetheart.

Our dark philosopher had prophesied not only the West's decline, but the world's end. And just last night, over national TV and radio, President Kennedy was trying his manly best to make Civilization look good. Jack's was a fighting, no-nonsense speech.

It is on the eve of my trip to Europe. Our President is letting Nikita Khrushchev have it. Pull back that Soviet ship. Or else. Remove those missiles from Cuba. Or else. Or else what? I'm scared.

I think of Einstein. During his last days at Princeton, after our tough little Give 'Em Hell President had dropped the two big ones on Hiroshima and Nagasaki, Einstein said he was scared. The way I figure it, if Einstein's scared, I'm scared.

I look into the mirror. My profile is sicklied o'er with the pale cast of fright. Our young President's profile is one of courage. Unconfutable. "It was an interesting day," he mused, sometime after the fever had subsided. Talk About cool. He is Clint Eastwood. I am Peter Lorre.

In 1975, Ben Bradlee relives the historic moment. The editor of the *Washington Post* is on tour, promoting his memoir, *Conversations with Kennedy*. Chicago is one of his ports of call. We are seated at the microphone.

Often, I open the program with a piece of music, if something appropriate can be found. Shall we try Casals doing Bach? In my mind's eye, I see a distinguished White House audience, with an intent young President, listening to the Catalonian master. I am saved from a gaffe by Ben Bradlee. He is privy to Jack Kennedy's true musical tastes. "He loved 'Big Bad John.' He played it again and again. He couldn't get enough of it." It was a quite popular song in the very early sixties. Its hero, whose exploits are sung out by a fighting, no-nonsense bass on the order of Ernie Ford, is one tough, brave *hombre*, who risks and loses his life to save his buddies; and, by God, you know there was a man. As it turns out, Mr. Bradlee's tip is an inspired one. It sets the tone for the conversation that follows.

Though the quicksilv'ry repartee at Hyannisport makes for pleasant radio reminiscence, I am more inclined toward gallows humor. On little cat feet, the subject of the Cuban missile crisis enters our conversation. I can't help my wretched self: I'm still haunted by that October of 1962. My guest has touched on it in his book. He agrees: It was a traumatic moment.

"What would have happened had Khrushchev not turned back?" I ask in a tremolo, ex post facto. "We would have been in World War III," says Bradlee. "Because we were going to get 'em. There is no doubt in my mind."

High Noon, by God. I am slack-jawed; no words come forth. I shake my head like a baby's rattle; my jowls jiggle loosely. I am Cuddles Sakall, the avuncular Hungarian film comic. I smack away at my left ear to clear it of sea water.

We were going to get 'em. My guest has a reputation as a fighting, no-nonsense newspaperman. Justifiably. With understandable hesitancy, I ask, No alternative? Mr. Bradlee patiently explains. His is a comforting, blues in the night, Jason Robards baritone. But why am I not comforted? "I'm afraid if the President of the United States had said, in the face of the Soviet fleet steaming to Cuba with missiles, 'Hey, fellow, don't do that. I'll take my guys out of Turkey'— I'm afraid that would have been viewed as the all-time gutless, yellow . . ."

"It's that gutsy *macho* matter again," I mumble, half to myself.

"It's a little more than that. It wouldn't have worked in the climate of that time."

To a slow learner, Bradlee explains Kennedy's pragmatism. The President, it seems, was well aware of our double standard of behavior. "It was okay for us to have 27,000 troops in Turkey right on the Soviet border, but it was not okay to have Soviet troops ninety miles from the U.S. border. That didn't seem right to him. He had an inner debate, but he kept it quiet."

"Suppose he had made those doubts public, might not the missile crisis have been avoided?" My naïveté is, I'm afraid, too much for Mr. Bradlee.

"The history of American politics is littered with bodies of people who took so pure a position that they had no clout at all," says the hard-hitting editor.

Maybe so. But why do my thoughts fly, higgledy-piggledy, to John Peter Altgeld? We remember this governor of Illinois, who in 1893 pardoned the surviving Haymarket riot defendants. He felt they had been framed. He spat into the prevailing winds. The Respectables were, of course, outraged. Altgeld was *seemingly* destroyed. But was he, really? He is remembered. Does anybody recall the name of his predecessor, a pragmatic governor who sent the others to the gibbet? Or the merchant princes of Chicago who damned Altgeld? They are not even footnotes. So much for pragmatism. Or, for that matter, so much for *machismo*. Need we ask ourselves who was the more gutsy of the two—John Fitzgerald Kennedy or John Peter Altgeld?

Meanwhile, back to reality. I mumble (listeners continually complain that they can hardly hear me), "It was a game of chicken. In Rusk's phrase, 'They blinked first.' "

Softly, Bradlee remembers, "Eyeball to eyeball."

My head is awhirl. I'm trying to picture what eyeball to eyeball looks like. All I can come up with is a Jules Feiffer cartoon. But why ain't I laughing?

I may not be as heavy as Herman Kahn, but I'm thinking the unthinkable, too. There is a difference. Kahn is brave and cool. I am craven and feverish. I find this strange, since there is so much more of him to be blown up than there is of me.

As one part of me is listening to my guest's straight-from-the-shoulder talk, the other part is talking to myself. Suppose the stubborn Russian peasant, instead of turning back, had replied, Okay, I ain't blinkin'. Big Bad John, being Big Bad John, would have let 'em have it, by God. And what would the rest of us have? The rest of us and the rest of them.

As my guest quotes Kennedy into my good ear—"taking a stand," "not getting shoved around"—my bad ear hears other sounds. An explosion somewhere behind the Urals that matches one in Alamogordo. A doubt expressed by Professor Sakharov that matches one expressed by Professor Oppenheimer. And a bang, a simultaneous bang.

And where do you think it all began? Unlike Ivy Compton-Burnett, I always ask myself rhetorical questions. At the University of Chicago, I reply to me. My alma mater. God help me. Ben Bradlee is saying something about eyeballs, but now I envision something else. Behind the stands of the abandoned football field, named after Amos Alonzo Stagg, the clean-livingest coach who ever lived, an "Italian navigator lands safely." It was the portent of this message in 1492 that, in 1945 via Alamogordo, hyped Give 'Em Hell Harry at Potsdam. He flexed his small Missouri muscles and, in that flash, became Charles Atlas. I ask myself wistfully, Why, oh why, did we ever leave the Big Ten? Robert Maynard Hutchins's greatest mistake.

Enough of this. I must turn my full attention to my colorful guest. "Wasn't Kennedy really thinking of the 1962 elections?" To show *us* as much as to show *them*? I offer this with some hesitancy. I don't like to think bad thoughts. I am much like W. Clement Stone in this respect. He attributes his success as a multimillionaire insurance man to having never disturbed his mind with black thoughts. "I don't believe in sadness," he once confided to me.

"That's not quite fair." There is an intimation of hurt in my guest's voice. I don't blame him. I'd be hurt, too, were some oaf to imply Jack risked blowing us all up just to win a damn election.

What an outrageous thought. I feel like such a snake. Still and all, I can't rid myself of a bad thought concerning a sequence of events: the Bay of Pigs, a sketch directed by Mack Sennett; though there are some who insist Harold Minsky was the genius behind it. An affront to the image of Big Bad John. Republicans breathing fire. And November just around the corner . . .

Why do I, in the manner of an alley dog, gnaw away at this old bone, better left buried? My guest is charming and friendly. It is not that I am an ungracious host. It is simply a matter of fear *ab initio*. The fear that some nut, of high or low degree, could push a doomsday button—that fear has clung to me ever since Big Bad John made that speech in October 1962.

Kid Pharaoh had no such fears. He is a Chicago free lance, employed on occasion by The Boys to collect small debts and things of that sort. At times, he finds his reputation as Tom the Tough Guy somewhat embarrassing, although in his secret heart it is a cause for delight; *machismo* being as essential to his self-esteem as it was to Big Bad John's.

One evening, Kid Pharaoh paid me a visit to explain some "bad paper." A newspaper report that morning had accused him of threatening to break a diffident debtor's arms and legs. Hurt, indignant, he flashed the results of a polygraph test to which he had submitted. Did you ever threaten to break the complainant's arms and legs? The Kid's reply was a thunderous and righteous no. The needle's constancy indicated a truth told. Did you ever threaten to kill him? The Kid's reply was a thunderous and righteous no. The needle went wild. "See," said a beaming Kid, wholly vindicated and righteous as John Foster Dulles, "I never threatened to break the guy's arms and legs, did I?"

Small wonder that Momo Giancana, Kid Pharaoh's *lieber Meister*, had, on a subsequent occasion, been called upon to dispose of the Troublesome Cuban. It has been alleged that Big Bad John and his small brother were aware of the matter and did not disapprove. It has been hotly denied by surviving members of the court. What an outrageous charge. Calling on gangsters! Malcontents and begrudgers, no doubt, still trying to destroy the good name of the young prince.

Still and all, literature and biology tell us of a common impulse and need that may attract members of a different species, one to the other, as the bee to the orchid: i.e., Proust's Baron de Charlus and

Jupien, the ex-tailor. In this instance, the endangered *machismo* of one and the endangered gaming tables of the other. And the culprit was, indeed, a common one.

There was, of course, no direct knowledge. Don't tell me, said Ben Hubbard in *The Little Foxes* to his wayward nephew Leo as the boy was rifling another's strongbox. "I don't want to know . . ."

During that October moment of 1962, Kid Pharaoh's was the cool of President Kennedy, Herman Kahn, and, I trust, Gordon Liddy, to whom every hour of every day was High Noon. "You can't imagine how many insecure people we have in this country," the Kid said to me one peaceful Chicago evening. "Say, in the Cuban crisis, remember? I was getting a manicure that day and the manicurist was so scared she didn't know if she was gonna have a heart attack. And I said, 'Look, Louise, don't be afraid, sweetheart. They're gonna turn back. The minute they get there, they're gonna make a U-turn.' You know what happened? They got no chance with the Uncle."

That is precisely what scares the crap out of me: Who has?

It was the day after our young President's ultimatum. Jim Unrath was driving my wife and me to the airport. We'd all have a stirrup cup at the Air France lounge. Jim, my colleague at WFMT, had collaborated with me in the making of a radio documentary, "Born to Live." Earlier that year, it had won the Prix Italia. UNESCO had sponsored this event, dealing as it did with East-West values. The irony of the moment was not lost on any of us: the program's theme being universal peace in the nuclear age.

Jim recalls the October evening. God had ordained it a salubrious one for flying. What Kennedy and Khrushchev may have ordained is something we hadn't yet figured out. The signs were telltale that their plans were not as nice as His.

"How could I ever forget it? It was weird. We were joking about it over brandies. I hadn't been aware of brinksmanship till then. I was twenty-four. It was the first time in my life that I felt the whole world might get blown up and there wasn't a thing I could do about it. It was the insanity of the whole thing. Two guys gambling with the whole world. The incredible gall. Luckily, Khrushchev turned back, but we didn't know it that night. What would Kennedy have done if he didn't? Start a nuclear war?

"I never gave much thought to the bomb. I was eight when

Truman dropped it. It wasn't fear in the traditional sense. Not a quaking in the boots. But this time I was feeling quite nervous saying good-bye to someone. All I remember is walking away, driving home, and wondering, Will I ever see you again?"

On the way to Bertrand Russell.
A depot. Bangor, North Wales. The man in the sheepskin coat is Meredydd Evans, the folk singer. He is our host for the night. I know it is he the moment I see him, though I've never laid eyes on him before. A case of *déjà vu*, perhaps? No, it's something else. As his story unfolds in the calm of the Welsh night, I suddenly remember him. He is another Evans: Morgan, the young miner-poet of *The Corn Is Green*. Meredydd laughs gently. It is the tale of many young workingmen of this land, he tells me. A hunger for knowledge, a respect for the book.

A Sunday morning in London. Two weeks before Bangor and Meredydd Evans. A Welsh miner is seated in an alcove of the Tate Gallery. He is studying a French Impressionist painting. It is quiet here. Elsewhere in the museum there are long queues of patrons, mostly young, passing by the works of Roy Lichtenstein, the American pop artist. Lichtenstein's exhibition has drawn more people than any other since Picasso's. "It's been well advertised. I saw him on the telly. That's why I came," says a young Londoner. "You can see those old-fashioned pictures any time. This is new. That's why everybody's flockin' to see it. Just one of those things."

"Perhaps I'm an old square," says the miner. "Lichtenstein may be a great man, but to be quite honest about it, his work is beyond me. It's just one of those things. My criticism may be very shallow. I hew coal all week, so how on earth can you expect a Bob like me to give you any sort of decision on Lichtenstein? He doesn't satisfy me. This fellow does." (He indicates a Renoir.)

"Of all the arts, I prefer music to anything else: orchestral works, opera. Choral singing? Of course. I was in New York in 1942. I did attend one opera at the Metropolitan. That was years ago. I'm getting long in the tooth." Do I detect a sigh? "You still strive to broaden your intellect, that is life."

He had come to London for the England-Wales rugby match. It

was a train of roistering countrymen. Somehow, I envision them in the company of a wild-eyed, wholly mad Hugh Griffith, with a harp slung over his back. "We had a sing-song, a pint or two. And today, Renoir." Might this not be a typical Welsh travel tale or is it something special? Twickenham Stadium yesterday, Tate Gallery today.

Though Meredydd Evans came from the people who worked in the quarries, his job, at fourteen, was in the shop. "It was the most soul-destroying thing I know." Today he teaches philosophy and literature to quarrymen and housewives. In Welsh. Tomorrow he'll be at a nearby village teaching Plato's *Republic*. In Welsh. Farmers are among his students too. Is this hunger pervasive? He's sure of it, if the encouragement is there. At this moment, he says, a village schoolmaster is trying to write a great Christian epic like *Paradise Lost*. In Welsh.

There's a dark music to his voice as he talks and sings of his life. I'm exhausted and sleepy, but I'm awake enough to suspect an unsung bard is on these premises tonight, who daily awakens mute, inglorious Miltons.

How did he get this way? His story is not unique, he quickly informs me. "There has always been someone to encourage you. It may happen to any Welsh boy who shows interest. The village minister gave me *Marius the Epicurean* when I was fourteen. Oh, I struggled with it. At fifteen, somebody gave me *War and Peace* and that was a tough battle. But I always felt something on the other side of the wall."

Across the room, his American wife, Phyllis, and his young daughter observe him with quiet joy, lasting pride. And yet, you sense the hurting in him, the unfulfillment. In Menai Bridge, where he lives, all the villagers look toward Meredydd Evans. It is a matter of course; he is Wales.

His young daughter speaks with deep feeling of an elderly gentleman whom she has never met, though he lives but a few hills and valleys away. "I admire Bertrand Russell more than any man I know because he, like my father, is a philosopher." Meredydd shakes his head and laughs. I hear the laugh of Kurt Müller in *Watch on the Rhine*, as his young daughter spoke glowingly of him: "My biographer and as unprejudiced as most of them." We turn in for the night.

Penrhyndeudraeth. It's a tough name to spell but an easy town to find. It's a well-traveled Welsh road that leads to a ninety-year-old man, Lord Russell. Phyllis Evans is at the wheel of the small car. My wife and I are passengers. Phyllis looks to the adventure with as much enthusiasm as we do. And, understandably, with a degree of awe.

Malcolm Barnes, an editor at Allen & Unwin, Russell's long-time publishers, had told me that the old man's life span was longer than any other's in history. He wasn't referring to the calendar, but to "human history." Russell's grandfather, with whom he was raised, knew Napoleon. Elba, 1815. And now the old boy himself was leading the world's young on the march toward nuclear disarmament. How did that old vaudeville song go? "I'm the Man Who Shook the Hand of the Man Who Shook the Hand of John L. Sullivan." Here am I, about to shake the hand of the man who shook the hand of the man who shook the hand of Napoleon.

It is cold, but somehow the drive toward Penrhyndeudraeth is invigorating. You're drunk with the verdure of the land and last night's song. Phyllis Evans points out the stone fences along the road—stones of varied size and shape, beautifully fused together. No cement; a jigsaw puzzle solved. Whose ingenious hand was this and how long ago? You see the serpentine road hugging a distant hill. It's a Roman *via* bearing the unlikely name of Watling Street. How many centuries ago did the conquering heroes lay out this freeway along which Welsh farmers drive Austin trucks?

Did the legions march along in quiet triumph or did they mumble GI profanities at their Caesars who led them so far from sunny Italy? No lemon groves in these parts. But it *is* always green. Astonishingly so.

As Bertrand Russell greets you there is a surprising spring to his step. Is that a twinkle in his eye as he welcomes my companions? I'm startled by the china doll delicacy of his appearance: the women by the vigor and pulse of his manner. A little dog scratches at the tall French window. Shall I open it? I make a slight move. He waves me away. He insists on doing it himself. We see the mountains clearly. And the sky.

The subject has been agreed upon beforehand: survival in a nuclear age. He will speak of nothing else. Some sixty-five books written and God knows how many essays and it all comes down to this. You're prepared for the nimbleness of his wit but not for the depth of his feeling. "I am ninety. In the course of nature, I will

soon die. My young friends, however, have the right to many fruitful years. Let them call me fanatic."

As I press down the ON lever, the clock chimes eleven times.
We have a half-hour. Does it bother me? he asks. I make a stab at
humor: It tolls not for us, I hope. He chuckles. He's a gracious host.
Wait. There's something on his mind. I push the STOP lever.

The Cuban missile crisis is fresh on his mind. At the most tense
moment, before Khrushchev had turned back, Russell had sent
cablegrams to the leaders of all the major powers. A plea for sanity.
He had received replies from Mao Tse-tung, Pandit Nehru, Charles
de Gaulle, Harold Macmillan, Nikita Khrushchev—he pauses. "I,
of course, sent one to your President. He is the only one who did not
reply." Bertrand Russell may know a lot about philosophy, *Principia
Mathematica*, and all that, but he obviously doesn't know much
about Big Bad By God John, who ain't blinkin' for nobody.

"I am not on either side. This contest is folly. What I'd like to
see is for it to die down, like the waves at sea after a great storm.
The US and the USSR have so much in common, this contest is
absurd. Ideology plays no part. It is simply dragged in to reinforce
armaments. The differences between East and West are as to power,
not as to ideology.

"Now, with these new weapons, neither side can win. War is now
beyond morality. It is just plain silly. These are not evil men at
work, merely silly ones. They don't seem to realize that dividends
are not paid to corpses."

I try out the fat man's theory on him, just for size. "There are
some who believe, though millions may go, much of the world will
survive."

He shakes his head sadly. "Survivors will be ill, hungry, miserable,
and savage. A very large percentage will be idiots or monsters.
During all that time, there will be horror and ghastliness. It would
take ages and ages for the wretched descendants of these survivors
to build up anything at all again."

I drop the fat man and go elsewhere. "In your writings, you spoke
of Gibbon describing man's lot as a stately historical procession,
and how cultural values survived even barbarism."

"Gibbon knew nothing of the nuclear bomb."

"Yet men of science have made it. We think of science and en-
lightenment. Aren't there some who say, I must discover. How it is
used is not my concern."

"Many have played an honorable role in trying to prevent nuclear

war. Einstein, for one. But I regret to say there are a fair number
of scientists who have been willing to sell their services to governments preparing for wars. None of their concern? If you see a
homicidal maniac and you give him a revolver, are you not responsible for the people he kills with it? Of course you are. Similarly,
these men of science who've given the world something much bigger
than a revolver wash their hands of responsibility and say, 'Oh no,
it is not my concern.' It's just a form of cowardice."

I mumble something to Lord Russell about Faraday and the
Crimean War. I had read somewhere that he had refused to work
on poison gas. That he had told the British government to go to hell
or something like that. Russell can't quite make out what I'm saying.
I half shout, *Faraday and the Crimean War!*

"Oh yes. That was very creditable of Faraday. He said, 'It's
feasible but I won't do it.' It may be a difficult thing to do, but a
scientist shouldn't shrink from it because it's difficult."

"You have been called an old fanatic leading fanatical young
people . . ."

"I wait for time to persuade them. Everybody who has ever stood
for anything that was any good has been accused of being a fanatic.
It's an occupational hazard, you might say. You just have to live it
down. Certainly, a great many of the young do not regard me as a
fanatic, because oddly enough they'd rather be alive than dead.

"I know that many people disagree with me. But one man can
be right and most can be wrong. All advances that have been made
of any importance have been started initially by a very small minority,
often only one. This man has always been ridiculed and persecuted
by humanity. It's a law of history."

I steal a glance at the clock against the wall. I'm trying to beat it.
So, obviously, is Bertrand Russell. I say something about its being
a long shot. Are the great many being reached?

He laughs. "Aren't we reaching them at this moment?"

Oh Christ! I'll bet he thinks it's a network program. Shall I tell
him he'll be heard over an FM radio station in Chicago? I think
I'll let it pass. Still, his words will reach some people. Is that a slight
twinge of guilt I feel? Yeah, but I suppress it rather quickly.

The idea of reaching out has caught his fancy. "I think you have
to behave in a manner that excites people's interest. However the
mass media are against you, the barrier can be overcome. That's
why we took to civil disobedience. We get more or less known. We

have reached a great many. It's a race against destruction. If we aren't wiped out, we'll somehow manage."

"Lord Russell, suppose someone says, I don't want to break the law. Civil disobedience is not for me."

I know this question will keep his motor running. "I should say, Now look here, my dear fellow, have you read any history? Have you heard of the early Christians? Didn't they disobey the law? They were told to worship the Emperor and they didn't. So they suffered. Galileo violated the law. He said the earth moved. The law said it didn't. So he was punished. Have you ever heard of anything of value brought into the world without somebody violating the law?

"The law represents what people thought right some time ago, because it takes time to enact a law. When circumstances change, what was right ceases to be."

There is something I want to ask him. Damn it, I forgot what it was. His secretary may appear any moment, giving me the high sign. What the hell was it I had in mind? Oh yeah. "Lord Russell, you had once offered a hypothetical case. Assume mad dogs were running around in Berlin today—rabies—wouldn't both sides be working together to eliminate the epidemic?"

"Of course. They certainly wouldn't stop to argue about politics. They wouldn't say, Oh, I hope the mad dogs will bite more people on the other side than on our side. Only politicians bite that way."

I let it ride. The old boy's juices are flowing. No need for a question here. My hunch is right. "You and I are talking here, still alive, thanks to Khrushchev. It would have been wiser had he withdrawn earlier. Nonetheless, we ought to give him credit. It has nothing to do with communism. It's a personal thing."

Time is really running out, and so is the spool of tape. This calls for the home run question. "Lord Russell, what is the world you envision?"

"I should like to live in a world where children were brought up as free as possible, freely, so they shouldn't be filled with rebellious impulses. I should like to live in a world where those of men's impulses that are not possessive should have free scope.

"I divide impulses into possessive and creative. If you write a poem, you don't prevent another man from writing a poem. If you eat food, you don't prevent him from eating food. If there is a shortage, you get conflict. Naturally, material comfort must be sufficiently supplied.

"What has happened in all societies that have ever existed, creative impulses are cramped by politicians or churches. The man who has a new idea or a new way of feeling is punished, although it would be a solution for a great many of our troubles.

"I should like to see our power impulses go into creativity— poetry, music, in lesser ways, gardening. There is always something creative a person can do . . ." He pauses.

Okay, I'll ask it. It won't matter too much to him personally, he said. He's ninety. "Is it possible in our time?"

"Hardly, I think. In our time, we can move toward it. It's a matter of degree. In some ways, things are better than they used to be. People used to be burned alive. Today they're only slowly starved. I suppose that's slightly better, but I don't know. You take steps. You can't get very far in our world. There is such a lot to do."

There is such a lot to do and he won't be around to do it. A touch of rue. A touch of weariness. And what a singular life. Shall I try a parting shot? "You liked Shelley when you were young, in your formative years. Do you still feel the same way?"

His eyes light up, ever so slightly. " 'Tis rather an exciting time. I liked Shelley because he had a vision of what the world might be. I still like him for that, but it's a much more difficult matter getting there than he thought. He thought kings and the Holy Alliance were the obstacles. If they were got out of the way, the world would be happy. They're all dead now, but we're not happy."

"I carry the words around with me," I say. "The ones you had chosen in your essay." There's no chance of cheering him up. Who the hell am I to try that on him? I need the lift.

"Do you have it with you?"

"Yes."

"Would you mind reading it to me?"

I fumble at my wallet. God damn it, where the hell is the poem? I know it's here somewhere. I had fingered it this morning, half-hoping we'd get to it during the conversation. I had no idea he'd ask me to read it. What's this? A matchbook, compliments Kit Kat Club, Waukegan. Oh, for Christ's sake. My library card. So this is where it's been all these months. I'd been looking for it like crazy. A note from a woman parole officer. What the hallelujah. Oh Jesus, where is Shelley? Here sits one of the world's wise men, whose days are numbered and whose time is jealously rationed. Waiting patiently. Is that his secretary to one side, about to give me the heave-ho? Damn, damn, damn.

*   *   *

Alec Wilder, a gifted American composer, has trouble finding things on his person. His is a constant state of indignation, usually directed at acts of meanness, lack of amenity, and loss of grace. Often at perverse gods, who have mislaid what he is, at the moment, looking for.

He and I are seated in the dining room at the Algonquin Hotel, of which he is senior in residence. It is breakfast. He can't seem to find a letter from some "idiot" who has misunderstood his cantata. I, it appears, have just lost two twenty-dollar bills. I *know* I had them on me this morning. Each of us is mumbling to himself, furiously. Though we had been seated side by side, we are now back to back. Furiously, he is emptying his suit coat pockets, out of which tumble, oh, just about everything. Furiously, I am emptying my trouser pockets, out of which tumble a couple of loose keys, a bus token, an orange business card from a Montgomery barber who claims to be Big Jim Folsom's second cousin, a pocket comb minus several teeth, and some crumpled dollar bills. Our soft curses, offered in counterpoint, grow louder. The other patrons, a number of whom are British, look up. They appear puzzled.

Here! I find Shelley. Oh boy. It's badly crumpled, but I can make out the words. I read it slowly, watching Bertrand Russell out of the corner of my eye.

> The world's great age begins anew,
> The golden years return,
> The earth doth like a snake renew
> Her winter weeds outworn,
> Heaven smiles, and faiths and empires gleam,
> Like wrecks of a dissolving dream.

He nods. I look down toward the Uher on my lap. He talks not at the microphone, which I now hold, somewhat self-consciously, away from him. "It's a hope grown rather distant, but it remains a hope. It's what human life could be. In gloomy moments, it's good to reflect how glorious and *splendid* and wonderful human life could be, if only human beings would let it . . ."

The spool of tape runs its course. He rises from the deep of his armchair. He nudges a live coal onto the fireplace flame. He wields the andiron in the manner of a putting golfer. Concentrating; both hands; effort. Only at this moment are you really aware of his age. Outside the tall French window, the green hills of Wales astonish you. It is mid-December. You mumble your surprise. "It is always green," he says. The flame shoots upward.

I never did get around to asking him about that letter, the fat, registered letter that Civilization had sent him so long ago. When he was the singer "of life immense, in passion, pulse and power" and I was a kid of fourteen.

8

A Free and Fair Election

The further I go back in memory, the more clownish the tricks it plays. There was neither Uher nor Sony to corroborate or contradict my testimony of long ago. But there is history. And, at awkward times, an old friend. Which is why I almost hauled out a clinker instead of a hot coal.

I should have known this from the experience of another: Victor Olander. For more years than any survivor may remember, he had been secretary-treasurer of the Illinois Federation of Labor. One day in 1944, I had gone to see him concerning a piece of history. In his late seventies, he was a portrait in ruggedness. As he told me all I needed to know, and much more, I was impressed that one so elderly was so full of piss and vinegar. And what a memory.

As I rose to leave, he had one more tale to tell. It concerned Bob La Follette, the senator from Wisconsin, and Andrew Fureseth, the Swede (or was he Norwegian?) who first organized the seamen. "Just the other day, Bob and Andy and I were having lunch at King's Palace . . ."

I have since forgotten the rest of the story. *Just the other day* was 1914. *Just the other day*, King's Palace was one of Chicago's better restaurants. In 1944, Fighting Bob and the Swede (Norwegian?) long since dead, King's Palace was a livelier image of Harry Hope's saloon; where a shot for its casuals was a dime and, at "cuckoo time," two for eleven cents. In 1944, outside Vic Olander's window, young cadets were in training for the war that had nothing to do with the assassination of Archduke Francis Ferdinand. *Just the other day.*

As for the accuracy of my remembrance, listen.

It was the first Tuesday in November. The year, 1934. FDR had been in the White House almost two years. Though the will of the electorate put him there, it was the lousy aim of a nut named Zangara that kept him there. The loony drew a bead on the President, but, Miami being Miami, the bullet went wild. Anton Cermak, our sainted mayor, took it instead.

Thus, Big Ed Kelly became our high monkey-monk. Thus, in his choosing Little Dick Daley as heir to this palatinate, the Hibernian line of succession was established. Were it not for an errant piece of lead, a Bohemian or a Pole might well have been the "greatest mare any city ever had."

November 1934. Though the breadline was beginning to resemble an endless, silent, gray snake dance, there was a salubrious note in the air. Flutelike. Something around the corner. Not prosperity, no. That had always been around the corner, but never quite made the turn. No matter how many incantations were offered by a shaman named Hoover, the snakeline had been sinuously growing ever since late in '29, when something funny had happened.

No, it was something else that lifted spirits. There was a deep Depression, true; but an elfin air pervaded, as insouciant as Roosevelt's tilted cigarette holder. There was an unexplained gaiety that November, forty-three long, lopsided, cockeyed years ago.

Less than a year before, the Volstead Act had been repealed, much to the astonishment, though delight, of H. L. Mencken. The Sage of Baltimore thought it would take decades before the Temperance people would holler Uncle. In less than one year after Roosevelt's inauguration, the water of life flowed legally as well as freely.

Which, of course, added a burst of creative energy to the polling place on Ohio Street, just off Wells. It was on other days a fire station. But on this cool November day it was a memorable place. At least for me. It was to be my instant school, my seminar, my arena of Revelation.

What the village of Combray was to Proust, the 42nd Ward was to me. As the ever-lingering taste of his Aunt Léonie's *madeleine* touched off his memory flow, so the sensation of a harsh dram of Chapin & Gore did it for me. Oh, remembrance of things past! In my mind's eye, I see it now . . .

All this is true, except for one thing. The memory I'm about to evoke was of a happening in 1930, not 1934. For some unaccountable reason, I had been positive it had occurred in the Roosevelt time. As I was telling this story elsewhere, a cantankerous somebody corrected me. And he was right. Old Olander had had a thirty-year lapse; mine was only four. All right.

November 1930.

Red Kelly corners me on the eve of Election Day. He is not related to Big Ed, though their forebears did come from that same poetic patch. How can I describe, after forty-seven years, one such as Red Kelly? Did he come out of some strange head of cabbage? Or some crooked alley? Or perhaps arise out of the waves covered with seaweed? He appeared ageless. He could pass for sixty. He could pass for twelve. His wrinkled face and puny body told us he was undoubtedly a leprechaun, who had migrated to the New World during one of those frequent potato famines.

Life in the big city had transformed him from a brownie under the mushroom to a child of the streets. Much like Hugo's gamin, Gavroche, Red Kelly was "gifted with an odd kind of unpremeditated jollity." As the gamin of Paris was "the dwarf of the giantess," so Red was the dogie of the heavy-titted cow Chicago. Sprung from her womb, she was his, and he was hers. Answering to no father, he grazed the pastures of the city at will. In one manner or another, he survived. It was not politic to ask how.

"Wanna make five bucks?" Red asks me in that unforgettable twilight.

"Sure." I reply without hesitation. Five dollars is no small potatoes in 1930.

"Okay, you be a poll watcher for Mary Daley."

"Who's Mary Daley?"

Red looks at me with forbearance. "Mary Daley's the grievin' widow of Johnny Joyce."

"Who's Johnny Joyce?"

"Who *was* Johnny Joyce." Clearly there is more here than meets the eye.

"Who was Johnny Joyce?"

"Johnny Joyce," Red patiently explains to me, "was our great state senator, may he rest in peace. *And* Republican ward committeeman. See 'at joint across the street? Da blind pig?" He points the bony stub of a finger toward an unmarked door, adjacent to an opaque store window.

"Blind pig?"

"Yeah. Johnny owned it."

We are, at the moment, standing near the alley where transactions of a sort take place. Where a small-time gambler named Froggy, by means of loaded dice, educates young newsboys to the truth of Horatio Alger. Where ladies of the evening meet scores of the morning. Where, as the gold of the day meets the blue of night, Red Kelly persuades me to enter Chicago politics.

"Johnny doesn't own it now." I volunteer this information.

"How can he?" Red is fast becoming impatient with me. "He's in the col', col' ground."

"How did he die?"

"You ast too many questions. You manna make five bucks or dontcha?"

"I wanna."

"Okay. You're poll watcher for Mary Daley."

"What's she runnin' for?"

Red Kelly sighs, weary of it all. His new recruit is slower than he had bargained for. "She's runnin' for state senator."

"Johnny Joyce's job?"

"Johnny Joyce's *old* job. He died four years ago, fer Chrissake! Charlie Peace is state senator."

"Charlie Peace?"

"Must ya repeat everyt'ing I tell ya? Charlie Peace is the Republican state senator an' Mary Daley don't t'ink he's clean. So she's tossed her hat inna ring."

"She's turned Democrat?"

"No. Ed McGrady's the Democrat. She's runnin' as Independent."

"She's not gonna win." I venture this well-considered opinion. Having been a devoted seventh-grade follower of Fighting Bob La Follette, the Progressive party candidate for President in 1924, I am profoundly knowledgeable in such matters.

Red Kelly takes a deep breath. "Who said anything about winnin'? She's runnin' as a spoiler. Who do you t'ink is payin' her to pay you the five bucks?"

"Ed McGrady?"

"You ast too many questions. Mary Daley is runnin' in the name of clean politics."

"Is Ed McGrady clean?"

"You wanna make five bucks or dontcha?"

"I wanna make five bucks."

"Okay."

An understanding having been reached, my mentor lays his right hand on my shoulder. "Since yer my buddy, I'll letcha in on a secret. Can you keep yer lips buttoned?" I nod. Red cups his left hand to his mouth. What follows is *sotto voce*. "Nobody knows how Johnny Joyce died. It's a mystery. Know what I mean?"

I nod, having not the faintest idea what he means.

"Dere are rumors afoot. They say somebody very, very close did it. Know what I mean?"

"Did what?"

"Shhh!" He looks around nervously, much like Elisha Cook, Jr., in *The Maltese Falcon*. Now that I think of it, he looks like Elisha Cook, Jr. Immediately, he cups both hands to his mouth, in the manner of a megaphone, and bawls out, his voice carrying halfway down the alley, "It was an accident!" To me, softly, "Accidents happen, don't they?"

"Sure." I knew he wouldn't contradict me on that one.

"Ya know what slogan Mary's runnin' on? Keep the Home Fires Burnin'."

"I like that."

"Who don't?"

Both hands are now on my shoulders. He is coach sending me onto the field with a play. Or George instructing Lennie. "Ya know what we gotta do tomorrow at the pollin' place?"

"Yeah, watch."

"You got it. You be there first thing in the mornin' an' stick it out till all the ballots are counted."

"What if I see somethin' wrong goin' on?"

He studies my face. Do I detect disappointment and hurt in his own? "What did I tell ya you're s'posed to do?"

"Watch."

"Okay, watch. That's what yer paid five bucks to do." Suddenly he pulls away from me. His face is hard. He is no longer Elisha Cook, Jr. He is Jimmy Cagney. "Hey, you ain't one of dem reformers, are ya?"

It is my turn to be hurt. "Red! Do I look like one of dem?"

"No, ya don't." He smiles knowingly. He winks. I wink back.

So it is that on Election Day, 1930, I am a watcher for Mary Daley. As far as I know, she was no kin to Himself; no more than

Red was to Big Ed. That she was a Daley and he a Kelly you may chalk up to poetic continuity and the peculiar ethnic nature of Chicago politics.

From early that day, as at the dawn's early light I salute the Stars and Stripes hanging outside the fire station on Ohio off Wells, until well past midnight—I watch.

There are five elderly men seated behind a long table: three election clerks and two judges. They are each to receive, if I remember right, seven dollars and fifty cents for their day's labor. They have been chosen by the precinct captains of the two major parties. I am acquainted with two of them. They are guests at my mother's hotel. Teddy Ruppert and Horace Bane.

Teddy, in his sixties, has a Van Dyck beard. It is always well-trimmed. He is courtly in manner. The guys at the hotel address him as Count. Sometimes they call him Yellow Kid, after the celebrated confidence man, to whom he does bear a slight resemblance. Not long ago, he was seen by one of the guys, in Lincoln Park, petting a little white poodle, held on a leash by an old dowager. Since that time, they've been wondering aloud whether he ever got into Mrs. Potter Palmer's pants. Teddy likes these jokes. It makes him feel the *bon vivant*. He barely gets by on his small savings. Seven dollars and fifty cents means a lot to him.

Horace Bane, a rugged fifty-odd, has been out of work since early in the year. He has made fairly good money as a stonecutter, but his savings have been going fast. He shoots a good game of pool, daily, at two and a half cents a cue. That isn't where his money goes. Horace is a horse player. He and my brother Ben often invest together. Their luck hasn't been that great. He doesn't mind the seven dollars and fifty cents at all.

Neither Teddy, Horace, nor their three colleagues appear to be bottle babies; but they are certainly not buddies of Mrs. Tooze of the WCTU. A carefree sort of bonhomie prevails at the polling place. And a faint whiff of bootleg sour mash.

Nothing too much is happening. There are a number of familiar faces among the voters. That is, they've become familiar, having entered the polling place several times this day; having done their duty as Americans, several times. In some instances, the X marked on the ballot has been in the nature of a proxy vote on behalf of some dear departed, whose name is still among those registered. You can't help being profoundly moved.

Who is to begrudge the familiar hangdog face a buck or two for each appearance? Outside, along the sidewalk, within saluting distance of the flag, the kindly precinct captain or an associate is generous to a fault. And there are still fifty-five days till Christmas.

There are, as I recall, about fifty more votes cast this day than there are on the official lists. How can this be interpreted other than as a tribute to the patriotic fervor of these citizens? What a sorry contrast is 1976, with such voter apathy.

It is at nightfall, after the polls are closed, that things begin to happen. I have no idea what's become of Red. Anybody here seen Kelly? K-E-L-L-Y. Nobody is singing, but I, for one, am wondering. Aside from myself, the other watchers are: a middle-aged woman, who is a laughing Allegra as well as a Democrat; a Fatty Arbuckle as well as a Republican, who can't make up his mind whether to laugh or sigh, so he does both; and a pale, earnest young man who will not crack a smile for love or money. He appears to have neither. He bears credentials from some sort of reform group downtown. Protecting us all, seeing to it that our sacred right to the secret ballot be not violated, is a Chicago policeman in uniform.

The paper ballots are piled high on the long table. The counting has begun. A sweep is in the making for the Democrats. U.S. Senator J. Hamilton Lewis is swamping his opponent, Ruth Hanna McCormick, the Colonel's cousin. The night before, Red Kelly let me know that J. Ham was his buddy. Senator Lewis was renowned not only for his oratorical flourish, but for his attire as well. From his pink whiskers, lovingly curried (he was called by his buddies Doctor Brush), to his pince-nez, to his diamond stickpin, to his pearl-gray spats, he was a portrait in elegance. He was, indeed, one of the most expensive servants our state ever had. He bore a remarkable resemblance to Teddy Ruppert, but more, in spirit as well as in appearance, to Yellow Kid Weil, that most exquisite of confidence men. It was hard to tell where one left off and the other began.

Nineteen sixty-nine. During my visit to his Washington law office, Burton K. Wheeler was full of Senate cloakroom stories. There was the time he stood up and damned, on the floor of the chamber, Hoover's reconstruction finance bill. "Its purpose was to bail out the bankers, the insurance companies and the railroads. . . . Old J. Ham Lewis came up to me. He used to call me 'boy.' That made me mad. 'Boy, give 'em the devil.' I said, 'Won't you make a speech on it?' He said, 'No, I can't. I represent a damn bunch of thieves. Thieves, I tell you, who want to reach their hand in the public coffers and pull all the money out. My God, if I were a free man, I'd tear this thing limb from limb.' "*

It is a shoo-in for Doctor Brush. But what about the race between Charlie Peace, Ed McGrady, and Mary Daley? J. Ham may be Red Kelly's buddy and all that, but I'm being paid to watch for Ms. Daley.

It is about ten o'clock when he enters. He is the Himself of our precinct. Prince Arthur Quinn. To call him a precinct captain tells you nothing. That he was to become state representative and lots more may be of passing interest, but it tells you nothing. That he left this side of the dark and hollow bound quite suddenly may be tragic, but it tells you nothing.

This glorious night, Prince Arthur strolls in. Stroll, did I say? No, it is a promenade; as members of royalty have so moved for centuries in all monarchical societies. *He is regal.* His pink flesh, a royal baby's. His green fedora, a crown. His is not the plump of a bartender. No, he is as round as Edward VII was round. We are all at attention. He is Upstairs to our Downstairs.

They called him Prince Arthur because he was the son of a king-maker, Hot Stove Jimmy Quinn. Hot Stove Jimmy was called Hot Stove because it was around the hot stove of his haberdashery shop, many were named but few were chosen. It is said that he was among the grand viziers who selected Carter Harrison the Younger as mayor. Prince Arthur came by his title rightfully.

On entering the polling place, he is greeted by his subjects as crowned heads usually are. The three clerks and two judges rise from their seats. With a benevolent smile and an airy wave of the wrist, he bids them down. He glances toward the rest of us, nods; we bow ever so slightly. No curtseys, no nothing. After all, we are not subjects of the British Empire nor of Imperial Russia. No, by God, we are a free and independent race: Americans.

Genuflection comes in the form of a greeting, an awed murmur: "Hullo, Artie."

"Hiya, boys, how's it goin'."

* Studs Terkel, *Hard Times* (New York: Pantheon Books, 1970).

"Great, Artie. It's a sweep."

" 'At's nice." He looks toward the policeman. "Any trouble?" The officer shakes his head. Again, Prince Arthur says, " 'At's nice."

To the five weary old men he says, "Finish 'at fifth I brung downstairs?" They all smile, shyly. Prince Arthur chuckles indulgently. "You guys better watch it. 'At's the third soldier ya killed. People might think you're alcoholics." Laughing Allegra can't stop laughing. Fatty Arbuckle laughs and sighs. He sounds asthmatic. The Prince turns to the pale, earnest young man and smiles cherubically. No response. He is Mount Rushmore, that one. The policeman looks away; a bashful child. I am watching. That's what I'm paid to do. Anyway, I like to watch.

Prince Arthur slips a beribboned package to Horace Bane. "A fresh one. We're celebratin'. A victory for da people. Take it downstairs. And one at a time, huh?"

"Thank you, Artie."

Prince Arthur Quinn, at length, seats his bulk on the long table, one well-shod foot touching the floor. Casually, he flips through the pile of paper ballots. He mumbles to himself: "McGrady, McGrady, McGrady, Peace, McGrady, McGrady, Peace, Daley. Atta girl, Mary. Peace, McGrady . . ."

"Hey! You're not allowed to do that!" We all look up in astonishment. It is the pale, earnest young man. The world stands still. Prince Arthur's mouth hangs open. A tableau. The young man is pointing a trembling finger at the Prince. The pink flesh of Prince Arthur is fast taking on a blushing hue. The others of us watch, transfixed.

After what seems forever and a day, Prince Arthur murmurs, ever so softly. "What'd ya say? Did I hear ya right?" Young Galahad insists. "You're a precinct captain. You have no right to sit on the table and finger ballots that way. That's only for the election officials."

Prince Arthur looks toward the policeman, who looks toward Prince Arthur. "Frisk that guy." The officer, in a businesslike fashion, goes toward the young troublemaker, spins him around, and pats all his pockets, administering a smart slap here and there. "He's clean, Artie." The young man, who obviously doesn't know up from down, is obstinately indignant. "You can't do that to me!" Prince Arthur shakes his head sadly. His voice is gentle, mournfully so. "T'row 'im out." Which the officer does.

Prince Arthur Quinn resumes the count of the ballots, which, during this untoward interruption, have never left his hands. The young man is banging at the door. The Prince sighs. At last, he says to the policeman, "Aahh, what the hell. Let 'im in." As the young man re-enters, Prince Arthur is the hurt parent lecturing the disobedient child. "Will ya behave yourself?" The young man nods. "Okay. Go downstairs and help yourself to a drink."

"I don't drink." This one is really righteous. The others have had a drappie or two of the sour mash. The breath of laughing Allegra is by this time one hundred proof. Aside from the young man, I am the only abstainer. I have gone downstairs several times, I have pretended to be one of them, but it hasn't touched my lips. (It isn't till that Christmas Day three years later that I taste the stuff. It is, poetically enough, a gift from the Prince: Chapin & Gore, and quite legal.)

The ballots are being leafed through, counted, and tabulated by the three clerks, two judges, and Prince Arthur Quinn. As the night is drawing to a close and the stack on the table is thinning out, something lovely happens; a moment I shall forever cherish. One of the judges, the cadaverous, phlegmy one, his glasses slipping perilously toward the end of his nose, appears bewildered by something he has discovered on one of the ballots.

"Hey, Artie, look at this, willya? I never seen this before. What should I do with it?"

Prince Arthur holds out his hand. The long pink sheet is put in it. He casually runs his finger down the ballot; and suddenly stops. He looks up, his baby-blue eyes wide with wonder. "What the hell! Communist!"

"Yeah, Artie. Some guy musta marked it 'at way an' wrote in 'at name. It's spoiled, ain't it?"

The Prince is bemused. His usually smooth brow is furrowed. "Communist. Communist."

"Should I t'row it out?"

Prince Arthur is lost in a brown study. Slowly, the crow's feet disappear and his face relaxes into its usual baby smoothness. He smiles. It is a beatific one, for all the world. "Aahh, what the hell. Leave it in."

It was in that *beau geste* of Prince Arthur Quinn that I experienced my moment of exultation. Let totalitarian states defy us, let dictators rave madly, let those who live in thralldom eat their livers. It matters not. We are blessed. How glorious to live in a society of free and fair elections.

The following night, at the headquarters of Mary Daley, in what had once been the meeting hall of a German *Turnverein*, where August Spies, the anarchist, had spoken, not too long before the Haymarket Affair and his subsequent hanging, I learn another indelible lesson.

We, the hard-working members of Mary Daley's watch and ward society, are about to be paid off. I look about for Red Kelly. He is, after all, my clout. I have never met the lady. She wouldn't know me from Terrible Tommy O'Connor. (Tommy, a convicted murderer, had escaped on the eve of his execution, not too many years before, from the jailhouse not too many blocks away. Rumor: He is still alive, if not quite well, somewhere in the city. Might he not be in attendance this evening? Surely, he could use a five spot.)

Will I get my five? I have it coming. Where, oh where, is Red Kelly? I see fat ones and skinny ones, pockmarks and harelips, gimps and bruisers, high-pockets and peewees. But where is my leprechaun? I haven't seen him since our alley transaction, our oral contract, on Election Eve.

Ed McGrady has won the state senatorship quite handily. Charlie Peace is o-u-t. The Great Depression has seen to it that all the Ed McGrady's, from sea to shining sea, have won quite handily. Herbert Hoover has been the Democratic party's greatest precinct captain since Hinky Dink Kenna and Bath House John Coughlan.

Mary Daley had not drawn enough votes to alter the result. In our precinct, though, I was proud to note, she drew five times as many votes as the Com*mun*ist. He drew one. In any event, Ed McGrady and the boys are grateful to Mary for the goodness of her heart.

At the headquarters—with the banner, slightly tattered, but flying proud, Keep the Home Fires Burning, Mary Daley speaks eloquently. "I personally wanna thank each and every one of ya for the wonderful job ya did. We made a great showin', no matter what anyone tells ya. What counts is we got our feet wet and Charlie Peace is high and dry." Cheers, laughter, and some applause. "We won a moral victory. 'At's as good as a real one, no matter what anyone tells ya. Mary Daley will be back. Remember that." More cheers and applause.

"All right, everybody, get in line. Angie will pay you off. Where's the fire? Get in line, get in line, boys and girls. You're all gonna get what's comin'. We got the fresh. An' don't forget, refreshments in the back room."

Angie, Mary's campaign manager, has one arm. It has been bruited about that he is a minor member of the Chicago Boys Club, and that, at one time or another, he had hurt the feelings of a major member.

The gimp, seated beside me, is licking an Eskimo Pie. He burbles conspiratorially. "Know how Angie lost dat arm? He had fat eyes for Louise Rolfe." Lovely Louise Rolfe! I don't blame him. The blonde alibi of Machine Gun Jack McGurn. Madonn'! What luck some guys have. Jack had celebrated St. Valentine's day in July Fourth fashion, just one year ago. Louise said he'd been with her all that time, and she's still with him. That Jack gets a bullet in his head some six years later is beside the point.

The gimp's ice cream is dribbling onto my mackinaw. "Lookit 'im, he coulda been in da movies." Come to think of it, Angie does look a little like Rudolph Valentino. Except for that missing arm. "He's takin' good care of Mary now, an' she ain't so bad."

"Takin' care of 'er?"

"Yeah." With his left hand, he grabs his right wrist and pumps his right fist back and forth. "Even wit' one arm, his cock is still workin'."

I stare at Mary Daley in a new light. Yeah, she's a handsome lady. My thoughts are distracted from my due money. But only for a moment.

The gimp leans closer. More ice cream dribbles. And I bought the mackinaw just a year ago at Klee Brothers. I back away, into the biceps of Stanislaus Zybysco. Or, at least a guy that size. He occupies two folding chairs. He pushes me away. I'm back with the gimp. "I had a chance to be in da movies," says the gimp. "D'ja know dat?" No, I didn't. "Yeah, with Lon Chaney in *Da Unholy T'ree.*" I am wiping melted chocolate off my new pants.

"Yeah, they chopped 'is arm off just like dat. He'll know better next time, eh?" He'd better. The lot of a quadraplegic is not a happy one.

I see a thick wad of bills rolled up in Angie's one fist. The manner in which he peels each off to pay the faithful is wondrous to behold. Though I am near the end of the line, I see fives, tens, and even twenties handed out. All brand-new bills. I even hear the delicious crackle. Angie is snapping them out with such style. Mary Daley is at his side, checking off each recipient. At last it is my turn.

"Who'd ya work with, kid?"

"Red Kelly." I say it hesitantly. Some inner voice is trying to tell me something.

Her smiles vanishes. Angie's one fist closes tight on the green. He bellows. "Red Kelly! Where is 'at miserable sonofabitch? Where is he?"

"I don't know."

"Ya don't know???"

"No." Am I trembling? If I'm not, why are my fingers pick-picking at the lint of my mackinaw? I stare at Angie's no-arm. Will this be my fate? He may have been a minor member of the Club, but I haven't even been that. Who knows? What Red Kelly may have done is worse than just making fat eyes at Louise Rolfe. I'm standing at attention. No blindfold, please.

"The kid don't know." Mary's smile is the most beautiful, compassionate, and forgiving I have ever seen. Perhaps a Fra Angelico could capture this moment. Madonn'!, indeed.

"Give 'im the fin."

Angie hands me the bill. A crisp snap.

I decide to skip the refreshments, though the gimp with a mouth full of liver sausage is waving at me. Feeling as guilty as Nelson Algren's Some Fellow Willie, who was born feeling guilty, I slink out into the Clark Street night.

Only later do I discover that Red Kelly had worked for all three candidates. He was buddy to Charlie Peace, too. He had even recruited the pale, earnest young man who had given Prince Arthur Quinn his moment of trauma. Thus, it was a second lesson I had learned that first Tuesday in November, forty-seven years ago. Election Day, 1930. Cover all your bets. You may never win; but you'll never lose.

Oh, rare Red Kelly! You were such a good teacher. Why have I been such a poor student?

9

A Bad Citizen

In 1934, too, I was a poll watcher. (Now I understand why I had the years confused.)

It is the March primary. A flag hangs outside the Moler Barber College. It supplements, colorfully and exaltedly, the traditional barber pole. On this day, the place is hyperactive. Naturally. It is one of the city's river wards and brings forth an astonishing number of votes; as well as astonished voters. It is on skid row.

I, along with other college students, have been recruited, at a day's fee of ten dollars, by one McQueeney. On other days, he runs a busy agency: Industrial Investigations. Watching is his business. I have no idea who engaged a labor spy to guarantee free and fair elections. A reform group, consisting of prominent Chicago businessmen, we are told. Report all unusual happenings, McQueeney advises us.

We work in pairs. My colleague is a cleancut, handsome young student of business administration. Bruce Berghoff. In my mind's eye, he bears a stunning resemblance to Dwight Chapin. There is no nonsense about him as he lays out our course for the day. "Watch these fellas. Keep notes. The scum of the earth. Look at them." He indicates the street, outside the window. I look.

I see faces and postures, vaguely familiar. I see the gimp and the harelip; peewee and high-pockets; Fatty Arbuckle and the world's thinnest man; old boys and young ancients; I see Bandhouse Babe; I see Civilization.

I lie back in the barber chair. No haircuts today and the hours are long.

"You're not going asleep on me, are you?" Bruce Berghoff means business. He's a take-charge guy, no doubt of that. I'll not fall asleep, I promise him.

He positions himself near the long table, where the election officials are seated. In his hand, a Parker pen and a notebook. He writes continuously. He will fill a couple of notebooks this day and evening. From time to time, he approaches me. Reproaches me.

"Why aren't you taking notes?"

"I'm watching," I reply.

"See what's happening?"

"Uh huh."

"I'm putting it all down."

"I know."

Bill Gordon, the Democratic precinct captain, escorts a wobbly old man toward the table.

"What's your name?" asked one of the clerks.

"Edward Butts," says Bill Gordon. "Butts is down there, ain't he? McCoy Hotel, right?" The clerk runs his finger down the registry.

"Yep." He gives the voter, of rheumy eyes, a ballot. Gordon, all solicitousness, leads Edward Butts toward the booth. He whispers to him ever so gently.

Bill Gordon is a kind man. I know this to be so, because as I look outside the window, he slips Edward Butts a dollar. Also, a pint of muscatel. He does it on the sly. Unlike other benefactors, he seeks no public acclaim for his good deeds.

Bruce Berghoff looks at me significantly and takes more notes.

Hank Romano is the Republican precinct captain. He, too, is a kind and gentle man. He leads by the arm a somewhat battered voter in a khaki coat, World War I issue. Was this one a hero of Château-Thierry?

"What's your name?" asks the clerk.

Khaki coat stares dumbly at his new-found friend. "Harry Wardwell," says Hank Romano. "He's down there, ain't he? Jefferson Hotel, right?"

The clerk runs his finger down the registry.

"Yep." He gives the voter, of vacant stare, a ballot. Romano, all solicitousness, leads Harry Wardwell toward the booth. He whispers to him ever so gently.

Outside, Hank Romano extends a handshake and a dollar toward

Harry Wardwell, who, having done his duty as a citizen, shuffles off.
I see no pint of muscatel. In that moment, I come to recognize the
basic difference between our two major parties: one offers the have-
nots more than the other. A pint of muscatel.

Bruce Berghoff is not missing anything. He writes away, furiously.
He is glaring at Bill Gordon and Hank Romano. And at me.

"Will you remember all this?" It is more than merely a challenge.
It is a stern teacher's ruler hard on the fat of my hand.

"Don't worry," I assure him. "I'll remember all unusual happenings."

It is late afternoon, as I luxuriate in the barber chair, that I feel
something shoved into the handkerchief pocket of my jacket? Bill
Gordon has slipped me a five spot.

"Buy yourself a hat," he murmurs. I feel that's carrying beneficence
a bit too far. I really don't deserve it. "I don't wear a hat," I tell him.
Softly, as not to hurt his feelings.

"Okay, kid." He isn't hurt, as he takes back the bill. Bruce Berghoff hurries over. "What were you and Gordon talking about?"

"Hats," I tell him.

Bruce Berghoff and I duly submit our findings to Mr. McQueeney,
who congratulates us on our work "for clean government." His
agency is quite busy on other matters. It is during the days of much
industrial dispute. He is a man on the go, trying his best to abort
aborning labor unions. Berghoff's report has the thickness of a
doctoral thesis. Mine is one paragraph.

Is it six months later? A year? I am served with a subpoena. I am
ordered to appear in court, as a witness to irregularities at a polling
place: Moler Barber College. Too bad, Bill Gordon. Too bad, Hank
Romano. You're shrimp, after all. (How's that go? "Big fish eat
little fish, little fish eat shrimp, shrimp eat mud.") I won't deny a
sort of ruefulness possesses me. It may be six months to a year for
Bill and Hank. I wish the fish were bigger. I'd feel a lot better.

I look about for the wretched men, as though to offer them a
shrugging condolence. I don't see them. That's strange. No Bill
Gordon. No Hank Romano. I see Bruce Berghoff, the avenging
angel. I smile at him, wistfully. Duty is duty, I guess. He nods,
barely. He's a cool one. And a righteous one. But I'll be damned,
where are the defendants?

Again, I glance around the courtroom. I'm quite casual about it.
I see five elderly men, shabbily dressed. They are huddled together,

as though for warmth. They appear apart from the rest. No. No. But I know in my bones it's yes. *They* are the defendants. The three judges and two clerks. The election officials. At seven fifty for the day's work, they never knew enough to get in out of the rain. Six months to a year—for *them*? Something's wrong here. Hey, Your Honor, something's wrong here.

A hard knot in my stomach. A cramp. My throat hurts. Do I have a fever? I'm in a cold sweat.

I hear my name called. I am on the witness stand. Judge Jarecki appears tired. John Cashin, Jr., is the prosecutor. He is a large man and has a deep voice. He asks each of the defendants to rise. They do so; one trembles more than the other. Can I identify them? I'm peering at each. I don't see very well. I know I need glasses. Surely, says Mr. Cashin, you should have no difficulty recognizing them. You were there all that day as a watcher on behalf of clean government.

I do recognize them. Teddy Ruppert and Horace Bane. And Harry Michaelson and Harry Hoffenbriedel. And John the Baptist. And Civilization. There's something terribly wrong here. Where are Bill Gordon and Hank Romano? And Prince Arthur? And the City Hall they serve? Mr. Cashin sounds impatient, as I mumble. "I can't make out what you're saying. Speak louder," says Judge Jarecki. His Honor's chin is in his hands. His thoughts appear to be elsewhere.

I raise my voice. "I'm not sure."

"Not sure?" Mr. Cashin raises his voice. "You were there all day. Were you asleep?"

"No sir. But it's been so long . . ."

The defendants are still standing. Someone has neglected to tell them they can sit down now. Is one of them trying to smile at me? Oh Christ! It is the most tremulous of smiles. He's shaking and I know damn well it's not the d.t.'s. Six months to a year. This old boy will never see the street again. Why doesn't the judge or somebody tell them to sit down?

"I've known old people with failing memories," says Mr. Cashin. "It's a sign of senility. I have never come across it in a young person before." I don't begrudge him his irony. I deserve it.

"I suppose you didn't see anything wrong there, either."

"I beg your pardon?" I heard the man all right.

"In your very brief report, you said you saw funny things. What were the funny things?"

Were Bill Gordon and Hank Romano on trial, I'd remember the funny things, I'm sure. But at this moment, I'm drawing a blank.

"Are you a college student?" Judge Jarecki interjects for the second, and last, time.

"Yes, sir."

"My, my."

Mr. Cashin has had enough. "You may step down. Fortunately, there is another young man. I'm sure he has a better memory." Bruce Berghoff takes the witness stand and his memory is perfect. Of course those five were the officials at the polling place. Of course irregularities occurred. He proceeds to cite chapter and verse . . .

I am studying the patterns on the courtroom floor. I hear Bruce's testimony ring out in firm, clear tones. I have the distinct feeling he is addressing me. I look up. Our eyes meet. I see the blue, the cold blue. He hates my guts. And I, at that moment, hate his. He looks away. Hey! *He* looks away. Well, well.

It doesn't matter. The five defendants are sentenced as expected: six months to a year. I seriously doubt whether there will be any effort from any quarter for a commutation of their sentences. The gavel sounds. There is a shuffling of feet. As I study the peeling paint on the wall, I hear congratulations offered Bruce Berghoff by the prosecutor. I am one of the last to leave. I do so, unobserved.

I am convinced that Bruce Berghoff is a good citizen and I am a rotten one. Why, then, don't I feel guilty? True, the statute of limitations has long expired. Still, guilt should last longer than that.

Perhaps Glenn and Betty Stauffer had something to do with it.

A postscript. Another year. Call it 1935.

Ben says to me, "Kid, don't worry. Everything's gonna be okay."

"What's gonna be okay?" I have no idea what my brother's talking about. It's out of the blue.

"You never knew Hank Romano, did you?"

It comes to me readily enough. "Yeah, he was the guy who . . ."

"No," said Ben, gently, "you got the wrong guy."

"Wrong guy?" I'm really lost.

"Take my word, kid, you're mistaken."

His hand is on my shoulder. Whenever he's dead serious, his hand is on my shoulder.

"What the hell are you talkin' about? Hank Romano was the Republican precinct captain who . . ."

Ben puts his finger to my lips.

"Shhh."

Tenderly, he pats my cheek. A sure sign that this is no laughing matter.

"I want you to live a full, healthy, happy life."

"Fer Chrissake, what's this all about?"

"Artie will explain."

"Artie?"

"Prince Arthur. He'll be here in a few minutes."

"What's he got to do with it?"

"Shhh."

Ben has a passing acquaintance with Prince Arthur Quinn. Often, my brother frequents a handbook shop on Clark Street. He and Horace Bane and Joe the Barber and nameless other two-dollar bettors, who dream of El Dorado. There are charts on walls. A couple of bank teller windows. A direct telephone from the track. A blackjack table. On the occasions I've been there, I have seen men tear up tickets and swear softly to themselves. I have never heard laughter. Other than from Prince Arthur. Whenever he shows up, his laugh is heard. He doesn't bet. He is there to accept a Christmas gift from the man who runs the place. For the Prince, every first of the month is Christmas. Between Prince Arthur and Ben, there is an understanding as old as time: the brotherhood, stronger than a blood knot, of winner and loser. Aside from that, our hotel carries fifty votes.

I have played the horses but few times in my life. I remember one instance. The Kentucky Derby of 1935. I picked the winner and lost twelve dollars. I suppose I should have informed Ripley, but I was too astonished.

I am working for the Federal Emergency Rehabilitation Administration (FERA). A New Deal agency, *ad hoc*. Its purpose: to determine the nature of unemployment in the large cities of our country. Each table, consisting of a foreman and six associates, is assigned a city. Mine is Omaha. The half-dozen young women who work with me receive sixty-five dollars a month. Some of them are the sole support of their families. I, the foreman, earn eighty-five.

"Omaha," I mumble aloud. A horse of that name is a Derby favorite. Why not? Have a hunch, bet a bunch. I'll put two bucks on the nose at the neighborhood bookie. The young women, in the spirit of the occasion, want a piece of the action. I hesitate. They insist. Each gives me a half a buck.

Saturday. Derby Day. I have second thoughts. Horse players always die broke, said Irvin Cobb. The young women work terribly hard for their money. A half-dollar buys a good meal. Damn, why did I open my mouth? I'll give them back the dough on Monday. No, a promise is a promise. All right, I'll place the bets, after I see a movie.

It's *Bolero*, with Carole Lombard and George Raft. It's so-so. But Carole Lombard can't act bad even if she tries. Like Joe Jackson, the old White Sox player. In the thrown World Series of 1919, he couldn't play bad even though he tried. It is not yet dusk as I come out. Slowly, somewhat guiltily, I stroll toward the bookie's.

I glance at a passing newsstand. Headline: "Omaha Wins Derby." I look at my watch, two fifteen. God damn Ingersoll. Omaha pays 4 to 1. I spend a frantic Sunday, borrowing a five here, a deuce there . . . no point explaining to my creditors. They wouldn't understand. I don't understand it myself.

It's no blue Monday for the young women of my table. They are ecstatic. I am embraced, kissed, and congratulated all around. I pass out two fifty to each.

"Oh," says one, "we listened to it on the radio. We jumped up and down. My mother blesses you."

"How much did you win?" asks another.

"A bundle," I say.

"You are so calm about it," observes another.

I smile my victory smile. And that goddamn George Raft can't even act.

Prince Arthur Quinn mounts our golden staircase. His green fedora. That hat always spells trouble for me. Something tells me this time is no exception. He breathes laboriously. He has been putting on considerable weight. His face is more flushed than usual; beet red is his normal complexion. It wasn't high blood pressure that did him in, several years later. It was an accident, as yet unexplained.

"I just saved your fuckin' life," he greets me. The Prince rarely has time for badinage.

"Huh?" What else is there to say?

"That bunch is crazy. They'd kill ya as soon as look at ya." Prince Arthur slowly explains the facts of life to me. I am about to be served with a subpoena by some of those reform bastards. They got Hank Romano, a wonderful guy and a dear friend of his, on charges of funny stuff at a polling place in the First Ward. A primary a year ago. Hank's boys are unhappy. And when they're unhappy, they don't act nice to whoever they're unhappy at. They are, quite obviously, unhappy with me. They had planned to pay me a visit. Prince Arthur stopped them.

"I told 'em I know this kid's brother. He's an old pal of mine." Prince Arthur's tone is confidential. "Got any idea how lucky you are? You mighta been in the drainage canal if it wasn't fer me. Anyway, you won't recognize him. It's been a year, for Chrissake. He's lost sixty pounds, wears glasses, an' got a mustache. Do you remember a skinny guy with glasses an' a mustache?"

"No."

"All right. Wasn't there another guy with ya?"

My right eyelid is twitching.

"Ya know where he is now? In Milwaukee wit' a broken leg." I can't quite figure out why I should be in the drainage canal and Bruce Berghoff suffer only a broken leg.

Prince Arthur congratulates me on having such a fine brother. "If it wasn't for him . . . Well, I saved yer fuckin' life."

I'm not sleeping very soundly for the next week or so. Each day, I await the subpoena. I'm thinking of New York City. I wouldn't live there, but it's a nice place to visit. I'm thinking of Tijuana, too. And Athens. Samuel Insull, when *he* was sought, found refuge there. Two weeks pass. Three weeks, no subpoena. Life can be beautiful. The sky has never looked so blue.

Months pass. A year. Two years. I see the morning paper. Hank Romano has been discovered in a doorway. He's in an upright, seated position, and hasn't moved for quite some time. Which leads me to believe there's no point in awaiting the process server any further.

After so many years, one question bedevils me. Why did Prince Arthur Quinn, a Democratic precinct captain in the Forty-second Ward, express such interest in the welfare of Hank Romano, Republican precinct captain in the First Ward? I don't know. But I begin to understand why wise investors, such as Howard Hughes and Dwayne Andreas, contribute to both parties. Red Kelly's dictum still holds good: Cover all bets.

As for Glenn and Betty Stauffer . . .

10

A Good Citizen

As Glenn and Betty Stauffer approach the hotel desk, I sense trouble. I'm not sure why. It has something to do with her, I believe. The way she smiles and frowns and glances about. Her bobbed hair is Clara Bow. Her look is Curley's wife. Why did they have to choose our place? There are others in the neighborhood. Damn.

Glenn Stauffer is a frail, tightly boned, mild-mannered small man. Come each Saturday, he pays his rent. My mother is delighted. Theirs is one of our few light-housekeeping rooms; and the most expensive. Eight dollars a week. With the early evening *Three-Star* under his arm, he offers no more than a brief comment about the weather as he urges the rent across the desk. Each morning at eight, he walks down the stairs. Each evening at six, he walks up the stairs. He never appears in the lobby. He is no trouble. Betty Stauffer is something else.

She is always in the lobby. She works but two days a week as a part-time waitress at the Victoria No. 2 down below. Otherwise, time hangs heavy on her hands. The pensioners, busy at cribbage, pinochle, hearts, and the perusal of obituaries, pay her little attention. Not so Bob Warner.

His work hours are irregular, too. He is often in the lobby. He tells amusing stories. Bob is foreman of a crew of ancients and little old boys off skid row. They distribute circulars for a department store celebrated for its one-cent sales. Unlike his charges, Bob Warner's

earnings are not squandered on drink. Women are his weakness and
delight. He lets Betty Stauffer know this. They spend a good deal of
time looking at one another, it seems to me. I don't like it.

I'm playing cribbage with John Barkie. Usually, I'm quite nimble
at this game. Not this day. For some reason I'm having trouble.
"Hey, boy, whatcha doin'? You got fifteen six. You only pegged two."

Damn. Why does she have to cross her legs in that manner? True,
I'm a hotelier and it's really none of my business. Still. The turn of
her calf is interfering with the turn of my card. Queen of Spades,
Jack of Diamonds. How can a boy who has just turned sweet sixteen
play a good game of cribbage under these circumstances? Damn this
daughter of Eve.

John Barkie calls all women daughters of Eve. Years ago, his
wife ran off with an IWW organizer. No wonder he expresses such
contempt for labor unions. The others call him scab, fink, scissorbill
during those violent arguments that erupt when someone mentions
Big Bill Haywood or Tom Mooney or Gene Debs. Though I am
not too sympathetic to John Barkie's economic philosophy, I understand his reasons. I, alone, know his secret. *Cherchez la femme.*

I look up from my cards. Betty has gone. So has Bob Warner.
Uh oh. Suppose Glenn Stauffer comes home unexpectedly. Ben,
who should know, says, "Watch out for those little guys. The quiet
ones. Don't ever cross a jockey. Murder." That's why Ben has never
fooled around with Betty Stauffer. God knows she's made fat eyes
at him often enough. Oh yeah, I notice these things. And it doesn't
help my cribbage game at all.

I toss in my cards. Mr. Barkie is surprised. I've never done that
before, especially a sixteen hand. "I guess I'll go upstairs and study
my catechism," I say. It's one of Horace Bane's catch phrases. He's
full of such folksay. Another: "I guess I'll go get my ashes hauled."
That's on Sunday morning, when he visits the girls on Orleans Street.
Horace Bane is always bragging.

I find myself in the darkened corridor, near Glenn Stauffer's
room. It's Betty's room, too. (I've never been an anti-feminist.) I
rap, tentatively, on the door of the adjacent room. "Lucille, Lucille."

Our chambermaid, Lucille Henry, had earlier in the day asked for
some fresh linen. On my arm are a Turkish towel, two pillow cases,
and a sheet, all freshly laundered.

No response.

I pause before the Stauffer door. I call softly into the dark,

"Lucille." Is that a bed squeak I hear? I have been blessed—or cursed—with keen hearing. Uh oh. Suppose Glenn Stauffer appears at the head of the stairs. As Lord Arling did at the head of the bed. Returning unexpectedly from Henry VIII's coronation, he discovered his new-wedded wife under the sheets with Mattie Groves.

> Oh, he took his wife by the lily-white hand
> He led her through the hall
> And he cut off her head with his bitter sword
> And he stove it against the wall . . .

How often have we read of mild little men who, on discovering betrayal, commit murder. Theirs is a sudden and gloriously gory transformation from bloodless vassal to bloody nobleman; kin to Lord Arling. God! In any event, Lucille did ask for fresh linen. Once again, I call out her name. My voice sounds so small and tight and far away.

"Lucille." I address the Stauffer door.

It opens. Bob Warner faces me. He is in his shirt-sleeves. He is having trouble with his belt buckle. His appearance, usually so neat (Ben calls him Beau Brummell), is disheveled.

"What's your trouble, kid?"

My trouble? His lips are smeared with lipstick. So is his chin. So is his neck. I am very quick at observing these things. Betty Stauffer is seated on the edge of the bed, looking down at the floor. Innocently. I look at Bob Warner.

"You haven't seen Lucille around, have you? She's supposed to fix Room Twenty-seven."

"She's not here." He's looking at me in a funny way. Quizzical.

"Have you any idea where she might be?"

He shakes his head.

"If you happen to run into her, Bob, tell her I've got fresh linen."

I hesitate. He merely stands there, shaking his head. As though in mourning. He is breathing like a stallion that has been, for no accountable reason, suddenly reined. She is staring intently at a specific marking on the linoleum. He turns away, studies her for a moment, and brushes past me.

At last, she looks up. Her face is sad. I stare at her. Imperceptibly, a slight smile appears. It's the way she looked at Bob Warner downstairs. My Adam's apple is bobbing wildly. "If you happen to see Lucille . . ."

My voice trails off. I walk away from the open door toward the other end of the corridor, bawling out, louder than need be, the name of our chambermaid.

I'm having a hard time of it for the next several days. My cribbage game is going from bad to worse. Bob, usually so friendly, ignores me. Even Ben is sharp with me, "Ever hear of the dog in the manger?" I have no idea what he's talking about. Betty hardly comes into the lobby any more. I barely glimpse her white dress as she flits up and down the staircase.

The following day—it is wintry in more ways than one—Bob Warner and Ben are in animated conversation. As I enter the lobby, they are guiltily silent. Bob appears to be in good spirits. I feel so much better. Perhaps he'll speak to me. He does.

"How you feelin', kid?"

"Fine," I say, feeling far from fine. Something tells me Betty Stauffer has a good deal to do with it. Daughter of Eve.

Years later, on hearing Cherubino's plaint, *Voi che sapete*, I get the drift. Cherubino, pageboy of the lovely Countess, has that feeling. He's about sixteen, my age. No wonder it's my favorite of all Mozart arias. But if you think for one moment I'll run Cherubino's risks, you're out of your mind. Imagine hiding in the closet of the Countess's boudoir, as the master returns. Okay, Count Almaviva, a dimwitted baritone, doesn't have too much to complain about, tom-catting around as he does. But suppose it were Lord Arling or, more to the point, Glenn Stauffer. It occurs to me that I may well have saved Bob Warner's "fuckin' life."

Ben is all business. "Kid," he says, "it's time we visited Orleans Street." He speaks glowingly of a girl named Laura. She's not too pretty but, he emphasizes, she's very understanding. Especially with novitiates. I have no idea what he's talking about, I tell him. All I want, as a young hotelier, is the avoidance of trouble. Ben insists on singing Laura's virtues. Who is Laura, I wonder, what is she, that all the swains commend her? Domestic tranquillity is all I seek. Peace on the premises. Bob Warner laughs. So does Ben.

Solly Ward, the Dutch comic, is at the Star & Garter. It is one of our better burlesque houses, 1926? '27? A sketch. He knocks on the door. The talking lady says, "Come in." She singsongs it. Solly enters. They embrace. Another knock on the door. "My husband!"

she cries. Solly hides in the clothes closet. A man enters. He and the talking lady embrace. Another knock on the door. "My husband!" she cries. The man hides under the bed. Husband enters, a gun in his hand. "Where is he?" demands the outraged spouse. He discovers the man under the bed. They fire at one another. The talking lady screams. Blackout. Lights come on. Silence. The talking lady, as Fay Wray in *King Kong*, trembles. Slowly, the door of the clothes closet opens. Solly Ward emerges. He sees the two dead men. He sees the terrified beauty. He studies the scene. At last, he says, "Iss ze var over? Goot. Now ve vill haff a little peace." Hands outstretched, he moves toward the talking lady. Blackout.

Lucille Henry is laughing, too, as she makes the beds. My mother hired her six months ago. She and Bob Warner and Horace Bane and Ben are always laughing about something. I can guess. She's singing that dirty blues again.

> What is it smell like gravy
> Good if you really wanna know
> Well it ain't no puddin' an' it ain't no pie
> It ain't nothin' you don't have to buy . . .

Oh, how I wish my mother were paying her a living wage so we could fire her. Ben accuses my mother of exploiting Lucille. They've had some hot arguments on this score. I agree with Ben. It's just this other matter that has lately soured me on Lucille. Ever since the Stauffers came, Lucille descends the staircase and approaches the clerk's cage in which I sit. I pretend she's not there.

"Honey dripper."

Why does she call me that? She knows my name. As though I haven't troubles enough. I had rejected Ben's invitation. I shall never know what Laura looks like, let alone her charms. Rather I court Lady Five Fingers than run the risk of Spanish ring. And now Lucille's laughter. Is there no right to privacy in these matters? They don't even have a warrant. Whatever happened to the Fourth Amendment of the Bill of Rights?

"She wants you to fix her radiator."

"Who?" As though I didn't know.

"The cute li'l girl. She says it's too hot."

"Why doesn't she turn it off?"

"Can't. Needs a wrench. Said for me to tell you to come up right away. She's meltin'."

I reach into the drawer and fumble for the proper tool. There is no need to hurry. I deliberately dawdle, determined not to be bullied by a chambermaid. Or a troublesome guest. Or Ben or Bob Warner or Horace Bane. I suspect they're all in on it. A conspiracy.

I tap on the door ever so lightly.

"Come in." Hers is the singsong of the talking lady at the Star & Garter. Am I Solly Ward?

She is in the middle of the double bed. Her knees are scrunched up against her chin. Her hands clasp her ankles, much in the manner of a little girl. She is smiling at me. I knew there'd be trouble the moment Glenn and Betty Stauffer mounted those stairs.

"Lucille said something about your radiator."

"Won't you turn it off for me? Please."

I turn off the radiator. There's no need for a wrench. A baby could do it. I show her. "It turns easily. See?"

As I walk toward the door, she shifts her position. Her legs are stretched out toward the edge of the bed. Her stockings are sheer, flesh colored. There is a slave bracelet on her left ankle. There flashes through my mind the whispered innuendoes of Joe the Barber concerning women who wear slave bracelets. Ow! The wrench is cutting into the flesh of my hand. I'm gripping it too hard.

"Is this bandage too tight?"

She runs her hand down toward her right ankle, where a piece of adhesive tape is visible.

"Did you sprain it?" My voice is of a lower register than usual. Rather this than the high squeak, which might be forthcoming, considering the dryness of my throat. Oh, for a Dr. Pepper. She nods.

"Feel it."

I move one small step toward her. I stretch out my hand but I cannot quite reach her ankle. She pulls me toward her. The awkwardness of my position causes me to drop the wrench and tumble onto the bed. She slowly runs my hand against her injured ankle and up toward her thigh.

I abruptly draw my hand away and lean backward. In so doing, I lose my balance and topple heavily onto the floor. Ow! I have fallen onto the open jaws of the wrench. I spring up, fumble my way toward the door. I shout at it. "Radiator's shut off."

I slam the door behind me and stumble down the murky corridor.

In the Mazda brightness of the staircase, I gently massage my wretched buttock.

That night, I notice a wild strawberry, a flaming red, to which I apply an ointment. It lasts about a week, as scarlet as the letter *she* deserves. To think that poor, gentle Hester Prynne had sinned so little and suffered so much. Would Hester have enticed an innocent sixteen-year-old boy onto her bed or under the elm? A boy so burdened with the troubles of the world. Yet, why do *I* bear the mark, and in so unlikely a place, rather than this wanton daughter of Eve? God is so perverse at times. Which side is he really on?

My wrestling with angel and devil is doing little good for my cribbage game and less for my sleep. If I did the right thing, why am I not sleeping the sleep of the righteous? The Puritan in me is having a hard time of it. For that matter, so is the pimp in me. And so is the Cherubino. As I struggle for peace of mind, the truth appears out of the blue.

It is Glenn Stauffer whom I've done it for. That's it, of course. Our hotel is his home. It is his castle. Man's castle is not a steer's barn. If Glenn Stauffer is to wear horns, let it be elsewhere. Oh joy, I am liberated. Let Bob Warner and Ben think what they will, I know the right.

On a Saturday afternoon, two large men lumber up the stairs. They wear fedoras. One is silent. The other speaks in a flat voice. "Let's see the register, son."

I hesitate. The spokesman flashes an open wallet at me. I see a police badge.

"We're from headquarters."

I push the long black book across the counter. The man shoves a yellow sheet of paper at me. "Came over the wire last night."

I read it: "George Simmons, using alias Glenn Stauffer. Bank robbery. Kansas City. With woman. Brunette. Information leads us to believe Chicago. Near North. May be armed. Caution advised."

"Anyone here by that name?"

I nod dumbly.

"Is he in?"

Again, I nod. I had seen him go upstairs about half an hour ago, with the Saturday *Three-Star* tucked under his arm. After paying his rent, he made a brief comment on the weather. Yes, she is upstairs too. The brunette.

"Got a key?"

"Yes, sir."

"Lead the way, son."

I take the ring of keys off the hook. They are close behind me as I mount the stairs and walk down the dark corridor toward the room. I am fingering the passkey. We pause in front of the door. We have arrived soundlessly. I hear a faint conversation inside. The crackle of a fresh newspaper being turned. Sounds of domesticity. Man's castle.

Shall I knock? My knuckles are poised. One of the men shakes his head, his fingers to his lips. He points to the keys in my hand. Very carefully, very slowly, soundlessly, I insert the key in the lock, turn the knob, and let the door float open. The men rush in.

Glenn Stauffer is reclining comfortably on the bed. He is in his polka-dot shorts. The *Three-Star* is spread out about him. The comic section is still in his hands as he is lifted off the bed by one of the men. He is held high, as a baby hoisted by a father. As with a frightened child, Glenn Stauffer's lips pucker, as though he is about to cry. How tiny and helpless he looks. The other man quickly frisks the bed, flipping away the punched-in pillow and turning over the mattress. Betty Stauffer, against the wall, covers her face.

Glenn Stauffer, in stocking feet and polka-dot shorts, is shoved against the bedstead by the other, who towers over him.

"You George Simmons?"

"My name is Glenn Stauffer."

His voice quavers. The other speaks softly now.

"Make it easy on yourself, George. Get dressed."

She rushes toward him. She is sobbing. He gently embraces her. The three of us look on——the three of us, for I am one of *them*. They are blubbering incoherently at one another. Betty is half a head taller than Glenn when he is fully dressed. Now, they both appear lost little orphans. He is blurting out brokenly.

"She don't know nothin' about this, honest. I picked her up——we met in a taxi dance hall. K.C. I been workin' here in the auto plant, Ford. Honest. You can check with my boss." He looks toward me. He is in tears. "Have I ever given you trouble?"

I shake my head. I feel funny. A hard knot in my stomach. A cramp. My throat hurts. Do I have a fever? I'm in a cold sweat.

She is mumbling at him, "I love you, I love you, I love you." Her wet cheek is pressed hard against his. One of the others gently suggests she let him get dressed. She can visit him at headquarters later; but now she must let him get dressed.

I ask if I might be excused. There is nobody downstairs minding the place.

"Sure," says one of the men. "Thanks, son. You're good. You opened the door so quick, you almost caught *us* with our pants down." He chuckles appreciatively. Obviously, I did well. I race down the stairs, hang the keys back on the hook, and rush blindly toward the toilet. I make sure the door is bolted. I try to throw up. I am unsuccessful.

I am back in the clerk's cage. Too soon. The two men and Glenn Stauffer or George Simmons are at the landing. He waves at me. So long. I wave back. We are both embarrassed. I mumble something about good luck, but he doesn't hear me.

It being Saturday, the lobby is busy. Cards played; racing form studied; politics and religion argued; women discussed, pro and con. All is silence as I enter. They have an idea. Horace Bane was near the desk at the time the detectives appeared. Bob Warner is staring out the window. I look toward him. He doesn't see me. I study the calendar, hanging crookedly on the wall. Its artwork: *September Morn*. It doesn't matter.

John Barkie breaks the silence. With unaccustomed ebullience, he tells of a bank robber he had known. I know the bastard is lying. John Barkie is a scab, a fink, and a scissorbill and I am glad his wife ran off with an IWW organizer.

Barkie's most appreciative listener is Peter Cousins. He and his wife Mary Jane have been our guests for only a few weeks. They are both very good-looking and clean-cut. They have a light-housekeeping room, too. Cousins will soon be appointed foreman at the plant and Mary Jane and he will move out. It's an accident that led them, so temporarily, to our hotel. A fire at his aunt's place, where they had been staying. They're from Indianapolis.

It's about eight o'clock. Betty Stauffer is walking down the stairs. Her eyes are red and her dress is lavender. In a voice hardly audible, she asks me how to get to headquarters. I tell her. The men in the lobby watch in silence. Bob Warner goes toward her. They talk softly. I have no idea what they're saying. She smiles tremulously. That's good. He'll take her to the station, he says. That's good, too. They descend the staircase.

Mary Jane Cousins has joined Peter, who has been lounging near the clerk's cage. She is an attractive blonde in a healthy, corn-fed way. Peter is tall and his teeth are a dazzling white. They smile, knowingly.

"There she goes," says Peter.

"Where?" asks Mary Jane.

"Where do you think?" says Peter. "To hustle money for her man."

Mary Jane laughs lightly. They exude a sense of self-satisfaction, these two. They are respectable and righteous. And the sooner they get the hell out, the better I'll feel.

A boy's daydream: Mary Cousins and Bob Warner. I have noticed Bob, seated in the lobby, facing the landing, glance fleetingly at Mary Jane, as she passes by. Mary Jane is aware of Bob, I'm certain. It's a whisper of a moment. Hot damn. I'll bet a fat man a brush fire could be set off. Mary Jane, so faithful, so cool, whose house-wifely lips turn up at the thought of Betty Stauffer. Mary Jane, who has just now laughed lightly. In bed with Bob Warner. Oh boy. Not caught, no, not that, too much trouble. No, just a twinge of guilt for Mary Jane, a moment of discomfort, a touch of terror. Especially, as Peter comes home that evening, after a rewarding, finky day at the plant. And Peter. He senses something. He knows not what. A slight ache. An intimation of unhappiness. (Johnny, a troubled Chicano kid, seated in an auto with me at one in the morning, some forty years later, mumbles something about "the hurts.") The hurts. Anything, anything to kick the bejeepers out of their all-American smugness. Oh, how I'd delight in playing Pandarus in this instance. A boy can dream, can't he?

What about me? And my respectability.

If a man's home is his castle—and surely that was the *raison d'être* of my behavior in the Stauffer affair, or so I convinced myself— why didn't I knock? There was that moment of uncertainty, outside the door. Why did I pause, with my knuckles poised, instead of doing the most natural thing: knocking on the door of a guest? Of course, the detective would say, Shhh, don't knock. That's his job. But I am not a detective. I am not a cop. I'm a hotelier. And as I have told myself, not once but thousands of times, a man's home is his castle. Oh boy. In that moment, at the age of sweet sixteen, I had behaved as a precocious advocate of the no-knock law.

George Simmons, alias Glenn Stauffer, was a bank robber. Perhaps he had a gun. Perhaps. The hard fact is: I knew Glenn Stauffer, not George Simmons. When I heard the *Three-Star*'s crackle outside his door, I envisioned Glenn on the bed, for I could tell whence the sound came. I envisioned him in his shorts, for on past occasions I had seen him thus. The hard fact is: *I wasn't worried about any violence on his part.* I was thinking of pleasing the detectives. Quite obviously, I succeeded.

Because of my righteous behavior, I still see a small man in polka-dot shorts, in the presence of his sweetheart, hoisted high, an absurd and helpless baby. In his home that is his castle. Talk about humiliation. I can't speak for Glenn Stauffer. I can only speak for myself.

That was 1928. I was the Good Citizen and I still feel guilty. Perhaps that mark on my buttock should have remained. In 1934, in Judge Jarecki's court, I was the Bad Citizen and I don't feel guilty. If that isn't perversity, what is?

BOOK
TWO

1

The Native

On a shelf against the wall of my workroom is something of a plant.
I don't know what else to call it. The flowers are of crepe paper,
the stems of wire. Their colors are green, pink, and yellow. The pot,
decorated with beribboned streamers of green, pink, and yellow, may
have been a vegetable can. Or a soup can. Campbell's, perhaps?
After fourteen years, the paper is faded. No matter. On the morning
of February 13, 1963, it was presented to me by Magwiana Hlachayo.
A gift. Something to remember him by.

   South Africa. The bus is taking the thirty-five of us pilgrims to
Kruger National Park, the celebrated animal preserve. It is raining;
a euphemism, if there ever was one. South African rains are tor-
rential. It is more of a cyclone, as the tall gum trees sway, drunkenly
and dangerously, above us. Bills Olds, our Gary Cooper of a driver,
is masterful, weaving and dodging along the sloshy roads. Frau
Weigel, seated beside him, is gallantly, though frantically, wiping
away at the windshield. She is young, handsome, and buxom and
doing one hell of a job. Some of my companions break into song.
"Muss i' denn." "Das Wanderlied." Even "Der Lindenbaum." It
may not sound as poignant as Schubert had envisioned, but ours is
a different kind of *Winterreise.* As a tribute to Frau Weigel, there's
"Hoch du lieber." As we all join in with "drei mal hoch," it is a
toast to our own well-being. We're feeling high, what with excellent
beers, fine brandies, and the wildness of it all. Nature is at its most
awesome, but we'll not be awed.

Outside the window, through the slashing rains, we see a black cyclist. Bareheaded, huddled against the wheel, he pedals on. We see scattered groups of black women and children walking along the road or whatever people do in these circumstances. Some of the women have bundles balanced on their heads. Where are they going? Must they be there at an appointed hour, even in this storm? Bill Olds manages a remarkably deft turn. The pedestrians are out of sight.

Pretoriaskop. It is the lodge where we shall spend this night. Each of us is assigned a hut. Mine is Number Fifty-eight. I seat myself on the cot. Am I Hemingway's great white hunter? What *is* across the river and beyond the trees?

There is a gentle rap at the door. I open it. A scrawny black man, a bantamweight, smiles wanly. His wrinkles and wizened appearance tell me he's way up there in years. He is wearing those small child pants.

"I am John, mastah. Your bedroom boy."

I stare at him, stupidly.

At last, I say, "Come in."

"I will make your bed, mastah. I will fill your basin. I will fill your jug. I will sweep your floor." He will attend to all my wishes, he says.

I wish for him to talk to me.

"Yes, mastah."

I shut the door.

I invite him to be seated. He hesitates. I sit on the cot. He sits on the chair. I scratch my head.

"What is it, mastah?"

Oh boy.

"I'm not your master."

"No?" He appears bewildered. "What are you, mastah?"

Oh Christ, I wish I knew. I'd be a millionaire. I'll try not to sound too stupid.

For starters: "How old are you?" Why did I ask that? Rude and awkward.

"I think about fifty-two," he says. "I'm not quite sure." I had him pegged as a young seventy. In any event, "my boy" is two years older than I am.

He had been at this job for six years. Before that, he had served "in madame's house" in a faraway city. His father, one of sixteen children, had been "a police boy" for the railroad. He himself has nine children: five girls and four boys. They live on a farm in White River. He has a few head of cattle. We had passed White River on our way here. It's a good forty miles off. Does he see his family on weekends?

"Weekends?" He repeats the word so slowly. It's plain he doesn't understand what it means. I soon find out why.

He works seven days a week. His hours: three in the morning to eight at night. His pay: three pounds a month. And whatever guests, such as myself, see fit to toss his way. He goes home every night. It is my turn to be bewildered. How does he do it?

"I manage," he says, managing a smile. "Everybody is suffering."

"What do you hope your children will be?" I ask. I try to be neither patron nor interviewer, but I'm failing on both counts.

"I will be very glad if they will clean up people who have hurt on their hands," he says. I squint at the microphone.

"When they got sores," he explains.

"Doctors?"

"Yes, doctors," he says. "Not native doctors. European doctors. My daughter says, 'I don't want to be fooled. I want to be well-educated.' I said, 'Okay. I must sell the cattle that you must be *well*-educated.' I am not well-educated. I am half-educated. Of course, I can hear when you people are talking." He laughs softly.

His people, he says, are Bush Buck Ridge.

"What is your name?" I ask.

"John," he says, as though speaking to a retarded child. "I told you."

"No, no," I say. "What is the name your father gave you?"

He looks at me intently. Who is this guy, anyway? He smiles. "Magwiana." He whispers it.

I take out a piece of paper. Slowly, he spells it out for me. Slowly, I write it down. I show it to him. He laughs. There is a touch of surprise to his laugh.

"Is that your first name or your family name?" I ask.

"My name is Magwiana Hlachayo." He pronounces it deliberately. I repeat it and get it wrong. Patiently, he enunciates it again. He spells it. Slowly, I write it down. He laughs.

"John is not my real name. The white people gave it to me because they can't say Magwiana Hlachayo." We both laugh. He must go now. He'll be back tomorrow morning to serve me.

At five in the morning, pale moon to the left, blazing sun to the right, Magwiana Hlachyo is at the door, bearing coffee. When I return from the excursion in the park and have seen all the animals, he has a surprise for me, he says.

From our bus, we see all manner of beasts wandering in the preserve, free and easy. Gnus, liberated from crossword puzzle squares; they are called wildebeests out here; warthogs, tusks at the ready, cousins to wild boars; a herd of small deer, taking their matutinal stroll; zebras, squat as fire plugs, huddled against bushes; clambering monkeys, nervous, busy, trying to take center stage and failing; buffaloes, out for their morning jog, minding their own business; an impala, posing in the bright sunlight, an innocent young maiden, unaware that a leopard has his eye on her and is poised to spring; a crocodile in the stream, half-camouflaged by surrounding greenery, patiently awaiting his breakfast—the impala is pigmeat to him; a couple of elephants, swinging their trunks, overwhelming all else within range; a baboon, hitchhiking, hopping onto our bus, and after a few hundred yards, hopping off, casually showing us his red ass . . .

(On the day of my departure from the country, a woman interviewer of the South African Broadcasting Company asked for my impressions. "Never," said I, much impressed, "have I seen a land where the sky is so blue and the animals so free.")

It is late afternoon at Pretoriaskop. There is a gentle rap at the door. It is Magwiana Hlachayo. He enters. In his hand is something of a plant. It is for me, he says. His twelve-year-old daughter made these flowers last night. She is his favorite child. The one who wants to be a doctor.

"I told her about the white man who asked for my real name," he says. I hold the plant in my hand like a hockey champion cradling the Stanley Cup; I am equally articulate.

"It is the first time a white man asks me these questions," he continues. "As long as I have been in this park, I have never seen a European sitting together with a native."

There is a knock on the door. Four black men, in small boys' pants, stand there. Magwiana Hlachyo invites them in. He introduces me to each. Everybody is laughing. Jack Wallace enters. It's as crowded as the Marx Brothers' stateroom. There is more laughter.

Emilio is Magwiana's brother-in-law. He is the petrol boy. My co-host urges me to ask him questions, which he will translate since Emilio knows little English. Emilio wants his small daughter "to be a mistress to look after people laying on the bed."

A nurse?

"Yes, a nurse," replies Magwiana Hlachayo. Emilio nods his head many times.

I recognize one of the others as the young floor scrubber from Swaziland. I had spoken to him before, while he was at his task in the office. Two white men, within earshot, had been talking about blacks as spoiled children.

Jack Wallace asks Magwiana Hlachayo, "When white men talk, do you feel they talk as though you weren't there?"

The other doesn't quite understand. "Will you say that again, mastah?"

Jack and I act out a European conversation with all the appropriate gestures. There is much laughter. Softly, Magwiana Hlachayo, who now understands, says, "I'm feeling bad on it. My heart is sore. I am also very cross because it is not very nice."

Jack says something about Magwiana Hlachayo having dignity. The other doesn't understand.

"What is dignity?" he asks.

"Dignity is a strange word," I say.

"Dignity is a strange word," he repeats ever so slowly, as though in the saying of it, he might understand.

"Whatever is it, you got it," says Jack.

In a few moments, we'll be taking off. It is time for good-byes.

"Can I get anything from the master when he leaves here?" asks Magwiana.

I surreptitiously shove a fistful of crumpled rand into his hand.

"Thank you, mastah," he says quietly. It doesn't seem to be exactly what he wants, though he certainly can use the dough.

"What?" I ask, not quite sure.

"I want a letter."

"A letter? To whom?"

"To me. Write something, mastah. Write to Magwiana Hlachayo. With your name."

I do so. It is, I imagine, an exchange of gifts, though I've a hunch I got much the better of the deal.

As, at this moment, I look at something of a plant, with its multi-colored paper flowers and wire stems, I wonder about the child who made it. She is now twenty-six. By this time, she may indeed be well-educated. If not in medicine, in other matters.

2

Meeting the Chief

I am in the back seat of a car, speeding toward Stanger. It is a suburb of Durban, where once Mohandas Karamchand Gandhi worked at the law.

Was I fifteen or sixteen when I first came upon Romain Rolland's biography of the Mahatma? How, though his practice was a busy one, humiliation was his daily fare. At this moment, on this highway, 14,000 miles from home, there rolls about in my head, unaccountably, like some loose ball of yarn, unraveling, the lyrics of a Leadbelly blues:

> Woke up this mornin'
> Blues was 'round my bed
> Ate my breakfast
> Blues was in my bread.

Did Gandhi hear the Hindi equivalent of these lyrics while listening to a raga "in the evenin' when the sun go down"? In any event, he said no to the sahib, Afrikaner style. Was it here in Durban that *satyagraha* came into being and the great soul was born?

Reading Rolland, I recall, did cause me some personal problems. At the hotel my mother ran in Chicago, there was the weekly task of applying the blowtorch to the bedsprings of our patrons: death to all bedbugs. I refused to serve, having been persuaded by the Mahatma's credo of *ahimsa*: non-injury to all living things. I conscientiously objected. We lost two guests that week. Such is the risk run when one truly becomes a true believer.

Jack Wallace is seated beside me. He is executive editor of the *San Francisco Examiner*. He has a camera. I have a tape recorder. George Jones is driving. We hired him last night. George is what much of this memoir is about.

We're on our way to see the Chief. Albert John Luthuli, a Zulu, is chieftain of the Groutville people, democratically elected, as was his father before him. He had been awarded the Nobel Peace Prize for 1961. Small good that's done him. He has been under area arrest for some time. George Jones has no idea whom we're visiting.

It is February 1963. It is cold as hell in Chicago, but it's summer down here, south of the Equator. George is driving at a pretty good clip. He seems to know what he's doing.

There are jacaranda trees to our right, lavender, trembling, and alive. To our left is the Indian Ocean. Never have I seen a body of water so flat, so without sound, so absolutely without life. Talk about a painted ocean. I see no painted ship, but was it here the Ancient Mariner experienced his moment of epiphany, as the bug-bird slipped off his neck into this dead deep? One day I'll run into a Coleridge scholar and I'm sure he'll let me know. It is evening and darkening fast. Call it moonshade. I am reminded of those Doré woodcuts I squinted at as a kid.

I had dreams, not at all bad, after peeking at Dante's *Inferno*. Forty years later, a wild, possessed street-girl named Lily offered me her vision of Hell: "It's just hands, reaching up, trying to get out. With sort of fire around them. The more that people on earth pray for them, the higher their hands come out and finally it touches God and He brings them up to Heaven." Lily had never seen Doré's stuff. Nor did I have the heart to tell her they were stuck down there forever and ever.

On a number of occasions, Mahalia Jackson tried to save me. One evening, during a concert of which I was M.C., she sang a soaring, absolutely awesome "City Called Heaven." I was pole-axed; to such an extent that I forgot my cue. Mahalia, triumphant, looked toward me: "I know Studs ain't a believer, but if I could save him . . ." I mumbled, "Baby, I'm beyond salvation, but if anybody could do it, you're the one." Even Mahalia failed.

*   *   *

A few days before, I had been in Johannesburg. Among the people I had visited was the novelist Nadine Gordimer. Aside from her giftedness, there is a tensile strength beneath her china-doll delicacy. On learning that my companions and I were due in Durban, she suggested a meeting with the Chief. I was, of course, delighted. But how is it possible if he's under area arrest?

Her suggestion: When you reach an Indian marketplace in Durban, find a public telephone and call this number. Ask for B. W. Medawar. He is a close friend and colleague of the Chief. His phone is undoubtedly tapped by the SB—Special Branch. It is South Africa's equivalent of the Gestapo, KGB, FBI, CIA, take your choice. Simply say you're a journalist from America and a friend of Nadine Gordimer. Say nothing else. He'll know what you want.

The next day, thirty-five of us, in a chartered bus from Louis Botha Airport, Durban, were taken to just such a marketplace.

Perhaps I should go back to the beginning of this *Winterreise*. It was an afternoon in January, early January 1963. I was in my slovenly hole of an office at WFMT, the Chicago radio station where I do my daily broadcast. A call came from Lufthansa. Would I be their guest on a premier flight: Frankfurt to Johannesburg? Two delightful weeks in South Africa.

Lufthansa was inviting five American journalists. They'd like one from the Midwest. I was flattered. I have hardly considered myself a journalist. Most of my years have been as a radio disk jockey and as an occasional actor. I was about to say: danke schön, aber nein, auf Weidersehen. I'm not especially delighted by our *de facto* apartheid, let alone Sou'frica's *de jure* species.

Sou'frica. Casually, as pronounced by Afrikaners, the two words are welded into one. It is not accidental, Cecil Skotness, a white painter, indicated to me. The blackness implicit in the word *Africa* is thus diminished.

Who said you have to bear sweet tidings? Why don't you go and simply report what you see? That's a fair paraphrase of what the voice on the Lufthansa end said. I must admit I liked the man's style. I agreed to go.

We descended at Jan Smuts Airport. It was dazzling, a beautiful summer morning. Green all around. Black shadows. Silent and soft-treading, moved along at a certain pace, carrying baggage and all sorts of containers. They were dressed in what appeared to be babies' rompers. The whites—Afrikaners, English, Huguenots—wore khaki shorts; stalwart as any Rudyard Kipling hero. And where was Errol Flynn on this great gettin' up morning?

At the Langham Hotel, the husky young black man was scrubbing away at the hallway floor. I was fascinated by an incongruity: his Muhammad Ali physique in rompers. At the lodge in Kruger National Park, two white men in khaki shorts were holding forth on the childish nature of "natives." Within earshot, a "native" was sweeping . . . He understood English well enough to carry on a murmured, slightly labored, though quite comprehensible conversation. He had come from Swaziland, he told me. As a small boy, he took care of his father's cow. Of course he understood the conversation across the room. God knows it was loud enough. He was in rompers, too.

One of the men let me know there was no point in talking to the boy: "He doesn't understand a word you say." I agreed. I'm known as an agreeable sort. (I was once informed that William Buckley, Jr., was a serious thinker. I agreed. It was three in the morning, I had had much to drink, and I was tired.) "Might as well talk to yourself," the man added. I nodded and grinned stupidly. "I always talk to myself," I said.

Each morning, as I shuffle down the alley, shortcutting my way to the bus, I mumble, curse, sing snatches of arias, pop songs of the twenties, and hymns. Occasionally, if the wind is with me and God smiles, I run into kindred spirits: the old lady in the long tattered black coat, lugging her brown shopping bag; the nasty old man, shaking his fist and hurling lightning bolts at the heavens; the young fat man, lonely, slovenly, furious, and hurting; the chortling one of indeterminate age. My crowd.

The man shook his head and laughed softly. So did his companion. What's to be done with these people? A black manchild and a whiteface clown. The "native" grinned stupidly as the man, in some sort of patois, gruffly ordered him to get on with his work.

During our Stanger Rendezvous, I mentioned these occurrences to Chief Luthuli. He laughed. Often, I've noticed, black people laugh at the moment a humiliation is recounted. Not a belly laugh; always from the throat. Big Bill Broonzy was rich in such laughter as he told of abrupt dismissals for no cause or restroom rebuffs. "Laughin' on the outside, cryin' on the inside" goes an old country blues. Raging on the inside is more like it today. Of course, said the Chief. "One of the sore points is that we are not regarded as human beings. But if occasionally we are, it is as ignorant children." And so, rompers.

In the light-filtered room at Jan Smuts, obviously reserved for Very Important People, we were greeted by General von Mellentin and his associates. The general, it was whispered to me, had served gallantly with Rommel in the North African campaign. He was director of Lufthansa, South Africa. Champagne and canapés. It was a most gracious welcome. Was this out of a Lillian Hellman play?

Talk about graciousness. A few nights later, we were feted at the General's house. His wife, a golden blond beauty, and his two daughters, equally golden and equally beautiful, were our hostesses. The wines, the food, the talk. I was seated next to Greta. My clatter-tongue had been at work a few moments earlier. I had mumbled something about "that fuckin' apartheid" to one of the other guests. He had undoubtedly passed it on to Greta.

"Nobody likes apartheid," she said to me. I leaned away to look at her anew. I was Raymond Griffith. "Yes," she continued, softly, "when people first come here, they're against it. But when you live here a while, you see that it is right."

Snap. I'm off again. I can't keep my big mouth shut. "Why, Miss Mellentin, I heard those very words last night. At the Cul De Sac."

"Cul De Sac?"

"A night club in downtown Joburg. Have you ever been there?"

"No."

"The SB is keeping on eye on it. They suspect it serves blacks. Anyway, I met this young advertising man. He had come from Amsterdam five years ago. He said just what you said."

"Of course. You'd feel the same way if you lived here awhile."

"I would?"

"I'm sure of it."

"But here's the funny thing, Miss Mellentin. As this young Dutch-man and I were talking, Rosie was singing a song."

"Who is Rosie?"

"A black girl who sounds very much like Miriam Makeba."

"Makeba sings beautifully."

"Rosie, too. So this Dutchman, he now likes apartheid, y'see, he stops Rosie, as she passes our table. He says to her, 'Are you doing anything later, Rosie?' "

Greta was murmuring to the guest at her left. I had no idea her attention wandered so quickly. Ah well, *la donna è* definitely *mobile*. The wine was really heady; I had no idea how the evening ended.

In the cab, heading back to our hotel, Jack Wallace let me know. He had been seated at the head table, what with his being a newspaper editor. He sat at the General's right; a Hamburg editor, who worked for Axel Springer, William Randolph Hearst's soul brother, sat at his left. The General, Jack recounted, proposed a toast to the three of them. "Your country, the United States of America, your country, Germany, and my adopted one, South Africa, have much in common. Our fates are one. May we always be together." Jack and I, bemused, puffed away at fat Havanas, courtesy of our host.

It was gracious living to which Cecil Skotness referred, as we sat in his house in Observatory. A middle-class suburb to the north of Johannesburg. "Life is very good. Look at the house I live in and the size of the grounds, a half-acre of lawn to the back. On the sort of money I earn, in no other part of the world would I be able to live this way. I have a very able servant as every other white person out here does. People eat well and drink well. The theaters and concerts are good. Lively conversations about art. Sport loving. And all the rest of it that goes to make a lush society. Decadent, perhaps. A happy society for whites." Skotness paused. A long pause. "One mustn't think too deeply, of course."

Bill Williams had no such problem. An Englishman, he had been performing for the past six years at the piano bar of the Prince Edward Hotel, Durban.

"South Africa has been very kind to me indeed. The servant situation is very much easy here. There are so many million black people here all looking for jobs, brought in from the jungle. They work for absolutely nothing. You can get a very good servant for nine pounds a month. They're not really downtrodden, these chaps, don't get that idea. The average house provides them with civilized amenities they've never really had. Really, life out here couldn't be better. It's a wonderful, wonderful life."

What would I like to hear? He noodled at the keys. I swashed the ice in my tall glass around and around. It made a pleasant sound in this air-conditioned room. All the more so, since Durban in February is unbearably hot and humid. "Fats Waller," I said. "Of course." He was delighted. " 'Honeysuckle Rose,' eh?" "Do you know 'Black and Blue'?" He didn't. I settled for "Honeysuckle Rose."

At Jan Smuts, a singularly tall young journalist came over. He called me by name. Was it my disheveled appearance? My red-checked shirt? We had a mutual friend, he said, who told him I'd be around. It was true; I had written letters to friends of friends. He handed me a note. Intrigue was in the air. I was Humphrey Bogart. Unfortunately, it was too hot for a trenchcoat. From the start, my much too lively imagination was at work. Or was it imagination? There was a dreamlike quality to the day; and to all the days that followed.

We were at the moment on an island, in this VIP room—no, it was more of a reserve. That was the exquisite irony. I was to visit some of the other reserves where the "natives" lived, where all had to be when the sun went down—Sophiatown, Alexandra, Soweto. This was the most isolated of all. It was delightful, Europeanly euphoric, if you didn't glance outside the picture window: vague black figures against the now blazing sun, bearing all sorts of burdens. Speaking only when spoken to, as properly brought up children have always been taught. As, in all civilized societies, children have been taught to address their elders as "Sir" and "Ma'am," so these blacks were taught to address all whites as "Baas" and "Mastah." Even I was called "Baas." I did a double-take each time it happened. Some dozen years have gone by and I still have a slight crick in my neck.

Durban. Our bus pulled into an Indian marketplace. Remember, I had to make that phone call to B. W. Medawar. We had but three days to spend in Durban. I had to work fast if I was to see Chief Luthuli. We were allowed one hour to shop. All sorts of bargains, we were told.

It was a huge arcade, off the corner of Brook and Victoria. Grain, spices, exotic foods, hundreds of stalls, it seemed, offering trinket boxes, lotus lamps, Siamese jewelry, African curios, works in ivory and bamboo . . . But I was shopping for a telephone booth. I fingered the tikki in my pocket.

The place was swarming with tourists, just off the buses, courtesy, Durban Municipal Corporation. An Indian, who appeared to be knowing, pointed me in the direction of the booth. He was Mr. Kenyaban, whose job was akin to that of hotel detective–housekeeper. "I see that it's kept clean and catch pickpockets." Oh yes, Indians and Europeans go about it very well. They get along fine. Africans? Oh no, you can't trust them. You must watch them all the time. He doesn't "mingle much with them."

The telephone booth was occupied. Damn. A sign on one of the walls: Natal Open Twist Championship. Jets vs Searchers. Saturday. 8:00 P.M. to Midnight. A small-boned man, red-faced, was at the microphone. "Right you are, folks." His was a sharp voice, piercing. He didn't need the mike, really. A touch of Cockney. He was a Corporation courier, who drives a Mer*ceede*s bus, and guides tourists to markets, factories, and the Zulu reserve. Mr. Dixon's accent may have been lower-class, but he spoke with upper-class authority.

"Anything you buy 'ere, you get a ten-percent discount, especially if you're off our bus. This is Mr. Naran's stall. If it's no good, or if for some reason you are not satisfied, bring it back to me and I'll settle *'im*." Mr. Naran, moon-faced behind the counter, seemed not to have heard. (Did Mr. Kenyaban know Mr. Dixon?) "You'll get a fair an' square deal 'ere. Okay, folks, carry on."

Ah, the telephone was free. Hold it. Two men in dark suits were loitering nearby. They were watching me. Oh Christ, not them! They *are* everywhere, aren't they? The secret police. Oh God, you know the type. I couldn't see their feet, but five gets you ten they wore white socks.

The Old Chicago Red Squad was euphemistically called the Industrial Squad. Their job, back in the thirties, was to break strikes, especially those of the aborning CIO. Today, their mission, and an equally dedicated one, is to hound-dog anybody who fails to see in Mayor Richard J. Daley the glow of Gautama Buddha. In the old days, they sported green fedoras and white socks.

The green fedora. Even now, I see it, silhouetted in all its verdure, as the unmarked car's big searchlight was turned on me. I was shuffling down the street one evening, in a vagrant's fashion, on my way to a rehearsal: *Waiting for Lefty* by Clifford Odets.

The Chicago Repertory Group had been organized the year before, 1934. The planned repertoire: plays and sketches, political in content. Some of the work was agitprop, performed in union halls, workingmen's taverns, soup kitchens, and along the picket line.

A workingmen's tavern. Sam's Place. May 31, 1937. It is within

hollering distance of the Republic Steel Plant on Chicago's far South
Side. On this spring afternoon, the place is crowded. The men are
on strike. They are members of the Steel Workers' Organizing Committee. Some of them have their arms in slings. Others have bandaged
heads. A couple are on crutches. All are in shock. They are among
the survivors of a Memorial Day picnic that was held yesterday on
the grounds of Republic Steel. Ten of their colleagues were killed
by Chicago police. Most of the wounds were in the back.

Three of us, members of the Chicago Repertory Group, were
called upon by Harry Harper, one of the union's organizers. Could
we perform at Sam's Place? Songs, sketches. It would help the morale
of the strikers. Harry himself is not there. He had lost an eye yesterday. Thirty-nine years later, George Patterson, an ailing septua-
generian, remembers me as one of the singers. Not quite. I can't
carry a tune if my life depended on it. I was an actor in one of the
sketches. George, an embattled young Scot, was a picket captain
during the 1937 strike.

A soup kitchen. It is within a block of Hearst Square. It has been
a long, tortuous strike, a critical one for the newly born American
Newspaper Guild. The management of the *Chicago Herald-Examiner*,
Hearst's big one in our city, has been adamant in its nonrecognition.
Only last week, a newspaper delivery truck driver, an alumnus of
my high school, had slugged a picketing journalist with an auto jack
and knocked him cold. In the soup kitchen, three of us are playing
out a sketch, written by one of our members, Red Bunning. It is
called "Guild-Edged Security."

A union hall. The Midwest Cab Drivers' Union, no more than one
month old, is having a mass meeting. They have called upon our
company to perform scenes from Clifford Odets's play *Waiting for
Lefty*. It is highly appropriate, dealing as it does with a cab drivers'
strike. Its locale is, poetically enough, a union hall. Something happens this evening, wholly unplanned. In the play, a striker exposes
his brother as a fink. The actor, portraying the fink, runs off the
stage, through the aisle, and out. On this occasion, he doesn't quite
make it. The realism is too much for the striking cabbies in the
audience. Several reach out and clobber the unfortunate actor. I,
playing the role of his brother, holler, "Don't slug him, don't slug
him, he's only an actor!" Only an actor. The unfortunate one sported
a beautiful shiner for a good week. Social realism in theater does
have its occupational hazards.

The members of the company, young and passionate, were non-professionals, though a number did have such dreams. The many of us were caught up in the radiance of commitment. A better world acomin'. Some of the gods did subsequently fail; but those were not doubting times. As Harold Clurman so aptly described the epoch, they were fervent years.

I was, on this memorable evening, wearing a gray fedora, tipped down toward my eyebrows. I had seen photographs of John L. Lewis thus glowering at the world; and so, too, it seemed, did his fedora. Unfortunately, it was not a cigar chomped in my jaw; it was a cigarette, loose on my lower lip. Though I felt John Llewellyn Lewis, I may have appeared Jimmy Cagney. I'd have settled for either image. In any event, the car swerved to the curb.

"C'mere, you!"

"Me?" I was astonished. Perhaps they thought I *was* Cagney.

"Yeah, you!"

"Wha-what is it?" That didn't sound like Jimmy Cagney.

I saw no face in the glare; merely the green of the hat. It could have been Iris March, for all I knew. My companion nudged me. "Red Squad. Don't argue."

I walked slowly, with deliberate step, to the car, trying to maintain an air of dignity and calm. I was thinking Leslie Howard, but it wasn't working. There were three of them. Three green fedoras. Three faces of baby pink and baby fat. Cherubic.

"What are ya doin' on the street?"

"Walking."

"Walkin', huh?"

"Yes, sir." I stood stiffly at attention.

"Where ya walkin' to?"

"To a rehearsal."

"Rehearsal, huh?"

Oh boy, I'd better watch my language. "Yes, sir."

There was a pause in the conversation. The three, expressionless, stared at me. I hope I looked presentable. At length, the talking one said, "Well, get goin'." There was a note of reluctance in his voice, as though he were beginning to enjoy my company and was sorry to see our *ad hoc* acquaintance end in so cursory a manner.

"If we catch ya loiterin', we'll pull ya in."

I had turned away, much relieved. His parting shot impelled me to mumble wretchedly to myself. "I'm a citizen."

"Whad you say? Come back here!"

Oh God, me and my big mouth. Why can't I ever let well enough alone?

"What was dat you said?"

"When?"

"Just now. What ya said?"

"I'm a . . . a citizen."

"Citizen, huh? Get in here!"

I found myself in the back seat of an unmarked car, between two large men. The driver, too, turned his attention toward me. Obviously, they had a live one.

"Wise guy, huh?"

"No, sir."

"What's yer name?"

"Terkel."

"Turtle, huh?"

"No. Terkel. In some parts of the South, they do pronounce turtle as turkle." I had been hearing some folk music at the time; I thought I'd be helpful. "A turtledove is called a turkledove. A mud turtle is called a mud turkle. The same way they call brittle, brickle."

A long silence, broken only by their heavy, labored breathing. I was holding my breath.

"A real wise guy, huh?"

"No, sir." I knew better. Had I been wise, I'd have kept my trap shut.

"You *are* a wise guy."

"No, I'm not."

"So you think we're dumb, huh?" It was said so softly, almost gently. But oooh, there was a nice razor edge to it. Slicing.

"Oh no."

"Shut up."

"Yes, sir."

"How old are ya?"

"Twenty-three."

"Twenty-three, huh?" I had no idea my comments were so provocative.

"Citizen." Even now, I hear the deep hurt in his voice. He sounded so wretched, lost, and put upon. Perhaps I should have apologized.

"One a them," said the other. "Let's take 'im to the station." The driver turned back to the wheel.

My companion came forth. "Officers, he didn't mean it."

"Citizen." It had a mournful sound.

"He doesn't know what he's saying." My companion was most helpful.

"What'll we do with 'im?"

"Aahh," said the second, "let 'im go this time."

To me, number one said, "We'll letcha go this time. But watch it, wise guy. Next time . . ."

As I stumbled my way out of the car, past fleshy knees and entangled legs, I noticed the white socks.

They're watching me, the two. Remember, I had been using my tape recorder rather promiscuously. And publicly. I had been talking to an inordinate number of black people. And here I am about to telephone someone whose wires are tapped in order to reach a black leader who's under area arrest. I knew it. Things had been going much too smoothly. I nodded toward them and smiled my stupid smile. They neither nodded nor smiled back. A bad sign.

If only they would go away. Mr. Naran was smiling at me, expectantly. I had been hovering near his stall. "May I show you something?" That's it. I'd clown. Ed Wynn, the Perfect Fool. I waved at the men near the phone booth, some fifteen feet away. I squeezed my right eye tightly shut; a wink, a palpable wink. The American tourist and the Indian merchant are about to engage in the classic pose: haggling.

"Mr. Naran," I was hardly audible, as I leaned across the counter. "Could we put on an act? Try to sell me something. I just want those men to hear. They're old friends of mine. Just a joke. I won't buy, but when it's over, we'll shake hands. I have ten rand in my fist. For your trouble." A rand is worth about a dollar and a half; not nearly the price of an Indian's daily humiliation in these quarters. Mr. Naran was delighted. He was good, too.

"See this lucky bean. Inside is the smallest family of animals in the world, And that's no lie. Have a look. Inside are six different animals. See? Elephants, lions, tigers. Look here. The Chinese call it one of the seven wonders of the world. You may have it for only fifteen pounds."

"Ten."

"It cost me twelve, sir."

"Eleven."

"Well, all right. I think I'll let you have it for eleven."

"Mr. Naran," I whispered hoarsely, "not yet! Don't give in so fast. Be tougher, please." "Oh, I'm sorry," he whispered. Loudly: "I changed my mind. I really don't know what possessed me. You see, sir, it cost me twelve, as I told you. Really, sir . . ."

We continued in this fashion through several more such exchanges. I looked up at the two; I shrugged helplessly. What can you do with these people? The men were smiling. They understood. They tossed a salute at me and wandered off. Mr. Naran and I shook hands and I hurried toward the phone.

Mr. Medawar's voice was quite friendly, though no words were wasted. I said I was a friend of Nadine Gordimer. "Of course. You'd like to meet my friend?" That was the general idea. Would I be in my room tomorrow night at eight? He'll phone, set the time, a day, and place of the rendezvous.

Were those two really SB men? I doubt it. I haven't the faintest idea who they were. I *imagined* they were secret police. It added a piquant note to the occasion. They might well have been, you know. Considering South Africa. Isn't it true of any totalitarian society? Or one approaching it? You imagine the Eye, even when it isn't on you. Isn't that what they want? Remember John Edgar Hoover's way with subversives. Make them think there's an FBI man under every bed.

I myself had been visited a number of times by an FBI pair. Especially in the fifties. Clean-cut young men, no nonsense, the Hardy Boys come to manhood. Efrem Zimbalist, Jr.'s, TV offerings always fascinated me. I invariably thought of Efrem Zimbalist, Sr. The concert fiddler. He was up there with Mischa Elman and Toscha Seidel. It was constant cause for reflection. Had Junior been taught to scrape away at Cui's "Orientale" or "Indian Lament," instead of spending so much of his childhood playing hide-and-seek, might not his soul have been saved as Mahalia Jackson tried to salvage mine? Obviously there was failure in both instances.

I am confident they have a fairly rich dossier on me. During the thirties and forties, I appeared at many "subversive" gatherings. God knows how many speeches I made. I earned quite a name for myself in the Midwest as an effective collection speaker. Years later, Mahalia was to say I missed my calling: preacher. I'd guess that half the organizations listed by Harry Truman's attorney general as subversive profited to the tune of a buck or two, thanks to my windiness.

I didn't miss a bet. The Anti-Fascist Refugee Committee. Beneficiaries: surviving Spaniards, exiles in Southern France and Mexico, who had been foolish enough to resist Franco. Friends of the Abraham Lincoln Brigade. Beneficiaries: young Americans stupid enough to volunteer in the fight against Franco; their stupidity compounded by the hard fact that El Caudillo had the help of Mussolini's Blue Division and Hitler's Condor Legion. The Civil Rights Congress. Beneficiaries: dissenters—damn commies—who were idiotic enough to lack sufficient funds for lawyers and court costs. And I quite volubly supported Henry Wallace for President in 1948.

My most perverse performance took place in that altogether fateful year, 1948. I agreed to act as master of ceremonies at the celebration of Paul Robeson's fiftieth birthday. It was at the Chicago Civic Opera House. For some inexplicable reason, it was a terribly moving experience. I had been advised by wiser heads to stay away. Keep your nose clean. I told them I always carry two handkerchiefs in my pocket.

Now I constantly ask myself this question, Why did I deliberately ignore the advice of these good people, who had my best interests at heart? Had I brains, I might have grown up to be Daniel Patrick Moynihan. Dare I dream the dream of Dr. Kissinger? I might have become a respected contributor to *Commentary*. Hell, I might have written a scholarly treatise proving Alger Hiss indubitably guilty. Being Jewish, I would most certainly have come out courageously, four-square, against the Rosenbergs. God, to think I might even have edited a celebrated journal for the CIA. Oh well.

Why did I behave as I did? I have been giving this a good going over for some time. Was it because I felt a certain compassion for the FBI? Possibly. One thing I knew: they needed work, redemptive in nature.

Consider this. For more than two decades, they had been clownishly inept in investigating the Chicago Syndicate. The Boys in charge of organized crime—I had a passing acquaintance with some of the boys who worked for the Boys—looked upon the white knights of Mr. Hoover (what other kind were there?) as more comical than the Keystone Kops. It was embarrassing to a law-abiding American boy like myself.

Consider this. Melvin Purvis, the tiny Virginian in charge of the FBI Chicago Bureau, almost blew the Dillinger kill. A battalion of

Chicago police came within seconds of a bloody shootout with suspicious characters hanging around the Biograph Theatre. The FBI, its mind on an exclusive, had neglected to inform the locals of the stakeout. John Edgar Hoover was choleric, as Purvis was publicly acclaimed: Dillinger's nemesis.

I once met Melvin Purvis. Was it 1933? He had written me a letter, on FBI stationery, inviting me to see him. It was an interview concerning a job. You see, I was unhappy at law school. My one ambition, at the time, was to get a civil service job. That's what I really wanted. Something steady. Something not too exciting or exacting. So that I might, without too much on my mind, see movies and plays and weekend baseball games and attend concerts. I felt I had the makings of a good spectator.

I had, a year or so before, taken a civil service examination. I assume I scored okay. Otherwise, Mr. Purvis would not have invited me. The job: fingerprint classifier for the FBI. Pay: $1,260 a year. Melvin Purvis was friendly enough; though I was aware he was studying me. Why an applicant for a civil service job paying $1,260 a year is subject to study is something I haven't yet been able to figure out. I remember his neatness, his diminutive size, and his soft Southern accent. It was a year or so before he would achieve renown as the FBI man who did in John Dillinger.

He asked me about myself. He was curious: Why should a University of Chicago Law School student seek so modest a job? I tried to explain. He didn't appear too impressed. What kind of books did I read? he asked. I told him Ring Lardner and Mark Twain. What else? Well, it happens that a month or so before, Professor Morris Raphael Cohen of the City College of New York had lectured at the university. I enjoyed it. So I said Morris Raphael Cohen, though I had read none of his writings. Mr. Purvis asked if I was of Hebrew extraction. I told him yes. I don't remember much else of the conversation, though it was polite. He thanked me and said he'd let me know. I never heard from him again. What did I do wrong? To think that I might have been a member of the FBI. Oh well.

Consider this. My mother's hotel was within a mile of the Biograph, now something of a national shrine. The neighborhood, unlike the country at large, was aware of the goof-up and near massacre. Were it not for a last-second recognition, there might have been memorialized, along with Ludlow and Attica, the Biograph Massacre.

Regard my neighborhood. Aside from transient men, there lived here the boys who worked for the Boys and policemen, who on more than one occasion worked for the Boys. I was one of the few law and order people on the block. My neighbors were laughing. Imagine my humiliation.

What was even worse, the director of the FBI bore a remarkable resemblance to Charlie Country, the fat first banana during the glory days of the Rialto, where Ada Leonard, Peaches, and other lovelies unzipped and stripped. Charlie wore baggy pants; the director was a fashion plate. But they were one, both in flesh and in psyche. The burlesque comic and the director shared the same hallmark: out-rageous pronunciamentos offered with the voice of authority. For some reason, best explained by critics of the lively arts, one was funny; the other was not.

Imagine my bewilderment. I didn't quite know what to do. My moment of decision came when the Cold War took over. Word had come to the land that the FBI was taking out after an alien breed that thought dangerous thoughts: commies, perverts, social workers, professors, union agitators, and certain kinds of housewives. My neighbors were delighted. They no longer laughed at the FBI. They were always patriotic. And wanted to do their bit. So did I.

I had been, from boyhood on, influenced, and not for the better, by certain dirty old men living at the hotel, who constantly favored me with little nickel blue books: writings of Eugene V. Debs, Clarence Darrow, Thomas Paine, Bob Ingersoll, Upton Sinclair, Voltaire, that bunch. I suspect that may have been why I was omni-present, in the thirties, forties, and fifties, at those gatherings that subsequently found their way onto the attorney general's list. Still, I was unfulfilled.

When the FBI, in the fifties, was on its way toward redemption in the eyes of my neighbors and taking out after the real enemy, I appeared more frequently than ever at those observed places. Oh, you have no idea how persuasive and eloquent I had become as a collection speaker. When I recognized an FBI man in the audience, I glowed.

You realize what I had in mind? The FBI needed some gold stars, desperately; certainly in the eyes of my neighborhood acquaintances. The more dossiers they gathered, the more such stars on their report cards. Naturally, I sought a dossier for myself; and one as rich as possible. It was not for myself I wanted it. You understand that. It was for the good name of the FBI. I was, in a sense, a double agent.

The occasional FBI visits to my house were not always pleasant.

With a sense of some shame, I say this. My wife, usually the most gracious of hostesses, was, for some unaccountable reason, inhospitable. There were at least two occasions I recall when she peremptorily showed them to the door. She always let in small boys who sold magazine subscriptions for the benefit of the nation's halt, lame, and blind; as well as to make points that would enable them to attend Harvard. But to the FBI, she manifested—how can I say it?—contempt. I was, of course, terribly embarrassed.

I myself was hospitable at all times. I seated them. I offered them choices of Scotch or bourbon. I had triple shots in mind. Invariably, they refused. Once, I suggested vodka, making it quite clear it was domestic. I thought I was quite amusing. At no time did our visitors laugh. Nor did my wife. I felt bad. I did so want to make them feel at home. I never succeeded.

They had questions in mind. They frequently consulted small notebooks. They hardly had the chance to ask any of their questions. It wasn't that I was rude. On the contrary; I simply felt what I had to tell them was far more interesting than what they had to ask me.

I read Thoreau to them; his sermon on John Brown. Passages out of *Walden*. Paine. I told them these are times that try men's souls. And so on. We hold these truths, I even tried out on them. Nothing doing. Their attention wandered. They were like small restless boys in the classroom, wiggling in their seats. At times, I showed them where the bathroom was and asked if they wanted any reading matter. No, they didn't. I have done some of my most exploratory reading there, I told them. No response.

After several such visits, with a notable lack of response on their part, my patience, I must admit, did wear thin. On one occasion, a visitor took out his notebook and studied it. Our son, five years old at the time, peered over his shoulder. The guest abruptly shut the book. The boy was startled.

"Why did you do that?" I asked.

"He was peeking in my book."

"He's five years old."

"This is government information."

"Is it pornographic?"

"I don't know what you're talking about."

"Isn't it fit for a child to see?"

"This is serious."

"Does it have dirty words or dirty pictures?"

"What??"

"Does it? Come on, be a sport, lemme see. I won't show it to the kid."

With the determined step of an FBI man, he stalked toward the door. He had trouble with the lock. I opened it. "One for the road?" I was determinedly hospitable. He walked out without so much as a thank-you.

The last time I heard from the FBI was a good fifteen years ago. It was a telephone call. I was not in the best of moods. In sorting through my records, preparing for my disk jockey program, I had dropped a 78 rpm. It smashed into a million pieces. It was a collector's item: "Joe Louis Blues." Lyrics by Richard Wright. Vocal by Paul Robeson. Accompaniment, Count Basie and his band. I was furious as I answered the phone.

"Are you Louis Terkel, known as Studs?"

"Yeah!" Damn my clumsiness.

"This is Martin Shea, FBI." It was a rich, stentorian bass. Strong, firmly American.

"Cut the shit. Who is it? Eddie?" I was in no mood for badinage.

"Shea of the FBI." A note of uncertainty. An octave higher than before. A baritone.

"Fer Chrissake, don't fuck around! Jimmy, ya sonofabitch!"

"I'm Shea of the FBI." An intimation of tremolo. A tenor.

"Look, you cocksucker! I'm not in the mood. I just broke a valuable record. Understand?"

"I'm Shea of the FBI!" Another octave up. A mezzo-soprano. I was quite certain it was he. My fury, though, was uncontrollable. All the more so because it was he.

"Look, fucko. Keep this up and I'll kick the shit out of ya!"

Really! I'm so flabby I can't swat a mosquito.

The voice was higher now. It was a countertenor. No, it was a despairing falsetto. A castrato, that was it.

"I'm Shea of the FBI!"

"You prick . . ."

A click. He had hung up. From Feodor Chaliapin to Alfred Deller. It was a remarkable piece of virtuosity, surpassing even Yma Sumac. That was the last I heard from the FBI. Oh well.

As we were about to board the Durban bus, past the crowds, I suddenly found myself in the middle of what was obviously a domestic dispute. The woman was shouting at the man, who was abject in his acceptance. A Zulu husband and wife. My Uher was at the ready; but not for this. A private matter, the world o'er. I had the tape recorder going for the purpose of describing a busy street scene, that was all. Sounds, voices. I'm crazy about *vox humana*, especially when it flows free and easy. But this was something else.

I was pinned against the wall, she on one side of me, he on the other. He had slunk against my shoulder; I was his shield. Her imprecations were pouring into my microphone. Trapped as I was, I couldn't reach the STOP lever. There was no need for me to know Zulu to understand what an indignant wife was shouting.

A black policeman came by as the crowd gathered. He listened impassively. I smiled my sick Stan Laurel smile. He was ignored by the disputants. He wandered off, well aware that discretion was, in this instance, the better part of absurd valor. But not I. How do I always get into these situations?

I was twenty-one and had just drunk my first real beer. Prohibition had been repealed. Much sooner than H. L. Mencken had expected. As I left King's Palace, feeling all was quite well with the world, I saw a man hit a woman. Hard. She fell down onto the street. She got up and hit him. Hard. He fell down onto the street. They were middle-aged. They, too, had been at King's Palace and had had a few. He got up and now they flailed away at one another. I stepped between them and held up my hands, in the manner of a referee: It's all over. The two stared at me for a moment. A moment was all.

"An where do you play piano, ya sonofabitch?" It was he who muttered. Or was it she? In any event, they swung at me, both of them. I held up my hands, protecting myself as once I saw Young Griffo (in a *Ring* magazine photograph); the man nobody could hit. The blows were not as devastating as I had thought. My dignity, though, took a terrific beating. A bystander informed me: "Dey been doin' 'at fer twenny years. Dey're married. A word to da wise. Don' never mix." Wisdom, to paraphrase Stephen Vincent Benet, is a hard bought thing.

The following night. Prince Edward Hotel. It is Friday. Seven-thirty. A half-hour to go. I'm ready, Mr. Medawar, any time you are. I'm sprawled on my bed, newspapers scattered about. *Rand Daily Mail* and *Johannesburg Star*. New repressive laws. Protest meeting broken up, leaders arrested.

Alan Paton. Of course. *Cry, the Beloved Country*. A mutual friend gave me his phone number. He lives in Kloof, another suburb of Durban. Perhaps he's free this weekend. I call. He answers. Sunday morning is fine. Done.

Did I hear clicks on the phone? It's about seven forty-five. I call Jack Wallace and tell him the news. Wait a minute. The wires are crossed. I hear a voice, Afrikaner accent: "If that chap is looking for trouble, he'll get . . ." It's disconnected. I hang up. Oh no. Chances are it has nothing to do with me. I'm tempted to look under the bed.

Eight o'clock. The phone rings. It is B. W. Medawar. His friend will be delighted to meet us tomorrow night. Could we be at Medawar's house at eight? It's in Stanger. A forty-mile ride. He suggests I hire a car. Allow a good hour. If lost, stop in any Indian gas station or grocery store along the way. They'll know.

Saturday is a busy night, we are told, but we're lucky, a car is available. The driver will come by the hotel tomorrow at about six forty-five. The man's name is George Jones.

Saturday. The thirty-five of us are honored guests of the Lord Mayor of Durban. It's a cocktail party at the Town Hall: five to seven. The South African wine is good. Not much for domestic whiskey. An American distiller would do very well here indeed, we are told. Do we know any who might be interested? Jack and I are vamping till ready. Luthuli is on our mind.

More wine. We stumble toward a small circle of three. The first is a German travel agent, one of our fellow pilgrims. The other two are man and wife. He is a Japanese Jew. His wife, a Caucasian, is a dead ringer for Sophie Tucker. The man fascinates me; for he is now, officially, European. South Africa has recently concluded a trade pact with Japan and declared, business being business, that all Japanese are white.

He is an industrialist and is here on a trade mission. At the moment, he is not talking business. In this society, all conversations, no matter how they begin, settle down to one issue: race. It has already settled down by the time we joined the circle. The New European is holding forth: "Sawages. They sawages just fwom the twees." I can't quite make out the dialect. A touch of Oriental, yes.

But something else, too. I once heard Michael Redgrave try out a strange accent as Shylock, but it isn't that either. It's an instant dialect; a fusing of Japanese tone and Afrikaans feeling.

"What you do wi' chilwen? Spank. Bwack peopoo, chilwen. We have thwee." Sophie Tucker nods proudly. "You have three black children?" I am astonished. He laughs. Sophie Tucker laughs, too. The travel agent shakes his head. This one is always shaking his head at me.

It is six-thirty. Just as the party is getting good. And the New European is amenable to being recorded. Jack Wallace tugs at my sleeve. It is time to go. Reluctantly, as in a Fitzgerald travelogue, we bid farewell to Durban Town Hall. The sun is setting in the west. George Jones would be waiting for us. And so, we hoped, would B. W. Medawar and Chief Albert John Luthuli.

There is a hint of Cockney to George's accent. It is as though his studied, deliberate speech is an attempt to transcend London East End origins. I'm dead wrong, of course. It turns out he's from the Midlands and his father was bandmaster of the Coldstream Guards. His wife, Zelda, is "not a bad old stick. A very clever girl. We always smile, have a tickle, have a laugh, and everything's okay. She's a very strict girl. She's German, actually. We have our fights . . ." A long pause.

There is something that is definitely eating at him. "The European is so full of himself. He'll drive past and see a stranded motor car. Which has happened to me many times on the open road. He'll drive past, smoking his pipe, cigar, or cigarette and not care a blow about anybody else. Whereas the native and the Indian . . .

"Which happened to me once near Mossel Bay. I ran out of petrol. My wife, my son, and my daughter were all pushing the car. Big cars passed me, small cars. Who should stop on the road but a native? He got an old pipe that he had in the back of his car. We sucked out some petrol, put it in my car, and I was off on my way. Now what would you think? It makes one so really against your own. You're really sorry to be a European at times."

He's unhappy about apartheid? Oh no, not at all. "When one goes to the cinema, you like to go as a European. You don't like to sit next to any other type. You're decently dressed and you go out to enjoy yourself." Even though the same fellow helped you out in a pinch? "Sir, you can't let him marry your daughter."

Silence. It is getting dark. George Jones can't let go. "That is the trouble with apartheid. You are friendly with the native but you can't hobnob with him. You can't bring him into your home as a neighbor. And—how shall I say it?—you can't allow sexual relations. If you allow that, you will in time create a bastard race."

Ten miles to go. A song would be nice. Does George know "Sarie Marais"? Every European schoolkid out here knows it. It is to the Afrikaners what "Sweet Betsy from Pike" was to the Gold Rush wagoneers of '49. It has the tug of "Auld Lang Syne." It was sung back in the seventeenth century when the voortrekkers moved north from Capetown into the insides of Africa. Afrikaners speak of the Trek as though it were only yesterday. It is to them what the Long March is to the Chinese and the handcart trek to the Mormons.

George knows the song, of course; but we should really hear Zelda sing it. She has a lovely voice. She loses it only when George annoys her with his chatter of that native on the road to Mossel Bay. He'll sing it, though, just for the hell of it. In broken Afrikaans, he half-sings, half-hums of the girl in the old Transvaal. Wistful, rueful. A song of homesick people. But where is home to the Afrikaner?

Alan Paton, the following morning in Kloof, in the sunny rotunda outside his house, explains: "South Africans are the most isolated white people in the world. Back in the seventeenth century, the Afrikaner cut himself off from Europe. He was strongly opposed to the Dutch East India Company. So he moved from Capetown into the hinterlands. Orphan girls were imported from Holland to be wives to the settlers. Then came the Huguenots, for whom Europe was an intolerant land. Afrikaners had no reason to be grateful to Europe. Homesickness is present in many of the songs about farms to which the Afrikaners in cities seem longing to return. A nostalgia, but for what?"

The song has stirred a memory in George. It has done something else, too. It has taken us off our course. George is embarrassed. He had traveled this road many times and never before had such a thing happened. I let him know it has happened many times to other experienced drivers in London, Paris, Stockholm, and even in Chicago. The common denominator: I, as a passenger. And my Uher. He feels better. I do, too, remembering B. W. Medawar's advice.

At a roadside grocery store, I ask the young Indian where Mr. Medawar's house may be. He smiles knowingly. He and his wife exchange glances. "Ahh, the bookkeeper." I have no idea what Mr. Medawar does for a living, but we're lost. He offers very specific directions to Jack Wallace and George Jones. I am ignored. How does he know I can't find my way around the block?

There appears to be much he knows. Jack and I are convinced he knows the purpose of our visit. Others may have passed this way on a similar mission. As with black people under siege, whether in a Mississippi town, pre-Freedom summer, or in a city ghetto, pre-alienation days, a grapevine is often at work. And certain strangers are not strangers at all.

As we leave the store, a young black woman, with a baby slung across her shoulder, smiles at Jack and me. Softly she says, "My baby no like black faces. She like white faces." I see smiles on the broad, square faces of Verwoerd and Vorster. I see the nod of certainty. And somewhere in Dr. Malan's Valhalla, the sun is shining. And why not, he being the father of apartheid?

B. W. Medawar's house. Neither the host nor the Chief has as yet arrived. I am much relieved. They are on their way, Mrs. Medawar tells us. She carries a pot of tea outside to the car, where George Jones has decided to catnap for the hour or so. We are immediately made comfortable. It is that not unfamiliar feeling, in a circumstance such as this: ease within the walls, a sense of unease out there. Does the SB know of this visit? If so, will the ruddy ones impound the tape? I have hardly time to indulge in fantasy. Two men enter the room.

The first is short, skinny, wiry, all nervous energy. B. W. Medawar. The other, Paul Robeson in size, is equally animated, though more composed. Chief Albert John Luthuli. Instantly, I recall a photograph: a tall Zulu chieftain accepting a plaque from Gunnar Jahn, a Norwegian. It is in Oslo. The Nobel Peace Prize. Hardly more than a year ago. As we greet one another, I wonder: Will he be punished for violating the law? Under area arrest, he can travel no more than fifteen miles from Groutville. Isn't this house further away than that? The Chief laughs. It is a rich laugh. He assures me it is all right. Mr. Medawar is laughing, too.

For a good hour, the Chief talks of a Zulu culture and history; and of the need to recognize the white man's offerings as well. He sees a multiracial society, with a synthesis of both cultures. "Unfortunately, human nature being what it is, the white man, when he settled here, concentrated on what he could get rather than on what he could give."

He recounts his learning years at Adams College, a mission school.

Though there was a muting of indigenous culture and religion by
the Christian fathers, the Chief is aware of sharp ironies. He is grateful to the school for having taught him much of the world beyond.
He had found Adams College "a pleasant place" and could have
spent his years there, untroubled, as a teacher. When the Groutville
people called him back to stand for election as Chief (a procedure
the government opposes), he agreed, and thus became embattled.
A moderate, he has become more and more disturbed by the im-
moderate ways of the government.

What had begun as an easy conversation has now assumed fervor
and passion. "The white is hit harder by apartheid than we are. It
narrows his life. In not regarding us as human, he becomes less than
human. I do pity him."

But he is not passive. "I am militant. Otherwise, I would not be
breaking the law, would I?" Since assuming the presidency of the
African National Congress, he has suffered three arrests. He expects
more to follow. He speaks of his "beloved country." And of his
vision: a vote for everybody. "An electorate free to choose, say,
Alan Paton or an Indian or anybody else. I wouldn't say: Why did
you choose a white man or an Indian? I am saying: There must be
a democratic government."

Without a trace of irony, he says, "America can do much to assist
in our liberation here." He takes the microphone from out of my
hand and addresses it: "Americans, you fought to free yourselves
from Mother England. With all your failings, you are trying to stand
for freedom for all. America should regard it as her duty never to
rest until all humanity is free." He says this with such deep feeling
that I almost believe it myself. Oh yes, he's well aware of our
corporate investments in South Africa, but he was taught to be a
Christian . . .

Mr. Medawar has glanced at the door a few times. Now he gives
us the high sign. It's time to go. As we leave, he murmurs that the
Chief is less moderate than he had been. As for himself, he gave
that up some time ago.

A few years after this visit, Chief Luthuli was run down by a
train and killed. He did not hear the warning whistle. I have since
been told by friends that, as a result of constant harassment, his
health, especially his hearing, had been affected. Said one: "He died
of apartheid."

On the way back to the Prince Edward, we pass Cato Manor. "It was a trouble spot in 1947." George Jones is a willing chronicler. "An absolute massacre. It went on for ten days. Natives went mad. We had to call out the army and the navy. The navy boys were the only ones who got the natives into submission. The men with the long knives. The native is very afraid of the long knife. The navy went in with fixed bayonets. Of course the natives didn't like that. So they stopped burning and killing each other. It was fierce."

Sunday morning. We are on our way to Kloof. Alan Paton is expecting us. I am seated beside George. My companion tells me he enjoyed last night's trip "immensely," especially the kindness of the Indian lady who had brought the tea out to him. The European lady at Kloof is equally kind.

In the rotunda, Paton's study, are pages upon pages of longhand. He's working on a biography of Jan Hofmeyer, who had been a minister in the government of Jan Smuts. He's been at it eight years. "His is *the* story of our times in South Africa. He not only tried to resist the drift toward neo-Fascism, but he proclaimed his Christian principles when it came to racial questions."

In Hofmeyer's dilemma, Paton sees a metaphor that became the theme of his play *Sponono*, based upon his own experiences as the principal of a boy's reformatory near Johannesburg. "What is involved is the difficulty in carrying out the Christian injunction if you are in a position of power and authority. This is fundamental to our human situation. Hofmeyer, of great Christian principles, was deputy prime minister and had to go to our native council to tell them he could not remove discriminatory laws. The good private individual behaves somewhat differently when a public man. No use weeping over that. If you accept a position of power, you must trim your sails. If you find that intolerable, remain in your private capacity; don't go fiddling around."

Alan Paton fiddles around. A founder of the Liberal party, which holds for one man, one vote, he is in constant trouble. "This book would normally have taken only a few years of solid work. One is inclined to resent being called away from the writing desk for this or that emergency, having to go to prison or hold, say, a protest meeting. I don't know whether the true writer doesn't so much isolate himself as go into a retreat when he writes. I have never been able to do it."

At the time of my visit his play *Sponono* was being performed in London. The government would allow him a visa on one condition:

silence on the subject of apartheid. He rejected the offer. Thus I found him at home.

A startling moment in Durban. A pale young bus driver, a "banana boy"—Durban-born are so called—giggles constantly as he talks of Alan Paton and apartheid. He himself is privately acquainted with blacks, though never associates with them publicly. "You are suspect immediately. You're thought of as pink or communist or liberal. I've had three warnings, though nothing has happened. They usually think I'm a seaman because I speak English."

He has attended some of Alan Paton's multiracial gatherings. There is considerable intimidation. "Everybody who visits his house is under surveillance. There is always a Special Branch policeman who attends such gatherings, invited or not. If Mr. Paton recognizes them he says, 'Ah, I see my friends are here.' Sometimes he says, 'Good evening, friends and the Special Branch.' " The banana boy giggles delightedly. "They take down the names and addresses of all the visitors and the numbers of the cars."

The *ad hoc* conversation takes place at the Louis Botha Airport as we're taking off for Johannesburg. God, I may miss the plane. I'm edging toward the gate, my companion following, giggling furiously; the microphone moving inches ahead of him. Carrot without stick. "At these gatherings, drinks are served. The police join in the conversation. Mr. Paton says, 'I know you're just doing your job.' Sometimes, one of them says, 'I don't enjoy it.' It does sound like Gilbert and Sullivan." We're both laughing, though we agree it isn't *that* funny.

One farewell word. Cupping our hands, the guard two feet away, we whisper. Between giggles, the young man speaks rapidly. "With all the bannings and exiles, no Africans can get experience in government. The African people will govern themselves some day. They must. There will be panic and confusion. And we'll all say, 'I told you so. They can't govern themselves.' "

The guard firmly urges me past the gate. Microphone extended toward the banana boy, we stage-whisper, tempo prestissimo, time really being of the essence. "WhatdoyoureallyseeasthefutureofSouth Africa?" He is more than my match. Not since Al Kelly, the celebrated double-talk artist, have I experienced such virtuosity. His is the pace of Samuel Beckett's Lucky. "Amultiracialsocietyistheonly hope. GeorgeBernardShawsawthefutureraceascoffeecolored. Maybe it'sutopianbutit'smyview." A pause for breath. A fond adieu. The guard turns away disgustedly. The banana boy giggles.

George Jones has been impressed by Alan Paton. "I know that man. I have seen him before."

Where? Paton has enough troubles, without a casual visit from an American busybody compounding them.

"Oh yes, his face is very familiar. I've seen him many times."

Christ, George isn't the sort who would report such things to the SB, is he? I chew away at my Ritmeester cigar. "Where have you seen him?"

"On all the billboards."

"Billboards?"

"Oh yes. Many times."

"What kind of billboards?"

"BVD ads. That man is a very popular model."

I am thoughtful as I bite away at a moist stogie. It takes times to sink in.

"Didn't you know that?" he asks.

"No. But now that you mention it . . ."

"Oh yes. I imagine he makes a great deal of money."

"I imagine."

Out of the blue, George springs an invitation. "Will you visit with us, sir? It's just on our way." "Now?" "Yes, I've told my wife all about you. You'll like Zelda. If you ask her nicely she might sing 'Sarie Marais.' She has a lovely voice. It's when I annoy her . . . but I did tell you that, didn't I?"

At the Joneses'. Entrance. "Mrs. Jones, George has been paying you great tribute. I can see why."

Liar. Vestiges of a once pretty face have long been overlaid with the diminished features of one who has disapproved of too many things for too many years. It is presumptuous of me, of course, to so assume. I have been wrong so often. With some effort, she smiles. Pursed lips make it difficult. "He had to say something nice."

For openers: a visitor's mail-order "charm"; a hostess's begrudging a gentle husband's tribute. Only George comes off well here.

It is one of those Durban midsummer afternoons. Zelda is trying to cool herself with a Japanese fan. No success. "How do you like life out here?" "It is hot, very hot indeed."

A long half-hour is in the making. "Oh," exclaims the visitor, "you should be in Chicago now. February. It is cold, I mean, cold. A blizzard! The wind cuts right through you. Blows you right off your feet. We call it the Windy City."

"I'd like to visit America. Americans are very clever people. They make it easy in the kitchen."

"Yes."

She reaches out toward a photograph. "My daughter is very beautiful. I wish she could go to America and get on the screen."

The girl is quite pretty. I look at Zelda. I look at George. Yes, Zelda was a truly attractive girl. George is leaning toward us, smiling tentatively. He so wants things to go well. I see a smart-looking young jockey. Once upon a time. "She takes after both of you."

George laughs a little boy laugh.

"My sons are very clever with horses," she says. "I still feel sick when I think of it."

"The poor dear," says George. "She has never forgotten it." A long sigh from Zelda. "You have to pick the last four horses and you can win quite a lot of money. You're made. I swear it happened to me. Arthur marked my book. I wasn't aiming to do any betting. It was a very hot day. I just sat in the car. And every horse he marked off for me came in. And my God, I could have died! When I picked up the Sunday *Tribune*, not a soul had the jackpot. Nineteen thousand pounds and I didn't take it. I swear to God, I felt sick. It would have cost me five shillings. It was meant for me and I was too lazy to move. I still feel sick about it."

"Poor dear," says George.

"George says you have a lovely voice, Zelda." I touch my tape recorder, hopefully. "I'd love to hear 'Sarie Marais.' "

"Oh, that George. He exaggerates." She seems to like the idea. Her husband encourages her as, hovering near, he hums a passage. She is softening.

"When I was a young girl, I used to reach the top notes. But seeing that my husband is a bit deaf, I've always got to strain and call him and call him. He's ruined my vocal chords, because he never listens. I've strained my voice calling him. He tells me he's deaf. I really don't know. He listens when it suits him. When it's something he doesn't want to hear, he doesn't hear."

George dances around her chair. He's having a good time, this young lover. She observes him. "The Germans aren't snobbish at all. My husband says the English are really snobbish. When you went to stay with your uncle, the one with the Grenadier Guards, you weren't allowed to mix with the gardener. They called my husband their colonial nephew. He loved to chat with everyone, being a South African. They talk about our apartheid, when they have apartheid themselves."

Here we go.

"I've never been unkind to black people at all. They come in, we sit them in the kitchen and give them tea. They think the world of us. It's just that marriage business. You'd like to stay pure. Otherwise, it would be such a mixture, a bit of native, a bit of Indian, and then we would look stupid.

"I've seen them, their children running around minus their little pants. It wouldn't be right, living next door to us. It wouldn't look nice. They're used to being like that, so they don't think it's wrong. Now, with all these robberies. When I was a little girl, we never had these things. Ooohh, it's shocking.

"These younger ones are the instigators. I've got an old girl that does my washing. I wouldn't change her for anyone. If she finds a tikki in your pocket, she puts it aside. She's a Christian type of native girl. She watches my clocks and bends down and says a prayer. She wears a blue frock with a white cross on it. She hates this barbarism that's going on."

It is almost time to go. I'll give it a whirl, what the hell. I take a deep breath. "Zelda, do you remember the time you and George and the family were on your way to Mossel Bay?"

An intimation of flickering eyelids. She stares at me as though I had just entered the room. She stares at George.

"You remember that, dear? We ran out of petrol and the native stopped . . ."

"An Indian would. They're clever enough. But not a native." It is said flatly. The room is silent. Zelda remembers something else. "Remember the native woman who poked into our car and put your hat on her head and ate my biscuit. She wouldn't be able to fix a car. It's the Indians."

George looks at me, then at his wife. "You remember when we got stuck at Mossel Bay . . ."

"Oh, they'd push, but they're not mechanical minded." There is a touch of stridency to her voice.

George, defensively: "Oh no, no, no. They're really uneducated where mechanical and scientific skill is needed. They're just ordinary, plogging people from the fields."

There is a tonelessness to Zelda's speech. It is as though she were talking in her sleep. "If they just happen to push a car a few feet, they want that tip. Some of them try to rob you when you're stuck."

The spool of tape in my Uher has been revolving during this time. I have neither the will nor the energy to stop it. I had no idea I was so tired. I wearily reach toward the STOP lever. Something makes me pause. George is talking. I let it roll.

There is a surprising insistence in George's soft manner. The deliberate speech, the cadence has returned. "That is true. But through the courtesy of those people, the natives, we got to get on our way. They will never see a person stuck on the road without trying to help them. Never has a European, my girl, ever done that for us . . ."

He stops. Zelda is reaching at her throat. She is staring at nothing. The two small birds in the cage have been singing. I switch off the Uher. I get up. I say, "They sound so beautiful, don't they?" George says, "Yes, it's lovely to hear the chirping of those two little budgies. You wake up to them in the morning and you always feel better."

"Mossel Bay! Mossel Bay! Mossel Bay! That's all I ever 'ear!" Zelda has let out a harsh, croaking sound. All is still. She whispers. She is hoarse. She addresses me. "George has ruined my vocal chords." Pitiably, an apologetic smile, hand caresses her throat. "That's why I can't sing 'Sarie Marais.' "

O triste il cor. Ah! I am suffocating. Boris Godunov, his conscience devils him. He cannot breathe. He falls into a swoon. Zelda Jones has trouble with her throat. She cannot sing.

I say good-bye, as George Jones, an elfin Papageno, tiptoes from behind and his spindly arms encircle his wife's tiny waist.

3

Singing Bird

I'm in the back seat of a car, speeding from Chicago to an affluent North Shore suburb. Seated beside me is Bernadette Devlin. It is 1969. She is touring the United States on behalf of the Irish Civil Rights movement. Money is desperately needed. At this gathering, she hopes, a fair-sized check or two may be forthcoming.

Bone-weary, from jet lag, lack of sleep, and just about everything, she is recounting a County Tyrone childhood. Is it a dream, a recurring one, my being slouched against the leather, listening to an impassioned wisp of a girl, observing the spool of tape whirling? Is it a feeling of *déjà vu* I experience, as she tells, softly, of a recent Derry encounter?

"Eamon and I went into a Protestant slum ghetto. This lady told us she hated us. We said we wanted to explain our position. To tell her how we felt about her plight. She took us in. The neighbors started coming in. It was tea time. We had not had any food. She gave us tea and biscuits. She brought out all her best. Even a bottle of sherry for afterwards. Something she was probably saving for Easter or Christmas. Typical hospitality that was natural to this woman.

"As she poured the tea, she kept telling us how she hated us. And if she had a chance, she'd finish us off. And every time she saw my face on television she wanted to break the screen, because she so hated us. She repeated this often during the conversation.

"So we asked, 'Why do you take us in? Why do you show us such hospitality?' She said, 'You're all right, one or two of you. You're human beings. But it's the whole lot of you and the things you stand for.' We said, 'Why do you live in this slum?'

"She said, 'Because there aren't enough houses.' I tried to point out that the government doesn't build enough houses. She said the government is doing the best it can. There are too many people. The answer is to get rid of all those Catholics. Then there would be enough houses for all the good loyal citizens.

"This was after the Belfast-Derry march, during which people were brutally beaten and eighty-seven were taken to the hospital. She told me quite honestly she had been throwing boulders and that she had picked me out as her target and was praying one of them would hit me. I said maybe we disagree, but we're both Christian. 'Ah no,' she said. 'You Catholics aren't Christians. You're anti-Christ. You don't worship God, you worship the Pope.' This is how she combines her Christian beliefs with her fears. She must rationalize.

"Yet all this time she was giving us tea and food. This is what makes one so mad at the government. It superimposes into the life of a decent, ordinary person the fears and prejudices she needn't have."

Derry. Durban. What was Zelda Jones's name in Northern Ireland? Did her hands tremble as she poured tea for her hated guests? Did she furiously clank down cup and saucer? Or was it a graceful maneuver, as natural to her as, at a crazy moment, her words were ill-natured? And Zelda—will she *ever* be able to sing "Sarie Marais" while being reminded of Mossel Bay?

We are approaching Lake Forest. A song is suggested. Bernadette recites the lyrics of "My Dark Rosaleen." It is a song, in poetic code, of another century. Rosaleen is Ireland. "It is a plaintive air," says Bernadette, "because it is so full of images and nuances; it is a song so appropriate for now." Would she give it a whirl? "I could sing it in Gaelic because the people, quite rightly, refuse to sing it in English. I'll try but I'll do it very badly." She sings. It is achingly beautiful. Even as she finishes, it hangs in the air.

Soon, all these people in the car, these others, will be going back home. Back home to what? Battle, weariness, confusion, battle . . . I'll be seated in other cars, other places, once again listening and observing the spool of tape going round and round. Observing. The listener. The spectator. Is it possible to be cool, detached? Perhaps.

Ivy Compton-Burnett was. She was the nonpareil of cool observers. Hers, though, was a different world. Or was it?

BOOK

THREE

1

Boy Seated

On a Chicago bus, only one day after my return from Verona, I lost my Prix Italia scroll. It had been hand-painted by a Veronese craftsman, who had no idea that his exquisite work would, so soon, find itself in the garbage can of the Chicago Surface Lines. I remember winged cherubs, tiny golden trumpets at the ready, a sort of Renaissance blue, something pink, words elegantly inscribed.

It had been rolled, by loving hands, into a slim cardboard cylinder. I hadn't as yet seen it. On the bus, I unwrapped it for a long, appreciative look. All came alive in the scroll: the North Italian light, the ceremony's grace, the sweet Veronese faces—My stop was called out. I shoved the scroll back into the cylinder. I hurried off the bus. I had neglected to seal it. Oh, somewhere the sun is shining, and somewhere children shout . . .

Perversely, I did not lose something of less worth: the tuxedo I had rented for the occasion. I had been told, damned if I know by whom, that the ceremony was black tie. Across the Atlantic, and from Rome to Milan to Verona, I had carried the Gingiss Brothers' oblong box.

"Why are you carrying *that*?" asked Lawrence Gilliam, as I arrived, after a few misadventures, at the Due Torri Hotel. Gilliam, daring and imaginative, had instituted BBC Features, the glory of British radio, during the blitz and for years afterward. He was the 1962 Prix Italia awards chairman.

"It is my rented tuxedo," I said. "It is *de trop*," he replied. "It is de *what*?" I cried out. "Do you mean to tell me I have borne my cross thousands of miles for nothing?" I loathe tuxedos. "Did you bring some Scotch?" he asked. "Yes," I replied. "Let's have a drink," said Larry Gilliam. And we did.

In earlier years, the ceremonies had been more formal, Gilliam recounted. It was his people, the British, who unstiffened them. In Venice, Jack Dillon, an award winner, was walking along the walk. He was talking wild and excited talk. Lost in his enthusiasms, he stepped off the curb and into the street. In Venice, there are no curbs. Nor are there streets. Dillon had taken a refreshing dip in the canal, black tie and all. That did it. Radio Italia (RAI), sponsors of the event, saw the unstarched truth in a clear Venetian light. No more black tie.

The first time I had rented a tuxedo was in 1945. I had a one-shot in "First Nighter." It was a weekly nighttime radio program, originating in Chicago. The audience was assembled into a large CBS studio to watch people read from scripts.

Les Tremayne, who had succeeded Don Ameche, was the leading man. Barbara Luddy, who had succeeded June Meredith, was the leading woman. Whereas June was singularly large, Barbara was singularly small. She read from her script while standing on a short stool or seated on a high one. During her romantic scenes with Les, who was tall, I looked about for W. C. Fields. You no doubt recall how he met a similar challenge, as film director in *The Bank Dick*. He set the leading man in a pothole.

Black tie was mandatory for all performers in "First Nighter." To my horror, I found this out on the day of the performance. It was my first acquaintance with Gingiss Brothers.

As I walked through the corridors of CBS in my rented tuxedo, a colleague was reminded of a bookie going to his sister's wedding. Remarkable. That was precisely my assigned role in "First Nighter." I was a crooked bookie and I was killed before the second commercial. I deserved it; as I did in other such past incarnations.

I first became a gangster in 1934. It had nothing whatsoever to do with Bugs Moran or Al Capone or Hymie Weiss or Murray the Camel or the Genna Brothers or Jake Guzik or that most ill-starred of horticulturists, Dion O'Bannion. How often after his sudden passing did I go by Scofield's Flower Shop, so near and dear to Holy Name, and reflect on God's will and *que será, será.* For it was in that bower, amidst roses and orchids and lilies of the valley, that dapper Dion, with a seasonal flower as his boutonniere, met his Maker. He was the minstrel boy who to the war did often go; in this instance, it came to him as a message from Al.

True, I did have a glancing acquaintance with the garage where the St. Valentine's Day Massacre occurred. I glanced in one day while looking for Upsadaisy Connors. He was a sometime mechanic, who owed my mother six months' rent, coming to about two hundred dollars. He had disappeared. Some weeks later, he was found floating down the drainage canal. A slight misadventure. My mother wore sackcloth and ashes. At least two hundred dollars' worth.

Happily, all was not lost. I inherited Upsadaisy's silk dressing gown. It was similar to the one worn by Clark Gable as Ace Wolfong in *A Free Soul.* Fortunately, Upsadaisy was my size, not Gable's. Unfortunately, Norma Shearer was not around. As I looked into the mirror, a study in subdued scarlet with thin black stripes, I missed Norma. Though she may have been slightly cockeyed and, as Lillian Hellman observed, had a lovely face unclouded by thought, I missed her terribly. Oh well.

No, my gangsterism had nothing to do with the precipitous demise of Dutch Gusenburg, his brother, and several comrades-in-arms. Jack McGurn was reputed to have machine-gunned their passage to Valhalla on that celebratory afternoon when boys and girls passed innocently erotic cards to one another. Fortunately for Jack, he had a blond alibi, Louise Rolfe.

In my silk dressing gown, I saw the vision of Louise. I missed her terribly, too. Unfortunately for Jack, he was remembered on a subsequent Valentine's Day and was himself dispatched by a cupid's dart in the form of lead. It was at a fine bowling alley. As he let the three-fingered ball go, he appeared to have made a strike. Jack fell down and broke his crown, but the ninepin did not come tumbling after. It was a bloody spare. Thus was the martyred Christian saint twice memorialized in Chicago. It was truly a love that passeth understanding.

No, my experience as a paid killer, safe cracker, and extortionist was, alas, ersatz. I was a soap opera villain.

My life of crime began in "Ma Perkins." Ma, a widow, owned a lumberyard. She and her lifelong friend Shuffle (was there a twi-

light something going on between them? We never really knew),
her son John, her daughter Fay, and her son-in-law Willie, did the
best they could. They endured small-town scandals, backdoor gossip,
serious illness, and trials Job had never envisioned. Yet, Ma and
her tribe of decent Americans persevered. For years and years and
years, Monday through Friday.

I had nothing to do with any of these American virtues, agonies,
and glories. Mine was the incursion of outside malevolence. I, and
smooth-talking colleagues from the Big City, would, on occasion,
slip into Ma's domain. Not on little cat feet. Ours was a heavy tread.

My first such appearance, indeed my debut as a gangster, was in
the person of Butch Malone. He was as brutish a knave as ever
terrified a Terre Haute housewife; especially the one who washed
her things in Oxydol, courtesy of Procter & Gamble. For six weeks,
off and on, I gave Ma and her loved ones an awful time. As Butch,
I wound up, if I remember right, in Sing Sing. A life sentence. What
was even worse, I was written out of the script.

It was a catch-as-catch-can existence. I'd reappear as someone
named Pete or Bugs or Bullets or The Chicago Kid. At times, my
well-deserved end came in more bloody fashion. I was run off the
cliff by some local constable; I was shot by a companion; in all
instances, I was disappeared. In despair, I once asked the director
if I couldn't play a good guy for a change, the hero, perhaps. Rue-
fully, he explained, heroes had pear-shaped tones; mine were
apricot-shaped.

Though Ma was my most frequent pigeon, I found myself un-
bearable to Mary Marlin, whose five-day-a-week martyrdom transcended St. Theresa's. On occasion, my menacing gravel came a
slight pause after the last chord of "Clair de Lune" was pressed by
Helen Westbrook on the Hammond. I was unspeakable to Kitty
Keene and obscene to Helen Trent (can a woman find love after
thirty-five?). Nor was I very nice to Girl Alone. I was even bad to
a girl who was bad to Girl Alone, in the person of Mercedes Mc-
Cambridge. I never got to slap her as Broderick Crawford did in
All the King's Men, but I said plenty of nasty things to her.

Let's face it. I was the most miserable of wretches. I was so vile
that in "Betty and Bob" I once threatened her mother with God
knows what. Or was it *his* mother? The lovely, gracious dowager was
played by Edie Davis, who eventually became Ronald Reagan's
mother-in-law. It's hard to tell, isn't it, where soap opera leaves off
and life begins?

The dialogue in all these adventures was like none other ever invented. It was truly *sui generis*. It wasn't Melville. It wasn't Faulkner. Nor could Chekhov ever have dreamed it up. It was, in short, astounding. Most often, it was offered *sotto voce*. My confederate and I nuzzled up to the microphone in the manner of Bing Crosby and Russ Columbo. What we crooned boded no good for the good folk.

BOSS   Ya know what to do?

ME   Yeah, boss.

BOSS   Synchronize our watches.

ME   Watches?

BOSS   Yeah, stupid. Watches.

ME   I gotcha, boss.

BOSS   What've ya got?

ME   Eleven.

BOSS   Ya got New York time, stupid. It's ten o'clock.

(We were in Middle America, of course.)

ME   I gotcha boss.

BOSS   Let's go.

ME   Okay, boss.

There was never in the history of drama, whether it be Euripides, Shakespeare, Ibsen, or O'Neill, a pause that was as pregnant as a soap opera pause. Especially when the distraught heroine murmured her troubles to the straight-arrow hero. He was forever WASP. He was Bruce or Charles or James. Sometimes he was Gordon. (Nothing to do with Scots, wha hae wi' Wallace bled; it was just a clean-sounding first name.) He was never Angelo or Eli or Wladek. He was certainly never Booker. Today, it's different. In the world of the banal, egalitarianism has been achieved.

He was usually a banker. Or a broker. Or a man of considerable property. He was as honest as the day was long. And God, *were* they long days! The cross he bore was invariably a ne'er-do-well younger brother. She, Cynthia, had a wild younger sister. Talk about troubles. Small wonder they spoke so deliberately, so softly, and, oh, so slowly. It was this air of monumental patience that enabled them to carry that weight, to gallantly see it through.

Awaiting my cue, I died each day. Each second flew by as quickly as a minute; each minute was as quicksilv'ry as an hour. Would that I were a Zen Buddhist. I read somewhere that when life is burden-some, take to the Bible. So I reflected upon Ruth amid the alien corn. I called on Ecclesiastes as well: And this, too, shall pass.

Thus, in these theological musings I, too, was enabled to carry that weight, to gallantly see it through.

Each of us, in his or her own way, was brave, off mike as well as on. It was chin-up all the way. In time, we came to believe the stuff actually was Flaubert and Brontë and Henry James. (Was it during these meditative moments that I first began to understand the power of the rationale? How what one does must be imbued with quality, though more imagined than real: whether it be a soap opera or a nation's foreign policy.)

Oh, those lovely pauses. What with three solid minutes for commercials, a musical signature, the announcer's introduction, integrating a summary of yesterday's tortuousness—and the pauses—it came to no more than eight minutes of script. And the sound man. A door opens. Thirty seconds.

There was such care taken: every word, every syllable—the manner in which the heroine said, "Oh?" Or the manner in which the hero said, "Oh?" I never said "Oh?" I always said, "Oh yeah?"

Nothing was left to chance. Humanity's fate hung in balance. Naturally, the performers were not inclined to an *ad hoc* approach. An ad lib was sacrilege. But life being real and earnest, as Ma, Mary, Kitty, Girl Alone, and Betty and Bob could well attest, an untoward event would occasionally occur.

Was it '39 that a terrible snowstorm hit our city? The cast of "Ma Perkins" was waiting for the scripts. The messenger, it appears, was lost somewhere in the drifts of Wacker Drive. No scripts. Time to go on the air. Let's improvise, suggested the director. Ma and her son John are plodding through a snowstorm. The wind is howling. Says John, at one point in time, "Ma, walk behind me. I'll break wind for you." Glory be. It is a memory that blesses and burns.

As for the directors, they were a singular lot. The mark of the master was mastery of the stopwatch. If we get off on time, to the precise second—and the words were spoken and the pauses taken—all else was of small consequence. Anxiously peering into the control room, we saw thumb meet index finger. There were smiles all around. All was well. Another triumphal day. We were Olivier, Edwin Booth, Eleonora Duse. Troupers, all. Artists, all.

One such choreographer, for it was a ballet of words, I shall never forget. He had the appearance of Albert Einstein. I have since met Bertrand Russell, Leo Szilard, J. Bronowski, Buckminster Fuller, Noam Chomsky, and Erich Fromm; but none of them compared to this one in intellectual bearing. He always sat, chin in hand, in the manner of Rodin's *Thinker*. He was the most impressive-looking man I have ever encountered.

During one audition, he advised, after considerable thought, "Give me Humphrey Bogart." I had just seen Bogey as Duke Mantee in *The Petrified Forest*. I let a cigarette dangle from my lower lip and muttered, "Get in dere, you guys." He shook his head. "Give me Humphrey Bogart as he was ten years ago." I said, precisely as before, "Get in dere, you guys." He smiled, nodded. "That's it. You got it."

On another occasion, Einstein's look-alike said, "Give me Jimmy Cagney." I jabbed my elbow forward sharply and said, trying out my tenor, "Get in dere, you guys." He was content. At still another time, he suggested, "Give me Eddie Robinson." (Eddie. Well, well. He once requested of another performer, "Give me Jack Barrymore." Jack. And why is it that every Middle European who has ever directed a community theater has worked with Reinhardt?)

I was confused because I once knew Eddie Robinson. He was a minor league hoodlum, who hung around with Prince Arthur Quinn, our precinct captain. And there was, subsequently, Eddie Robinson the baseball player, who wound up with the White Sox. "You mean Edward G. Robinson?" I asked tentatively. He replied, somewhat snappishly, I felt, "Give me him." I pulled out a dime cigar and commanded in my finest nasal, "Get in dere, you guys." Einstein smiled. I was in.

There were times when dialects were called for. Foreign. Especially bad guys. I had an all-purpose dialect, known as Continental. It was guaranteed to baffle, indeed destroy, Henry Higgins. It, more often than not, was acceptable because it sounded so un-American. Once I slipped into something that sounded Swedish to him. I was supposed to be a Middle European assassin. He stalked impatiently the length of the studio. "That's Swedish. I want something foreign." I was stuck.

"How about Mediterranean?" I wanted to be helpful. "They're loaded with assassins." He paused; he studied me. "Hmm. Give it to me." I did my usual Continental. He beamed. "Marvelous. You got it." It *was* marvelous; a three-week job. And I never got to assassinate anybody. Somebody got me first. Even now, I remember my last words, as I faded away from the mike, collapsing on the studio floor: "Fuggive me, Mudder of ———— Ooaaawwow!" Thus I died.

"I want Levantine." It was another director. Could it have been

"Captain Midnight" or "Little Orphan Annie"? I think it was Daddy
Warbucks, who was having trouble with a smuggling ring somewhere
in the Middle East. Or was it Daddy as Samuel Insull, being hounded
by foreign agitators? Or was it Jack Armstrong, the All-American
Boy? (Oh, Jim Ameche's pear-shaped tones. They were even more
pear-shaped than his brother Don's.)

I stared dumbly toward the control room. "Levantine?" He
pressed his finger, testily it seemed to me, on the talk-back button.
"Yes, of course. Something from the Levant." The only such one
I'd heard was Oscar. I called upon my Continental. He nodded. That,
I'm delighted to say, was four weeks' work.

My most formidable challenge came during the several auditions
of a projected nighttime half-hour drama, "Martin of the Mist." It
was based on the theme of *The Flying Dutchman*. Horlick's malted
milk was interested in sponsoring it at one time. Later, General
Mills appeared excited. And still later, the ubiquitous Procter &
Gamble wanted to run it up the flagpole. There were, if my count
is right, four different auditions. Each time, we had a new skipper,
a new Martin. John Hodiak was the first. He went to Hollywood.
MacDonald Carey was the second. He went to Hollywood. I forget
who the third and fourth were. They, too, went west. In all instances,
I was the Polynesian bosun. Einstein directed all the versions. For
some reason, he felt I was the perfect Polynesian.

The opening lines were mine. "Ma-a-arrr-tee-eeenn of de Mee-
eest!" It was repeated about five times. "Sing it," Einstein said. "Be
mellifluous. Remember, you're from the Islands. A child of nature.
Sing it!" I sang it, thinking all the while of Cio-Cio-San in *Madam
Butterfly*. And of Paul Robeson in *Sanders of the River*. It helped.
"Now, run around the studio as you sing it." I looked in despair
toward the control room. It was NBC's huge studio, the size of a
small racetrack. It was here that Joseph Gallichio and the whole
symphony orchestra played. They, in fact, supplied the musical
background. "Run around the *whole* studio?" I mumbled, thinking
of Joey Ray and Paavo Nurmi. *They* never sang while they ran.
(The only singing runner I ever saw appeared in an early Soviet
film: a young Tartar, going like the wind, as he was being shot in
the back by a band of counterrevolutionaries, along the Siberian
border.) "Don't you understand?" Einstein was testy again. "You're
calling from a distance. A mist. This is a ghost ship." Oh, I got it.

I ran around the studio, singing out "Ma-a-arrr-tee-eeenn of de

Mee-eest!" Five times. By the time I reached the mike, I was Phidippedes at the end of the Marathon. I carried no torch, but I didn't collapse. I was breathing rather laboriously, I must admit. The musicians honored me with a *Tusch*. Even now my heart leaps as I hear the violin bows tapping the music stands.

Einstein had another leap of the imagination. "Take your shoes off." I looked dumbly toward the control room. "Don't you understand?" He *was* in a mood. "You're Polynesian. They don't wear shoes." Oh, I got it. Method acting. "May I keep my socks on?" There was a touch of desperation to my voice. I wasn't sure I had showered that morning; I was worried about athlete's foot. I waited. So did the whole symphony orchestra. Came the order: "Bare feet. Polynesians don't wear socks. We want to hear the slap-slap-slap of your feet on the deck." To this day, I am somewhat bewildered. How could the slap-slap-slap of my feet be heard a hundred yards away from the microphone? And why couldn't the sound man do that? Let *him* earn his wages. Slowly, I took off my socks. It was okay; I had taken a shower that morning.

It's better with your shoes off. I was thinking of the Stanislavsky technique. A touch of realism can't hurt. It's better with your shoes off. I was thinking of Beatrice Lillie, too. And her refrain in *I'm a Geisha Girl*. It's better with your shoes off. Thus reflecting, it helped.

Once more, I sang as I ran, a child of nature. When again I reached the mike, I was expecting a standing ovation from the orchestra. Nothing. A fine thing. They stand up for Solti, for Gilels, for Horowitz, for Rostropovich. Was my performance any less virtuoso? Oh well.

Polynesians. Levantines. Mediterraneans. Smugglers, assassins, children of nature. Glory moments. But none of these experiences ever matched the perverse delight of playing the American gangster. Even now, as in a mist, I hear my voice, "Get in dere, you guys." I am Bogey, Cagney, Little Caesar. But it is small consolation. I am not Clark Gable. Though that silk dressing gown has long since been taken away by the sanitation man, I think of Norma Shearer. And how I missed her something terrible. Oh well, I did scare the daylights out of Ma Perkins.

At the railway station in Milan. It is noon, Saturday. I am expected, I believe, in Verona that evening. A banquet has been arranged to honor the Prix Italia winners. At binario #2, the departure track: Milano-Verona. It takes off in fifteen minutes. I double-check with the station master. He's a dead ringer for the big guy in *The Bicycle Thief*; the one who drove Bruno and his father around town. He nods, "Sì, sì."

The train is crowded; six people in each compartment. Women, children, families are here; but most of the passengers are young men. Everybody is waving at everybody. I join in. I am smoking a cigaretta Scanelli, small, Milanese, and bitter. I feel very Italian. But as I fumble my way, in sign language, gestures, and a word or two, I am really Blanche du Bois, depending on the kindness of strangers.

A little old man is seated at the window. It is open. A woman shivers slightly. "Chiudere finestra, per favore?" she asks him. He closes the window. She leaves. A young man takes her seat. He dabs at his brow with a handkerchief. "Aprire finestra, per favore?" he asks. The old man opens the window. "Grazie," says the young man, as did the woman before him. "Prego," says the old man for a second time. At that moment, I realize *prego* is the most lovely word in any language. Name one that matches it for good nature and grace.

The young men who work in Milan are, this weekend, visiting their home towns, scattered along the way. All are voluble and genial. It is assumed I am Italian, too. I shrug as they shrug. I sigh as they sigh. "Ah, *Corriere della Sera*," I say to the passenger seated across the aisle.

It is easy enough to make out the name of the newspaper. I am not that myopic. "Sì," he says, smiling a big smile. I sigh. He sighs. It is safe enough. The news in 1962 isn't all that good.

He points out a news item. I nod. He speaks excitedly. He appears none too happy about it. I shake my head. "Madonn', Madonn'," I mumble. He shrugs. I shrug. What's my destination? His hands and eyes ask the question. "Verona," I say, rolling the "r." "Ahhh," he says. And you? My hands and eyes ask the question. He names a town I don't quite catch. "Ahhh," I say.

He now unwraps a sandwich. A small bottle of red wine appears. He offers me some. I shake my head, smiling wistfully. "Grazie, signor." He insists, I take a good gulp. I wipe my mouth. I say, "Mille grazie." He says, "Prego." We both feel fine. He is obviously curious. "Tedesco?" Holy Christ, he thinks I'm German. So much for my Milanese air. It has worked, though, on other occasions.

*   *   *

At the Caffè Canova, in Roma, my wife and I are waiting for her sister and husband, Alberto Burri, an artist. There is a traffic jam. They are late. Anyway, it's Italian time, unlike German time. Our waiter is wizened, middle-aged, and haunted. It is a terribly busy hour. He's having a rough time.

Enter: a tall, beautiful blond woman, who may be Anita Ekberg. Straining at the leash is her large dog. He leaps toward the waiter, who gasps. He is terrified. As I am. She says something in Italian (was there a slight Swedish touch to it?) to her dog, as she tugs him away.

In despair, the waiter catches my eye. I shrug my shoulders, my hands raised imploringly toward the heavens. He does likewise. He tells me the story of his life. I know it, though I don't understand a word. I interrupt the first sequence after four minutes of it. "Scusi, per favore," I say. I explain to my wife. "You see, he has four kids. He works like a dog. Why must he daily suffer all these humiliations."

My wife sighs. She has been through this before. Often, she has threatened to tell my sudden companions of my fraudulence. But it isn't fraudulent, I insist. That's what he told me, I *know*. The waiter, feeling better, now that he has someone to tell his troubles to, continues. This time, there is passion in the telling. The put-upon air has vanished. It's a long and quite dramatic sequence. "Scusi," I say. I tell my wife of the many years this man has spent, doing his work as a skilled craftsman. Ever since he was a small boy, he's put in a hard day's labor. He doesn't have to take this crap from anyone. Dogs or humans. He nods. He knows I know and he appears quite satisfied. My wife has no recourse other than to smile at him with great sympathy and understanding. He leaves us, his dignity reclaimed. Says my wife, "One of these days . . ."

Strolling along Boulevard St. Germain, I occasionally steal a glance at my Larousse French-English dictionary. I am heading for 16 rue St. Simon to see Sonia Delaunay, the first of the Cubist designers.

She is the widow of the artist, most celebrated for his vision of the crumbling Eiffel Tower. He called the shot on the fall of Paris. I have known her son Charles, the jazz discographer. He is an admirer of Mahalia Jackson and Big Bill Broonzy; and any friend of theirs is a friend of his. His mother, he assures me, has stories to tell of Picasso, Braque, Apollinaire, Diaghilev, and even Rousseau. She is to arrange an appointment with Tristan Tzara, the dadaist. And possibly one with André Breton, the Pope of surrealism, if his health permits.

As I stroll along the boulevard with an independent air, I'm the man that broke the bank at Monte Carlo. I lose my way.

"Pardon, s'il vous plaît," I say to a pleasant young man.

"Yeah?" he says.

Slowly, with the deliberateness of Eliza Doolittle, I say, "Ou est dee see Rue San Simon?" I finger my Larousse, stuffed deep in my pocket.

"Two blocks to your right and one to your left," he replies.

"Merci beaucoup," I say.

"That's okay, buddy," he says.

It is a delightful journey to Verona. At every village stop there are parked rows upon rows of bicycles. As the young men get off, they hop onto their two-wheelers and speed down the road. Ah, I say to myself, De Sica again. I am at the window, waving. They wave back. Men, working along the ties, gandy dancers, Italian style, are calling out to everybody, myself included. I have thrown my coat across my shoulders; a cape; I am a Bolognese. *Salute.* I propose imaginary toasts. The spirit is festive.

It is only now I notice the sudden quiet on the train. I am the only passenger in the car. I walk through the train. I encounter nobody. A scene out of Kafka. A Bergman dream sequence. My heart sinks, I know not why. We pull up to a siding, near the hill. Hey, this doesn't look like Verona. I look out the window. The sign: Brescia. Ah, Pope John's home town. I feel good. Below, an arrow: Verona, 60 K. I feel bad.

I study my ticket stub. Yeah, Milano-Verona, that's what it says. I walk all the way toward the front. In the last compartment is a lone passenger. He is tightening his suitcase straps; he is about to disembark. I hastily leaf through my small, fat Collins Italian-English Dictionary. I show him my stub. "Treno a Verona, eh?"

"Sì, sì." He nods. I feel better.

I point to the sign outside. "Brescia."

"Sì, sì," he nods. I feel less better.

He is wearing dark glasses. He smiles and shrugs helplessly. Could this be Marcello Mastroianni? There is compassion in his voice as he says, "Non parla italiano?"

I shake my head. "No. Inglese."

"Americano?"

"Sì."

"Parlo solamente italiano." He looks very sad. I mime, I indicate my plight. I point toward the distance. He doen't understand. Once again, that shrug and compassionate smile. He must be Marcello. It is the final scene from *La Dolce Vita*. I am the young innocent girl, the Umbrian angel, calling out, across the rivulet, to his creative nature. Nothing. Two lost lambs, we stare at one another. Is this train bound for glory, this train?

He escorts me off toward the depot. The stationmaster is the identical twin of the one I met at Milano. He, too, is fat and genial. He studies my ticket. "Sì, sì," he sighs. I sigh. Marcello sighs. My train companion says "Buon giorno." He shuffles away. The stationmaster says, "Buon giorno." I say, "Buon giorno."

A porter takes my valise and walks me toward the desk. A tiny elderly lady is furiously scribbling away. She bears a remarkable resemblance to Emma Grammatica, the actress; wraithlike, wild-eyed. She looks up, smiles pleasantly. She studies my ticket. A young man, her colleague, studies my ticket. In unison, they say, "Sì, sì." I point to my wristwatch. Four o'clock. The young man studies the timetable. "Otto," he says. The next train to Verona is eight o'clock. He points toward the trees and grass and flowers and benches. It is a beautiful afternoon.

I slap my cheek. I know the woods are lovely, dark, and deep, but Christ! I've got promises to keep. "Piano, piano," he says softly, gently. The old lady nods. "Sì, sì." There is a *ristorante*, he says. *Mangiare*. Not a bad idea. I'll never make that banquet.

The young man at the oven is aware of my despair. And my sense of mission. And my clown smile. He sets the marvelous veal before me that he had himself prepared. The waiter is, at the moment, otherwise occupied. Never mind, he'll serve it himself.

As I leave, I notice that the young man and the waiter are arguing, not heatedly; it is a dispute, nonetheless. Something tells me I am responsible. It is the tip, a rather large one, I have left on the table. The proprietor shakes his head. He says a few words. He is chiding me, I know. It is I who had induced the young man to violate protocol; it is I who had brought chaos out of order. My wretched

"Scusi, scusi" does little to assuage hurt feelings. I am the serpent in the garden. I've done it again.

Romila Thapar, a young Indian scholar, is visiting Chicago. She is eager to hear some of our city's blues artists. There is one catch. It is but ten days after Martin Luther King's assassination. The black neighborhoods are still on fire. The rebellions are hot on everybody's mind. And so is Mayor Daley's edict: shoot to kill. My common-sense self says, Let's take a pass. My perverse self says, Turner's Blue Lounge. It is in the heart of the South Side ghetto. I know J. B. Hutto, who is playing there. It is an early Sunday evening.

Mr. Turner is not at all pleased to see these three patrons: my wife, Romila, and me. Though our guest, in her sari, is obviously non-Caucasian, she is as much an outsider as the white couple. I have been here a number of times before, but this occasion is something else again. My common-sense self says, Some other time, Romila. Let's head north. But Mrs. Turner is effusive; and J. B. Hutto seems delighted. Still, the old man, I feel, knows more than anybody. It isn't Turner's Blue Lounge for nothing. My perverse self, as usual, prevails.

The musicians are in fine form. So are the customers. Tomorrow, another week of hard, dull labor will begin. Today, there is singing and dancing and laughter. The time of mourning is ending. Perhaps the old man's discomfiture is baseless.

We are seated in a corner booth, drinking discreetly and hearing good Chicago blues. Romila Thapar would come to know something of our city's singing, though unsung, artists. Two young men, feeling no pain, join us. Willie Hightower and Jimmy Johnson. I have no idea where they came from. I order a round of drinks for everyone. O'Neill's Hickey had nothing on me.

Mr. Turner comes over. He asks Willie and Jimmy to leave at once. "They're okay, Mr. Turner. Everything's fine." I'm a blithe spirit, all right. He is furious. "This is *my* place. Don't tell me how to run my place." He calls the police. J. B. Hutto never sounded better.

Two young cops appear, one black, one white. They are quite friendly. They invite Willie and Jimmy outside, to talk things over. No sweat. Willie suggests we keep the drinks fresh until their return. "Fine," I say. Romila and my wife don't think it's fine. They suggest we've heard enough blues for the night. I'm feeling mellow; Old Grand-Dad is a tranquil companion. And J. B. Hutto's blues are *so* good. However, if that's the way they feel . . .

Outside, the cops and our sudden companions are chatting amiably; and laughing. The four wave at us. As we cross the street to the car, I call out, "See you around, Willie Hightower and Jimmy Johnson."

"Can't you leave well enough alone?" my wife inquires. Does she know something I didn't know?

Willie and Jimmy are in the back seat with Romila. How did that happen. My wife looks at me. I look at them. "Where do you guys wanna be dropped off?"

"We're goin' with you," says Willie.

"We're heading for the other side of town," I say.

"That's okay," says Willie. "You came to see our neighborhood. We'll go see yours."

How do you answer that one?

My wife is driving. It is decided that Romila should hear some folk music. How do they feel about folk music? Long, sad songs about shepherds and kings and shipwrecks; songs that go on and on and on. "Fine," says Willie. He is clearly the talker of the two, though Jimmy gets a word in now and then. Romila Thapar isn't saying much of anything.

There is talk of the two assassinations. Both Willie and Jimmy feel that Kennedy and King were done in by the Syndicate. Many black people feel that way, they say. As we come to the white part of town, Willie's voice changes. "You ain't gonna let 'em jump us, are you?" He and Jimmy have in that moment become *our* hostages. Before, I had felt funny. Now I feel sad.

Edwardian-dressed singers are performing at the club. The songs are mournful and go on forever. Willie and Jimmy aren't too crazy about it. Nor, for that matter, are the rest of us. "Where's the jukebox?" asks Willie. "I'd like to dance."

"Nobody dances here," I say.

"I don't like this place," says Jimmy. Willie agrees. Our table has lost its *esprit*, much to the relief of the singers and the other patrons. We are all sleepy. It is time to drive Romila back to the university on the South Side. "You ain't gonna leave us here?" Willie sounds scared. We'll let them off on the way.

Willie is impressed by Romila. He'd like to see her tomorrow. What does she do? She is a professor, I say.

"You're a dumbbell," says Jimmy to Willie.

"I'm smarter than you," says Willie to Jimmy.

A heated argument begins. Each is out to humiliate the other. It is getting serious. My wife interjects. "You work in a garage, you said. What kind of work do you do?"

Willie glows. "I spray cars. I bet I could spray this car; it'd shine like new. Nobody sprays cars like me."

Jimmy says, "I can fix *a-n-y* car. You got trouble with this car, I'll get it right in nothin' flat."

They get out at Pepper's Lounge. They invite us to join them. I'm half-tempted. Junior Wells is holding forth and his style is great these days. The women are not very enthusiastic. Oh well, let's call it a night.

In parting, Willie says to Romila Thapar, "You make me tremble all over."

Jimmy says, "You're dumb. Let's go."

"You shut up," says Willie.

"We had a good time," Jimmy tells us. Willie agrees.

Romila Thapar says it was a memorable night. It was, in a way. My wife agrees. She adds, "But Mr. Turner was right. Things might have turned out differently." I know. Why can't I leave well enough—or bad enough—alone? Oh, I do mean well, sure.

At the station, Emma Grammatica and the young man are delighted. Yes, I assure them, the meal was eccellente. Grazie. There is something about their eyes. Are they grandmother and grandson? Sì, sì. They laugh. They seem even more delighted now. They study me; a curiosity. Where do you come from, Cotton-Eyed Joe? I tell them Chicago. The young man's eyes widen. He is definitely impressed. Aahhh, Chicago. He aims his two index fingers at me, two forty-fours, Boom! Boom! Boom! He thinks I'm Scarface. I shrug helplessly. I smile forlornly. I am Marcello. If Fellini could see me now, I'd be his next existential hero. Why not Chicago? Rome ain't the only decaying apple in the barrel.

December 1962. It is toward the end of the day. Fellini is weary as hell. He has been dubbing *8½*. "Rome happens to be where I live and work. That the squalid city depicted should find its historian not in a Suetonius or Tacitus but in a gossip columnist seems right to me. Concerning the unmerciful look at each scene: everything is seen through the same curious, negative eye. This way of looking seemed typical of our time: a tragic or a great event is given the same importance as the election of a beauty queen; all are given the same value."

Fellini's English isn't bad, but he'd rather say it in Italian. My Bolognese friend, Carlo Baldi, is our interpreter. He is a marvel, but on occasion he engages in poetic flights. "For Chrissake, Carlo, give it to me literally." Carlo smiles. I don't understand. "Studs, my dear friend, Federico Fellini is a poet. To translate as you suggest might lose its flavor." Aahhh, what can I say to that? He's *Italian*.

I am haunted by Fellini's being haunted by the waste of human beings, of possibilities that may never be tapped.

"Actually, I am very optimistic about human beings. I do not feel I have adopted a negative, judging attitude toward human waste. This wandering around today in search of some truth has a certain value, I feel, and I view it with a sympathetic eye. This sympathy, this solidarity, this participation in everything we do, I attempt to express formally in my work."

Now give it to me straight, Carlo, I say to the party of the third part. Oh God, Carlo, I silently pray, don't be Montale or Ungaretti now, give me Fellini straight. And Carlo does just that (I think) beautifully.

"Decay can bring liberation and growth. Men tend to become free through it. The hero of *8½*—the movie director Guido—out of the decay of doubts and confusions, recognizes himself. Only by admitting that decay can he start fresh, free of doubts given him by wrong education, and free, too, of the way of life imposed on him by his environment. By admitting them, Guido is free to start all over again. He finds a new humanity.

"I try to reveal a certain element in all of us and to vibrate a core in our spirit. I am concerned not only with social implications; I care for the poetry in us.

"Guido becomes aware of the value of man as he is. Man's recognition of his limitations is a way to freedom. Only when man understands that he is free can he know where he stands and then make a free choice. Only at this point can he jump into faith. This faith can be religious, political, or whatever. That choice exists is the point."

Did I mention the color of Rome? Burnt orange, the earth, melding into a Mediterranean sky. As in North Wales, the grass is green in December. The beauty is breathtaking. So is the auto. Heart-stopping is, perhaps, the more apt phrase. Villainous as it is in Paris, it is altogether diabolical here. Medieval streets, too narrow even for the Fiat 500's—not to mention the larger cars, horns honking, drivers gesturing, passengers thin-lipped: unhappy all. In the shadow of ancient ruins. *La Dolce Vita.*

Fellini has been lighting my cigar that is forever going out. He finds it amusing. My cigar is Tuscany grown. It is crooked, black, hard, acrid of taste. It is maddening, though highly satisfying. Cheap, too. Because it is more often out than not, it lasts a long time.

Shall I try to light one of these dark weeds? I have a good three hours before the train to Verona. The young man looks for a match. His grandmother comes up with one of those tiny boxes. She holds it high, triumphantly. "Fiammifero!" I lean across the desk, but it is not the striking of the match I hear. "Signora, un momento!" Is that a bus outside, about to pull away? I hadn't noticed it before. This is a bus terminal, too. Do any of them go to Verona? "Sì," says the young man. One is leaving at four thirty-five. I look at my watch. It is four thirty-four. Madonn'!

I hold out a crumpled wad of lira before him. My Tuscany cigar falls into the money. He gently removes the cigar, hands it to me. He carefully picks out the proper amount. He slowly makes change. "Presto! Presto!" I moan. "Piano. Piano," he says. I rush out, ticket in my sweaty palm. They call out to me. I had forgotten my valise. I rush back, and out through the door. "Ciao," the young man calls out. "Ciao," cries his grandmother. "Ciao," I shout. I turn back at the door. "Grazie, mille grazie." I stumble off.

As I clamber onto the bus, the driver is finishing a cigarette. "Verona?" I gasp. "Sì," he says. He takes my bag. I flop into a seat. He flips the cigarette in a practiced manner toward the paved walk. We zoom off. The passengers are merry. It is Saturday night.

There are many stops. As we pick up and let off people at the different towns, we see walkers. Everybody, it seems, is at the square, the center of the village. They promenade slowly, arm in arm, in most instances. A few cyclists, here and there, but the strollers have it. The spirit is holiday.

I think back to my behavior in Brescia. It was execrable. I was the gross businessman of *Mr. Hulot's Holiday*. An absurd one, he was, with his important telephone calls to the city. I realize now how lovely a word *piano* is. It has class. As *prego* has class. As the Bresciani have class. It may be no accident that Pope John was that way.

As for schedules, were they, on a night like this, that important? Perhaps the people were getting back at Mussolini, who, it is reputed, made the trains run on time. I doubt that generally accepted premise, as I doubt just about anything William Randolph Hearst or his trained seal, Arthur Brisbane, had to say about Il Duce's efficiency.

The banquet at the Due Torri is almost over. I apologize for my tardiness. No apologies are necessary, I am told. They are astonished to see me. The award winners are not expected till Monday. I have arrived two days ahead of schedule.

Does my face, at this moment, betray my befuddlement? I am Basil Radford and Naunton Wayne. Their pole-axed moment in *The Lady Vanishes* is now mine. On the train, where so much was happening—Dame May Whitty kidnapped, Michael Redgrave imperiled, Paul Lukas murderous—Basil and Naunton, wholly oblivious to drama and danger, *had* to get to the cricket match on time. They arrive at last. A poster greets them: Match called off on account of rain. And I, after all my trials . . .

My hosts ask if I am hungry. I have eaten, I tell them. They don't believe me. I look famished. I am escorted into the large hall. The word is out: the first award winner has arrived. A delightful surprise. Everybody applauds. I wave. The way Richard Nixon waved. Uncertainly.

I am served much food and drink. I still taste the Brescian veal, but I can't let these good people down. Everybody assembled—the man from NHK in Japan, the Swiss, the Israeli, the Yugoslav, the Swedish radio and TV people, the Australian, the West German, the man from Radio Eire, the young woman from the Indian Embassy in Rome—all, all are watching me eat. They have already had their cognac. My table companions are gracious and charming people. I am a bloated mackerel. I raise my glass. "*Salute*," I say. Everybody laughs.

At the Caffè Dante, outdoors, we drink grappa and observe the Veronese. I have a funny feeling I have seen them, all of them, somewhere before. Where? The Etruscans were here. The Gauls were here. The Romans were here. These people are of the twentieth century, no doubt of that; yet they are of another time as well. So, too, with the buildings. They are of another time, yet they are no museum pieces. Very much part of this city, part of now, and yet . . . I wish I could put my finger on it.

Dante observes us. He is everywhere, in bust and full-bodied. The Florentines may not have wanted him, but the Veronese sure did. And do. As Larry Gilliam and I have another touch of grappa— and how diabolically deceptive it is—his countryman, a Mr. Sutherland, is studying a small book. He is lost to all else.

"What are you reading?" asks Gilliam.

"Charlotte Brontë," says Sutherland.

"Only an Englishman would read Brontë in the shadow of Dante," moans Gilliam.

In the lobby of the Due Torri, I stare up at the ceiling. We have been appreciating the Veronese grape too well, yet they are not pink elephants I see. They are Renaissance paintings. No, this is not a museum. This is a hotel, where twentieth-century people are guests. I get that feeling again. I'm not Leslie Howard in *Berkeley Square*. I'm not out of my time. All my companions are my contemporaries. And yet.

A Sunday outing. Vincenza. Near the Austrian border.

The North Italian light pours into the castle from all sides. Is it my imagination? My companions appear transformed. They are all handsomely Renaissance people. I whisper this to Larry Gilliam. "Of course," he says.

After the meal, Count Carravisi, chairman of RAI, offers a small speech; more of a toast, really. "Here the past and present meet. Thus there is harmony in this region. There is tradition behind it. Not a dead past, not a quaint past. It is a throbbing, living past. Thus the people who live here have a sense of their history. The more they are aware of the past, so much more is the present fruitful. So much more will the future be richer."

At the art gallery in Vincenza. Busts of the Caesars, their cousins and their friends and foes, make up quite a party. All the Beautiful People of the Empire, in stone. I am face to face with one who stops me cold. "Your face is familiar," I mutter to myself. A young Roman. Was this Augustus on the make? His laurel wreath is slightly askew. A crack runs across his face, on a tangent. A piquant touch; his saber scar, let's say. His eyes are directed heavenward. That certain smile. He has just pulled a fast one.

Oh God, I've seen that look before. Last week in Chicago. A month ago in New York. A year ago in Washington. The young ad exec. The young lobbyist. The young White House aide.

Monday. Presentation Day. Ambassador Talliani, who will do the honors in my case, doesn't like my tie. Aside from Gingiss Brothers' black tie, I have one pretty badly wrinkled and soiled; a memento of Saturday's misadventures. He suggests a little shop along Via Mazzini. Get something *grigio argenteo*, he says. He thinks silver-gray becomes my suit and complexion.

Three o'clock. The siesta is over; the young boy gracefully approaches and opens the door to the shop. He makes a beautiful knot and slips the cravat around my neck; as though indeed he were honoring a prince. I look in the mirror. It is the boy I see. His face, of such serenity and repose. Where have I seen him before? Damn. It really bugs me.

The ceremony at Palazzo Vecchio. Of medieval military architecture, it was built in 1354. Trumpets sound. Each of the six of us steps onto the stage and receives a scroll, enribboned. No speeches. It is a simple gift they have. I am so moved, all else is forgotten. Fortunately someone has retrieved the scroll I had left on the bench. He will encase it in a slim cardboard cylinder: I must not lose it on my way back to Chicago.

Down below, in the cellar of the castle, a buffet has been prepared. As the guests promenade toward the feast, we pass through corridors; on the walls are the work of Renaissance masters. It has become an art gallery. Larry Gilliam tells me they were brought down here by the curators during the Allied bombings of Northern Italy.

I stop suddenly. *Bambino Seduto* by Paolo Veronese, 1528–1588. A boy seated. That's *him*! Larry glances at me. He sighs. "What is it now?"

"That boy, Larry! I saw him this afternoon. The kid who sold me this tie. That's him in the picture! I knew I'd seen him before!" A face of such serenity, such repose.

"Of course," says Larry Gilliam.

I turn around and around. The people, the men, women, and children of Verona, whom I have seen and run into during the past two days—they are alive on these walls. There! A boy and a girl. Girolamo dai Libri, 1474–1555. I saw them, too, earlier this day.

They were seated in the piazza, speaking softly to one another. "A throbbing, living past," said Count Carravisi yesterday. "The people who live here have a sense of their history."

"Of course," I say to myself.

Nineteen sixty-six. Atlantic Hotel. Hamburg. It is first class. They say Goering slept here. During the war, it was favored by members of the General Staff. Was it their headquarters? Hamburg, with its long-time democratic tradition, was not one of Hitler's more *gemütlich* haunts. No matter. This room has a *gemütlich* air, as it faces the gentle River Alster. I wonder who occupied it some twenty-five years before.

Kalle Freynik, twenty-one, is visiting me. He is one of Hamburg's more popular rock artists. He has gone in for producing—"That's where the power is." He had, until recently, sung protest folk songs, but gave that up for better things. His girlfriend accompanies him.

The phone rings. It is the desk clerk downstairs. His voice is ice. In a precise British accent, an attribute of most young Hamburgers, he informs me, "You have a woman in your room. This is no saloon."

"How dare you, sir?" I, of course, assume his accent. I can't help it.

"If you rent a suite, you are permitted," he lets me know.

"Permitted to do what?"

He hangs up.

Kalle takes a dim view of history. "During my folksinging days, I believed in it. That was before I discovered the truth."

"The truth?"

"That history is really a mystery. History is written by people and it changes. It's not a lasting thing. It's nothin'."

"The past is nothing?"

"You can't really believe what you read or what you see or what you learn from parents or from school. You can't really find the truth. Everybody lies. So I don't bother about it. I don't really care very much about politics."

"Do you believe what happened in Hitler's time. The killing, say, of six million Jews?"

"Sure. They are facts. Should I say, Well, I'm sorry for them? I don't feel anything about that. They're in the past. It's gone. The world is changing. Our generation—and if not ours, definitely the next—will change this world completely.

"I don't want to be a loudmouth, but I think I'm a very progressive-thinking young man. I'm in the music business. I'm expressin' my thinkin' through pop music. And most of 'em believe what I say. It's spreadin', man, it's really spreadin'. Everything is happening."

"What's happening?"

"Love, man, love."

Scene: a sprawling, modern supermarket at Olympic Village, on the outskirts of Rome. Dramatis personae: two employees, assistants to the American manager (a merchandising pro from Kansas City). They are a handsome young man and a lovely young woman. They are deeply in love, though not with each other. They love The Store. Their passion is all-consuming. The issue is joined between the Organization they adore and the small Italian shops. "We will destroy the shops." Confidently, they ride the Wave of the Future. Nineteen eighty-four is now, for them. Their ecstasy is as quiet as their voices. Romantic music is heard in the background by customers as well as by The Couple. It is piped in by the Italian variant of Muzak. "For us," they say, "there is no past. Forget it."

On a Chicago bus, I lost my Prix Italia scroll. Somewhere, long since burned in some incinerator of the Chicago Surface Lines, was the loving handiwork of a Veronese craftsman. On that damn bus, I lost more than a scroll, much more.

2

The Architect

In my desk, among an eraser that doesn't work, an old typewriter ribbon, dull pencils, and spent ballpoints, I find a memento of my Italian adventure: bits of tobacco that crumble to the touch. They are remainders of a Tuscany cigar.

Carlo Levi is his usual ebullient self. He is smoking a Tuscany cigar. He offers me one. We light up. It is the hallmark, he says, of the true Italian aristocrat. Certainly not a high-priced cigar, I observe. That's what I mean, he says. The true aristocrat can't afford the others. We puff away contentedly. I try blowing smoke rings. I fail, but it's okay. The climate of his studio, behind a full-flowering Roman garden, is salubrious.

He is something of a painter these days. But writing is the greater piece of the man. *Christ Stopped at Eboli*, his novel of Fascist Italy, came about under most unusual circumstances. An active anti-Fascist, Levi kept one step ahead of Mussolini's *arditi*. He wrote as he fought. There were close calls. A chapter at the home of one friend; a knock on the door; a chapter at the home of another; a knock on the door . . . Not accidentally, it was a powerful work.

Today, he is hounded by another dictator. The telephone. Being the most sociable of men has its drawbacks. The ting-a-ling is maddening in its persistence. He is congenitally unable to say no.

As I stop the tape for the hundredth time, I bawl out, "Mussolini again!" He laughs and his Samuel Johnson belly bounces up and down.

Salvatore Baccaloni, the amply set up basso-buffo, laughed loud and gloriously. It was too much, too much for even the cork-lined walls of the radio studio to absorb. He was remembering a moment of truth and art: Chaliapin's Boris. He himself had sung Varlaam a number of times in the company of the giant. The memory, after so many years, overwhelms him. He speaks in the present tense.

"He is the mos' great actor, the mos' great personality in the worl'. When he sing Boris—oh yes, there are many Boris aroun', some good, some lessa good." He chuckles softly; the forgettable ones worth no more than a soft chuckle. "But Chaliapin, he remain meister."

Baccaloni was, at the moment, whispering in hushed, awed re-membrance. "He go down in the street, near to deat'. I remember he attack the monologue wit' one littla breat' of voice." Caught in the magic of it, Baccaloni sings ever so softly a few passages from *O triste il cor*. "He's atremble on the stage, he's near to fall down. Many Boris today sing . . ." He bawls out the same passages full voice. "What kind of sick man is this?" The laugh is bubbling up from deep in his belly.

"Chaliapin was not merely a great singer," I interject. "He was a great actor, too."

"Chaliapin is a no great actor, he's a no great singer. When Chaliapin sing Boris, he's a *Boris*!" His laugh erupts like an antic Vesuvius and envelops us all.

As Carlo Levi laughs, he bears a striking resemblance, in spirit as in appearance, to Cesare Zavattini, whom I had visited yesterday. Zavattini, Italy's most gifted screenwriter, had collaborated closely with De Sica in the making of their memorable films. I am aware that he and Levi are friends. Does he agree with Zavattini's disturbing observation?

Yesterday, he had said, in a passing reference to Italian mores, that when the husband comes home at night, he leaves the twentieth

century and enters the sixteenth. Levi agrees. He adds: The
new Italian woman, especially to the north, is fast changing all that.
He suggests, as have others, that I see Anna Magnani. She'll have
plenty to say, and passionately so, on this matter.

I look forward to meeting the volatile Magnani. It has been
arranged by a mutual friend, Perle Cacciaguerra. My last day in
Rome. What a way to say *arrivederci, Italia*! Who can ever forget
that searing moment in *Open City*, as she raced down the street,
her hand reaching out toward the sky and the *fascista* police truck
bearing away her lover?

On the appointed day I buy a bunch of red roses. Mine is the
excitement of a high-school kid. Word comes that her gardener has
died. Suddenly, unexpectedly. An old, old friend. She is distraught.
Another time, I am told. Another time it is. Several years later, I
am back in Rome. Anna Magnani is dead. Damn. Damn. Damn.

In Carlo Levi's studio, as I damn less cursed matters, he talks of
man triumphant: his friend, Danilo Dolci. On a wild hunch, I had
mentioned the name. Dolci, the living legend. The Gandhi of Italy.
The architect from Trieste, who gave it all up when he visited Sicily.
He saw men, unaware of being men, and revealed to them their
humanity. Dolci, rather than Levi, becomes the subject of the conversation. It is at my host's insistence.

In a Chicago hotel room—is it five, six years later?—Danilo
Dolci reflects on his experiences and discoveries in the bleakness of
western Sicily. Though he has been compared to the Mahatma, he
is uniquely himself. A heavy man, his hands are rough and calloused;
not those of an architect. They are the hands of a laboring man.
Why did he do what he did? I ask. A question that has no doubt
been put to him scores of times. Who knows? He might have become
a respected associate of Pier Luigi Nervi, perhaps.

He laughs. His manner is easy and gentle. "It's wonderful to build
things with *pietra*, with stone. But men interest me more than stone.
To help them be built. I've always wondered, 'What was life like
before me? What was life like *outside* me?' Oh, it was a hard and
terrible thing for me to do. But it was fascinating."

I had heard that during one of his fasts in western Sicily he had
played Bach and Vivaldi. Did these people ever hear this music
before? I ask.

"People need an organic vision of life. What you see in Bach is a kind of organic unity."

An organic vision of life. This has been the harsh and exhilarating challenge to Dolci in the land "where the man who plays alone never loses." One of Dolci's books has this title. "It is a bitter proverb in Sicily. Of one who has a terrible experience in life. It comes from a people who have had to defend themselves, by themselves, from everyone else. From the mafia and the police, who've worked together. From the politicians and the judges. A feudal life. It's very difficult for men to work and live together anywhere in the world. But it's *very* difficult to form alliances, to better their lives, in an area where the ideal is the man who plays alone."

How was he able to accomplish what observers have described as a near miracle? Alliances of the dispossessed in Sicily—peasants and workers—in defying centuries-old, established ways: in the building of roads, dams, and schoolhouses. In getting jobs. As Dolci patiently explains, I realize he has transformed himself.

A man from the north, who is a professional, Dolci says, is always going to be different. But in another sense, he is the same. When they can see the blisters on the hand, when they can see the back . . . It is not spending a week with the hoe in your hand. It is more like two years with a hoe in your hand. *Then* people will trust you.

Danilo Dolci, in coming to Sicily, did not appear as an organizer, let alone a savior. For two years he worked as a manual laborer. He worked with the fishermen, with the farmers. He married the widow of a peasant, who had several children. "Knowing with the head is not enough. One must know some things with the bones." He began to understand, through his conversations with people at work. He had become one of them.

"Of course this does not come about spontaneously. It's not possible that spontaneously the fields are going to produce grain and potatoes. Oh yes, by accident the wind can carry the seeds and you're going to have one or two stems of grain or a potato, but that is all. But to change a society, and to give a man a pair of clear eyes . . ."

He tells of such a change in one area. He never speaks in abstractions. They are meaningless, he says—at least, to the people he has been living with. There must be something they can see grow before their eyes, something they themselves have done with their own hands.

"I once worked with some people in a completely underdeveloped area. Many, many acres of nothing. At first, bulldozers and mechanized plows had to be brought in, to take away the stones, to clear the field of weeds. Then we sowed the grain. Then the houses were finished. And the grain was coming up. First, there was chaos. Now, there was a life. We, they and I, discovered that the face of the earth can be changed.

"Once chaos, now life. This is the real work of man. In the world today, much of human life is chaos. Yet each of us can experience bringing real life out of chaos. Not alone. It isn't possible. Together, we can be artists and create this work of art. Life is a work of art.

"It was interesting to see what happened to people in one week's time. At first they were very unsure. They never had such an experience. By the second, third, fourth day, slowly, through conversation, discussion, they became more animated, more excited, more bound to it.

"The same people. Day by day they became more beautiful. Became more themselves. In the last days, it was so beautiful—they never believed they had it within themselves.

"One day we were at a house with children and friends. A poor house. A great many difficulties in the area. There was much tension in the air, unhappiness. One of the little children in the house had an accident, as it were. Another person, not his mother, went to clean it up. Within ten minutes, someone started to sing. The atmosphere in the house slowly changed until it was utterly changed."

Is it any wonder that his friend, Cesare Zavattini, wrote *Miracle in Milan*? In the De Sica film, there is a scene involving a lonely old woman and a small orphan boy, whom she has adopted. While she is away at work, the boy spills a bottle of milk onto the floor. He is frightened. On returning home, the old lady, beautifully played by Emma Grammatica, sees the white rivulets and the scared child. At once, she makes a game of it, hopping and skipping across them, as though they were indeed little rivers. She and the boy laugh delightedly.

"Children have the imagination to see this," says Dolci. "And they are curious. How come this is so? they ask. They have fantasy, but they also have reality. If a broken leg is not fixed, it will be troublesome. It must be made whole. Children will not accept a broken reality."

When, I ask myself, will this heavy man with calloused hands be awarded the Nobel Peace Prize? He has been nominated, as a matter of course, during these past several years. I thought he was a cinch in 1973. I was wrong. It was awarded to a doctor who had done so much to heal the world's wounds. Henry Kissinger. So much for the Nobel Peace Prize. Still, forty thousand dollars would have done a great deal for the peasants of western Sicily.

3

The Scotsman

"Children will not accept a broken reality."
—DANILO DOLCI

An early Sunday afternoon. November 1962.

It's four fog-bound hours from my London hotel to Leiston, Suffolk County. One hundred miles to the east. The clouds are lowering fast, as we see the word: Summerhill. A small girl—is she Alice?—is perched on the wall, quite comfortably. She waves at us.

We enter the bare room. In the center, seated in a frayed arm-chair, Sunday papers strewn about, an old cap on his head, is the seventy-eight-year-old Scot. A. S. Neill. He's about, oh, six feet two, six three, shoulders slightly stooped, as though from years of reaching down and out toward small children.

At the moment, he's not too happy about things. He sounded terribly tired on the phone. "Why do you want to see me? There's no point to it." He made a passing, forlorn reference to the missile crisis of three weeks ago. All the more reason to see him, I mumbled. As if he hadn't had his fill of visitors, saying pretty much the same thing. "Come along," he said.

"Are you sure it's working?" Neill indicates the Uher, posed uncertainly (and unhappily?) on my lap. Astonishing. How could the man ascertain so immediately the uneasy détente between the machine and me? As I absently punch at the levers—a wanton boy swatting at flies—I think of Jacques Tati.

*   *   *

Shambling, loose-limbed, long of face, Jacques Tati, with a dollop of White Russian in his French, is animated as he talks of his film *Mon Oncle*. Not only his words (they mean little to him), but his gestures, artfully awkward yet, paradoxically, graceful, delight me and the young engineer in the control room. His constant theme: technology as against the vulnerable, human touch. It is a rich, rewarding hour. A tape to be preserved.

The young engineer appears in the studio. A ruddy-faced, confident winner, he is, at this moment, a pale, slightly trembling loser. He calls me over.

"I don't know what to say," he whispers.

"Say it." My heart tells me more than I care to know.

"I feel terrible." *He* says. As though I never felt better.

"You didn't press the record button." I say it matter-of-factly. I had been dipping into a British novel of manners.

"Yes," the culprit cries.

"Shhh!" Hush, little baby, don't say a word, papa's gonna buy you a mockingbird.

Jacques Tati, it seems, feels pretty good about the interview. He contrasts it with others, on national TV, where the host sits at a table and "shuffles around papers, a nervous man." I am flattered. And slightly devastated. And more than slightly nervous myself. I've heard of the White Russian–French temperament.

"Mr. Tati." I don't know how else to begin this colloquy.

"Yes?" He is full of good cheer.

"I don't know what to say."

"Say it."

"I feel terrible."

He looks toward the young engineer, who looks away. He looks toward me. I look beyond the silver of his hair toward the action painting on the far wall. Isn't there just a touch of Jackson Pollock? What would Harold Rosenberg think? I squint as I study it. I address it.

"This is the first time this has ever happened." A happening, that's it.

"Nothing is on the tape?" Though he puts it as a question, it is really a declarative sentence.

"Oui! Nothing!" I cry.

Jacques Tati's laugh begins quietly enough, swells slowly, and erupts volcanically. It is almost a Baccaloni special. He slaps his hands delightedly. He slaps me on the shoulder. "Beautiful! Beautiful!" This is the point he's been trying to make in all his films. We couldn't have planned it better, he shouts exultantly.

The following day, at his hotel suite, the young engineer and I appear. There is another hour of conversation. The large reel of tape—Jacques Tati's reflections on technology and the vulnerable, human touch—has an honored place in the library of radio station WFMT, Chicago. Yet, what happened the day before is even more blessed in my memory. And, I hope, in Mr. Tati's. A dark thought: suppose the guest had been a computer programer?

On the flyleaf of Neill's book are four lines of William Blake. They'll do for openers.

> Children of the future age,
> Reading this indignant page,
> Know that in a former time,
> Love, sweet love, was thought a crime.

"It's my credo," says Neill. "People bring up their children with what they think is love. With discipline. The two things are contradictory. No mother can smack a child unless she hates the child at the moment. We don't use discipline here. It's another name for hate."

My mother walloped Ben one evening in the spring. He had been late and missed supper. In a fury, unconstrained—where it came from, only God and Sophocles know—she hit him good. His head struck the chair and he bled slightly. My father clutched him to his breast and, in one of his rare moments of anger, told her off good. My mother lay her back against the wall mirror and, in one of her rare moments of silence, trembled. Her face, a study in remorse. I see the tableau. Ben was nine. I, four years old and never been struck—nor at any time in my life—observed the scene. It was my first attendance at Aristotelian theater: I experienced terror and pity.

What is freedom? What is license? To Neill, it's an easy rocking-chair question. "In this school, if a boy or girl doesn't want to go to lessons, it's nobody's business. But if a child wants to play a trumpet while others are sleeping or studying, that's everybody's business. You get people who are antisocial. They're in every society. The whole community deals with them. Not I alone.

"We meet every Saturday night and make our own laws. Last week, the chairman was an American boy, fifteen. Offenders are punished. A small fine, as a rule. We never advocate beating. I think they keep the laws far better than if I made them. There's always resentment against the lawmaker, the father. If they themselves make them, there's no such feeling. If a boy's punished sixpence for riding someone else's bicycle, it's accepted without question. But if his father or mother docked him sixpence, that'd be something else.

"I have as much right here as anybody else. The other night, I objected to someone pulling up my spuds prematurely. It wasn't a moral question. I didn't say, It's evil, you'll go to hell, God won't love you and I won't love you. It was a matter of my spuds and nothing else."

I'm somewhat bothered by Neill's throwaway manner in the matter of class attendance. What if a kid decides never to go, to just horse around?

"Nobody asks him to go. A new boy said to me last week, 'I'm bored. Shall I go to lessons?' Nothing to do with me, I told him. If a child has come here young enough, he'd never ask that. If a kid had come at five, and at sixteen asked the question, I'd be shocked.

"We don't tell 'em what to do. We only teach them a way. If a boy came to me with a piece of copper and said, What'll I make? I'd say, I have no idea, you decide. But if he asked how to chain two pieces of copper together, I'd show 'im.

"I remember where a kid did something bad and they decided to punish him by keeping him from classes. Others said, No, it's too harsh a penalty. Almost every new child goes to lessons for a fortnight and drops out, because kids hate lessons, as a rule. But when they come back, they're fresh and learning is easy then."

Neill is in a reflective mood on this bleak Sunday. "My father was a schoolmaster in Scotland. We had ten in the family, eight survived. I was the only one who challenged. Why was I challenging? Nobody knows. Challengers in any society are very few. The whole of our environment lies, but few challenge. Even in an ordinary household.

"As a small boy, I broke a plate and my mother spanked me. My father broke a plate at the next meal and she smiled. I thought, There's something wrong here. A lie. A child knows when his parents are lying. 'If that's Mrs. Smith, tell her I'm not at home.' Children are frighteningly honest themselves. Lying is put into a child, it's not natural. A kid comes up to me and says, 'Neill, I've broken a window.' He won't tell his father for fear he'd smack 'im. So he lies."

Didn't Neill ever lie to a child? In all his forty years at this school? That's what he said in his book. Is that really *true*?

He sighs. "Oh my. Oh yes. I have lied. A problem girl was accused of stealing a pound. At the public meeting she said, 'Neill gave it to me.' The chairman asked me and I lied. I said yes. I knew if I went against her that night I could never help her. I'd be her enemy. I'd be classed with all the others who let her down. That was a legitimate lie. I expect if I'm busy digging a deep hole somewhere and a kid comes over and says, Have you got a nail?—I'd probably say no, though I might have one. I don't mind that too much. To live a lie is unpardonable."

But how, I wonder out loud, if we live in a lying society, is the wholly truthful, generous, openhearted, vulnerable child to survive? He'd be clobbered unless he has the luck of my old friend Frank, the radio engineer.

"We meet a lot of our old students, some we haven't seen in thirty years. We don't keep track, but we know something about them. They're in all sorts of work. I don't know if many of them are successful in a Cadillac way. But I'd rather see a contented dustman than a neurotic Ph.D. I have a feeling that their lives are, in the main, happy—living a life without hating and struggling with other people to get somewhere. They have a certain charity toward people, a sort of balance. I couldn't imagine any one of them becoming a Fascist or anti-Semitic or anti-colored.

"A lot of people came here hateful, brooding, savage, stealing. I've seen them become nice, friendly, ordinary citizens, simply because they were free. I had to conclude that if people are free from outside compulsion, this good side can come out. My dog is a very friendly creature but if you chained him up, in six weeks he'd be biting. We chain our children."

Neill is wondering where mankind went wrong. He feels man is innately good. We've been taught of Original Sin. If this were so, he feels, every village in the world would be criminal. "Some people say it began with private property and man became hateful because of his goods. Delinquency isn't growing because people are too soft. It's because we've been taught to be hard.

"You can't pretend to be master or saint. Just human. That's what children like. A playful quality. No child gets enough play. I don't mean football, cricket, or tennis. I mean fantasy play. I object to the teacher who, seeing a child playing in the mud, makes it an occasion for a lesson in coast erosion. Play has nothing to do with learning. There should be no strings to it.

"If people are not free to be children, they cling to childhood in adult life. They stand by and watch others decide. All the juice was taken out of them when they were taught to say nay to life. Symbolically, they were castrated in their cradles.

"What happened three weeks ago? We were all on the verge of being blown to hell. And we couldn't do a thing about it. One of the two K's might have pressed a button. Humanity was waiting because it's been emasculated in the cradle. We leave it to father, we leave it to God. God's in his heaven, Kennedy is in the White House, Macmillan's at 10 Downing Street, and Khrushchev is in the Kremlin. Let's trust them. We've remained children, I think."

It is at this moment that Neill's shoulders appear to stoop, perceptibly. He who had been teaching the young freedom from fear finds himself on this island surrounded by a world in thralldom to fear.

"How afraid we are of sex. A small child discovers his sexual parts and some stupid mother or father or nurse or teacher says, 'Naughty, mustn't do that.' A woman complained to the police when my daughter went into the sea naked. 'How old is your daughter?' he asked me. 'One year old,' I said. 'My God!' he said.

"There are three ways of dealing with sex. One is to be religious and say God doesn't approve. The second is to say sex is normal, but for grown-ups only. I follow the third way. An example. Some years ago, a new boy of fifteen fell in love with a new girl of fifteen. They said they'd like to have a bedroom for themselves. I said, 'I can't give you one.' 'Why not? It's a free school,' they said. 'Yes,' I said, 'but it's not a free civilization. If I gave you the bedroom and the Minister of Education heard about it, he'd shut my school.' To the girl I said, 'If your mother heard about it, especially if you got pregnant, there'd be a hell of a row, because she is, as you know, not pro-sex.'

"It's not a matter of sin. You just can't go very far ahead of civilization. Maybe a step ahead. If you go two steps ahead, they'll chuck you in prison and ruin you . . . We don't say this is good or bad. We say, Smashing windows costs money. It's not a moral question."

There is a message for Neill. A parent is waiting for him outside. We'd better call it a day. "Oh," says Neill, winking at me, "she's the one I was just telling you about. The one's who's against sex. I'll be but a minute. Wait."

Stealing. Since private property may be what all the shooting's been about, what of the kids who pinch stuff that belongs to others?

"Most kids steal, at one time or another. With a real difficult case, with a child who's had no love at home, I give him sixpence every time he steals. If he's punished, he gets worse. So I get on his side by rewarding him. He's stealing love. It doesn't always work. A woman wrote and said, 'I did as you advised. Every time he stole, I gave him sixpence. He's worse than ever now.' I replied, 'The sixpence is symbolic love. He doesn't want the damn sixpence, he wants real love. Next time he steals, take him on your knee and hug him.' "

"What happened?"

Neill laughs. "I don't know. She never answered."

He offers one for the road. Call it a parable on crime and punishment. "The uncle of a new boy phoned from the north of England. 'My nephew has written me and asked if he could come for the weekend.' I said, 'I don't mind, but who's goin' to pay his fare?' Half-hour later, his mother phones. 'We've heard from Uncle Jim. He can go. The fare is two pound ten. Give it to him and add it to the bill.' I gave it to him.

"A friend of his came to me. 'Neill, you've been had. I was with him when he made the calls. He's a great mimic. He imitated his uncle's voice and his mother's.' I didn't ask him for the money back. I went to his room and said, 'You're in luck. More than you know. Your mother just phoned again. She made a mistake on the fare. It's not two pound ten, it's three pounds. Here's another three bob.' He took off the next morning, and left a note: 'Neill, I've discovered you're a better actor than I am.' He never tried it again."

Neill chuckles softly to himself, as though it were a private joke. "The heavy, moralistic way doesn't work. How long will it take for us to find this out? People say I'm brave. I'm not at all brave. It's just the natural thing to do. I'm not the last one. I don't want to be the last one. I think freedom should go on and on and on."

Another parent is waiting. Outside is grows darker by the minute. One of those heavy English pea-soup fogs is setting in. He'd invite us to tea, but suggests we go now or we'll never make London to-night. As he escorts us to the gate, the small girl on the fence calls out, "Neill." He waves at her. I look through the rear window of the auto and see the tall Scotsman, shoulders stooped, shambling past the cottage toward the main building. It's been a long, old lonesome road, but he shambles on.

4

The Midwife

Malcolm Muggeridge was having a hard time with Joan Littlewood. And when her tam, perched precariously on her head, fell off, as it had been threatening to do throughout the BBC television program, she scrambled under the table to retrieve it. It was all so discombobulating to poor Muggeridge, who seeks a preordained order to things. At home in Chicago, watching these two, I was enjoying the best theater in years. The born-again Christian, solemn as a periwigged judge, didn't know what the hell the exultant pagan was talking about. It wasn't really his fault. She was a visitor from another planet. Or was he a stranger to earthly delights?

I was bound to run into her, I know.

New York, 1964. A small dressing room, backstage. *Oh! What a Lovely War*, Joan Littlewood, director. Not really. Kenneth Tynan said it: "She doesn't direct a play. She creates theater." Same thing with Brendan Behan's *The Hostage*. She didn't direct it; she was its midwife.

We pick up the conversation where we had left off. The fact that I have never met her before is of small matter. "What are you trying to stir up?" I ask. I had just come in to get out of the rain and was curious.

"I have nothing to do with it," she protests. "It's lying all over the shop, like gold and rubbish and diamonds."

"What is?"

"People. I'm sick to death of all these silly old political and social and educational systems which have got in the way of human expression. You've got a parliament—your Congress—our parliament that represents a frizzled old excrescence from the past. With life bursting out all over the place, you've got a Broadway theater, like a calcified turd, where people line up in black dresses and gloomy faces. Here you have this great country, and, my God, what a mess you've made of it." She laughs. It's the sort of laughter that so bewildered Malcolm Muggeridge. Suddenly gentle, "Except for the people you bump into on the streets. There's a million Brendans out there. And yet there's nothing geared to human delight.

"Here we are on a planet, life's short. For a few times in human history, there's been a crossroad and there's been great theater, like Shakespeare's. Now we're at a crossroad again. We can move forward out of prehistory and we can pull down the walls of these terrible blocks, where the posh people and the poor people are trapped alike. And open the door to having perhaps more pain in our life and more delight. Rilke said it: Every day, a woman locked in her little flat is for one moment a poet. All along the back streets of this world."

Walls were pulled down in a Chicago neighborhood back in '61, but not in the manner Joan envisioned. An old neighborhood, pulsating with the life she was celebrating, was demolished by the Mayor, realtors, insurance companies, and banks. It is now a cold complex, euphemistically known as Circle Campus, University of Illinois. It is surrounded by ribbons of cement, called expressways. No people.

Observing the scene, Joan, some three years after our first encounter, said it was a historical sport: a throwback to another time. When medieval armies invaded a town, they drove out the inhabitants and made it a fortress. She painted the portrait in such live colors that I actually saw the moat and drawbridge some fifty yards away; and those young soldiers, euphemistically called students, dutifully going about their chores. Separating this fortress from the civilians, driving by, was a stone fence. It was a portcullis, I saw, thanks to Joan Littlewood's sense of history.

And when, that evening, she chose Louis Sullivan's *Testament of Stone* from off the bookshelf, was it an accident? He had visions, too. Tall ones, too. "He was cut down, Joan. And his visions with him. He died on skid row." She knew that, too. But it doesn't appear to stop her.

The cast is waiting outside the dressing room for a few words from her; it's all right, they're laughing and having a good time. It's

Brendan Behan she's thinking about. "Life was a bit too much for him. He didn't die of drink, he died of love. He was not a tough man. He was a very shy, gentle lover. The old woman on the corner, the penniless old tramp, the outcast, the prisoner, these were the people he made laugh. These were the people who followed him to his grave. Not the rich and powerful, the politicians, the stars from show business. I didn't see them. But thousands and thousands of the poor of Dublin that always followed him like the Pied Piper, and who stood as he went by and said, 'Oh, Jesus, he may never get there.' Because he gave them laughter, apart from sharing every penny he got by throwing it around every bar. And by the fish market early in the morning when the dead fish were laid out on the marble slabs and giving them all the last rites after a night of booze." There's that laugh again.

The Hostage was playing in Chicago—was it 1961? St. Patrick's Day was near. As is the Daley custom, the Chicago River is dyed green that day. As is the Daley custom, the Big Dumpling himself leads the parade. It is a festive day for our city; a tribute to the Irish. Brendan Behan had passed the good word: he'd love to come to Chicago and join the parade. The Big Dumpling had passed the good word, too. Behan is not welcome. Of course not. Had I met the man, I could have told him so. It would have saved him the price of a telegram. To Richard J. Daley's Irish, Brendan Behan was an affront.

The official apostle of Daley Irishness in our city, indeed in our country, is Father Andrew Greeley. For that matter, all known as ethnics are officially defended by him. Not that any have chosen him as their champion. But when the call comes, what other course has a man of God, such as he?

Twice a week in the *Chicago Tribune*, occasionally on our educational TV station, occasionally in the *New York Times*, and God knows where else, Greeley scourges all the dark forces that demean the "neighborhood people." Righteous, gimlet-eyed, stern as any Aunt Emma, he has sprung out of Molière's *Tartuffe*.

> Hang up my hair shirt, put my scourge in place
> And pray for heaven's perpetual grace.*

* Translated into English verse by Richard Wilbur (New York: Harcourt Brace Jovanovich, 1968).

And with what ease does he shift from saint to sycophant. On Richard Daley's sixth consecutive election triumph, Greeley was picking canary's feathers out of his teeth. A victory for the neighborhoods, purred this cat. And a hammer blow at the "Lake Shore liberals."

Do he and I live in the same city? What neighborhoods was he talking about? The neighborhood that is no more, where the academic fortress stands? The bungalow people, who like Horatio are holding off the Mayor's cement mixer, putty-put-put, that would make rubble out of their homes for the Crosstown Expressway? Need we mention the unmentionables, the project people? A pavement truth is of small value to this Tartuffe, who calls upon higher values.

As for the "Lake Shore liberals," I see them each day on the bus: lawyers, accountants, brokers, realtors. And their ancient, loyal secretaries. And young advertising agency executives. Their vote was overwhelmingly Richard J. Daley. Tartuffe, when caught in *flagrante delicto*, pleaded, "I may be pious, but I'm human, too." Not so our *buffo* Chicago monk. He is merely pious. To err is human.

And he does find errancy where you'd most expect him to find it. The scourge is often applied to our permissive society.

> Cover that bosom, girl
> The flesh is weak and unclean thoughts
> Are difficult to control
> Such sights as that can undermine the soul.*

"Poor old suffering Jesus," says Joan Littlewood. "Hanging up there, having a miserable time that we've had to live by. There was another theory, you know. Kit Marlowe said He danced with the apostles. They had a ball." The laugh, again. And the vision. "And we are that side of the penny, the clowns. That's what theater is, love, communion.

"I'd like to see people realize their full height. Did you ever see people who never danced dance? They become so beautiful and alive. A little boy at home is told he is dull. He's an A, B, or C. How dare they judge? We know we're all chemically different. How dare they judge the unique genius, these so-called educators? How dare they put up these old buggery cloisters from the Middle Ages and call it a place of learning?

---

* *Tartuffe*, translated by Richard Wilbur.

"Each man, each woman is part bird, part fish, wishing to fly, to dance, to fuck well, to eat well, to think. And we will. We've got to risk as artists. More pain, as Brendan knew it, but isn't it worth it? Who wants to be a vegetable? The woman who's shut up in her room parades as Cleopatra, we know. We only have to say, We're good enough. Let there be war, but *real* war between man and man over an idea. We've slapped the backside of the moon, yet we know nothing about you and me.

"We're part of the herring fleet, we're part of this flight of birds across the planet. Life is short. But there's more joy than we know, more brains than we know, more ability to learn. But learn for what? We learn quickly in times of war and disaster. But in life, there's a disaster all the time. The waste of human possibility. And we don't face it."

Joan Littlewood and I, in the dressing room, have some coffee. "I pick up what's in the wind," she says. "All these things I love and believe in. It's easier to cling to the past. Now people are so lost, it seems, so barren. But the time must come when all those funny old freaks of distinguished politicians and kings, queens, presidents, who tread their paranoid way through dreary corridors—their time must come. We've jumped into the future without knowing it. And we're gonna win!"

Should I bet on it, Joan? Didn't Blake sing out of a new Jerusalem during the Industrial Revolution?

"Yes. Raleigh, the intellectual, and Marlowe, the poet, dreamed of a republic of clowns. Of laughter, of bringing the stars to man's knowledge. Later came Hasek, the Czech Brendan, and his *Good Soldier Schweik*. He made war laughable and the soldiers threw down their rifles and went home. Before I die, I'd like to push open the door, so that people can see the absurdities of the calcified turds and recognize the genius in themselves."

As the young clowns of her company file into the dressing room, I ask Joan to call upon Blake's vision again. We sure could use it. She looks past me, way, way out there, somewhere out there, and she sings it:

> Bring me my bow of burning gold!
> Bring me my arrows of desire!
> Bring me my spear! O clouds, unfold!
> Bring me my chariot of fire!

I will not cease from mental fight,
Nor shall my sword sleep in my hand,
Till we have built Jerusalem
In England's green and pleasant land.

"That's what he said. Poor old bugger." She gets up to go to work with her young clowns. It's not a rehearsal, she says. It's a renewal.

BOOK
FOUR

1

The Whole World Is Watching

James Cameron and I watch. A wounded young man is being helped into a tent. A skinny, freckle-faced girl, with hair all the way down to her waist is the *ad hoc* nurse. She is bandaging his battered head. Another young recruit, his arm in a sling and his horn-rimmed glasses comically askew, stumbles in. "They got me again," he mumbles through bruised lips. An air of the absurd pervades. It is a Civil War photograph. It's not a Brady. He's long since dead.

It is a Chicago battlefield, August 1968. Across the street is one of our city's most beautiful parks. The glory of the Garden City. It was this verdant scene that so excited the imagination of Frederick Law Olmsted, in his search for outdoor delight. That was back in the 1870s. Here, on this night, will be staged the Battle of Lincoln Park. Again, Cameron and I shall watch. And we shall cry. There is as yet no immunity from tear gas. Talk about Living Theater.

James Cameron is astonished by what he sees and experiences. This is, in itself, astonishing. He has been called an Orwell, a Burton, a Lawrence; perhaps pieces of all three are in him. No matter. He is uniquely Cameron: Edwardian in manner, yet aware of the uneven pulse of this century; vulnerable, yet the consummate journalist— "It is my trade." It is no accident that so many young Englishmen, contemplating journalism, have looked toward him as their bright and morning star. Home, to Cameron, has been wherever he's hung his hat. And yet he's never really been at home.

*   *   *

I cannot remember when these curious moments of suspense first began, when I would find myself unanchored and adrift in the dark, groping for clues as to where I was. These moments came, and still come, at the exact transition between sleep and awakening, lying on the edge of uncertainty: what is this bed, where is this room, what lies beyond it—Egypt, England, Berlin, Jerusalem, Moscow, Minneapolis, Peking; there have been so many places, and any of them could be the background of this vacuum.*

From the beginning, I have been caught and held fast by his autobiography, *Point of Departure*. From the day I first met him in 1966, on his return from North Vietnam—he was among the first Western journalists to visit Ho Chi Minh—I recognized a man who answered only to himself. No wonder he was clobbered at the time by American television commentators, who have since come around to the truth he saw. Though apologies to him have long been overdue, he expects none. He judges only himself.

In all his writings, Cameron reveals himself and thus pieces of ourselves. And he's been around. Whether it's the Six Day War, the Algerian conflict, the volcanic boilings of Latin America, Verwoerd's South Africa, Franco's Spain, Ho's Hanoi, the death of Gandhi, or the psyche of Nehru, whom he, of all Western chroniclers, knew best—Cameron, like Kilroy, has been there.

Despite his giftedness, he is perhaps the most self-deprecatory of our journalists. Nor is it a sense of undue modesty that causes him such self-doubts. Rather it's a vision he has followed from his first days as a young newsman in the industrial bleakness of Dundee: the fragile possibility as against the brutal fact. From the late twenties on—in the depressed Scottish town and in more exotic places—Cameron has known where he stood; and how so often the ground beneath proved treacherous. Even now, battered as the young man in the Chicago tent, he pursues the ideal: "a sense of mortal community."

With an elegance of style, he has recorded on the run, in the rain, or at some weekend refuge his feelings as well as his observations. The double sense of his writings is evoked, while watching the A-bomb tests at Bikini:

---

* Here and below from James Cameron, *Point of Departure* (New York: McGraw-Hill, 1967).

It was not a bang, it was a rumble, not overloud, but it thudded into all the corners of the morning, like a great door slammed into the deepest hollows of the sea. Beside me a heavy wire stay unexpectedly quivered like a cello string for a moment, then stopped. . . . Now standing up unsteadily from the sea was the famous Mushroom. . . . The only similes that came to my mind were banal: a sundae, red ink in a pot of distemper. From behind me I heard a frenetic ticking of typewriters; very soon I found I was fumbling with my own. The reportage had begun. Many of us will never live it down.

From the first, Cameron's life and work have made a mockery of the mythic credo of the "detached" journalist. Following the Bikini scenario, he participated in the Campaign for Nuclear Disarmament and the Aldermaston March. "This annual ritual naturally attracted the derision of the press." Naturally. How could—a seriocomic case in point—Malcolm Muggeridge, a charming master of irrelevancies, understand a man like Cameron? No more than the court fool could interpret the haunted spirit of the saga man. Yet Cameron has always been gentle toward his detractors. That "sense of mortal community" again.

Inevitably, his personal concern—can't the man mind his own business and tend to his trade?—has led to troubles, though he has never quite seen it that way. Take the 1945 brouhaha, for instance. Lord Beaverbrook's *Evening Standard* carried a scurrilous headline concerning John Strachey, Labor's newly appointed war minister. Cameron was, at the time, the highest paid correspondent of the Beaver's other paper, *Daily Express*. Doing what comes naturally, he resigned, though he had never met Strachey. It was a *cause célèbre* along Fleet Street. Not to Cameron. It was simply a matter of personal standards.

Again it happened, while he was roving Korea for *Picture Post*, during that wretched war. In a startling coup, at least for the Western world, he revealed the noble little patriot, Syngman Rhee, to be an ignoble little brute. Firings and resignations followed. To the credit of British journalism, jobs found Cameron.

A remarkable chapter in his autobiography deals with his visit to Lambaréné, while another myth was still extant. In the rain forest, he discovered Dr. Schweitzer to be somewhat less than saintly . . . "The Hospital existed for him rather than he for it. It was deliberately archaic and primitive, deliberately part of the jungle around it, a background of his own creation which clearly meant a great deal

more philosophically than it did medically." Bach, it seemed was
one thing; the blacks, another. Yet it is the journalist's "reverence
for life" that makes this sequence a deeply moving, perhaps because
it is not worshipful, study of Albert Schweitzer.

And Churchill. Some fifteen years after Cameron's tempestuous
good-bye, he was invited by Beaverbrook to his Cap d'Ail home.
The publisher had a project in mind. Cameron was his man; at least,
so he thought. As *divertissement*, there was a dinner for four: the
host, the journalist, a senile Winston Churchill, and a rugged
Aristotle Onassis. Cameron, caught willy-nilly in this rare circle,
observed.

What Cameron captured becomes a tragicomic study of the
passing of power. It is, at once, *Lear* in its tragic overtones and
burlesque in fact. While Churchill snored, the two infinitely lesser,
semiliterate men talked the arcane language of big money. Theirs
was the power, if not the glory. As for Churchill:

> After dinner somebody put a cigar in his mouth and lit it; it seemed
> a ritual gesture without dignity; the completion of an effigy. Already
> I had begun to find this a profoundly melancholy occasion. My own
> admiration for the old gentleman's vigorous and abrasive qualities
> had always been qualified by opposition to almost every one of his
> public attitudes; nevertheless . . . it was sad to see him, for the first
> and last time, diminished into a totem, part of the social image of
> a rich Greek patron.

So it had been, and unfortunately still is, with James Cameron;
the heart of the innocent, the eye of the experienced, and the style
of the master. It's been said he changed the whole character of
English reportage by offering it a model that transcends journalism.

There is a fine irony to his being here, at this moment, on the
streets of Chicago, 1968. Here, it appears, the ghost of "objective"
journalism is being once and forever laid. Cameron needs no billy
club on his gray head to tell him this; though a good whiff of Lincoln
Park tear gas will, no doubt, add an acrid note to his London
dispatches.

Last night, a gathering of the young in the park was broken up by
Chicago police. Clubs were swung and heads were busted. Several
young journalists were among those clobbered. The ministrations in
the tent, a moment ago, brought to mind the wild night before.

Would there be a repeat performance tonight? The indignant young, and a surprising number of the middle-aged, plan to gather once more in the park. Mayor Daley has ordered the police to disperse all at eleven o'clock. That is the park's official curfew. For years, it has been more honored in the breach than in the observance. For years, smelt fishermen have lingered and hoped all night long for a good catch. They have sat along the banks of the lake, in the area that is officially Lincoln Park, from nightfall to well past dawn. It has been a Chicago ritual ever since the Potawatamies. But tonight, Mayor Daley, with Nestor-like wisdom, has decreed that the curfew shall ring at the appointed hour.

Led by young clergymen of the North Side Ministry, a raggle-taggle band is marching toward the park. A huge, rude wooden cross is borne at the head of the parade. James Cameron and I join the procession.

It is a lovely midsummer evening. Thousands are seated upon the grass. Brief speeches are made. Familiar songs are sung. "Amen." "Down by the Riverside." "Come by Here." Even "We Shall Overcome." Cameron is "instantly transported back seven or eight years to Aldermaston." The feeling of *déjà vu* overcomes a number of others, too, including myself. The occasion is both tender and sad.

Cameron notes that this ceremonial of what appears to be genuine dedication, touched by anxiety, anger, and some fear, is almost deliberately masked by outrageous costumes and fancy dress. A few youngbloods, hot out of Radcliffe and Amherst, protest the tranquil spirit. They are gently hooted down by the others. It is something of a religious occasion.

Testimony is offered by one or another, caught in the spirit of the occasion. Even I. A young clergyman recognizes me as one who talks a great deal, to others as well as to himself. At a microphone, one doesn't have to bear too much witness. "I am glad to be here, where life is," I intone preacherlike, "rather than at the Amphitheatre where life ain't." It doesn't really matter; the mike isn't working very well.

I am certain, I let James Cameron know, that nothing will happen tonight. After all, last night's bloody encounter was chronicled by the world's press and television. The Whole World Is Watching. It was certainly a black eye for Chicago. Mayor Daley may not be Pericles, but he's not really so dumb as to stage an encore. He'll just let the kids say their say, shout their shouts, sing their songs, and wander off. A few stragglers may spend the night in the park, but that's about it. James Cameron accepts my word, because I know such things. He and I shall soon wander off ourselves and toast a peaceful night with a martini or two.

The era of good feeling is short-lived. About three minutes after my pronouncement, Cameron says, "Look out there." So does the young clergyman at the mike. All eyes peer into the semidarkness across the green field. About two hundred yards away, in what appears to be a ghostly light, from lamps and headlights of cars speeding down Outer Drive, is gathered a Roman legion. So it seems. We see helmets and shields, face shields of plastic. We see no faces. We are, all of us, transfixed.

Have I seen this before on some wall tapestry? Or in some well-thumbed pictorial history of ancient times? Here, a band of raggle-taggle Christians and all sorts of outcasts. There, a battalion of armed soldiers of the Empire. Or is it a summer festival of young pagans, about to be disrupted by figures out of some primordial myth? One thing is certain: we are dreaming awake.

Several police trucks are faintly visible. From one, a voice on the bullhorn is heard. It is impersonal in tone. "You are ordered to clear out of the park by eleven o'clock." We shall be allowed to go peacefully. Those who remain will be in violation of the law.

The young clergyman suggests that those who wish to leave may do so now. We have about an hour to go. Hardly anyone moves. A band of young men uproot the huge cross from its original position, carry it some fifty yards forward, and implant it in the field. It stands between us and them. In the night vapors, it is awesome. Will it, as in medieval times, ward off the devil, wherever he may be? "I have never seen the crucifix more symbolically used," murmurs Cameron.

It has been made clear that tear gas will be called upon. Thus the trucks. A young man says to Jim and me. "You two elderly people better go. We don't want you hurt. Tear gas is nasty." Cameron and I harrumph indignantly. Elderly, indeed! Yet, our indignation is muted by something deeply felt. At first, there had been a gratitude expressed by a good number of the young that so many Over Thirty are here, to help them bear some sort of witness. Now, as Cameron observes, they are solicitous. Rather they be hurt than us.

Advice is offered by young veterans to middle-aged rookies. When the gas comes, hold your nose. Breathe through your mouth. Moisten your handkerchief. A pretty girl comes by and applies vaseline to our eyelids. Several years later, I encounter a young man who informed me it was *he*, not a pretty girl, who came by. My memory lapses may be attributable to nothing more than a middle-aged man's fantasy.

We are waiting. Waiting. A lone voice sings out a snatch of song and trails off. There is easy banter, yet an air of unease pervades. It is nearly eleven o'clock. Now, the tension cannot be disguised. The helmeted figures across the field are motionless. So are the trucks. "They always have the advantage," observes Cameron. "The decision is theirs. They can keep us waiting as long as they want."

Eleven o'clock. A last warning from the voice on the bullhorn. Nobody moves. The faceless images come alive. They are coming toward us. So are the trucks. "I don't believe it," somebody says. A sound is heard. Another. And another. Canisters of tear gas are being shot out from the tanklike trucks. Held noses and wet handkerchiefs do little good. We are coughing, hawking, crying, spitting, phlegming, cursing . . . We are helpless. And humiliated.

The humiliating attributes of tear gas are astonishing. During the Grant Park fracas, one day later, the gas floated across the boulevard and affected casual passersby. Among them were two Chicago industrialists, one of whom I recognized as an admirer of Richard J. Daley. From inside the bar at the Conrad Hilton, I saw him coughing, crying, and angrily waving away his companion, who sought to comfort him. It was a remarkable dumb show: a powerful man, powerless and humiliated by something he could not quite put his hand on.

We are stumbling, helter-skelter, across the park, toward Clark Street. It is a retreat of stumblebums. James Cameron and I, among others whose presence we hardly sense, are two characters out of Samuel Beckett. We are Estragon and Vladimir. We are Hamm and Clov. We are Krapp. We cling to one another. We cough, we spit, we hawk, we curse. Like blind Pozzo, we stumble on.

A canister falls at our feet. A tall young man, of flowing blond beard (I note, tearfully), immediately behind us, kicks the canister away, toward himself. "Are you all right? Are you all right?" he coughs at us, solicitously. "Grrrhhgg," we reply. "Are you sure?" "Grrrhhgg," we insist.

We are huddled, refugees, a good fifty of us, on the safety island in the middle of Clark Street. Sirens are sounding. The whole city, it seems, is possessed by the wailing of banshees. Nobody is in his

right mind. Cars are racing past. We see the faces of the occupants.
They are crazy with fear. Of us. One car deliberately swerves toward
the island, on which we hover. I see the driver's face. It is distorted.
Hate and terror. Of us. His hand is on the horn; stuck to it. Noise
and confusion. We cry out.

The car's fender scrapes against a young islander. It knocks him
down. He howls, jumps up, and beats against the window. Others
join him. Banging away at the car, they almost overturn it. Sirens.
Horns. Rage. Madness.

Was it at this moment that the Weathermen were born? Hardly
more than one year later come Days of Rage. Hardly more than one
mile to the south of this island cars are overturned. And "trashing"
is added to our vocabulary. Officially, 1969 was the year of their
birth. But weren't they conceived in 1968? And was Richard J.
Daley their unnatural father? Who, then, was the mother? And who
the midwife?

Study the portrait of Mayor Richard J. Daley as you would a
Rembrandt or a Goya. It's awesome, his startling resemblance to the
Buddha. A touch of Gaelic, perhaps, but godlike nonetheless. It
bears a religious significance.

Of the fifty members who make up Chicago's City Council, forty-
five (give or take a wretched fall-away or two) genuflect toward the
Big Dumpling with a love that passeth understanding. On Holy
Wednesdays, when the priestly aldermen gather, Himself presiding,
meditation and flatulence are the first order of business. There are
moments of ecstasy, too. The ritual may begin sedately enough: "I
just wanna say, God bless Mayor Daley." Gradually, the syllables of
an argot, uniquely Chicago, fall one upon the other and the language
is the talk of tongues. A portly alderman, who'd never dream of
doing it at Sunday Mass, becomes unashamedly Pentecostal. It is
the time of the jollies. It is glossolalia, Chicago style.

August first—as though in rehearsal for Richard's summer festival—was one such occasion. A black ghetto street was to be named
after Martin Luther King. To the dismay of the faithful, Alderman
Leon Despres, the Council's most unrepentant sinner, suggested a
Loop area as King Plaza! It was an apocalyptic moment; a theological switch was mandatory. The kindly Buddha became the wrathful
Yahweh.

Thundered He: "You and your ilk are trying to tell me you're being stepped on. As long as I am the Mayor, no one will be stepped on and that goes for you too." Yelled back Despres: "I don't want you or anyone else to call me an ilk." And God said, "I did not mean to call you an ilk. I meant to call you an elk." The faithful roared. Could Fred Allen have done any better?

Our Mayor is more than the city's most acerbic wit. He is our leading historian. During his seven-minute peroration that followed Despres's irreverence, He observed, "I was in Ireland a few years ago. I was told they had no feelings against the English because all that was behind them. That's how it should be here. We have the police and we have six commanders who are Negroes." So much for Parnell; so much for Frederick Douglass.

When Picasso's statue was unveiled at the Civic Center and the folk could not decide whether it was a woman, *Winged Victory*, or an Afghan hound, a city employee, studying it hard and long, mused aloud, "If it's okay wit' Mayor Daley, it's okay wit' me." He is our city's cultural arbiter as well.

For a time, after Chicago '68, His name was regarded with less than reverence throughout most of the "Free World," but hardly any of our Responsible Citizens had spoken out. We were told there had been reservations, privately whispered, at the Mid-America or the Tavern Club. Perhaps the wives of the Civic-Minded had been somewhat disturbed. Robert Motherwell, among other artists, had canceled his one-man show at the prestigious Arts Club—until such time as Chicago rejoined the community of the civilized. But it was not talked about publicly. Not in these circles.

The Chicago Press Photographers Association did speak out. They paid public tribute to Him and His police. When questioned, the head of the outfit explained, "Only two of our members were beaten up."

Knock on any door. Any cab door. The response is Johnny-One-Note: "Daley's okay. He shoulda busted more heads." Student cabbies don't give a hoot one way or another. They've had it. Black cabbies smile knowingly. They've been there before.

And what of *the* University, boasting more Nobel Prize winners than any other campus on earth? The silence is the silence of the dead. No, that's not quite right, either. Three of its most respected faculty have been quoted in the Daley Report (a brief, in the spirit and language of W. C. Fields, explaining the need for busted heads in Chicago '68). Out of context, no doubt. Where, then, the disavowals? Or at least some show of dissociation?

Dissociation? Hell, no, they go with God, these honored members of Academe. At the Quadrangle Club, to which *the* University's established professors belong, a student-waitress heard conversations that would put Vito Marzullo to shame. Alderman Marzullo considers Richard J. Daley not only "the greatest man any city ever had in the history of the world," but one of the greatest men who ever lived. Undoubtedly, there are members of the faculty who may be horrified, but mum's the word.

And well it should be. Chicago police spies are as energetic as Gordon Liddy in his palmy days. And as bold. In 1975, Larry Green and Rob Warden, two of our investigative journalists, made public what had, for years, been whispered in dark corners. Tapped telephones of troublemakers. A troublemaker: any Chicagoan who does not see in the Big Dumpling the light of life. Infiltration and sabotage of community organizations. Buddying up to the Legion of Justice, a merry band of local *fascisti*, whose specialty was breaking and entering radical bookstores. And the offices of those damn Women for Peace. Outside, a squadron of the city's finest lay in wait for any busybody who might call the *police*.

Though editorials have condemned these violations of law and order by the Apostle of Law and Order, and the United States Attorney has investigated further, Himself defies them all. Thus far, it's no contest. He's way ahead on points. Why, He asks rhetorically, if people got nothing to hide, should they object to a tap or two? Why, indeed? As Nelson Algren observed on another occasion, as the night's last Indian lay beaten to a pulp at the hands of neighborhood cops, "If the bastard ain't guilty, why is he bleedin'?"

How did the literary palatinate that produced Dreiser, Hemingway, and Lardner come up with this one?

> One man was carried by four policemen and he grabbed one of the lead policemen by the ankle and all four of the police fell to the ground. The police got up and kept hitting the man with his nightstick. The policeman whose leg had been grabbed was yelling, "The bastard is biting me." It took two policemen and an assistant corporation counsel to disengage the policeman's leg from the mouth of the prisoner.

We find ourselves, under siege, bedraggled though still breathing, in the lobby of the Lincoln Hotel. Its grandeur has long since gone to seed. Old people, making do, petty gamblers, no longer dreaming of the big score, and less affluent tourists are among its guests. We, sudden casuals, are a wretched lot. Twenty, thirty of us. It is Ellis Island. Nobody has any idea what it's all about, where to go, what next. Jim Cameron reads from a large tourist attraction poster: Six Good Reasons for Visiting Chicago.

I am furious. My fifteen-cent panatela is crushed in my pocket. During the rout, no doubt. I had envisioned more than a good smoke. It was my psychological weapon. Years before, I had seen the Russian film *Chapayev*. During its climactic battle scene, White Russian troops march toward the Bolsheviki, rifles at the ready. Each man is puffing a panatela. Psychology. My Lincoln Park plan: when the legion comes toward us, I shall casually light my panatela. But no. Tear gas. Put to flight. Humiliation. A crushed cigar.

I'm in no mood for badinage. One of the guests, a small-time horse player, murmurs dolorously, "I hear they killed one a the police officers." After some reflection, I reply, "You're fulla shit." To make matters worse, he is puffing a White Owl in my face. Outside, down the darkened side streets, long-haired young visitors are being chased by short-haired young cops. It's a crazy game of hide-and-seek. If caught, wham! right in the kisser.

A policeman, no more than twenty-five, rushes into the lobby, his club held high and menacingly. Everybody backs away. He stalks the lobby in circles. He appears to be looking for somebody. Who? What? He doesn't seem to know. His eyes are wide, wildly opened. He's scared. Of whom? Of what? He races out into the dimness.

Among others, high and dry in the lobby, are members of the *Esquire* crew: Allen Ginsberg, William Burroughs, Terry Southern, and Jean Genet. The Paterson poet has lost his voice. He is laryngitic. Did he hold the consonant too long during his constant Om? Nothing disturbs his good nature as he plays the mummer. Burroughs, owl-eyed, appears slightly bewildered, but not too much. Southern is bemused. It is Genet who seems most at home. Though the language and city are alien to him, he has obviously made this run before. "Genet observed the scene with the seasoned eye of a connoisseur," writes Cameron for his London paper.

It is late. A cautious, gradual dispersal is taking place. In pairs, in threes, in fours, the vagrants are making their way back to hotel rooms, friends' pads, or home. Something is still out there, so be careful.

It is too late for a drink. The bars are closed. I live a fair distance away. The Yellow and Checker cabs are on strike. The buses run irregularly at this hour. Once again, the young come to our aid. A boy of scraggly beard and two girls in the dress of gypsies offer us a ride. His car is across the street.

Across the street, on the Lincoln Park side, are no civilians. Only young policemen in groups of three and four. As we slowly approach, one of the girls says to me, "We're glad you two are with us. We feel safer."

"Why?"

"You're middle-aged and you're wearing ties."

A reversal of roles. In the park, they were our guardians. Now, we are theirs. One good turn deserves another.

"Where you goin'?" The young cop challenges the young man.

"This is my car."

"Yeah? Well, you better get in fast." The young cop smiles at us and at his colleagues, who fail to respond.

The car owner says something about constitutional rights. I quickly suggest this may not be the most appropriate occasion for a forum. Let's get in and fast.

"H'ya, Studs." It is the young cop. I look at him. He is grinning. He turns to his companions. "You know Studs, he's on radio." They don't know. "Whatever happened to that TV show? 'Studs' Place.' My family loved that, used to watch it every week."

"That was eighteen years ago."

"I remember it. I was nine years old."

Jesus.

"You hang around funny people these days, dontcha?" He turns his attention to the car owner. "It was better tonight than last night, wasn't it?"

"What do you mean?" asks the other.

"Last night we had the hitters. Tonight we had the pitchers."

"Very funny," I say.

"You think so? Maybe you'll have me on your show some day."

"Maybe."

He opens the car door for us, comically bowing from the waist. "Allow me." As we drive off, he calls out, "Be careful, Studs." From the rear view mirror, I see him turn toward his companions. They look at him.

There is a silence as we head north. I'm thinking back eighteen years. This uniformed man, his billy at the ready, was a kid of nine. The television program he and his family loved was, I had always thought, gentle in nature and concerned human frailty and, whimsical though it was, some sort of sense of community. Oh boy. Obviously, in my arrogance, I had assumed much too much. It was just a weekly half-hour show.

Jim Cameron breaks the silence. "He was letting us know something, wasn't he?" Yeah. He was making it clear to us that he had a face. Under the helmet, behind the plastic mask was this particular somebody, who knew another particular somebody, me. A few years hence, Vincent Maher, police officer, lets me know something: "Because I wear a uniform, people that are garbage will say I'm a pig. They don't look at me and say, 'This is a human being.' They look at my dress. I'm a representative of the law, of you, the citizen. You created my job, you created me. To you, I am a robot in uniform. . . . But I'm also a man. I even have a heart."* Vincent Maher laughs, as he pouts babylike.

This night, the young policeman was letting his colleagues in on something, too. He knew somebody they didn't know: a small winner, a small-time celebrity. And thus, perhaps, in their eyes, he was something of a winner, too.

In his introduction to the third edition of Earl Blackwell's *Celebrity Register*, Cleveland Amory observes, "I now believe the idea of registering celebrities is at least as valid for our time as the *Social Register* was for its time—circa 1880." He is right, of course. They are of equal value.

Blackwell's index does reflect our time. Several years ago, C. Wright Mills pointed out, "In the world of the celebrity, the hierarchy of publicity has replaced the hierarchy of descent and even of great wealth." This heavy book—it runs to almost six hundred outsize pages—contains about two thousand names and faces from A to Z: Hank Aaron to Adolph Zukor. Athletics, finance, the fine arts, the raffish arts, politics, science, fashion, sex: the achievers in those worlds are here celebrated. The *sine qua non* for making it in these pages need not be accomplishment. It is being famous. Having a name, face, or reputation. The arbiter is Earl Blackwell, cofounder of Celebrity Service, Inc., whose own face, in the company of others equally celebrated, has graced whiskey ads.

---

* Studs Terkel, *Working* (New York: Pantheon Books, 1974).

The late Vince Garrity had one of Chicago's most famous faces and reputations. "My life," he once told me, "has been a life of knowing everybody, regardless of who they are." His life as a celebrity had begun that memorable summer evening in 1937, when he hopped onto the running board of President Roosevelt's car. From that moment on, Vince was on his way.

"I happened to be with Tim O'Connor the day he was replaced as police commissioner." (The Summerdale scandal. Chicago policemen were assisting a burglar named Morrison in his endeavors. He blabbed. O. W. Wilson was chosen to replace O'Connor.) "I was with Pendergast the day he replaced John Allman. And I was with Allman the day he replaced Alcock as police commissioner. . . . I became the office boy of Mayor Kelly. He liked me because he saw me around and saw me with big shots. . . . I worked the telethon on TV to raise money for a good cause. I brought Snite, the famous boy in the iron lung, Downtown.

"I got known during the milk strike many years ago. The dairy I was working for was bombed. I picked it up and gave it to Jimmy Gallagher. [J.G. subsequently became the G.M. of the Chicago Cubs.] He threw it out and we saved the dairy. That's how I first got to know Walter Winchell.

"When I was seriously ill . . . , Father O'Malley, Rabbi Binstock and Preston Bradley of the Protestant faith were all three at my bedside. I'm sure their prayers helped me a whole lot."*

As I strolled along the streets of Chicago in the company of Vince—he had the air of the Man Who Broke the Bank at Monte Carlo—everybody waved at us, pointed, murmured, gawked. Hardly a day passed without some admirer requesting his autograph. I assume, were my friend among us today, he'd have made *Celebrity Register*, third edition. Certainly he had the requisites as set down by Earl Blackwell.

A minor Syndicate tiger of my acquaintance—occupation: juice man—reflected on his big brother's glory moment. "He was in trouble. They accused him of threatening to break a guy's legs. All the papers had him on the front page. They had him on television. He was scared. What was gonna happen to his income? People would shy away from him. I said to him, 'Fool, you'll be able to raise all the money in the world. You're *known*.' He came back in a week.

---

* Terence Ignatius Boyle in Studs Terkel, *Division Street: America* (New York: Pantheon Books, 1967).

He says, 'I've raised fourteen thousand.' I says, 'Fool, you could've doubled it. People want to help people, especially a celebrity.' He was on *television*, for God's sake! People worship celebrities."*

Unfortunately, my acquaintance's big brother would be rejected out of hand by Mr. Blackwell. "Sometimes one spectacular event," he informs us, "can catapult an unknown into instant celebrity (Neil Armstrong, Mark Spitz), while another spectacular event of less savory import can banish a formerly powerful person to non-celebrityland (H. R. Haldeman, John Mitchell)." Mr. Blackwell, one sees, is a moralist though not a seer. Spiro Agnew is listed, having the longest profile. Blackwell's style and perceptiveness are stunning; he concludes this entry: "Of the future, no one can guarantee that the odyssey of the first Vice President of Greek origin will not be as filled with suspense and turns of fortune as that of Homer's epic hero." *Celebrity Register* obviously went to press before Agnew's troubles went public. Howard Hughes is, of course, listed.

Blackwell is wistfully aware of fame's evanescence and the risk of chroniclers. Some time ago, I accompanied Alger Hiss as he checked in at a Loop hotel. The credit manager, on seeing the signature, blinked. "Oh, you recognize the name?" I asked. "And how!" He was, it appeared, somewhat impressed. "You know who I had last week? Shep Fields of Rippling Rhythm!" The manager was, I must admit, somewhat advanced in years.

Celebrity Register is, in the manner of the hotel credit manager and the academician who works for the Pentagon, value-free. Thus there are endearing juxtapositions, the list being alphabetical: Ralph Nader and Joe Namath; Heinrich Böll and Pat Boone; Lewis Mumford and George Murphy; Pablo Casals and Johnny Carson; Pablo Neruda and Peter Nero: Edward Dahlberg and Richard J. Daley.

Remarkable though this work is, the editor might have done still better had he called on the services of David Lefkowitz, a professional autograph hound who doubles as a Good Humor man. Charlotte Curtis quotes him: "I like big people. I like mayors, governors, presidents. Or famous stars or secretaries of state." Though he disdains Henry Ford, he is impressed by Alfred Gwynne Vanderbilt because "he's a millionaire and a gentleman. I mean he's loaded. I can tell you that."

In this instance, Lefkowitz and Blackwell are in agreement:

---

* Kid Pharaoh in Studs Terkel, *Division Street: America* (New York: Pantheon Books, 1967).

Vanderbilt is listed in *CR*. But where is W. Clement Stone? He's a millionaire and a gentleman and I mean he's loaded. I can tell you that.

Mr. Stone, president of the Combined Insurance Company of America, was the largest single contributor to Richard Nixon's 1972 campaign. He is a celebrated philanthropist who was listed in *Fortune* as one of America's new centi-millionaires. And talk about personality. (As Blackwell does.) Stone has a pencil-thin mustache ("In those days, movie stars Ronald Colman, John Gilbert, and others did it"); he wears a wide bow tie ("It's an indication of an extrovert, someone with a high energy level, someone who has drive, who gets things done"); he smokes long, thick Cuban cigars ("When we had our Castro troubles, I bought up the equivalent of three warehouses. If you take the label off, you'll see it's '59"). His laugh is unique; it has a five-note rise. He was just one gaffe away from being our ambassador to the Court of St. James.

I had phoned Mr. Stone, after a second look into Blackwell. He was his usual ebullient self. "No, I'm not bothered at being left out. Not in the least. There isn't any part of the world, whether it's downtown Chicago or Hong Kong, that an average minimum of six people on the street don't stop me to tell me how much their lives were affected by my writings, speeches, and TV appearances." Mr. Stone is an apostle of PMA (Positive Mental Attitude) and has written *Success through a Positive Mental Attitude* and *The Success System that Never Fails*. Rudi Gernreich is in *CR*; W. Clement Stone is not. Do six people in a Hong Kong street stop Rudi Gernreich and ask for *his* autograph?

I don't mean to cavil. *Celebrity Register* is a book that, after its own fashion, illuminates our times. Jerome Zerbe, who is still in, explained, on some other occasion, the difference between Then and Now. It was he, during the Depression, who photographed socialites. Alchemist that he was, he transmuted them into celebrities. "They were the top, top social. These were the people whose houses, one knew, were filled with treasures. These were the women who dressed the best. These were the women who had the most beautiful of all jewels. These were the dream people we all looked up to, and hoped we and our friends could sometime know and be like."*

Zerbe may be speaking for himself and that legion of Zerbes who

* Studs Terkel, *Hard Times* (New York: Pantheon Books, 1970).

sup at the welcome table of the "dream people," in return for the flattering word. Yet, as Mills suggested, the new element of publicity, instantaneously offered through the new technology, radio and TV, changed the hallmark of the celebrity. To the anonymous many today, the celebrities are "the dream people we all look up to," but hardly hope "we and our friends could sometime know and be like."

The presence of the celebrity, black or white, evokes a set response: awe. Occasionally, there is a tentative brush with familiarity; a touch, as one might an ikon; but it's genuflection all the way. Neither circumstance, place, nor race matters. It may be on the street, in an auditorium, or at a funeral.

At Mahalia Jackson's funeral service in Chicago, directed with reverence by Mayor Richard J. Daley, the exciting response came forth as Sammy Davis, Jr., appeared on stage. An awesome murmur arose from the thousands of mourners. He approached the microphone, some ten feet from the casket, and read a message. It was a touching tribute to Mahalia: "She made a joyful noise unto the Lord," et cetera. Toward the end of the eulogy, the performer paused—a soulful moment—and intoned softly, "Signed, Richard M. Nixon." The applause was thunderous, wave after wave, enough to drown Pharaoh's army.

The medium and the message were one, via the voice of the black celebrity and the words of the white celebrity (or those of his PR man in charge of such ritual). Sammy, having done his turn, apologized to the assemblage for "rushing off" and left in the company of a White House courier. Again, applause. It was, after all, performed without a hitch. And we had been amazingly graced by a celebrated presence, brief though it may have been.

That the President may never have heard Mahalia Jackson sing, let alone understood the meaning of, "Move on Up a Little Higher," "I'm on My Way," or "Hold On" is wholly beside the point. It is possible that the Mayor, too, may have been thus underprivileged. No matter. It was to him, Richard J. Daley, that tribute was paid that morning, as much as to the dead artist. For certainly, he is Chicago's number-one celebrity.

On another occasion, I was hurrying toward the O'Hare Airport terminal. It was not till I was near Baggage Claim that I sensed an excited, indeed exhilarated, peering, whispering, craning, and turning of heads. They were pointing toward something behind me. I turned around. An elderly man in white (Mark Twain?)—suit, mustache, and goatee—was acknowledging the tribute. Genially he nodded and grandly waved his cane. It was, of course, Colonel Sanders. Life was indeed finger-lickin' good.

For the anonymous millions, whose actual lives are somewhat less than finger-lickin' good, there is a surrogate life to be daily lived. It makes the day go faster for Teddy the doorman, who watches human traffic at a Loop office building. "Hey," there's a fever to his usual monotone, "who was that just came in? I seen that face, I know. He's supposed to be somebody famous." It matters little whether the face, probably one that has appeared on a TV talk show, represents a commercial, a political idea, an art, a science, or a call house—for Teddy it is enough. Two, three such winners a week and he has it made.

Consider this Blackhawk Indian. The Chief, as he chose to be called, was doing quite well at the all-night poker game. Nelson Algren, the host, had, hours before, introduced us, one to the other. The Chief was impressed that I was a disk jockey. That the furniture dealer, across the table, was a far wealthier man, meant little. I was speaking over the radio, the magic box. Whether I sold bulletproof Bibles or barnyard perfume, whether I played Mozart or Lawrence Welk, was of no interest to the Chief. Mine was the voice of the turtle, heard throughout the city. A celebrated voice.

Others less fortunate must make do with images on the TV screen. On rare occasions, when the image in some occult manner materializes on the street, at the airport, or in some lucky somebody's cab, the anonymous one experiences the shock of recognition. If the face is Bill Russell's or, God willing, Charlton Heston's, it may provide conversation for an otherwise lost weekend. In any event, it helps the faceless face survive the day.

Came the dawn. The Chief and his colleague, a defrocked Chicago cop, were the big winners. Algren was convinced they were cheating, but he could offer no proof. A heavy loser passed his personal check on to the Chief; he had lost all his cash. The Chief glowered. "I don't know you. How do I know this check won't bounce?" "It's okay, Chief," I assured him. "Take my word for it." The Chief turned to me. He nodded. Softly he said, "If it's okay with the disk jockey, it's okay with me." Thanks to my bush league celebrityhood, my clout at the table on this newborn day was the clout of Richard J. Daley.

A few days before the Battle of Lincoln Park, I had appeared as a guest on the "Today" show. My portrait of the local Buddha hadn't been flattering. The following evening, as the usual dog days of August had assumed a wolfish air for some Chicagoans, out of uniform as well as in, I found myself in a neighborhood bar. I was in Daley territory. A patron bawled out, "Hey you! I wanna talk to you!"

"Me?" I smiled shyly, lacking only Charlie's derby, mustache, cane, and baggy pants.

"Yeah, you!"

Reluctantly and somewhat perversely, I came toward him. Was the bottle of bourbon I had just bought enough of a weapon for a preventive strike? He had the mark of the true believer. "Were you on the 'Today' show yesterday?" I mumbled something. He sidled off the stool and shoved his face close to mine. He exuded the attar of Four Roses. His hands heavy on both my shoulders; his voice of gravel and menace: "I want you to tell me somethin' an' tell it straight."

"What?" I leaned away, gripping the neck of the fifth as I would a billy.

Reverently, he murmured, "What's Hugh Downs really like?"

The awe of the celebrated image did not come into play with television or with radio. It's been around ever since Born Losers were many and Successes few. Propinquity has, however, heightened the illusion of the Loser's delight as it has diminished his sense of self.

I have not run into the young cop again. It is eight years since '68. And twenty-six years since "Studs' Place." He should be a rugged thirty-five now. Does he still joke around? Or does he find less to laugh at these days? How are the wife and kids? And how does he become a particular somebody?

As for Officer Maher, I've encountered him frequently. He's had his troubles, domestic and otherwise. He has been separated from his wife and, on occasion, from the force. As a non-policeman, he's felt himself a non-person. The last time I saw him he remembered his moment as a particular somebody.

"Oh yeah, the Democratic Convention." There is a show of hurt and the small boy's pout once more appears. But there is also an intimation of excitement, which he doesn't try too hard to suppress.

"There was this radical garbage piece of thing, dirty, long-haired, not a human being in my book, standing by the paddy wagon. Not a mark on him. He spotted the camera and disappeared. In thirty seconds he came back. He was covered with all kinds of blood. He's screaming into the camera, 'Look what they did to me!'

"Lincoln Park. This group was comin' down on me. I'm by myself. They're comin' down the hill, 'Kill the pig! Off the pig!' Well, I'm not a pig." The tone of hurt changes to Gary Cooper. "There's only one of me and a whole mess of them. Well, *c'est la guerre*, sweetheart. I folded my arms, put my hand on my .38. I looked at them and said, 'What's happening?' They stopped. They thought I was gonna pull out my weapon and start blowin' brains out. I didn't lose my cool. I'm a policeman, I don't scare. I'm dumb that way." His laugh is not a laugh of someone who thinks he's dumb. "These kids were incited by someone to do something. They said, 'Those guys up there with the cameras.' I blame the media."*

Visiting journalists, quite a few, are nursing drinks in the Haymarket Lounge of the Conrad Hilton. It is one day after the Battle of Lincoln Park. It appears that another is in the making, across the street, kitty-cornered. It is to be commemorated as the Battle of Grant Park. The other Civil War had its Chickamauga and Gettysburg. This one's bloody encounters are named after parks named after Presidents.

The journalists, having but a moment ago sent out stories from the press room upstairs, don't quite believe it. Not again. They are fast becoming aware of the week's surreal nature. And Chicago's. Drink up gentlemen. Here we go again.

The hotel, advertised as the largest in the world, is on the southwest corner of Balbo and Michigan. Until the Chicago World's Fair of 1933–34, the street was called Seventh. During that celebratory season, General Italo Balbo, Mussolini's air minister, led an armada of *fascisti* planes onto our city's lake front. It was a triumphal experience for the blackshirt, who had, in 1922, led the March on Rome. He had come a long way. Our city fathers, who are gracious in such matters, decided to name the street after him. What more appropriate way to honor the memory of Italo Balbo than the event to

* Studs Terkel, *Working* (New York: Pantheon Books, 1974).

follow. If our city fathers have nothing else, they have the touch of the poet.

The battle begins. Nobody quite knows how. Or why. Clubs swing. Whistles blow. Sirens sound. Tear gas has come to Michigan Boulevard. Crowds and panic. Run. They have no idea where they're going. The police have an idea. They're in pursuit of these middle distance runners. They win a few, lose a few.

There is a crush at the revolving doors of the lounge. And at the hotel. No, nobody can get in. Locked. It's the other way round, too. The journalists can't get out. They are indignant. In one of the booths sit Jim Cameron, Jules Feiffer, William Styron, and myself. We are truly a captive audience, as outside the window we see fights, uneven, but fights nonetheless. We hear shouts. Screams. What's to be done? Is that a line out of Beckett?

It is at this moment that the voice of the maître d' is heard. It is he who adds the surreal touch that crowns the experience. A small man, a mouse of a man, with a touch of Middle Europe to his accent, stands at the door and demands our attention. "Gentlemen," he announces with some firmness, "you cannot leave." Having established authority, he becomes his usual gracious self. "Please enjoy your drinks. Thank you." Oh where, oh where is Jean Genet today? Somebody has just lifted a scene from his play.

In recalling Chicago '68, it is these moments that most immediately come to mind. A fusing of mindlessness to the Theatre of the Absurd. For James Cameron, it shall always be a unique experience. Only a few weeks before, he had observed the Paris riots. There, too: the police versus the young. The French police, he believes, are more calculatedly cruel; there is more style to their sadism; they are more personal. "Here, it was mindless and thus more shocking." And, perhaps, as consequences appear to indicate, more numbing to the young.

Several years later, by remarkable coincidence, Cameron and I found ourselves on the campus of Lewis and Clark College in Portland, Oregon. He as writer-in-residence; I as a lecturer. At an assembly, we jointly recalled Chicago '68. During the question-answer period, we asked the students what they were doing in 1968 and how the event the great many of them saw on television affected them. Almost without exception, they, who were twelve and thirteen at the time, spoke of being "paralyzed." Said one young man, who, it appeared, spoke for many, "And I've been so ever since."

2

A Study in Clout

A chapter, hitherto muffed by history, of another such gathering, during another Chicago summer. The Republican National Convention, 1952.

I am in a parked car. It is two o'clock in the morning. My buddy, Vincent De Paul Garrity, and I have captured a randy voice or two for our night owl radio program. It is 1954; and though Vince is somewhat content, his heart is with 1952. It is his glory moment.

Every man is Parsifal seeking the Holy Grail. For Vince, short, squat, and squinty-eyed, to be known was not quite the ultimate meaning in life, though it was close enough. He went along with Ecclesiastes: to everything there is a purpose under heaven. To be known for its own sake was not quite what this Pilgrim, traveling through this world of woe, had in mind. Any clod seen often enough on the tube or heard over the air waves, day to day, can achieve that. Any oaf can score through a well-publicized scandal. Any peacock can make it big as a "world statesman" in this Sino-Soviet Era of Hard Feeling. Consider Henry Kissinger, Peter Sellers's most deadly deft mimic.

No, what Vince had in mind was wholly something else. He was determined to be known to every cop, every ambulance chaser, every City Hall coat holder as well as those whose coats were held, every hood, no matter how large or small his enterprise, and all such citizens who have helped to make this Frank Sinatra's kind of town. And he was so known.

Unlike most red-blooded American boys, Vince did not want to grow up to be President. He didn't even want to be Mayor. All he wanted was to be "da power behind da t'rone." The ultimate clout on his own turf. And, in some wondrous, cockeyed way, he succeeded. At least in one memorable instance.

Much has been written and spoken of the 1968 Democratic Convention. And of the Big Dumpling's lack of *élan*. Little has been said of the 1952 Republican Convention and the Little Dumpling's exquisite show of *élan*. Vincent De Paul Garrity admired Richard J. Daley, as Little invariably admires Big. Yet, the worshipper in this instance was much more hip to the religion of clout than his idol. By a country mile.

To begin. Red Quinlan was, at the time, station manager of WBKB, an affiliate of ABC. Derring-do was Red's most singular attribute. While other TV executives were ciphers, superfluous in swivel chairs, Red risked. He made errors, the kind a wide-ranging shortstop, say Marty Marion, was impelled to make. Hiring Vince for this special occasion was not one of them.

To refresh memories, the American Broadcasting Company won every award in the books, Peabodys and etceteras, for its coverage of the 1952 convention. Its most celebrated recipients were John Daly and Martin Agronsky. Know who really won it for ABC, though he was, of course, accorded no recognition? Vince. He was truly "da power behind da t'rone."

An explanation is in order. Red had decided to put Vince on the payroll for the express purpose of easing the way for the networks' visiting firemen, who, on the tube, appeared to know much, but who knew little of the city they were visiting. Vince knew it, not in spades, perhaps, but certainly in blue. He knew every cop who stood guard at the Amphitheatre, the convention's arena. What's more to the point, they all knew him.

So it was that Vince advised the officer at the press gate, "Watch me for the high sign. If I shake my head, don't let 'em t'rough. They're a bunch of New York wise guys. If I nod my head, it's okay. Let 'em in. Got it?"

"Got it, Vince. Whatever you say."

It came to pass that H. V. Kaltenborn, NBC's most authoritative voice, accompanied by his producers and assorted go-fers, was barreling toward the gate in an NBC special limousine. As is the wont of such Eastern hotshots working the benighted hinterlands, the air was of towering confidence and, by its very nature, of cool contempt toward the natives. A card was flashed, *en passant*. The Red Sea did not part. The cop said, "Just a minute."

"We're NBC," somebody said clarion-clear.

"I said, Just a minute."

The officer turned away. He was peering intently, it seemed, at somebody several yards distant. Somebody short, squat, and squinty-eyed. He waited for a sign. After what seemed an appropriate passage of time, the mysterious figure slowly, and with an air of dolor, shook its head.

"Sorry," mumbled the man in uniform. "Can't get in."

"Are you crazy?" A caterwaul in Manhattan nasal. "We're the *National Broadcasting Company*! And that's *H. V. Kaltenborn* back there!"

"I don't care if it's Gabby Hartnett. Ya can't get in."

"We *must!* He's got an important interview with Senator Taft's campaign manager. Can't you read our credentials? N-B-C!"

"I can read. Move to one side, please."

Another limo was pulling in. Again, the indolent, languorous flash of a card.

"Just a minute."

"Just a minute? We're CBS!"

The gentleman in blue turned away. Again he peered toward the short, squat, squinty-eyed body several yards distant. After what seemed an appropriate passage of time, the mysterious figure, slowly, and with an air of dolor, shook its head.

"Sorry, ya can't get in."

"Are you crazy?" Another caterwaul—this one in Scarsdale nasal. "We're the *Columbia Broadcasting System*! Do you know who's sitting back there? *Ed Murrow!*"

"I don't care if it's Luke Appling. Ya can't get in."

"We *must!* We've got an important interview with Eisenhower's campaign manager. Can't you read our credentials? C-B-S!"

"I can read. Move to one side, please."

Another important car was pulling in. Again, a card flashed. The policeman turned away. Once more he looked for guidance. This time the short, squat, squinty-eyed man of mystery nodded. Determinedly, quickly.

"Okay, sir. Sorry for the delay."

The car whizzed by.

Thus it was that ABC scooped its two rivals, again and again and again, during that unremarkable convention of 1952. ABC was duly honored with plaques and plenty of adulatory ink. It is not that John Daly and Martin Agronsky deserved these tributes less, but that Vincent De Paul Garrity deserved them more.

There's the story of Taft conceding the nomination to Ike, via ABC. As Vince passes it on to me this night, it goes something like this:

Taft is staying at the Congress Hotel. Or is it the Blackstone? Vince and an engineer, fully equipped, get off at the Senator's floor. They are grabbed by Secret Service men.

"Where do you think you're goin'?"

"To see the Senator."

As Vince and his colleague are shoved toward the button and DOWN is pressed by a hammy hand, he loudly proclaims. Though his voice carries through the corridors, the announcement is casually offered. Its import is thunderous.

"You know who's waitin' to talk to Senator Taft on the other end?" He looks up at the Secret Service man who has him by the collar. "Cardinal Stritch."

The heavy hand falls away. "Stay right here." In a moment, the SS man returns. A touch of apology. "Okay, go right in."

In the Senator's room, whatever needs hooking up is hooked up; the telephone is beeped. The Senator, stiff and formal, is ready. On the other end is John Daly of ABC. Another coup. As Vince explains to a quizzical me, "John Daly's Catholic."

Consider this Vincentian tale of the same affair. He, Vincent De Paul Garrity, is experiencing some difficulty getting into the Amphitheatre on the night of Eisenhower's acceptance speech. The members of the Secret Service are, for some reason, less than appreciative of Vince's stick-to-itiveness. They are, patently, not Chicagoans. So he does what comes naturally. He bedecks himself in the uniform of a Chicago policeman. "I was the shortest cop in the history of the force." He finds himself on the platform. Of course, Ike is in the wings, awaiting the moment.

Do you understand that moment? There is always an anticipatory ten seconds or so, when nobody is quite sure what to do. The nominee is nervous, clutching the papers in his hand, waiting. The network commentators whisper softly, reverently, waiting. Millions of Americans are watching, waiting. All is sweaty pomp. Suddenly, there appears on the TV screens, coast to coast, a singularly short, squat, squinty-eyed, bespectacled policeman, leading by the arm a bewildered, bald-headed national hero—toward the ABC microphone. Of course.

Huge figures grab at the cop; he is spirited off the screens. That he is unceremoniously booted out of the hall is of small matter. A friendly member of the local constabulary spirits him back in, so he, seemingly another face in the crowd, may taste the fruits of his existential heroism.

History may indicate that General Eisenhower, in the year 1952, made his acceptance speech, haltingly perhaps, but muddling through, into a microphone on which were writ large the letters: ABC. Where did Teddy White chronicle that? Do any of these eminent observers know what time it is?

Apocryphal, these happenings? True, it is Vincent De Paul Garrity himself who is my murmuring source, as we shuffle into an open-all-night beanery. Nor will I deny that, at times, he engages in flights of fancy. I'd be among the Doubting Thomases, too, were it not for the fact that Vince and I have worked together for two memorable years. And astonishing ones.

By what means he appeared at the scene of a robbery no more than thirty seconds after it happened was no business of mine. When I'd ask, the index finger of his right hand tugged ever so slightly at his right eyelid. Nor did I ask how he came across the ecdysiast, whom he grandly led into the studio as "the best dancer since Pavlova. Even better than Irene Castle."

And when Johnny Groth, star outfielder of the Detroit Tigers (and a Chicago Latin School alumnus), was seriously beaned by a wayward pitch from Billy Pierce, it was headline news. That very night, the injured Groth called in from his hospital bed.

"Everything's fine, Studs. Tell everybody I'm okay."

It was thoughtful of Johnny to call me, especially from the intensive care unit.

ME   Is Vince there?
GROTH   Yes, he's right here.
ME   Put him on.
VINCE   Your old pal, Johnny Groth, wanted you to have the news
        first.

I was terribly moved, especially since I had never met Johnny Groth. Vince explained it all the next day. Nobody was allowed to see the ballplayer; it was that serious.

ME   How did you get in, Vince?

VINCE   They barred the door.

ME   How'd you get in, Vince?

VINCE   I got a little black satchel and I said I was Dr. Garrity, the Groth family physican.

Do you still doubt that Vincent De Paul Garrity deserved all the kudos won by the others in 1952?

3

A Brief Vacation

Another summer day, 1924.

Madison Square Garden is, for the greater part of this July, my home away from home. Thanks to the wonder of radio. This one is a superheterodyne, encased in a huge, rococo-ugly cabinet. Is it a Majestic? An Atwater-Kent? I forget. It belongs to the couple that runs the summer resort in South Haven, Michigan. The place is called Mount Pleasant, though I doubt these two hard-working people find it so.

They put in a good twenty-seven-hour day in a vain effort to please their suddenly sybaritic guests: small merchants, salesmen forever scuffling, marginal entrepreneurs, assorted wives, children, and flatulent grandchildren. The country air has a magical effect on these *petit-bourgeois*. They have become khedives, caliphs, sultanas, princesses. Regally impatient and demanding. Rarely has anyone suffered such bullyragging as the unlucky couple.

I am no trouble to them at all. They hardly know I'm around. Nobody does. I am scrunched in an old armchair, listening hard to the gavel-to-gavel proceedings of the Democratic National Convention. One hundred three ballots and God knows how many Michigan mornings and afternoons. Some vacation. My mother has sent me here, having convinced herself that I am an asthmatic child.

"Why aren't you outside playing?" It's a fat woman, laboriously navigating her way toward the porch beyond. Her tone is not especially friendly. I am about to tell her the doctor said sunshine is bad for me. She doesn't wait for my reply. There is one seat open at mah-jongg.

"Why aren't you on the beach?" a pasty-faced old man who runs a dry goods store asks me rhetorically. He carries a crooked walking stick and is always suggesting hikes. I tell him the doctor said water is bad for me. "Sorry to hear that," he says. He doesn't sound sorry at all, as he walks toward the skinny young woman wearing glasses. She sits at the table next to mine in the dining room and is forever smiling. I find it disconcerting. Some years later, in seeing a film version of Hugo's "The Man Who Laughs," I thought of her each time Conrad Veidt appeared; he had a carved grin. Pasty Face and Smilin' Sadie walk out together. I was afraid he'd ask me to join them. I was prepared: The doctor said walking is bad for me.

"How's it coming, kiddo?" It's the woman who runs the place. She has just come in from the kitchen for a brief respite. She wipes her brow with the back of her hand. A portrait in weariness. I like her and her husband more than I do my fellow guests.

It's a hopeless deadlock, I tell her. Al Smith won't give in to William Gibbs McAdoo and William Gibbs McAdoo won't give in to Al Smith. There is talk of a dark horse. "Six of one, half a dozen of the other," she says. She and her husband are anarchists. There's a book by Kropotkin lying around; and another by Emma Goldman. How they became resort-keepers, and why, is something I never did find out. Slowly, as though husbanding her energy to make it through the day, she walks back toward the kitchen.

As for the Madison Square Garden turbulence, I am nonpartisan. I study the convoluted designs on the radio cabinet and listen to the voices. I have become most familiar with two. The delegate from Alabama, whose name escapes me, but never his orotund pronouncement: Alabama, twenty-four votes for Oscar Underwood. It is as regular as mealtime at Mount Pleasant. And as heavy.

The other voice, that's the one: it rings out with an authority that comforts and a power that overawes. It is the gravel bass-baritone of Thomas J. Walsh, Permanent Chairman of the Democratic National Convention of 1924. In later years, on hearing De Wolf Hopper declaim "Casey at the Bat" (via victrola) and Hal Holbrook re-create Mark Twain, I think of Walsh: his boom, a crossbreed of the other two.

Through much of the steamy summer, the senator from Montana

bangs the gavel and I am with him all the way. When he says that's
it, there's no question about it: it most definitely is it. His voice is
as a balm to me. On hearing him, I forget about my asthma. I doubt
whether I really have it, but if it makes my mother feel good, being
so cursed by the fates, who am I to argue? On encountering my
fellow guests, the bad signs appear. I have trouble breathing. Why
is this so? Oh no, I'm not about to abandon this armchair, this radio,
come hikes, dominoes, or a cool dip in the lake.

It is not that we're unfamiliar with Tom Walsh's face. His craggy
features and furious mustache appeared in all the newspapers the
year before. It was he who doggedly investigated and laid into the
big-time crooks of Teapot Dome: oilmen, bankers, and members of
President Harding's cabinet. Warren Gamaliel Harding . . .

Mount Pleasant. An early August morning, 1923. The guests
have had a much too hearty breakfast. There is a lounging around
and a satiety that is beyond the merely vulgar. An occasional belch.
A discreet fart. Somebody makes a joke. Somebody laughs.

"Have you no respect? The President is dead."

Sudden silence. It is not so much the tragic news of Warren
Harding's death. We knew that yesterday, moments after it had happened. It is the Judge who has spoken and when he speaks you'd
better listen. He is Mount Pleasant's most prestigious guest. His
pockmarked face in no way diminishes the awe with which he is
regarded by the others. He is a municipal court judge and a good
friend of Mayor William Hale Thompson. He is very patriotic.

How come there is no American flag being flown from the porch?
he demands to know. There certainly should be one at half-mast
this morning. There was none on the Fourth of July, you say? The
fat woman is quick to offer this information. Some people don't
know how lucky they really are to live in a great country like this.
You know who I mean. Heads nod. They turn toward the couple on
the grass, some distance away. The Judge has been staring in that
direction. Balefully.

The couple that runs the resort is resting. The grass is as good a
place as any. I saw them but a moment ago flop down onto it. They
chat softly to one another. I have no idea what they're saying. A
couple of times before, they had invited me to join them. I did. They
asked me if I was really enjoying myself. I said sure. They asked me

what I was reading. I showed them my copy of Ring Lardner's "You Know Me, Al." My brother had bought it for me as a vacation gift. He knew I followed baseball. They'd rest in this manner, the couple, for about fifteen, twenty minutes. As they are doing now.

The Judge announces that at eleven o'clock everybody is to stand at attention and face east. One minute of silence in tribute to our late President, Warren G. Harding. The Judge appears angry about something. I think it has to do with the couple on the grass. The Judge takes out his gold watch. He is counting off the seconds. Eleven o'clock, he announces. The guests are standing up.

The fat woman, stretched out on the hammock, is having considerable difficulty, but she is making it. Her patriotism is overcoming her sloth. The pasty-faced man is the first to arise. He is standing ramrod-straight, his crooked walking stick clasped in the manner of a riding crop. The owner of the dry goods store is, at this indelible moment, a pukka sahib, somewhere in Bengal. Menashe Skulnik is C. Aubrey Smith. The ever-smiling girl in glasses is trying her desperately damnedest not to smile. She fails, but it's all right. E for effort; P for patriotism. And I, eleven years old and American, all 95 pounds of me—I, too, stand and face east. It is an impressive minute. Except for one thing. The couple on the grass.

They are seated. Not so much seated as stretched out. They appear not to notice what's happening. The man lies, belly down; his chin is cupped in his hand, his eyes are closed. The woman, reclining, her open palms pressed downward on the grass, her head tossed back, is gazing up at the sky. They are out of some French Impressionist painting. Impression: a bone-weary man and woman, delighting in this precious time out. Rest.

The Judge nods. The minute is up. We plop back into our seats and hammocks and swings, having paid our respects to a departed statesman; more to the point, having abided by the Judge's wish. He is nobody to cross.

"Those Goddamn bolsheviks."

The Judge is glaring in the couple's direction. The others glare, too. There are dark murmurings.

I feel funny. Suppose, this day, I had been invited by the couple to share their moment of respite. Three of us on the grass. Would I have arisen at the Judge's signal? Or would I have lain back in the grass, my eyes closed, my face toward the heavens, in a moment of quiet communion with these two? Would the Judge have called me a Goddamn bolshevik, too? And me, only eleven years old and possibly afflicted with asthma.

It is the last time I see the Judge in the flesh. Years later, I see his photograph on the front page of the morning newspaper. He has been found guilty of accepting bribes and making all sorts of crooked deals. He is sent off to prison. Standing next to an attendant, he doesn't look like a judge. He looks like an ordinary crook.

As for the couple that ran the resort, I had heard—and that was many, many years ago—that they had gone west to find some sun to warm their weary bones. And read more of Prince Kropotkin.

As for the Democratic nominee of 1924, it was somebody named John W. Davis, a big-time lawyer. His hair was silver and his clients gold. It didn't really matter. Come November, he was clobbered by Calvin Coolidge and that didn't matter much, either. In any event, I was a Bob La Follette man and that did matter. At least to me. It still does.

4

Glasses

I still see that girl at Mount Pleasant, the plain one with her glasses and her tic. I feel bad, in retrospect. She may not have been aware of it, but the eleven-year-old boy, transfixed by radio voices, was silently putting her down. I was judging her by the company she kept. As though she had much choice. Wasn't she Judith Hearne experiencing a lonely passion? A set-up for the first oaf who came along with a soft word.

Glasses. Once upon a time, they were the mark of the vulnerable. At least to me. Not the pince-nez of Woodrow Wilson; his was the emblem of the Sunday schoolmaster, the wrinkled prune, the bloodless. Nor the pince-nez of FDR, which, in its off-again, on-again behavior, became as insouciant a sign as his tilted cigarette holder. Nor the pince-nez of my mother, which, considering her tough credo, became as antic and outrageous a symbol as Bobby Clark's painted-on glasses. No.

When Lee Meadows appeared on the pitching mound for the Pittsburgh Pirates, it was, for me, a revolutionary moment. He was the first major leaguer to wear glasses. And then came Carmen Hill. And George Torporcer. And when a slugger, Chick Hafey, decided to wear them, I knew that a corner had been turned. And when, some time later, another bespectacled slugger, Bull Connor, turned the hose on people, I no longer had to worry about the daily fate of "four-eyes." Nor feel inordinately tender.

It was, apparently, not so for Billie Holiday. As recently as 1956, she was soft on those who wore specs. I had gone to see her at the Budland. It was a short-lived jazz club in a South Side Chicago cellar. I was in the process of working on a children's jazz book. "Sure, baby. Come on," she said at the other end of the phone. Nelson Algren accompanied me. He was, at the time, wearing glasses.

Billie's voice was shot, though the gardenia in her hair was as fresh as usual. Ben Webster, for so long big man on tenor, was backing her. He was having it rough, too. Yet they transcended. There were perhaps fifteen, twenty patrons in the house. At most. Awful sad. Still, when Lady sang "Fine and Mellow," you felt that way. And when she went into "Willow, Weep for Me," you wept. You looked about and saw that the few other customers were also crying in their beer and shot glasses. Nor were they that drunk. Something was still there, that something that distinguishes an artist from a performer: the revealing of self. Here I be. Not for long, but here I be. In sensing her mortality, we sensed our own.

After her performance, Algren and I shambled into her dressing room. Dressing room, did I say? It was a storeroom: whiskey cases stacked against the walls, cartons of paper napkins, piles of plastic utensils strewn about, this, that, and the other. It didn't matter. She was there, with the gardenia in her hair. Lady, in the gracious manner of a lady, bade us be seated. Algren slouched into a chair against the far wall, in the semidarkness. He appeared a character out of one of his works: Bruno or Frankie or Sparrow or Dove.

Patiently, she answered questions that I'm sure had been put to her too many times before. About the white stoops of Baltimore, of the others for whom she scrubbed, about Miss Bessie, about her grand-mother, about club owners, the honest and the venal. When there was trouble remembering, her eyes half-shut as in a slow blues, her hands poised in midair. If, by chance, I hit upon the right name, her fingers snapped. That's it, baby. No words were needed; the gesture said it.

And when the conversation ended, as casually as it had begun, and the waiter had brought her a tumbler of gin—"Lemon peel, baby"— she indicated the man in the shadows, Nelson Algren. She had been aware of his presence from the beginning; there had been mumbled introductions. Now she murmured inquiringly, "Who's that man?" Algren explained that she and he had the same publisher. *The Man with the Golden Arm* and *Lady Sings the Blues* had both been put out by Doubleday.

"You're all right," she said to him.

"How do you know?" he asked.

"You're wearin' glasses."

He laughed softly. "I know some people with glasses who got dollar signs for eyes."

"You're kind."

"How can you tell?" he persisted. How could she tell? He was half-hidden in the shadows.

"Your glasses." She was persistent, too.

Nelson Algren no longer wears glasses, but he's still a funny man. He may be the funniest man around. Which is another way of saying he may be the most serious. At a time when pimpery, lick-spittlery, and picking the public's pocket are the order of the day— indeed, officially proclaimed as virtue—the poet must play the madcap to keep his balance. And ours.

Unlike Father William, Algren does not stand on his head. He just shuffles along. His appearance is that of a horse player, who, this moment, got the news: he had bet her across the board and she came in a strong fourth. Yet, strangely, his is not a mournful mien. He's chuckling to himself. You'd think he was the blue-eyed winner rather than the brown-eyed loser. That's what's so funny about him. He *has* won. A hunch: his writings may be read long after acclaimed works of Academe's darlings, yellowed on coffee tables, will be replaced by acclaimed works of other Academe's darlings. To call on a Lillian Hellman phrase, he is not "the kid of the moment." For in the spirit of a Zola or a Dreiser, he has captured a piece of that life behind the billboards. Some comic, that man.

At a time when our values are unprecedentedly upside-down— when Bob Hope, a humorless multimillionaire, is regarded as a funny man and a genuinely funny man (until his bad choice of lock-pickers) was regarded as our President—Algren is something of a Gavroche.

"The hard necessity of bringing the judge on the bench down into the dock has been the peculiar responsibility of the writer in all ages of man." It was something Algren wrote in 1961, as an added preface to his prose-poem, *Chicago: City on the Make*. The original work had been composed a decade earlier. It's a responsibility to which he has been obstinately faithful. He's openhearted to Molly-O and

Steffi and Margo and Aunt Elly's "girl," who are forever up against
it; who are forever in the pokey for turning a five-dollar trick with
the wrong guy. (That fee is absurd today. You must remember his
heroines subsisted long, long before inflation.) He's mail-fisted to
their judges, the Respectables, who turn a trick for no less than a
hundred G's. So, too, this piece of writing from the same essay:

> "We have to keep Chicago strong and America mighty." I heard
> his Honor proclaim before sentencing the girl with a record for
> addiction. "A year and a day! Take her away!"
> Blinking out of the window of an Ogden Avenue trolley at the
> sunlight she hadn't seen for almost a year, "I guess I was lucky I
> done that time," the girl philosophized. "Chicago still looks pretty
> strong and America looks mighty mighty."
> Still nobody seems to be laughing.

What Algren observed fifteen years ago applies today in trump.
And in that prose-poem put down some twenty-odd years ago—and
what odd years they've been—the ring of a city's awful truth is still
heard. Only louder. As with all good poets, the guy is a prophet.

It was no accident that he wrote *The Man with the Golden Arm*
so many centuries before posh suburban high schools fretted about
junkies in their blue-eyed midst. The fate of Frankie Machine
presaged adolescent hells to come.

In *Never Come Morning*, Algren gave us Bruno, the doomed
young jack-roller. How different is he, the desperate city ethnic,
from the young black mugger? Law and Order is the cry today, as
Algren so eloquently italicized the old poet's prophecy: "The slums
will take their revenge." Call it ghetto, if you wish.

Yet, I'm thinking of Nelson Algren, the funny man. The antic
sense is there, of course, in Dove Linkhorn, the innocent, of *A Walk
on the Wild Side*. It's there in Frankie's colleague, Sparrow, the
hapless shoplifter. It's there in Some Fellow Willie, who always
looked suspicious because he always suspected himself of one thing
or another. It's there in Lost Ball Stahouska of the Baldhead A.C.'s.
He was something, that one. Remember when his conscience bothered him because he shoved an in-play baseball in his pocket, though
he was unperturbed when cracking a safe with the help of three
Chicago cops? As to the latter caper, Stahouska explained, "Oh,
everybody does that."

Again, you have it. Turning a two-dollar trick is a sin and prickly
to the conscience. Turning a hundred-thou trick, that's something

else again. Lost Ball, were he around today, could well appreciate the workings of ITT, Lockheed, Penn Central, and the late Howard Hughes. Recurring in all of Algren's work—novel, short story, poem —is the theme of the rigged ball game. Offered in his unique lyric style, they are memorable.

In his poetic evocation of the Black Sox scandal of 1919, he asks the ever-impertinent question: How is it that front office men never conspire? However do senators get so close to God? Or winners never pitch in a bill toward the price of their victory?

Though today's literary mandarins treat the man with benign neglect—he has in the past twenty-five years become something of a non-person—he is highly regarded in unexpected quarters.

About two years ago, in the streets of London, I ran into a voluble Welshman. On learning I was an American—let alone a Chicagoan —he bought me a whiskey. I had no idea Americans were so popular with the people from Rhondda Valley. But it wasn't that at all. He could hardly wait to blurt out, "You're an American, you must know of Nelson Algren." He proceeded to rattle off, in mellifluous tongue, all the titles of Algren's novels and short stories. On discovering that I actually knew the man, he bought drink after drink after drink. And on miner's pay, at that. How I got back to the hotel shall forever remain a mystery to me.

In New York, an old freight elevator man, a small battered Irishman, whose one claim to immortality was an encounter with Fiorello LaGuardia, asked me, between floors, if I'd ever heard of a writer named Algren. He had read *The Neon Wilderness*. As far as I know, he owned no coffee table.

Recently, in a conversation with a woman on welfare, his name came up. It was she, not I, who introduced it. She had been reading one of his paperbacks and saw herself in it. She had also been having her troubles with the Welfare Department and neighborhood cops. As far as I know, she owned no coffee table.

Maybe Nelson Algren's horses usually run out of the money. Maybe his luck at the poker table is not that good. Maybe he'll never be endowed by a university; nor be earnestly regarded by literary makers and shakers. But he has good reason to just shuffle along like a laughing winner. And he may be the funniest man around.

*　　*　　*

Glasses. When did it come into vogue: the new twist? The offhand young woman, wearing her glasses, usually aviator and tinted—not parallel to her eyes, but upstairs, in the manner of an old-fashioned Spanish comb or a mantilla. There, adding a piquant touch to her locks, raven, blond, or auburn, is a pair of spectacles. Are they prescription glasses? If so, does she ever drop them onto the bridge of her nose. Does she use them for reading? For seeing movies? Or is it something vaguely erotic? Or, perhaps, not so vaguely.

Dorothy Parker's observation about four-eyed girls not being subject to passes has long been passé. It is not the material of this query. I'm curious about the new positioning of glasses. I have a theory; take it for what it's worth. It has something to do with Ada Leonard.

In the glow of yesterday, Ada Leonard was the most exciting and truly erotic of all strip-tease artists. She was something new on the Rialto. *At* the Rialto, I should say, that wondrous burlesque house on State Street.

Sure, there was the Star & Garter. There was the Haymarket. There was the Empress. There appeared the queens of the Columbia Wheel: Ann Corio, Gypsy Rose Lee, Margie Hart. And there was always Peaches, the regular. Sure, Ann stepped down into the audience and kissed bald pates. Sure, Gypsy was considered clever, witty; and she was. But Ada Leonard at the Rialto was something else. She was a college girl.

Ada was probably the first ecdysiast with a bachelor's degree. Imagine her impact on the audience: old gaffers, dreaming never-never dreams; delinquent law students, their thoughts far, far from torts; serious young men in specs, observing the phenomenon for "sociological research"; an occasional broker-looking guy, who may not have found on the North Shore what he found here; and assorted casuals. They had become somewhat jaded with the expected: the weary bump and grind; the mechanical strip tease, anticlimactic, with a cute face peeking out from behind the curtain and the wave of the G-string. Ada Leonard was something else.

Before her appearance on the scene, we had become well acquainted with the music of the strip tease. Buster Lorenzo, "the little man with the big voice," appeared against the proscenium and sang in honey-sweet tenor, "Songs My Mother Taught Me." To these poignant strains, the artistes did what they were paid to do. The flowing gown, crinoline or gingham; visions of the Southern belle or the girl next door; a summery straw hat, wide-brimmed; and, of course, the elbow-length white gloves.

It began as the gloves were unsnapped; and slowly, delicately tugged off each finger . . . and the rest of it. Good-bye to all that. As Edvard Grieg was memorialized in song, as the crinoline, silks, gingham fell onto the wood of the stage, we were strangely unmoved. There was no astonishment. It was all so one-dimensional. And along came Ada.

The music had progressed to Ellington. "Mood Indigo" had become the ecdysiastic anthem. With Ada's appearance, the boys in the pit struck up "Bolero." They knew class when they saw *her*. But it was something else that caught and held us. That intangible something else. We were aware that she was an intellectual. The public relations man at the Rialto had seen to that. And she was aware that we were aware. What did she read in the dressing room? Joyce? Melville, Dostoyevsky? Was there a passage she was savoring at the moment she touched the zipper? We were poignantly aware that her thoughts were elsewhere—on a higher plateau—as she stripped.

Hers was not the audience-pleasing smile. Oh no, there was hardly a trace of Mona Lisa. She was bemused. Imagine the challenge to all the lost males; each hoping it was *he* who caught her eye. *He* who dwelt, if only for a moment, in the mansion her mind. What Ada thought about at such times, we'll never know. But we knew what it was she possessed. And what possessed us. It was *simultaneity*.

There was the body, yes. Observable, magnificently so. There was the face, yes. Classic Grecian features—memories of the young Arletty in the film *Children of Paradise*. But the killer was the hidden, the cryptic, the beyond-our-ken, the "intellect." She had us.

Today, as the self-possessed young woman strides, businesslike, *with her glasses on her head*, I think of Ada Leonard. Is this her daughter? Is hers the psyche of the most erotic of all strip-tease artistes? What goes on *in* her head as she wears the glasses *on* her head? Is she so busy that she has no time to remove them and put them in a case, as she goes out to lunch? Or is she preoccupied as Ada seemed to be. If so, she, too, is possessed of simultaneity. And that's pretty good. But if it is nothing more than a vogue, a Virginia Slims "You've come a long way, baby," I am grievously disappointed. The Commercial has won again.

*   *   *

I still see that girl at Mount Pleasant, the plain one with her glasses and her tic. How would I remember her had she worn her glasses on her head? She might have bumped into walls and fallen down stairs. In that event, I'd have rushed to help her; she'd not have been ignored. But what would I have done about the Democratic Convention of 1924? And what about my asthma?

5

The Impertinent Question

Is it hearing Tom Walsh, though a thousand miles distant, or One-Arm Cholly Wendorf, closer at hand, or Civilization, face to face, that impels me to join McKinley High School's debating team? No, it is the persuasive power of Jimmy Two. It is but two years before his unfortunate alley accident and departure from this life. He is breathing, breathing a glowing promise: "If yer gonna be a criminal lawyer an' represent us, ya need lotsa practice as 'n orator." I have no idea I'm so highly regarded by the Forty Two's.

Nineteen twenty-seven is a casual year, what with a casual Calvin in the White House. As a matter of course, we are casual in debate. In McKinley High School as well as in Congress. True, there are a few aberrants on the Hill, such as Bob La Follette and George Norris. The overwhelming others are less troublesome; pliable and purchaseable. At McKinley, there are neither troublesome teachers nor troublesome students. So it is with our debating teams, affirmative and negative. We take either side. Winning points is what it's all about.

Resolved: Capital punishment shall be abolished. Understandably diffident, I murmur to Miss Olive Leekley, our coach, when she is not letting us in on Caesar's triumphant adventures in Gaul, "May I be on the affirmative side?" I had come across Clarence Darrow in one of those E. Haldemann-Julius nickel blue books. The gentle lady persuades me that the other side needs my eloquence desperately. I

am deeply touched. I soon discover that my colleagues in righteous-
ness are a boy who stutters and a girl who whines. In a ringing boy–
baritone, I invoke the Biblical injunction of eye for eye and tooth
for tooth. We win on points. Virtue and vengeance simultaneously
triumph.

Jimmy Two is in attendance; he and three companions. He had
laid out a dollar for the four admission tickets. He has an astonishingly large roll of bills in his hand. He pulls off a five-spot and urges
it into the lapel pocket of my new blue serge.

"No no," I say.

"Oh yeah," he says.

Out of the others' hearing, his *sotto voce* is hoarse. "Ya tryin' to
insult me in front a my pals?"

I have no intention of insulting him. His tribute subsequently buys
me an awful lot of chocolate malteds and second gallery seats at the
Palace. Is this the first installment of my retainer as his mouthpiece?

He is proud of me, he says. His companions, too, are impressed.
I wanted to argue for the other side, I tell them. They stare at me,
uncomprehendingly.

"You against capital punishment?" His voice is suddenly steel.

"Yeah." My voice is suddenly small. "Ain't you?"

"Hell, no! All traitors should be strung up by da nuts."

His companions nod, righteously. I feel so subversive, I'm tongue-
tied. I knew Jimmy Two was patriotic but I had no idea he'd gone
that far.

Resolved: We shall grant the Philippine Islands their independence. Miss Leekley assigns me to the affirmative side. I feel good. We
lose on points. I feel bad. Something's wrong here. But what? In
the climate of casualness, we had neglected to ask the impertinent
question: Who the hell are *we* to grant the Philippines their independence? How did they come to lose it? And how did we get to
own the joint?

The impertinent question. It is 1962. Late at night. I am at the
home of a friend in Highgate Village, London. Jacob Bronowski,
the physicist, is another guest. The Cuban Missile Crisis is still in
the headlines.

I'm wondering how the hell we got into this mess. "We haven't
asked the impertinent question," says Bronowski. "Until you ask an
impertinent question of nature, you do not get a pertinent answer.
Great answers in nature are always hidden in the questions. When

Einstein in 1905 questioned the assumption held for three hundred years that time is a given, he asked one of the great impertinent questions: 'Why? How do I know that my time is the same as yours?' Now the artist asks the same kind of question; not about dead, but living nature; not about the outside, but the inside world; not about facts but about the self."

I ask myself, fifty years after McKinley glories, if the impertinent question is demanded of poetry and science, why not of politics?

Hopefully, doggedly so, I sit before the television set every Sunday and await the question. I watch "Meet the Press," "Face the Nation," "Issues and Answers," you name it, wherever and whenever journalists and commentators square off with statesmen. I await the impertinent question. I'm still waiting.

It is an April Sunday afternoon, 1:05 (CST), I am sitting through a discussion program. Our Vietnamese adventure is nearing its end. Brigadier General John Flynn, a returned POW, is being questioned by two celebrated commentators, whose names and faces have escaped me. It is a subdued occasion. Understandably so. Reverence is in the air. That, too, is understandable.

As the General recounts the courage of the men under torture, he murmurs, "We all knew why we were there." At that moment, I cretinesquely assume one of the interrogators will ask the impertinent question: Why? Why *were* we there, General? There is no telling what the General would have replied. Perhaps a lowering look would have been enough. At least, the interrogator might have experienced the perverse delight of feeling impertinent.

The General further advises them that South Vietnam has a more stable government than North Vietnam and that, by virtue of its democratic spirit, it will survive any onslaught of socialism. The impertinent question—How did you come to that conclusion, General?—is not forthcoming.

Toward the end of the half-hour, the General lets it be known that he and his gallant fellows are pursuing "our national objective." Again, I hold my breath. Would impertinence make itself felt here? What is our national objective, General? But no, they appear to understand. I don't. I feel guilty about it, much like Algren's Some Fellow Willie.

The hosts express their profound appreciation of the General's presence. It is over. I am strangely dissatisfied. It is as though I've had a Chinese meal. Nothing stays with me. Fortunately, there immediately flashes the trailer for a coming attraction on the network: "Searching the Unknown." I feel better already.

It is a casual, friendly program all around. I assume some conversation follows the sign-off. For some reason, I think of Archie Moore and the time he clobbered a club fighter of sorts. It was no contest. He made a mess of the boy. The pug enters Archie's dressing room and mumbles through his bloody pulp of a mouth: "May I have your autograph?" I'll forever wonder: Did the commentators get the General's autograph?

In his salad days, George Wallace had a high time with commentators. They never laid a glove on him. The champion of the little man was never asked about his lickspittlery toward the big man. How can you fault the auto worker in Pontiac for confusing this three-dollar bill with the real thing? He is never afforded information. Perhaps it's just as well he sticks with replays of the preceding Sunday's football games. Had Peggy Terry been on these panels, it might have been otherwise. She asks impertinent questions.

Peggy Terry is an Appalachian migrant living in Chicago's Uptown. "They talk about welfare bums. They mean me. They mean that black woman across the street. How come they never talk about Howard Hughes?" I am visiting her. It is mid-November 1975. She searches for something. She finds it. The torn-out front page of Sunday's *Chicago Tribune*. She indicates the two column headline: "U.S. Paying $1.7 Million a Day to Howard Hughes' Enterprises." "How come," she asks impertinently, "he's never called a welfare bum?"

On a more recent occasion, she asks about our military budget. One hundred thirteen billion dollars. Onward and upward. How come? she wonders. "If just a few of our newer and bigger H-bombs can knock off the Russians and just a few of their newer and bigger H-bombs can knock us off, what are the other bombs and bombers for? *Who* are they for? The people on Mars? Aren't they *welfare* bombs?" Peggy is impertinent, as any fool can plainly see. She'll never make it as a network commentator. But wouldn't it be something if she did? Perhaps the auto worker in Pontiac would watch.

And on the six o'clock news, is the impertinent question ever asked of double-speak? I still hear authoritative voices, during our Indo-Chinese experience. A communiqué: "American soldier wounded, three communists die." Isn't anybody impertinent enough to ask why our boy is described by his nationality and the others by their ideology? Shouldn't an investigative journalist, be he foreign correspondent or police reporter, investigate the matter? Wouldn't he perhaps come upon four human beings, three of whom are dead— assuming the body count is accurate? He might very likely report: "One American wounded, three Vietnamese die. The first represented the capitalist side; the others the communist side." Talk about impertinence.

Perhaps high-school debates are less casual and more impertinent today than they were at McKinley in 1927. Or is winning points what it's all about even now? I am afraid to find out.

Finding out a truth is sometimes awful. I guess that's why it's called the awful truth. In that time of innocence, Ben Hecht and Charles MacArthur were regarded as Chicago's two most irreverent and impertinent journalists. Were they, really? Or were they merely winners of points? And was the flesh-and-blood editor they honored in aspic as Walter Burns in *The Front Page* really that great a newspaperman? If it is so, why do I, on seeing a revival of this comedy hit, feel like Sheridan Whiteside? I think I shall vomit. It was not always so with me.

6

A Farce

It is one year after my McKinley glories, more or less. I am seated way, way up in the last row of the second balcony of the Erlanger Theatre. I am with my brother Ben. We are crazy about what we see. It is a touring company of *The Front Page*. We are falling all over ourselves with laughter, as is everybody else in the house. The irrepressible Hildy Johnson. What a reporter. The daring Walter Burns. What an editor. "The son of a bitch stole my watch!" What a curtain line. Hecht and MacArthur. What irreverence. And ever since that year, revivals have been greeted with equal enthusiasm. What a play. Why is it, then, I am unable to join in the spirit of bonhomie, as I did, a laughing boy of sixteen?

On occasion, I have run into old-timers who had known Hildy in the long-gone *Herald & Examiner* days. Was he really a good police reporter? They have little to say. What were his sources, other than the police blotter? They have little to say. How did reportage of this sort usually go? "The gun was accidentally discharged," our hero blithely informs city desk. "The police allege that Mr. Nobody lunged at Officer Friendly's gun." By the time the news appeared, Mr. Nobody was either dead or lying in a county hospital bed, charged with criminal assault. Hildy was, of course, busy reporting another such crime. Which is what made him so irrepressible.

Did Hildy ever expose venality in high places? The old-timers have little to say. Perhaps all officials in those days were Knights of the Round Table. The trouble with me is I'm so damn suspicious.

Discovering Lincoln Steffens in the Newberry Library Reading Room may have had something to do with it. But God, Hildy was a joy to watch on that stage. Hecht and MacArthur were cockeyed wonders. That's the trouble. Ben and Charlie were perhaps the two most non-investigative journalists in Chicago's history. They were quite marvelous cosmeticians. Color, yes; truth, hardly.

Mike Royko writes colorfully. Five days a week, he puts together a column on page three of the *Chicago Daily News*. He is not a cockeyed wonder in the tradition of Ben and Charlie. Oh, he writes funny stories, all right. As funny as anything they ever tried in their most raffish days. There is one difference. Whereas Hecht and MacArthur were irrepressible as cute little wayward boys are irrepressible, carefree, and careless, Royko is possessed by a demon. He obstinately, doggedly digs away at the bone of truth. More often than not, he takes us to high places. As a matter of reflex, he does what the celebrated two never dreamed of doing: he asks the impertinent question. Naturally, he discomfits the powerful. On occasion his demon gets the better of him and he wings the sparrow rather than the vulture. Those are rare occasions.

I see him in his cubbyhole of an office. His glasses have slipped down toward the tip of a sharp nose. He is listening. Some nobody is at the other end of the phone. Sometimes it is a cry for help. Sometimes it is an astonishing tip. Sometimes it is just a funny story. The human comedy has him on the hip. Most often, it's from somebody up against it. The other calls are from some fat stuff with clout, whose venality Royko has exposed to the light. Ben and Charlie, anything-for-a-gag men, would never have understood Mike Royko. Not in a million years. Nor could he ever play the hero of *The Front Page*. Never Hildy Johnson. Never, never Walter Burns.

Walter Howey was editor of the *Herald & Examiner* in the good old days. It was he whom Ben and Charlie celebrated in their portrait of Walter Burns. It was he whom the gifted actor Osgood Perkins portrayed in the New York production. I saw a fine performer here at the Erlanger. Unfortunately, his name escapes me. But he was good and it is a juicy role: nimble-wit, derring-do, brass and sass. Endearing.

What sort of man was the flesh-and-blood Walter? And what sort of editor? George Murray lets us know. In his memoir,* the veteran Chicago journalist, an admirer of Howey, recounts a celebrated 1919 crime and its denouement.

Carl Wanderer, a World War I hero, killed his wife and a ragged stranger. It was Walter Howey who, by virtue of fast thinking, made the discovery. It was a great scoop for the *Herald & Examiner*. Howey had solved what might have been the perfect crime. So far, so good. Let Murray pick up from there:

> Carl Wanderer was brought to trial, charged with the murder of Ruth Johnson Wanderer. He had a sharp lawyer and a soft-headed jury. He was found guilty and given twenty years in the Illinois State Penitentiary at Joliet.
>
> Walter Howey was outraged at what he considered a miscarriage of justice. He daily ran photographs of the jurymen who had been so lenient with Carl Otto Wanderer. He printed the jurymen's names, addresses and telephone numbers. He urged the readers of the *Herald & Examiner* to call these men—preferably in the middle of the night—and tell them what their fellow citizens thought of them.
>
> The *Herald & Examiner* demanded that Wanderer be brought back from prison, indicted for the killing of the ragged stranger, and tried on the second murder charge. A fighting newspaper editor can rouse a community. . . . This time Wanderer, upon being found guilty, was sentenced to hang. A juror later said that he and all his colleagues were so fearful of what Walter Howey might say about them in print that they never considered any other verdict.
>
> On March 19, 1921, Carl Otto Wanderer was put in the death row at the old Cook County Jail on North Dearborn Street. Two of the irreverent reporters who covered the building were Charles MacArthur for the *Herald & Examiner* and Ben Hecht for the *Chicago Daily News*. . . . They teamed up on a variety of pranks to keep the place from succumbing to boredom.
>
> . . . The two learned that Wanderer had been a choir singer in his boyhood. At the request of MacArthur and Hecht, he rendered his favorite, "Old Pal, Why Don't You Answer Me?" . . . Sheriff Hoffman dropped the mask over Wanderer's face in the middle of the second chorus, which ended with "glub, glub, glub." Then there was a signal to the deputy behind a partition and the trap was sprung. Carl Wanderer fell with a jerk to the limit of the rope. . . . In the deathly quiet that followed, MacArthur commented, in a voice meant to be a whisper but which carried to every corner of the still area: "That son of a bitch should have been a song plugger."

Wit, I suppose, depends on what end of the rope you find yourself. As for the law-and-order editor, the vigilante man, Walter Howey,

---

* *The Madhouse on Madison Street* (Chicago: Follett, 1965).

another newspaperman had something to say. The late Ray Brennan was one of Chicago's most highly respected and stubbornly honest of police reporters. In asking the impertinent question, he did as much as any journalist to expose the Syndicate. If anyone knew the folkways of the Mob, it was Brennan.

Occasionally, I'd meet him on the bus. We took the same one to work. He was tired and ill, but his conversation was easy. He spoke several times of Walter Howey. He knew, of course, about the Wanderer case. He spoke of the irony. Irony? I asked. Yes, says Ray, Howey was a buddy of Al Capone's. Often he was feted at the Lexington, one of the gangster's cathouses. "He was Al's errand boy." It was this Ray Brennan phrase that most stuck in my mind. Al's errand boy. Walter Howey . . . Walter Burns.

A true life bully-lickspittle transmuted into an endearing comic character. Ben and Charlie did it. Alchemists, yes; journalists, no. As for *The Front Page* . . . oh, that delightful memory of 1928, way, way up in the furthest reaches of the Erlanger, when I was a howling sixteen and innocent of the awful truth.

7

A Seminar

Years after I was floored by *The Front Page*, I was knocked out by *The Three Penny Opera*. What a lesson it was for me: life and art. As Ivy Compton-Burnett saw life as no more than a mounting block for art, Bertolt Brecht saw art as no more than a mounting block for life. Though I'd never in a million years meet Hecht and Mac-Arthur's journalists, I did meet Brecht's people. One fine summer day, they knocked on my door.

Americans of all strata, it would seem, had been polled concerning the Watergate break-in and its consequences: congressmen, clergymen, industrialists, journalists, teachers, students, blue- and white-collar workers, housewives, Sun City septuagenarians, small children . . . in short, all who qualify as "legitimate."

That's the catch. It had precluded the opinions of Doc Graham and Kid Pharaoh. These two hard-working Americans were professionals in the craft of illegal breaking and entering. Doc, silver-haired and distinguished in appearance, has retired from the race; he is not as swift as once upon a time. The Kid's endeavors are more quasilegal these days.

On July Fourth, 1974, three of us met in an informal seminar: Doc Graham, Kid Pharaoh, and myself. It was in a modest Chicago apartment, a mile or so from the Biograph Theatre, where John

Dillinger had so suddenly met his Maker. Doc had been acquainted with the man. "Actually, Dillinger was a country bumpkin."

Their credentials were in order. Doc, the older of the two, offered his first. "I have delved in any number of nefarious activities. I am almost considered a Fagin by the amount of students I have turned out. Some successful, some not so successful. I have never been adequately rewarded for my talents, such as they comprise. But let that be as it may. That's for posterity to judge.

"I was once associated with the late Jack Freed, the hardest-working burglar the United States ever saw. He worked three shifts: afternoon, late at night, and in the early hours of the morning. He was the most proficient artist I have ever known. He accused me of rattling a coat one night, making entrance. But I had to quit later on, due to the fact that he didn't have time to open the door by conventional methods: celluloid, a screw driver, or a credit card. He merely kicked the glass in. It was so unprofessional. How the mighty have fallen."

Kid Pharaoh's précis: "I'm dedicated to one principle: taking money away from unqualified dilettantes who earn it through nepotism. Take it away from them—hook, crook, slingshot, canoe, we must shaft these guys. But don't hurt them. How do I take money from these guys? The Freudian theory. Long may Freud live. They are all biologically or physically insecure. They're all scared. We sell them the item of fear and we give them the security they never had in their life.

"I work on contracts, like in business. They come to me with some trouble. If called upon to perform, I perform. If not, I subcontract. Example. They're usually in debt. Or someone owes them money. Or their wife is an infidelitist. I muscle the guy she's making love with. I run him off. If he owes somebody money, somebody's after him, I chase the other guy away. See? Now he's in debt to me. The biggest mistake of his life . . .

"There's a song I love. 'A man with a dream, a mighty man is he, For dreams make the man the man he wants to be.' You can be anything in this world you want to be, if you dream hard enough, long enough."

DOC   Watergate? A motley bunch of small-time Square Johns employed by a Square John President.

KID   I disagree. The President had the pontifical right to do as he did. His mistake, he engaged a bunch of incompetent dilettantes who couldn't do the job. But he did have the right to break in. It's all in the game. Politics is a warfare game. It happens. So what?

DOC In my lengthy record of similar activities, it was without a doubt the most ill-conceived job I ever saw. All on earth they had to do was get out of the way of the helpless, pathetic Democrats, who had aligned themselves with a neophyte from Dakota. But no, he had to hire a bunch of idiots who shouldn't have been entrusted to deliver a good-will package to the right address. They were as capable as Francis the Mule.

KID It was the Peter Principle. They reached the height of incompetence.

STUDS How would a craftsman, such as Jack Freed, your mentor, have done it? In his better days . . .

DOC He would have called up first to see that the place was empty. Went there; in a matter of seconds, he'd have picked the lock, went to the index, and just stole *all* the material and left. Photographing and putting it back is just another attestation of the Square Johnery of these inept creatures that want to be kings, dictators, criminals, but with no know-how. They couldn't stand up. As soon as a little white heat got on them, they melted.

KID All they had to do was to go to a federal penitentiary and found certain guys who'd perform this kind of function, and cut their time. I assure you to this day and their dying days they would never have abandoned the Commander-in-Chief. No one would have ever known about it. The job would have been done.

DOC Two could have done it with no trouble. I myself know fifty could have handled it. You just knock twenty, thirty years off their time, and let them do thirty days more after they delivered the mail. Instead, they had six men who were as greedy as their boss and just as incompetent. It cost sixty-six million dollars to put Nixon in the job. Sixty-six dollars would have been overpay. The end result is, all amateurs get caught.

One guy would have rifled the desk. The other guy would have stood at the door with his pistol, with his back to the wall. If the guard would have come in, me or my associate would have quietly shoved a .38 pistol up in his kidneys and asked him not to move, and disarmed him, handcuffed him to the door. We'd have some in case of emergency. And that would have been the end of the score.

There was one guard, a colored North American. If it was Jack

Freed, he'd have heisted him, removed his revolver, handcuffed him to the door, wished him well on departing. And one other thing, would have called the police and said there was an idiot involved with the door, and give the address.

We would handle it in about one minute, depart quietly as gentlemen, with a brief case or an attaché case. We'd have carried two in case the voluminous files were that many. If it overflowed, we'd have wrapped them up in a coat and put it under our arm like it was a warm evening and been wiping our sweat in front of the idiot policemen.

KID   We'd have included Mr. Smith and Mr. Wesson.

DOC   Good point. I prefer a Luger, but the Kid's entitled to his opinion.

KID   We would never have taped the door. If the passkey didn't work, we'd have used a certain kind of puller and pulled the lock right off, reinsert it, go about our function, and that would have been the end of it. The guard wouldn't have noticed anything.

DOC   Had the guard come to the door, one of us would have handled the matter. In case it was necessary, the other would assist.

STUDS   The guard didn't come in. He called the Washington police.

DOC   We wouldn't have been waiting there for a reception committee. In case of supreme emergency, we would have held court right there.

STUDS   Held court?

DOC   The Kid prefers a Smith & Wesson, as he informed you. I like the German make. It would have been how many times we would have reloaded. We would have contested the issue immediately.

KID   You need strong men for a function of this type. If I was in charge, I would screen the people first. I would quiz the guy and ask him if he managed his own dick. If he's weak before a broad, he ain't gonna work for me. I would ask him, "Do you chat with your wife about everything that happens, dear boy?" If he does—out.

DOC   A good point. I strongly suspect that every one of these men are dominated by a woman.

STUDS   May I assume you are referring to the cooperative witnesses before the Ervin Committee?

KID   *(Furious, righteously indignant)* Yes, of course! Those who are now betraying the President of the United States. Has it occurred to anyone that if these men were performing a function for the national security of this country, they would have betrayed us? Dean,

Magruder, and the guy with the big neck—what's his name?

DOC Ehrlichman.

KID No.

DOC Haldeman.

KID No.

DOC Colson.

KID No.

DOC LaRue.

KID No.

DOC *(Despairing, shouts)* There are so many of them! Which one of them do you want, for God's sake? There are twenty-three. I'm not a mental recording wizard! How the hell do I know which one you mean?

KID Ervin thanked him for his integrity. *(Suddenly)* McCord! The sonofabitch betrayed the Commander-in-Chief. These guys should be punished. You can't betray the top officer of the country. What's happened to honesty? You must show respect to authority. We're still the boss of the world. If somebody gives you a contract, you must fulfill it. If caught, you must pay the penalty. This is the game.

DOC The contract was to carry out their assigned duties.

KID Dean, the way he testified was unique. He had his red badge of courage. She was sitting behind him. A ring on his finger, to show that his wife, someone cared for him. Magruder, the same thing. What has happened to the masculinity of this country? Can't males think for themselves any more? Betraying their Commander-in-Chief . . . In the past, we had a code of honor.

STUDS Are you implying we are no longer a moral society?

KID We've gone feminine. The little boys are going to grow up fags. They want to be like their mothers, not their fathers. We're a gutless, coward society.

DOC To go a step further, we are thoroughly deteriorated. I was in Havana fourteen years ago, speaking to a sporting girl. I speak a minute amount of Spanish. *(Diffident)* This is rather risqué. I asked her if she was inured to the French way of intercourse. She replied, "Oh, you mean the *American* way." We have stolen complete depravity from the French. We are the lowest country moral-wise on the face of the earth.

STUDS Is this the lesson of Watergate?

DOC Yes. A breakdown in organization. Look at Colson. A successful young man on the go. Without scruples, as long as he's wielding the hammer. He claimed he'd climb over his grandmother to get Nixon re-elected. But when it goes against him, he runs like a scared tabby cat. Where to? To Jesus.

STUDS   Don't you believe in religious conversion?

DOC   Religion is a case of longitude and latitude. It depends whose gods you're operating with. If you come from Japan, Hirohito's your man. If you come from Beirut, Mohammed's your man. If you come from China, Confucius is your man. If you come from India, a starving cow is your man. The one we're stuck with—our theology— we're waiting for the job we haven't seen, hope to see, aren't gonna see. This is difficult for me to reflect because He died for my sins and I haven't sinned against nobody. I am a believer in the Neanderthal man that was here 250 million years ago.

STUDS   I take it you are both in favor of free enterprise, as it is currently practiced?

DOC   What other enterprise is there? If you don't take first count, where are you? You can keep second count. It's no good. There's nothing left for the weak. Whoever said the meek and lowly shall inherit the earth, I would like him to prove his point. It's never been proven and never will.

STUDS   So this is what Watergate's all about?

DOC   Of course. Had Nixon any sense, instead of being as stupid as he is, he'd have hired seasoned thieves to play thieves' roles. If you're a dedicated thief, you take pride in your work. You don't wait around for underlings who have no proven record of *modus operandi*. You go do it yourself. Nixon was not truly dedicated. If Nixon had more pride, *he'd* have been there in the party at Watergate. An Indian chief does not wait four or five miles behind the attack. He leads it.

STUDS   Yet Al Capone and Bugs Moran, for whom you on occasion worked, didn't do the actual jobs themselves . . .

DOC   Bugs Moran and Al Capone were proven products. They wouldn't ask anyone to do what they hadn't already done. They could size up a man for his capabilities or lack of them. Nixon is incapable of this. These people were so unworthy . . . The exorable law of retribution is in force.

KID   It's a chain reaction of traitors. Liddy is the only guy who kept his mouth shut. When he walks in the penitentiary mess, the prisoners give him a standing ovation. Were you aware of that? As a man. When he sits down, they sit down. When the other guys go to jail, particularly Dean—what do you say, Doc, will they tap him biologically?

DOC   Since he has the semblance of youth, I believe Kid Pharaoh is imputing there will be a blanket over his head when he takes a shower and he'll be used, shall we say, for female purposes.

KID   It's very feasible. Liddy is a man among men.

DOC   I concur. The only other men were the Cubans that never once opened their mouths.

KID   True criminality is not rewarded. Liddy, were he not the man he is, would have got religion like Colson or cried like Magruder or showed up like Dean, the traitor.

DOC   Liddy is dedicated to his trade. He knows Nixon is totally worthless, but he's a dedicated thief. You have to admire the man.

KID   Why do you call him a thief?

DOC   There's nothing wrong with that. Momo Giancana, when they asked him his profession, said, "I'm a thief." When they asked Titanic Thompson what he did, he said, "I separate gibbering idiots from their money." Yellow Kid Weil has never denied his profession. Three of the top hustlers of this era are proud of their work. Why should Gordon Liddy be an exception.

If you accept a commitment in an enterprise, you, so to speak, play the string out. Or don't accept the commitment. The commitment in the world Kid and me come from is inviolate.

There is no backing out; there is no hedging. There is either fulfillment or you pay the price, which may be extremely unpleasant. There is no if, and, or but.

A good example: If four or five engage in a venture and one doesn't fulfill his obligation and the venture is not successful and two lose their lives, the fellow that caused this inconvenience is usually left beside the road. It's a permanent resting place.

STUDS   Adolf Eichmann said he fulfilled a commitment, loyalty to his boss . . . he just did his job.

KID   Eichmann, whatever he did, was dedicated. He stood up. In the glass cage, he said, "Long live Germany." He went out like a man.

DOC   Exactly. He asked for no mercy. He had no illusions.

KID   I'll tell you another great man. Abel, the Russian spy.

DOC   A step further. Abel was undoubtedly a top spy, undoubtedly the arch-spy since Cicero. The Soviet government turned over Powers and three or four more worthless slabs of garbage for him.

KID *(Furious)* Francis Powers of the U-2. He had the needle. His contract was, if captured, he was supposed to spike his leg with it and die instantaneously. He reneged on the contract. The sonofabitch. Was it Nathan Hale who said, "I have but one life to give for my country"?

DOC Maybe it was Patrick Henry. Be that as it may, he was correct. When Abel crossed the bridge from West Berlin to East, six Soviet officials ran up and embraced him. They respected him as a man.

KID I know of no American today capable of doing it. Do you, Doc?

DOC Yes. James Earl Ray delivered the mail. For some rightist group that perhaps controls quite a bit of our country. He was double-crossed in the process, but he's another dedicated man. No matter how much you don't like him, he's dedicated. Such as they didn't have in the Nixon party, except for Liddy. Also, Ray was a heist man in Canada, in England, Wales. He was a professional. He never opened his mouth. None of this testifying: "I was on the haydon-gaydon waiting for you on the moden-toten."

KID Our great President Harry Truman said it: "If you can't stand the heat, get out of the kitchen."

STUDS Where does this leave us. We're two years away from our Bicentennial . . . on this very day.

DOC We're coming to the end of this form of government. To quote an eminent professor, Friedrich Hayek—he wrote a book, *The Road to Serfdom.* Thirty years ago. I bought it. It was seven fifty I believe, which was a strain on my purse. But it was a revelation I've never forgotten. Since the government is as wasteful as they are, there can be no blandishment, which we used to call American conservatism. The future generation has nothing to look forward to . . .

A postscript: After the seminar had come to a close, an unexpected dispute arose.

DOC I think Kissinger is guilty of everything they say he is. The fair-haired boy. I suspect he is guilty of wanting his associates' phones tapped, which is un-American, undignified; it's sneaky, it's snide, it's underhanded, it's no give and take. Kissinger should be tried and sued for redress. He's just as guilty as the rest. He just happened to stay hid longer than the rest.

KID Dr. Kissinger's talent goes back to the German disciplinarian school system of education, which gives them an advantage over the

Americans. If Dr. Kissinger said the phones should be tapped, he was a hundred percent right. The German system is much superior to our respect for authority.

DOC   But he's guilty.

KID   Not guilty.

DOC   Guilty.

KID   Not guilty. He has the authority. The others don't.

On this Day of Independence, two years before our Bicentennial celebration, I am wistful. I think of other Americans, kindred spirits of Doc and Kid: Jimmy One and Jimmy Two. The silver-haired businessman from Omaha who told off a senator from New Hampshire. Upsadaisy Connors, whose silk dressing gown I inherited. These lost and by the wind grieved ghosts sure as hell won't come back again, but oh, how Macheath and Peachum keep green their memory. And Brecht never lived in Chicago. Nor did he ever attend McKinley High.

BOOK
FIVE

1

La Divina Claudia

I am seated way down front in the McKinley auditorium. I am
floating up, up, up. Claudia Muzio is on the stage. It is bare, save
for a piano. A nervous, storklike man had tuned it no more than
half an hour ago. Carlo Pirelli and I had been watching him. We
were the first ones here.

She has just sung a Neapolitan song, this most glorious of all the
Milanese. I know she's from around there. Carlo just told me. Piave,
he said. Carlo's glasses are misty. He wipes them with his tie. He
has the appearance of a serious scholar. He is proud, though he tries
not to show it. His father, who runs the bank on the triple corner of
Halsted, Milwaukee, and Grand, has arranged things. Mr. Pirelli is a
good friend of the Italian artists who are members of our Chicago
Civic Opera Company. He has persuaded *la divina* Claudia to sing
at his boy's school. Who needs Groton?

Usually, I choose the last row at Assembly. I like to see what's
going on down here as well as up there. The acoustics of the place
are not quite as good as those of *the* Auditorium. Louis Sullivan
and Dankmar Adler had nothing to do with this auditorium. Often,
from the back row, I've observed Mr. Page, the assistant principal,
giving the student body a piece of his mind and challenging the
toughest one to step out in the alley. I cannot truthfully say I've ever
heard him; his words have always died before reaching me. I got the
drift, though, watching the hurt on the faces of the more promising
among my classmates. Who da fuck's he talkin' about? Just because

we gang-shagged Rosemary in da boy's toilet. She didn't object, why da fuck should he?

On this stage hardly more than a week ago, our debating team won on points. Resolved: United States should recognize the Soviet Union. We took the affirmative. We won on resonance. One of my colleagues was a member of the school's choir; a boy basso. I am unaccustomedly down front, so as not to miss a note of The Voice. It is a memorable afternoon.

I have no idea this may be one of the last times I'll see Carlo. No more than a few days after his glory moment, and mine, the newspapers are full of scandal. Mr. Pirelli, a respected banker, has absconded with a considerable bundle. He was accompanied by a young woman. I feel a terrible sense of personal loss. I just know I'll never see Carlo again. I know he's in town. One of the other kids told me. I pass by his house four or five times. The window shades are down. I stand across the street hoping Carlo will appear at the window, so I may wave at him. He never shows.

As I talk these words some fifty years later, I hear Claudia Muzio on the phonograph. *Addio del passato*. On her deathbed, Violetta is reading aloud the letter of old man Germont, father of Alfredo. He asks forgiveness for goofing up her life. Too late, too late. Listen to that voice, will you? The reading, the singing, the passion. Nobody quite like her. Even now, I see her on the high-school stage. They say she was short and dumpy. You couldn't prove it by me. Nor, I'm sure, by Carlo. Damn it, Carlo, why didn't you come to the window?

I am on the stage of the Opera House. I am one of the villagers in the Sevillian square. Carmen is about to flounce out of the cigarette factory and onto the stage. She doesn't know that a villager in short, black velvet pants and long white stockings is about to steal the scene. Poor Coe Glade. She is the mezzo playing the impetuous gypsy.* It is 1934. Aside from being a troubled witness in Judge Jarecki's court, I am, that ill-starred year, a troubled super at the opera.

Mr. Sens, a willful old German, is in charge of the costumes. He

---

* Paul Hume, music critic of the *Washington Post*, reminds me that Coe Glade was no small potatoes herself when it came to scene stealing. He had been a super, too, in those days.

arbitrarily assigns the shorties the dress of villagers and the tall ones grenadier costumes. They are the buddies of Don José. I hate long white stockings. Further, they will accentuate my bowleggedness. I suggest to Mr. Sens that the tenor playing Don José is shorter than I am. Can't I be a grenadier? "Pudt it on or oudt!" he says, indicating the mass of black velvet and white. I put it on.

The stage manager, Désiré Defrere, is a volatile Italian. A colorless baritone for a number of years, he has caught fire backstage. He is a terror. He advises the villagers, men and women, to dance around and around, as the curtain rises. It is not so much a dance, as trotting around and around in a circle. He says it's a tarantella.

The grenadiers are idling about, doing nothing. Nor, for that matter, is Don José. We, the peasants, are getting pretty winded. At least, I am. Carmen rushes out and sings the *Habanera*. Now it's our turn to stand around. I am at the edge of the crowd, when I sense that my stocking is slipping. I tug at it. The elastic is loose. Coe Glade is fiery as she's vamping Don José. He is getting goo-goo eyed. I am slightly frantic. My stocking has slipped to my ankles. Is it a tittering I hear from out front? I am afraid to look. My eyes are on Carmen but my heart is elsewhere. I hear a voice other than the gypsy's. It's the Italian's. It is truly a stage whisper. Désiré Defrere is in the wings and out of his mind. "Coma 'ere! Pleeza! Pleeza! You! You! You!" I know he means me, me, me. I'm quick at sensing those things.

Fortunately, I'm not too far from the wings. I shuffle backward, ever so surreptitiously and slowly. I am grabbed by somebody, beyond view of the audience, as Carmen reaches a crescendo. It appears that she has won them back. I am happy for her. Désiré Defrere is pushing me away, out of his sight, toward the dark, vast recesses of backstage. "Se ne vada! Se ne vada!" I guess he just doesn't want me around.

"I got two passes coming," I tell him.

"Upastairs! Upastairs! Pleeza! Pleeza!"

I shuffle up the narrow staircase toward the precincts of Mr. Sens. Though Signor Defrere and Mme. Glade may think otherwise, it is a not inauspicious operatic debut.

I make two other appearances this season. I am part of the Cathay crowd in *Turandot*. In this instance, I do nothing to distract from Rosa Raisa's performance. I can't. I'm stuck in the middle of the mob. Anyway, we're in semidarkness.

My third and farewell performance is in *Lohengrin*. I appear in the last act as a Teutonic knight in the court of King Henry. Though it may seem so, it is not an easy role. The uniform Mr. Sens insists I, and about fifty others, wear is of heavy mail. The helmet is much too large and too weighty. Somebody has put a spear in my hand. It, too, is inordinately heavy. Fortunately, we don't move around much. We don't move at all. We are standing behind the throne. I am resting much of my weight against the shoulder of the sturdy fellow next to me.

I doubt whether any member of the audience sees me. I am directly behind a knight, who may be Wilt Chamberlain. I must peek under his elbow to see Lohengrin's good-bye to Elsa. He, a young Ukrainian tenor, Dmitri Onofrei, about to embark on the swan, is singing *In fernem Land*. Maria Jeritza, all in white, doesn't appear too attentive. She is sniffling.

We have been told by her tiny Viennese maid, backstage, that the diva has a terrible fever, "vun hundertd und two." The tall blond super raises his eyes towards the heavens. He casts a significant look at the rest of us. He seems to know all the backstage gossip. He has a way of enrapturing us; indeed, mesmerizing us. Though his voice has the timbre of Truman Capote, his air of authority is William Buckley's.

"Jeritza's heart was set on Turandot. Poor dear. And when they gave the plum to Raisa, she was *livid*. She may look like a cool Austrian, but her temper, oh *God*! She's a tiger, that one. Don't *ever* cross her, darling, if you value your sweet tender skin."

I have no intention of crossing Maria Jeritza.

"And, I have it on good authority, she threatened to walk out. And they threatened to sue the *pants* off her. So, kiddies, she's doing *Lohengrin* under duress."

Jeritza, if our source is reliable—and who dare doubt him?—is sniffing rather than sniffling. As I observe, past the sweaty arm of the tall knight, Elsa ignoring her champion, I am indignant. After all, Lohengrin, coming out of nowhere, saved her honor in clobbering Telramund. The least she could do is look at him as he sings his big aria. Oh well, that's how things go in the court of King Henry. I promise myself never to appear in Wagner again. Nor, for that matter, in any opera. *Addio del passato*.

*   *   *

I move toward the phonograph. Violetta's letter scene has become Leonora's prayer. Muzio has just sung *Pace, pace, mio dio.* And who has ever done that better than her? I fumble through the haphazard stack of albums on the floor. I find Mahalia Jackson. "Jesus Met the Woman at the Well."

When did I first hear that voice? As I talk into my Sony, it comes to me that the exaltation I experienced in 1927 on first hearing the Italian was equaled in 1947 when I first heard the black woman. Mahalia.

2

Mahalia

It is Mozart's birthday. January 27. It is the custom of WFMT, on this occasion, to devote all twenty-four hours to his music. I am listening to a replay of the conversation with Maestro Josef Krips. Once again, I hear the soft Viennese accent. "Beethoven's music is heavenly. Mozart came to us from heaven." It is 1972. Somebody opens the studio door. He holds a news dispatch in his hand. He has just ripped it from out of the ticking machine in the hallway. "Mahalia Jackson died this morning."

I am listening to the Maestro. I hear nothing. Elisabeth Schwarz-kopf is singing *Dove sono*. I hear nothing. Richard Tauber is singing *Il mio tesoro*. I hear nothing.

The news has come as no great surprise to me. Mahalia had been ill, better, worse, better, worse, for some ten years. Not that it kept her from working: one-night stands, concerts, television appearances, recordings, Europe. Nobody was pushing her. Or were they? Perhaps it was her own demon, too. Lately, she had been failing. So they told me. If her death was not unexpected, why am I, at this moment, so furious? Why is my pulse going crazy?

We had visited her a year or so ago. My wife danced in with a bunch of red roses. Mahalia was low; yet she wasn't. I clowned. We had a laugh or two. She clowned. We laughed some more. From under her mattress, she brought forth a pint of Old Grand-Dad. She was saving it for me. I took a good swig, made a face, shuddered, and staggered drunkenly around the room. She laughed some more. It was an old routine. It worked every time.

And now, no more.

It is a harsh, wintry day in Chicago, 1947. At a record shop, George Hoefer, a critic for *Down Beat* and a friend of jazzmen, works behind the counter. He insists I hear something that has just come in. It is on the Apollo label. He plays it. It is gospel. "Move On Up a Little Higher." It builds and builds and builds for six minutes. I am floored and lifted. Who is she? George tells me she lives on the South Side and sings in a lot of black churches. I am caught.

As a disk jockey on a weekly radio program, I play Ellington, Caruso, Armstrong, Chaliapin, Leadbelly, Lotte Lehmann, and those others of the God-possessed. Now I add Mahalia. I'm flying high. (I play the Goodman Sextette, too.) It is an exhilarating time for me. And, I hope, for some of the listeners.

On Sunday mornings, I visit the Greater Salem Baptist Church. It is on the city's West Side. There are intimations of rubble around and about. Urban renewal is just getting under way. Here are parishioners, bone-weary after a week of unsung work, for a wage not worth singing about; here they are, listening to song, such as I, whose work is so much easier and whose wage is so much better, have never heard.

It is at such time and circumstance that I become aware of my own arrogance. For a stupid moment, I had thought *I* discovered Mahalia Jackson. On occasion, I run into somebody who obtusely insists it is so. Most disheartening are those quite gifted singers of gospel music in this city, who, God help us all, attribute Mahalia's "success" to me. It is cause for tears as well as laughter. The people of Greater Salem know better.

Consider this. A single voice. A piano and an organ. A record label little known. Consider this. More than two million people, way more, have put out hard-gotten cash for "Move On Up a Little Higher." In scores of thousands of homes, among the devout and God-fearing, oh yeah, and in taverns and pool parlors, too, lowly spirits are lifted by a soaring, winged voice. Again and again and again, this record is played on phonographs and jukeboxes. The grooves are worn deep and the needles are dulled, but they keep on listening, through scratch and static, to this voice. And hardly a white has heard of her.

It is the story of Bessie Smith all over again. They say, a couple of generations ago, when a Bessie record came out, people would line up for blocks. Many who could not afford coal would derive warmth enough from the glow of "Backwater Blues" or "Baby Doll" or "Nobody Knows You When You're Down and Out."

I kid her about this. "If you took up the blues, you'd sound like Bessie Smith. If Bessie had ever sung spirituals, she'd've sounded like Mahalia Jackson." She laughs. She gets a kick out of it. Funny or not, it's true.

We're seated in her Prairie Avenue flat, oh, shall we say about twenty-five years ago? It is just before she moves into that ranch house, one of the first blacks in a white neighborhood; a few broken windows and a few phoned threats. She stares out the window, toward the setting sun, miles away and centuries ago. "Mahalia, she was a girl in the slave days. She was dreaming of Jubilee all the time. Of better days to come. My people gave me her name."

Her hands are clasped on the kitchen table. They are delicate, graceful hands. Not dainty, not soft. The calluses are eloquently there. She had scrubbed floors of other people's parlors. She had laundered other people's finery. She had nursed other people's children. A bitter reflection some years later: "I nursed little Jimmy like he was my own. Do you think he was in that mob that threw rocks at Dr. King?"

I stare at her hands. She opens them and lays them on the table. "You got to work with your hands. All artists should work with their hands. How can you sing of Amazing Grace, how can you sing prayerfully of heaven and earth and all God's wonders without using your hands? My hands demonstrate what I feel inside. My hands, my feet, I throw my whole body to say all that is within me. The mind and the voice by themselves are not sufficient."

She was part of an early migration to Chicago from the Deep South. Her people wanted her to have a better chance than she'd have in Louisiana. Perhaps beauty culture. She tried. She didn't make it. She worked as a factory hand and as a domestic. Come Sunday, she found respite and exhilaration. She sang open-voiced and freely at Greater Salem. For that matter, she sang at any church you could name on the South Side, on the West Side, wherever black working people gathered to find a one-out-of-seven-day solace.

"When did I first begin to sing?" She laughs. "When did I first begin to walk and talk? When did I first begin to breathe? I remember singing as I scrubbed floors. It would make the work go easier. When the old people wasn't home, I'd turn on a Bessie Smith record and play it over and over. 'Careless Love,' that was the blues she sang."

" 'Careless Love,' Mahalia?" I act out horror.

Her eyes suggest a twinkle. "That was before I was saved. I don't sing the blues now. The blues are wonderful, but I just don't sing 'em. When I imitated Bessie Smith, I was just a little girl, remember that." Significantly, she repeats, "Before I was saved."

Uh oh, I know what's coming. And she knows I know. "An' I'm gonna save you, too, Studs." It isn't the first time she offers this challenge; nor is it the last. It is to become our Chautauqua debate: believer versus atheist. The studio audience at her radio programs, during the warm-ups, have come to delight in this theological dispute, knowing quite well who will come off the laughing winner. I always lose. Don't misunderstand. I have never in my life thrown a match of this nature. I am, in this instance, pitifully overmatched. All my Bob Ingersoll arguments are demolished by her soaring song. And her humor.

Will she ever sing the blues? She laughs. I know she loves the blues, but there isn't a ghost of a chance. Big Bill Broonzy, who sings a country blues like nobody ever, before or since, understands. "It ain't right for Mahalia to be asked to sing the blues. They all respect her because she sticks to her beliefs. I feel funny when they put me on the same platform with her. It don't seem right. 'Course, you know Mahalia. She don't complain about it, 'cause that's the way she is.

"I guess it's all right, though, if we're on two separate parts of the program. Like that time in Oxford, England. Those Englishmen liked the both of us. Just between you an' me, I don't think they knew the difference. But they were very nice just the same.

"No, Mahalia shouldn't be made to sing the blues. They should just let her sing only what she believes and feels inside. Without feelin', there's nothin'. That goes for all kinds of music."

Mahalia is equally fond of Bill. One day, as she lies in the hospital bed, gaunt and emaciated, she talks of Bill. As by magic, she feels better. She is wildly comical doing Broonzy. She recounts their joint triumph at London's Albert Hall. "I'm scared. I never sang for those

British people before. Bill, he says, 'Just sing, baby, they won't know the difference.' " As she captures his voice, his inflection, his throw-away manner, her visitors laugh uproariously. She's getting a great kick, too. She no longer looks gaunt and emaciated. Only the clergyman, at her bedside, is not amused. He is praying. Mahalia, though, is Here rather than There. And not about to die.

Under other circumstances, Mahalia might have become an outrageously wondrous comedienne. She could do Moms Mabley and then some. Her gift in mimicry; her sense of the absurd; her nimbleness in repartee. Oh yeah, easy. Were it not for her voice. And something else.

"I don't know what it was all the time. All I know is it would grip me. Bessie's singing gave me the same feeling as when I'd hear men singing outside as they worked, laying the ties for the railroad, working on the docks . . ."

Her reminiscences are always interrupted by friends and strangers. The doorbell rings; it is always ringing. And the telephone is always the hot line. A blind bass and four women singers enter. They are a gospel group from Washington, just passing through. They've dropped in to rehearse. Mahalia's piano is available.

Mildred Falls comes by. She is Mahalia's accompanist. She knows every breath the singer takes. What Paul Ulanowsky is to Lotte Lehmann, what Gerald Moore is to Dietrich Fischer-Dieskau, Mildred is to Mahalia. And more. In their early travels, they suffered humiliation together. And glory. It is in every chord, in every song.

If one thing disturbs me, it is Mahalia's attitude toward Mildred. She is, at times, and without apparent reason, curt and abrupt with her. Even cruel. And so, too, with the gentle Ralph Jones, who often backs her on the organ. They are scared of her. On occasion, I have heard them crying. I have a feeling she is unaware of the hurt she causes them. Shall I tell her? No, it might complicate matters. And who the hell am I? Have I not, in my higgledy-piggledy journey, hurt others without being aware of it? My mother's genes, perhaps. Oh boy. The next moment, Mahalia is tender and generous toward them. I guess the demon is at work, even in the best of us. Or the worst.

In my mind's eye, I see Princess Stewart at the door, sightless and, oh, so wondrously rich of voice. And small, wizened Willa Jones. And Big Alice from upstairs. And Brother John Sellers. And Robert Anderson, young and gifted and black.

It is nothing more than a matter of reflex for ministers from all parts of the country, this reverend and that one, she knows them all, it seems, and gospel singers, whom she knows and doesn't know, to drop in on Mahalia. It's the most natural thing in the world. She belongs to them.

She belongs to the people on the street. How often in my stumbling along with her has she been stopped by the old lady with the absurdly heavy shopping bag, who effusively greets "Mahalie." And the waiter, the garage mechanic, the young schoolteacher, the pretty girl who makes sandwiches at the mostly black drive-in. They'd heard her at such and such a church; she's a friend of an aunt or a cousin or a neighbor; they'd worn out "In the Upper Room" or "Even Me" or "Didn't It Rain."

And yet, Mahalia is discontented. There is a plaintive note to her voice as she calls late at night. What's the trouble? She can't put her finger on it. Something about not being "successful." I kid her because I think she's kidding. She's not. There are Carnegie Hall triumphs, Columbia albums on more than coffee tables, college professors paying her tribute, an appearance at the White House, an honorary degree—what is it? She can't explain, she, who is usually so deft with the telling phrase, so quick at getting to the heart of the matter. It is something she is reaching out for that may not be there. But it is. And it appears quite suddenly.

Is it 1956? 1957? Another call in the dead of night. Her voice has an unaccustomed ring. She says something about a phone call from Alabama. A young Reverend Abernathy has called on behalf of another young reverend, a Martin Luther King. Something about a Montgomery bus boycott. They'd like her to sing at one of the church rallies. What's her fee?

I know what's coming and I delight in it. She's having a high time.

"You ever hear of these people?" she asks.

She knows very well I've heard of these people.

"Don't you think the colored are pushin' too fast?"

I am rolling off the bed.

"Why they lookin' for trouble all the time?"

When I laugh uncontrollably, it sounds like a cackle. I am cackling.

She is doing Moms Mabley now.

"Mmm, chile, you laugh at crazy things. 'At's why you get in trouble all the time you'self."

"I can't help it, Mahalia, I don't look for it. It just seeks me out. What did you decide?" As though I didn't know.

She lets out a long sigh. "What do *you* think I should do?"

"When are you goin'?"

"Day after tomorrow. Reverend Abernathy asks how much I'll charge." She laughs.

"What'd you tell him?" As though I didn't know.

"I said, 'Reverend Abernathy, I don't charge the walkin' people.' " Mahalia has found what she was looking for.

Time passes, cataclysmically. The walking people of Montgomery set hearts on fire. So does song as well as the word. Martin Luther King knows what he's about in calling on Mahalia Jackson. He has found a way; so has she.

It is Sunday afternoon. The phone rings. It's Mahalia. Her voice is reassuring; she been ailing. There is laughter and a touch of excitement.

"Come over right away."

"Why?"

"Martin wants you to interview him."

"Are you sure?"

"Bring your machine."

I am aware that Martin Luther King has a back-breaking schedule in Chicago. The papers are full of it.

"Don't force him, Mahalia."

"I made some gumbo. Martin's had two helpings. You have some, too."

She's at it again. Naturally, I'm delighted that Martin Luther King wants me to interview him, especially since he's never heard of me. Not until this moment. Mahalia is gifted in hyperbole as well as in song.

Dr. King and I are seated at the edge of her bed. She, propped against two pillows, is regal. She's in charge. Of course. He is manifestly bone-weary. He smiles resignedly. I do, too.

"Go on, Studs. Ask Martin questions."

Her running commentary is hilarious. She's given me my cue: the role of humor in the lives of those up against it. I'll lead into it casually. There is one catch.

I'm being tapped on the shoulder by a visitor. I recognize him. He is the rabbi of one of the city's most affluent reform synagogues. It seems that Dr. King is due at the other side of town. *Now*. A dinner, preceding his lecture, has been planned for him by this shepherd; his most influential parishioners will be there. "Can you hurry it up?"

Dr. King tells of influences: his father, Gandhi, Thoreau, Amos, the Old Testament prophet. My questions are hurried. His replies, though unhurried, tell me his thoughts are elsewhere. Clearly, he's in a time bind. The visitor, impatient, paces the room. He attracts our attention; he slaps at his wristwatch. Only Mahalia is unconcerned. She beams.

I'm getting to what I want: laughter through adversity. Not quite. The shoulder tap again.

"Time's up."

I'm tense to his touch. I shrug off his hand, though he is wholly unaware of it.

"You ready, Dr. King?"

I surrender, dear. MLK has troubles enough. I press down hard on the STOP lever.

"Did you get what you wanted, Studs?" Mahalia asks.

"Oh yeah." Almost.

As Martin Luther King is hustled off by one of Mayor Daley's favorite clergymen, I head into the kitchen and dig into some of Mahalia's fine cooking.

Later.

"Who was that man?" she asks.

"A famous Chicago rabbi," I tell her.

"I thought he was an agent."

"Oh no, he's the shepherd of a flock."

"I thought he was from William Morris."

That Mahalia. She always gets to the heart of the matter.

Is it 1953? '54? Another CBS radio program has come to a rousing finish. The studio audience won't leave. Mahalia tells them, though delighted with their response, she's all worn out. She says something funny. They howl. Slowly, quite satisfied, they straggle out. Three of us—Mahalia, Mildred, and I—are famished. Across the hallway, no more than twenty feet away, is the entrance to the Wrigley Restaurant. The food is superb, I tell them. Mahalia and Mildred look at one another. I know the look. The hell with it.

"Let's go," I say.

The women hesitate. Did you ever see Negroes eat there? Mahalia asks it.

"No, but they will now."

The funny thing is I don't like scenes. But I don't think there will be any. For Christ's sake, Mahalia is the star of the program just across the hall.

"The eatin's good, huh?" I know Mahalia loves food. Too much. She must lose weight. But not tonight. We're celebrating.

"Fantastic," I reply.

I don't think Mahalia knows that Les Atlass, the station's owner, has referred to her as "that black gorilla." An anthropological sport, Atlass has a scary reputation among white performers, too. Especially women. He quite obviously delights in his power to abuse. He may be dining here now. Who knows? P. K. Wrigley may be in here, too. I am feverish, I know. Let's *do* it!

I am at the entrance. The women haven't moved.

"There's a nice little place down the street," says Mahalia. I know the place: a one-arm joint; just a counter, no chairs. Hamburgers and hot dogs. We eat there all the time, the three of us. Oh, Christ. I am still at the entrance. I talk to the door. My voice is small, though the women hear me well enough.

"You don't wanna eat here?"

"They got pork chops, too." Mahalia is referring to the one-arm joint. "Mmm, you know how I love pork chops, Studs." She's trying to laugh. She's not doing too well. I am furious at myself. They have suffered these humiliations, not I. Who knows better than they? I follow them out into the street. I am cursing, talking to myself.

How green is the memory of 1963 and the March on Washington. The Lincoln Memorial is the backdrop. The reflecting pool is ahead. As the assembled thousands await Dr. King's memorable plea for mankind, the heavy woman, wearing a new multiflowered hat, celebrates life. She is singing "Precious Lord, Take My Hand." It is Dr. King's favorite hymn. Professor Thomas A. Dorsey wrote it. Once known as Georgia Tom, accompanist of Ma Rainey, he has, since being saved, written scores of hymns for Mahalia Jackson. She has never sung this one better.

As she goes into "I'm Going to Live the Life I Sing About," an airplane—or is it a helicopter?—for some unaccountable reason, is impiously buzzing overhead. We all look up, slightly distressed. Mahalia looks up, too, without missing a beat. She outsings the flying machine, as it vanishes into the blue. Even now, I see those scores of white handkerchiefs waving as banners of triumph . . .

"Mahalia Jackson died this morning." The bearer of the news says it softly and closes the studio door. Have ten minutes gone by? Half an hour? I hear Erich Kunz. He is Papageno. *The Magic Flute*. It is beautiful.

3

Oh, Freedom

I am standing on the corner of Bibb and Commerce in Montgomery, Alabama. I am swearing softly at my wayward Uher. It is behaving in a maddening, eccentric fashion. For no accountable reason, it goes on and off, on and off. I bang it against the mailbox. It doesn't seem to help. It is ten o'clock at night, Wednesday, March 24, 1965, and I am furious.

It is the eve of the Freedom Movement's great trek from Selma to Montgomery. Tomorrow, at eight in the morning, begins the last lap: from St. Jude's, a Catholic complex on the outskirts of town, through dirt roads "where the pavement ends," and on into the wide, magnolia-bowered avenues, toward the steps of the capitol building, hardly more than a spitting distance away from the Dexter Avenue Baptist Church, where Martin Luther King, Jr., has his pulpit.

Earlier this evening, I'm standing in the soft, red Alabama clay, along with ten thousand others, at St. Jude's. Celebrated singers, musicians, and actors are performing. The only artist missing is Mahalia Jackson. She's back in Chicago, ailing. There are rousing songs and speeches and much laughter. Dick Gregory is in rare form. Spirits are high. And tomorrow, feet will be winged.

Most impressive are the kids in the high trees. Montgomery's black children are delighting in this, the most exciting moment in their young lives. They don't quite believe what they see and hear. Faces they may have occasionally seen on television or in tattered fan magazines; voices they may have heard on scratchy phonograph records in battered jukeboxes. Here, in the flesh, and for *them*. And the crowd—never have they seen so many people, black and white together, in one place. And friendly. Oh yeah.

These small acrobats balance themselves on the skinny branches, with the aery air of the Flying Wallendas. Is that Jimmy McGee, on the top of the tree, saying, "How is this for high?" Through the greenery, their wide eyes dance. "It's *bootiful*," says one.

It is a Rousseau painting. Leaves trembling. Eyes peering through leaves. Color brilliant, even in the night light. Alive, alive O. In this instant, I am elsewhere: Kruger National Park. A South African bus, carrying thirty-five wide-eyed passengers, has stopped somewhere in the world's largest natural preserve, where, ironically, the animals are free.

An impala is posed against the blazing sun, trembling, delicate, lovely, and vulnerable. From behind a green bush, a leopard leaps. He tears away at the impala's throat. He sees the bus. He lopes, ever so casually, back to behind the bush. His prey lies in the tall grass, a red trickling onto the green. He's in no hurry for his dinner. He peers from behind a leaf. I see his one eye. It is wildly Rousseau. Horror in the preserve. Delight at St. Jude's.

The wizened old black woman stands beside me. We can hardly move; there are so many of us celebrants. She has marched from Selma, where she has been doing domestic work ever since she was ten years old. "Mmm yes, Lord, an' ain't gettin' nothin' for it. My son in Detroit's upset. I been to jail an' he's worryin' hisself about me. He called me long distance. Yeah, sonny, I been to jail. Mama, I'm scared for you." She laughs softly. "Jim Clark's horses run over us an' the gases. I just didn't make it home. An' they come down with the hoses." Will she march tomorrow? "Yes, Lord. I'm marchin' tomorrow. I been sick but I'm marchin'. Greatest feelin' I ever had in my life."

The entertainment is first-class, but I'm restless. I must get back to the streets of Montgomery. Now. It is clear how the people out here feel. But what's happening along Bibb and Commerce? And at the bar across the street? And at the service station? I and my Uher maneuver our way through the crowd onto the street and into a cab, as Nina Simone is singing "Mississippi God Damn."

Visitors from all over the country have been converging on Montgomery all day. By plane, bus, and jalopy. Priests and nuns and historians and students and housewives and labor people and journalists and entertainers. Our chartered plane comes in from Chicago via Atlanta. We are greeted by Freedom Summer volunteers, who carry us to our assigned hotels and motels. In charge is an ebullient and altogether charming young woman from Detroit. Her name is Viola Liuzzo. She doesn't tell me her name, but I recognize her photograph the following Friday morning on the front page of the *Montgomery Advertiser*.

As I smash the perverse Uher against the mailbox, two sudden companions offer all sorts of advice. They have come from the bar across the street. Unfortunately, they are not technicians. They are barbers, local craftsmen, who have had a few and feel little pain. I, too, have had some bourbon and branch, though not in their company. Their good natures assuage my distress. After all, I am no mad Ahab, asea, out to destroy some dumb beast of a machine.

E. J. Blount is squash-faced, gravel-voiced, stubby, and bluff. He is a dead ringer for Wallace Beery. Will Holmes is slim, handsome, *soigné*, and equipped with a slight blond mustache. He is a dead ringer for David Niven. For no accountable reason, the Uher, suddenly, is working beautifully. I am no longer furious.

We are facing the lobby of the Greystone Hotel. What goes on inside is startlingly visible through the large plate-glass window. What has gone on inside, through much of the afternoon, has discombobulated the people across the street: merchants, clerks, truckers, and aimless young men on the corner. They have been getting an eyeful, enough to last a lifetime of fantasy.

The celebrated entertainers have been put up at the Greystone. By accident or lot, I'm staying here, too. As they arrive, the celebrities recognize other celebrities. The greetings are effusive and theatrical. There is much embracing, kissing, and a laying on of hands. It is a matter of ritual with these folks, a show of affection. It is, of course, interracial. To the stunned and bewildered observers across the street, it is something out of Hieronymus Bosch. All this and the March, too.

Now Wallace Beery, David Niven, and I are deep in conversation. Baseball. For two years, Montgomery has had no season. But this year, the Montgomery Rebels of the AA Southern Association, a Detroit Tigers farm club, will be playing to paying customers: an integrated team. "I hope Detroit will send us their best nigra players," says Wally. "You'd rather see integrated ball than no ball?" Sure, Niven says. Beery nods.

For some reason, we are speaking softly, though I have my tape recorder's volume turned high. Wally winks at me. I'm sure it has some significance. Four men, standing against the Greystone's wall, are staring beyond us toward some point in the distance. "City detectives," whispers David. "They don't like us standing here talking to you."

"Oh well, let's call it a night," I say.

Wallace Beery winks again. He lightly jabs my arm. "Nothin' to it, nothin' to it."

The detectives' eyes are slits. Nor have they any lip among them. They, collectively, bear a remarkable resemblance to John Connally. I need a cigar, desperately. I waltz up to the four. "Pardon me, but would you know if the cigar counter's open. Damn it. I should've . . ."

One opens his eyes. They are hazel. He goes into the hotel. I mumble to myself as much as to the others: "How could I be so dumb? Here I am without a cigar to my name." They say nothing. There really isn't too much to say. Hazel Eyes returns.

"Sorry. It's closed," he says.

"Thank you," I say. I mumble wretchedly as I return to my companions.

"You know what they're thinkin'?" David Niven indicates the detectives, whose deadpan, even in thoughtfulness, I find disconcerting. I'm more at home with the glower of a Chicago cop.

"What are they thinkin'?" I ask Niven at last.

"They think him and I," he thumbs at Wallace Beery, "want to make a date with those girls in there." Through the lobby window, I see two pretty young black women.

"What makes you say that?"

He laughs softly. Wally grins. Another wink.

"Don't get me wrong," says David Niven. "They very nice fellas." Wallace Beery nods. "Oh no, they're not go-to-hell types."

"You see," David Niven explains, "Montgomery County is not hostile to the colored. We're against rabble-rousers and troublemakers and agitators. This march won't accomplish anything. What are they trying to prove? I don't hate colored people. Neither do I have a personal affection for them. I'd treat them just the same as I'd treat any other human being. Every man should have his chance."

I understand. He pauses. He seems uncertain whether to continue. I stare at the revolving reel. I hear his voice again.

"But if I served a colored man in my shop, I'd have to close my doors." He nods at an elderly, heavy-set man who passes by. "He's

a judge. Think he'd come to my shop if I cut a colored's hair?"
Wallace Beery looks hurt. Why don't I understand these things?

"Take him," David Niven puts his hand on Wally's shoulder. "He
doesn't personally dislike colored, but he'd be afraid of reprisals from
his cohorts."

Beery nods. He appears even more hurt than before. The other
continues. His words are flowing now.

"Do you think all these realtors here and all these doctors and
all these executives are going to sit in the same chair? No, they'll
boycott this man. That is what he's afraid of. If he serves colored in
his barber shop tomorrow, he comes down here, he doesn't have a
barber shop. Somebody has thrown dynamite in it. Let it go at this,
one word: tradition."

Wallace Beery grins. He has an idea.

"Let's all go for a drink."

"Wait a bit," says the other. "This man's from the North. He's
takin' down our words with that machine. Right, sir?"

I nod solemnly.

"I'm thirty-five years old. I've been taught all my life a Negro is
supposed to go in the back door with his hat in his hand. As a kid,
I couldn't understand this myself. My kid asks me, 'Daddy, what is
the difference whether I go to school with colored or white?' He's
fifteen. I tell him I don't know. All I know is what I've been taught.
'Do what your heart tells you to do.' That's what I tell him.

"Martin Luther King. My personal opinion, he's a brilliant man,
one of the smartest men of our time. Had he not been a smart man,
he'd have been a dead man. If he stood before me now, I wouldn't
feel hostile to him. I respect intelligence whether it's white or colored.
But I also respect tradition. If I go up North and they tell me I'm
not supposed to do something, I don't do it. If they come down here
and tell me they're *gonna* do something, that's all right. Today, I
couldn't take my normal route home. This I didn't mind. I don't
mind anybody doing what they feel in their heart is right. But don't
push me all over my place. Don't tell me I've *got* to. It's not Lyndon
Johnson's problem or Mr. Katzenbach's up there. It's my problem."

A young man, wearing a NEVER button, strolls by. I ask the
question. "Never is a long time," says the slim barber. His stubby
friend nods. "My father is sixty-seven years old. With him, it is
never. If he lived here, he'd take his squirrel gun and get him some.
He'd shoot Martin Luther King for a snake. Me, I'll tolerate Martin
Luther King. My kid will accept him. With his kid, it will be the

custom. My grandson, if I have one, will probably admire Martin Luther King. There's no such thing as never. Sheriff Clark is crazy."

As for today, tomorrow, the march, the aftermath, my companions are worried. "When I go home tonight," says David Niven, "I'm gonna pray this thing goes off without a hitch, that nobody gets killed. I'm just a simple, uneducated barber. What they hope to prove, I don't know."

Wallace Beery cups his hand over his mouth. As for his prognosis, "I'll tell you privately, sir. In the morning." He invites me to visit his barber shop. We make a date for eight A.M. I envision being seated deep in the barber chair, getting a Montgomery trim, and listening to Lardnerian talk, Southern style.

At the suggestion of Wallace Beery, the three of us are seated in the cocktail lounge of the Greystone Hotel. Somewhere on the mezzanine, it is far removed from all else. The entertainers and the others have come back from St. Jude's. All have retired to their rooms. Tomorrow is an early rising for the march. I am the only Yankee on these premises; it is clear to the other guests. They appear to know one another; I am the only stranger. I curse my stupidity for having, in the high spirit of the moment, forgotten to sneak my Uher back into my room. It poses on the small table like some obscene creature. I shove it against my chair. Someone stumbles over it. I testily kick it under the table. It skins my shin. Damn the machine.

My friends, having had a couple in short order, are ebullient. I sense the other patrons staring at us. It is not a high-spirited moment for them. The softer I speak, the more effusive my buddies, especially Wallace Beery. His gravelly voice carries across the room beautifully. Oh boy.

Lily is our waitress. I order another round. I call her familiarly by her name. I had slipped her a ten-spot earlier that afternoon. She had agreed to talk into my Uher, after hours: impressions of bar talk on this night. "Sure, honey," she had said.

A tall man comes to our table. He bears a remarkable resemblance to John Wayne. He is the owner of the lounge. He is not especially cordial. He warns me against using the tape recorder here. I tell him I haven't the slightest intention of doing so. See? I show him the microphone. It is a bulge in my pocket. Uh oh, it has torn my pocket. A new suit, too. He shows no sympathy. He reaches down under the table and carries off my Uher. I rise and follow him to the bar.

"You've been talkin' to my help," he says. "I don't want any trouble here." Neither do I, I tell him. "Ah'm jus' buyin' mah buddies a coupla drinks." The bourbon and branch has affected my accent. "Well," he relents slightly. He returns my Uher on the condition that it remain inoperative on this night. I promise. And how.

As Lily puts down our drinks, I mumble up at her ample bosom, "Lily, you betrayed me."

She laughs lightly. "Ah'm just doin' my job, honey. I ain't lookin' for trouble." Oh, I understand. She makes no effort to return the ten-spot. She'd have gone great at the Winchmere.

Wallace Beery nudges me under the table. His knee is sharp for a fat man's. "Everything's okay. Don' worry about a thing. We're all friends." David Niven wonders whether he and Lily are ever gonna have that heavy date.

"Sure, honey," she says.

She remembers something. "The Colonel would like to buy you all a drink."

"The Colonel?" I feel better already.

She points out a squat man in the uniform of the National Guard. He wears thick-lens glasses and leans heavily against the bar. He's had more than a few. My companions are delighted. I raise my glass toward the bar, in salute and gratitude. I rise from my chair somewhat unsteadily. The Colonel stumbles toward our table and eases me back down. He joins us. Wallace Beery, once again, nudges me, under the table. I rub my bruised knee. David Niven is seated stiffly, smiling at nothing in particular.

The Colonel shoves his face close to mine. "Ah wanna talk in youah tape recorder." He is loud. "Ah got things to say an' ah don' care who knows it. Ah got one hell of a lot to say." I glance up toward the bar. John Wayne is looking our way. I stare at the tape recorder. What an ugly centerpiece. That Ahab feeling is coming over me again. "I can't record here," I say. "See?" I tug the microphone from out of my pocket. The wire extension almost upsets the Colonel's glass. I hold the microphone high. Any fool can plainly see it is alien to the tape recorder. John Wayne is unmoved. After several vain attempts, I jab it back into my torn coat pocket.

"Hell with it," says the Colonel. "You can remember what I tell ya, cantcha?"

"Sure." Maybe I can, maybe I can't. Booze has never been known to make wits more nimble. That fucking John Wayne. That fucking Lily. That fucking Uher.

"My name's Al Munson," says the Colonel. "Ah hate mah job.

But ah'm gonna do mah job tomorrow an', by God, ah'm gonna do it right. Ah'm in charge of the National Guard that's gonna protect youah niggers tomorrow. Anybody so much as scratches a nigger in that march is gonna deal with me. By God, I mean they'll have me to deal with. After four o'clock, they're all youahs. What happens to 'em after that ain't none of mah business."

President Johnson had federalized the National Guard until that hour. What happened to Viola Liuzzo on the road back to Selma happened in the dark, considerably after four o'clock. Would what happened to her have happened had the troops been federalized until the following day? On occasion, I ask myself this question.

Colonel Munson orders another round. I insist it's my turn. Wallace Beery kicks me again; he shakes his head. David Niven is smiling at the distant wall. Colonel Munson disagrees. He squeezes my arm. Later that night, in my room, I detect black and blue marks on my biceps as well as my shins.

John Lukwinski is staggeringly drunk. A foreman at the vinegar works, he has been all this Saturday afternoon at King's Palace. How he has clambered up the golden staircase and into the lobby of the Wells Grand is, to my mind, even after all these years, an awesome accomplishment. Falling back two steps, ascending three, falling back one, ascending two, he has transcended Sisyphus.

I grab the keyring from off the hook and urge him up three flights. As we enter his room, he squeezes my arm and, with his free hand, falteringly points toward the two photographs on the wall: oval, in golden frames. A woman, severe, in a black, high-necked Sunday dress; a lavaliere, delicate on her bosom. A man, equally severe, in a suit of Sunday black and a mustache, twirled, and equally black. They stare down upon us, disapprovingly.

John Lukwinski is blubbering. "My mudder," he sobs. "My fodder," he sobs. His grip on my arm is viselike. I shove him onto the bed. He is immediately snoring. I remove his shoes. I softly shut the door behind me. That night, in my room, I detect black and blue marks.

"Ah've always hated mah job, but ah've done it, by God, the best ah could." Colonel Munson is furious about something. His voice carries across the room. They are listening at all the other tables, I know. I am hunched up, sneaking an occasional look around and about. The others are staring at their drinks; and when they take a sip, it's, oh, so casual. I am glaring at the dead Uher.

"Put that thing on, ah want to talk."

I shake my head, palsied.

"You're on the radio, aintcha?"

I nod, palsied.

"Youah from up Nawth, aintcha?"

"Yeah," I mumble inaudibly.

"Ah want all the Yankees to heah me! Colonel Al Munson speakin'!"

"Shhh." I say it without realizing what I'm saying.

"Don't shush me; ah wanna talk!"

Wallace Beery kicks me again. "It's okay." He mouths it.

I fondle the microphone in my pocket. The metal and my palms are sweaty. I casually look up toward the bar. John Wayne's eyes are slits; he is studying me. Sonofabitch. I *know* Colonel Al Munson has one hell of a story to tell. And that Uher is as dead as the Mariner's albatross. No wonder I loathe John Wayne movies.

"When ah went to Auburn, ah played fullback. Made All-American, ah forget whose. Somebody's All-American. Don't believe me? You c'n look it up!" Al Munson is challenging more than me or the others on the premises. He is challenging the world.

"Ah averaged five yards every carry. Mah teammates all hated mah guts. But ah did my job, by God! Five yards every time. Bam!" Fist pounds into palm. It is more than flesh on flesh. It is a thunderclap. The lounge is still. Silence at the tables, silence at the bar. No sound from the cash register. Nothing, other than the lone voice of a furious man.

"Did you know ah was in the Berlin airlift? Didn't know that, didja?" I shake my head.

"Sure. Captain Al Munson. Crew all hated mah guts, but ah delivered the goods, by God! Ah did mah job. Think they appreciate what ah did? Nahhh! Ah don't give a good goddamn. Tomorrow, not one nigger's gonna have one scratch, all the way to the capitol. After four o'clock, ah give 'em all to you 'thout one kinky hair outa place."

He drains his glass. It is empty. "How 'bout another round?" he bawls out. There is no reply. Lily is near John Wayne. She casually leans against the bar. Hers is the smile that kills. It is fixed. At this moment, I sense, her contempt for the Colonel is even more pro-found than it is for me.

"Do you have a family?" I ask, apropos of nothing. His laugh is wholly without mirth.

"*Had* a family. *Had* one. Mmm hmm. Wife and two girls. Ah was a good husband, good father. At least, *ah* thought so. One day, she up and leaves me. The girls, too. Hated mah guts. They *tol'* me that. Ah didn't know what the hell they were talkin' about. Ah provided, damn right ah provided. Ahhh, ah don't give a good goddamn." He pounds the table. "Where're the drinks fer me an' mah buddies?"

Is Al Munson out of a William Faulkner short story? A Gwendolyn Brooks poem? "Dry September" is about a scrawny maiden lady, who passes the word, excitedly, that a black man has made a pass at her. He is lynched. The leader of the vigilantes is in a furious mood as he comes home. He tears off his sweaty shirt, terrifies his wife, and curses life. In the poem, one of Emmett Till's killers, the morning after, slaps his mewling child at the breakfast table, terrifies his wife, and curses life. Al Munson, at this moment, has no wife to terrify, and though he has killed nobody as far as I know, curses life, as he goes about his job. I am cursing life, too, especially John Wayne, Lily, and my Uher.

A woman comes over to our table. She has been seated nearby, in the company of two men and another woman. They must be important, because Lily has been waiting upon them with the servility especially reserved by people like Lily for people like them. Her chin recedes slightly; she bears a resemblance to Dorothy Kilgallen.

She lays her arm gently, ladylike, on Al Munson's shoulder. She smiles. Hers is not Lily's smile. She is a forbearing mother telling her recalcitrant child enough's enough. "Colonel, you've been talk-ing too much. I suggest you go to your room and get some sleep. Tomorrow's a hard day." She urges him up. "That's a good boy." Somebody leads Colonel Munson out of the lounge.

"You're a charmin' man, I know"—is she talking to me?—"but isn't it time you went to bed?"

Vaguely, I look up at her. My head is heavy.

"Ah'm about to finish mah drink, ma'am, if you don't mind." It's a weary effort to match her charm. My smile is a sickly one. She has me buffaloed.

It is a sign for further activity. John Wayne moves toward our table. He puts his hand on David Niven's collar and tugs him out of his chair.

"He's my guest." I am fuzzily indignant. I sound stupid.

"I'm showin' him out an' this is my place an' don't you tell me how to run my business."

Uh oh. It is Turner's Blue Lounge all over again. I've got to cut this stuff out: telling others how to run their business. It's happening too often. Perhaps I should go into some other line of work. Why did I stop being a disk jockey? The radio studio is so cool, distant, and detached.

David Niven, released at the doorway, returns to finish his drink. John Wayne makes a move toward him. The barber holds up his hand. "I'm goin'." It isn't his drink he seeks to retrieve; it's his dignity. "He says I've been agitatin' all day, I'm unwelcome here." He is hurt and bewildered. Agitatin'. For the past hour he had been seated, absolutely smashed, silent and smiling. He may not know what the owner means, but I do. The barber had talked to me downstairs and brought me upstairs. The enemy alien. Funny. It was the word David Niven himself had used in reference to tomorrow's marchers: agitatin'.

Wallace Beery, with another under-the-table kick, lets me know "it's okay, it's okay." He winks. David shakes my hand and says, "I'll see you tomorrow." Where or how, I do not know. Neither, do I suspect, does he.

A large man enters and sits in the chair vacated by the Colonel. I recognize him as one of the four men who had been observing the three of us on the street corner. He takes out his wallet and flashes his credentials. "It's time you went to your room," he says. His tone is fatherly. If Wallace kicks me once more, I'll kick him right back. He doesn't.

"I'd like to finish my drink," I say. There is nothing in my glass, but I put it to my lips as David Niven did. I'm trying to retrieve what he tried to retrieve. I have as much success. As I rise with some difficulty, my knees being stiff and bruised and unsteady, the surviving barber reminds me of our appointment at his shop, but a few hours from now. At the doorway, I hear the detective tell my buddy, "Time you left, too."

In the elevator, I ask the elderly black operator if he knows the number of Colonel Munson's room. He looks scared, so I shut up. I don't want to go to my room. I've changed my mind. Could he take me downstairs, to the lobby floor? I'm too restless to sleep. And too stupid.

The night clerk at the Greystone is a middle-aged woman, matronly. She is smiling. She has a secret. A dirty little secret, perhaps? I ask her how things are going. I slip her a fiver, just for the hell of it. She crushes it in her hand and slips it into her bosom. Hers is an awkward maneuver. My mother's was one graceful swoop. Oh, you just wouldn't believe it, she says. I tell her I'd believe anything these days. She drops dark, though titillating, hints about goings-on among the visitors. Well, what? I am matching her in prurience. Oh, she says, you know. I tell her I don't know. She lets me know that black men and white women, those civil rightsers, are engaged in more than civil rights. She giggles knowingly. Hers is the excitation of Faulkner's scrawny maiden lady. No kidding? Oh yeah, she says, they're having a real good time. She's a real dirty-minded old woman. I keep that considered opinion to myself. I'm interested in something else.

"What's Colonel Munson's room number?" I ask it casually.

She is no longer smiling.

"What, honey?"

"Al Munson. He's a guest."

"Nobody by that name here, honey."

I yawn. I'm really groggy. The day, the night, the booze, the encounters, have caught up with me. Damn. I've got to get the Colonel on tape. It's a once in a lifetime affair.

"Oh sure, he's staying here, ma'am. I'm supposed to see him."

Solemnly, she shakes her head.

"Nobody by that name here, honey."

She sounds practiced. Did Alfred Hitchcock direct this one? It's a replay of *The Lady Vanishes*. I'm Michael Redgrave looking for Dame May Whitty, who has disappeared. Nobody knows the lady's whereabouts. Nobody knows the Colonel's whereabouts. Shit.

I stare hard at my wristwatch. It reads two-twenty-five A.M. The lobby is empty, save for one. He is slouched deep in an armchair against the wall. He is not asleep. I stumble toward him. I'd like to check the time. My watch is as constant as my Uher. I sway in front of him. "Sir, any idea what time it is?"

I know him. He's one of the other detectives who had been observing the barbers and me. He appears not to have heard me.

"My watch is on the blink."

He is staring past me. I can't tell the color of his eyes. They're slits. For want of anything better to say, I volunteer an observation. "It's been quite a day, hasn't it?"

His eyelids blink. Imperceptibly. Whatever he's studying, and he's studying it hard, is beyond the horizon. Something tells me it's time to retire. I shuffle toward the elevator. I move to the tempo of Duke Ellington's "East St. Louis Toodle-oo." I'm that tired.

The door of my room clicks shut behind me. Click. Instantly, I'm cold sober. I am trembling. I fumble for the chain. I scramble into bed. It is dark, but my eyes are wide open. Sheet at my neck, I go over the events of the past few hours. What if . . .

What if I had found the Colonel's room. What if I'm seated on the edge of his bed, the reel revolving and the Colonel half-reclining, mumbling out the hurts of his life. What if a couple of detectives enter. What if I'm given a good going-over. Considering a fury, barely repressed, and a Yankee pest, irritating sore spots, it may be more than a going-over. If a battered clown is found the next morning in the Colonel's room, with his smashed Uher beside him, it is easily explained. A homosexual had made a pass at a grizzled soldier. The soldier, righteous, indignant, had lost his temper. Who's to fault him?

What if the one in the lobby, who blinked imperceptibly, feeling as put upon as Jean Gabin was by Jules Berry in *Daybreak*—goaded beyond forbearance—takes me outside. Two-forty-five A.M. There's no-o-o-body around at that hour. You can shoot a cannon down the street. Or a hard jab to the kidney and a right cross to the heart. And I ain't Harry Greb. I am truly smashed.

What if . . . I pull the sheet over my head. I sleep fitfully.

Thursday morning. March 25, 1965. The March has not yet begun. People are assembling at St. Jude's. I shall improvise around town. First, I must visit Wallace Beery's barber shop. It is hardly more than a block from the Greystone. There will be a few early customers, a couple of old-timers, he has promised me. There is a checkerboard and a golden cuspidor. Some are George Wallace aficionados; others take a dim view of the little one and remember Big Jim Folsom with affection. I can stand a slight trim myself. I gently pat my Uher. We're gonna have a good time.

The barber is at the window. He sees me. He waves at me to come in. On the sidewalk, I am embraced from behind. It is a fond embrace, but why does my heart turn to stone? It is Mary of Peter,

Paul, and Mary. Peter and Paul embrace me, too. Mary has long, lovely blond hair. Peter and Paul have trim beards and are Christlike in appearance. They were among the performers last night at St. Jude's. They will be among the marchers this morning. They have been guests on my radio program. They are delighted that I am among the visitors and will I be in the march, too? They are a sweet, gentle three, but they have just ruined me. I look toward the window. Wallace Beery turns away. He pulls down the wide shade. Damn. It might have been a born-again *Haircut*.

I am on the bus that is taking last night's performers to the March's starting point. We are passing the Dexter Avenue Baptist Church. On the steps are black people. They are old, very old. I hop off the bus.

I find some room on the top step of the church. An old woman tells me she's been here since six this morning. So have many of the others. It is a favored spot. We face the capitol building. The March will end here. The old people are quietly excited. They are murmuring to one another. I ask the old woman how long she's waited for this. "All my life," she says. An old man in fresh laundered overalls and a baseball cap hears her. "Everybody here's been waitin' their whole lives for this one. Oh yeah."

There is a slight drizzle. I hope the rains hold off, I say to the man in Sunday black. His fedora, you sense, has been saved for special occasions. "It don't matter," he says. "Been rainin' all our life. A little wet won't hurt us none. Not this day." He chuckles. He tells me he just up and decided to take the day off. I ask him if his boss said anything. "He didn't say anything. I didn't tell him, he didn't ask me." Think he knows why? "Oh yeah. He knows why all right." The man laughs. It is one of those deep from way inside the belly laughs. It rolls out and swells. A couple of old women hear him. They laugh, too.

"Brownie! Brownie, come 'ere!" A wizened old woman is calling out to a little dog. It's a little spotted brown mutt on the pavement below, trotting back and forth, back and forth, tentative, lost. "Brownie, up here!" she calls. Others cry out, "Brownie, lady's callin' you!" The dog looks up. He sees her. He scampers across arthritic bones and ample flesh onto the bosom of his mistress. She caresses him. "Brownie," she says, "he come here with me. He want freedom, too." Everybody laughs.

A woman leans across another and talks into my microphone,

clearly and distinctly, a proclamation: "Never dreamed I'd live to
see this day." There are appreciative murmurs. Oh yeah.

The man in black judges that the youngest person here is about
seventy years old. Oh yeah. He points out a man, seated in a straight-
backed chair, at the foot of the stairs. "He's a reverend. Know how
old he is? One hundred and four years old." He suggests we talk to
him, both of us.

Reverend William Franklin Paschal says it is so. He was born in
1861. He has been brought into Montgomery for just this day by
his daughter, with whom he lives in Columbus, Georgia. He is seated
erect in his chair. His mustache is iron-gray; his cigar is a fifteen-
center; and his voice is rolling thunder. No childish treble here,
piping and whistling. Yes, he says, he had baptized Dr. King's daddy.

Reverend William Franklin Paschal puffs thoughtfully at his cigar.
Slowly, emphasizing each word. "Keep your mind free. Your body
is nothin' but a servant of your mind. We can poison our minds just
like we poison our bodies. Takes the same thing to poison your mind.
People who carry prejudice, malice, hate, their minds become
poisoned, they do most anything, without any feelin's at all. Man
ain't nothin' but an animal. After all, he's just the highest type of
animal. If you don't put some God in him, he's liable to be just the
same as an animal."

A Montgomery policeman comes by. We must all move. This
place must be kept clear. There are sighs, murmurs of discontent,
and a weary, resigned raising of old bones. It is an old, old story.
This favored place gradually empties. The ancients, who had been
here since six in the morning, move on. But it is a jubilee day, no
matter what.

The sky is lowering; a few umbrellas appear. The rains are
heavier, though not enough to drive people for shelter. It is the last
lap of the march. From curb to curb, thousands walk down Dexter
Avenue toward the capitol building. From the flatbed truck, at the
foot of its steps, Martin Luther King and others will speak. A public
address system will carry their voices several blocks. Did the curtain
move ever so slightly, from one of the upper floors? Is the little toy
soldier peeking out?

I'm resting along the curb. My neighbor is a genial sort. Though
he lives in Montgomery, he's come from Illinois. Pleasantries are
exchanged. Oh yeah, he's disturbed. Plenty. And so are the merchants. Can you blame them? It's giving Montgomery a bad name.

"I never thought I'd live to see the day to see what I'm seeing." How did that old black woman put it? "Never dreamed I'd live to see this day." Ahhh.

His name is Lincoln. "I was raised in an atmosphere of tolerance and non-prejudice. But this is not the proper way. In Oakland, just the other day, they were protesting armed shipments to South Vietnam. If this keeps up—it hurts. I'm proud of my name and as Abe said of the Civil War, this too will pass."

The assistant police chief is shaking his head. He has never seen a crowd this size before. The demonstration is due to end at three o'clock. It is nearly that hour now and the speeches haven't yet begun. Lincoln chuckles. "This reminds me of Cinderella. If they're not home by midnight, their carriages will turn into pumpkins."

The circuit solicitor joins us. He's bewildered. Why are they doing this to us? "I've never had any trouble with a nigra any time in my life. Most of the nigras here are uneducated, they have no ambition and like to be the way they are. Very few of them are demonstrating. We arrested twenty-three of them the other day and twenty-two were from out of town."

He's warming up. There is so much on his mind. He is about to unburden himself. He likes my style, he says. I'm not like the others from the North, who push and push and push like those people out there. As we speak softly, confidentially, a woman is walking toward us. She has stepped out of the line of march. She is smiling. No. Yes. It's my wife.

She, among other Chicago women, had chartered a bus. They had arrived this morning, in time for the march. Oh, she and the others are fine people; I'm not gainsaying that. She is humane, intelligent, and charming. But she's just ruined me, that's all. Peter, Paul, and Mary, encore, encore.

"Well," she says brightly. Hers is an engaging smile, for the others as well as for me. I introduce her to my companions with the ebullience of Buster Keaton. They are polite as Southern gentlemen are. She is quick to note the weather and gracefully vanishes into the crowd. Too late, too late. My buddies suddenly find other business at hand. They bid me a friendly, though brisk, good-bye. So long, it's been good to know you. Oh, God.

I need a cigar. A grocery store, gas pump outside, is nearby. Several young men in T-shirts are horsing around. They Indian wrestle. Flex muscles. One throws the other against the Coke machine. They laugh. Mostly, theirs is a running commentary on the marchers. It's about queers and commies and nigger lovers. An older man in a flowered sports shirt is holding forth. "Ah killed a nigger in World War II. Shot him in the back." Oh yeah. I've a hunch he's saying it to impress me. I'm the only outsider here. I'm having trouble lighting my Roi Tan. One of the kids says, "I'd like to get me a couple now." They laugh.

Two black kids come in. Tentatively, they move toward the Coke machine. They look beat and hot, bandanas tied around their necks. "Go 'way, *boys*," says one of their fair-haired contemporaries. The intruders about-face and vanish. There is more laughter. Two young whites, obvious out-of-towners, enter. They, too, move toward the vending machine. "Broken," proclaims another T-shirt. The intruders move out, shuffling backward. Scared. There is much hilarity.

"Goddamn cigar won't light." I bite off the tip and spit it away. I'm out of matches. I smack at my pockets. No matches. "Damn." I gesture to one of the kids, who's smoking a cigarette. He ignores me. The man in the flowered shirt tosses me a matchbook.

"On the house," he says.

"Much obliged."

"You're welcome."

I doubt that. I light up.

They are studying me.

The man in the flowered shirt addresses my Uher. "Got that on?"

"No."

"Put it on, we'll give you an earful."

"Batteries run down. Damn batteries."

They're back to the theme of queers, commies, and nigger lovers. Maybe I am welcome. Talking among yourselves can get rather boring. An alien in the midst can make for a little excitement. Diversion, at least. They're dying for a round-table conversation. I sigh. "It's been quite a day, heh?" My needle is stuck in the groove.

"It ain't over yet," says the man in the flowered shirt. They laugh.

I'm in a drugstore phone booth. I'm calling a few of Montgomery's distinguished citizens. The more powerful ones. I'm interested in their thoughts on the march. Cliff Durr has bet me they'll be "out of town." A voice answers. It is male, soft, and polite; black, I think.

"Is Mr. —————— in?"

"Mr. —————— is out of town."

"Mrs. ——————, too?"

"Yes, they're both out of town."

"Any idea when they'll be back?"

"They gone for the rest of the week."

I try three others. They're all gone for the rest of the week. Cliff Durr has won his bet.

Many of the marchers have dispersed, though the speeches continue. Cabs are hard to find. I share one with a young woman journalist who's on the staff of the evening newspaper. She is downcast. "I saw my Southern heritage really shot down today. I'm appalled, actually."

She is an alumna of the University of Alabama. Of course, qualified people should have a right to vote. *Qualified* people. She dislikes mass demonstrations, white or black.

"Montgomery doesn't have many of these redneck types. Ours is more the old Southern genteel tradition. Somehow, I was surprised to see an integrated march. In Tuscaloosa, just the nigras marched. Even though I played with nigra children when I was a child, today shocked me. I didn't particularly like it. It gets my dander up to be told I've got to associate with these people."

I don't think that's quite the issue, I murmur. It is something else that bothers her. What?

"I spotted the faces of two girls in the march."

Yes?

"I had gone to the university with them. It made me sad."

"Why do you think they did it?"

"You've got to know the girls. They were not accepted by their peers because they were unusual, even then. One was really intelligent and that's the pity of it. The other was pseudo-intelligent. I'd expect it from her. But the other . . ."

"Why weren't they accepted?"

"Their ideas made them somewhat eccentric. And their unconventional dress, of course."

I get off here.

It is open house at the Durrs. It is always open house at 2 Felder Street for outcasts, scholars, libertarians, dreamers, troublemakers, waifs, and eccentrics. Clifford and Virginia Durr have lived in Montgomery and its environs all their lives. And their parents and grandparents before them. Cliff had been Rosa Parks's lawyer when she was arrested for refusing to move to the back of the bus. Virginia was forever speaking out. They didn't court trouble; neither did they run away from it; naturally, they were always in trouble.

He had a distinguished career as a lawyer in Washington. As a member of the Federal Communications Commission during the administration of Franklin D. Roosevelt, he wrote the Blue Book, an affirmation of radio listeners' rights. When, during the administration of Harry S. Truman, he was asked to sign a loyalty oath, he refused and resigned.

I first ran into Virginia Foster Durr, a sister-in-law of Associate Justice Hugo Black, back in the early forties. She and Mary McLeod Bethune were touring the country on behalf of the Committee to Abolish the Poll Tax. Naturally, she was called before Senator Eastland's Internal Security Committee. On the stand, she was most uncooperative, regarding Sunny Jim with undisguised contempt, and his questions as irrelevant, impertinent, and vulgar. During most of the inquisition, she ignored the massa of Sunflower County, taking out her compact and powdering her nose. Rumor hath it that haunch, paunch, and jowl almost had a stroke then and there.

Cliff's once lucrative law practice had become a shambles. Nonetheless, he was richly endowed with clients: mostly blacks and indigent. If anything, his sense of grace, always there, had deepened.

They are a stubborn pair.

All sorts of visitors parade in and out of the old house on this late afternoon. And last night, too. C. Vann Woodward, the Southern historian; two frail seventeen-year-old girls from a staid Chicago suburb, who have just spent a week in the city jail for picketing; Lou Pollak, Dean of Yale Law School; E. D. Nixon, ex–sleeping car porter who organized the Montgomery Improvement Association, a client and old friend; an English schoolkid with sleeping bag and God knows what else; Myles Horton, founder of Highlander School, burned out of Monteagle, Tennessee, now in Knoxville; a genteel elderly neighbor; a genteel young neighbor; Carl Braden, who, in trying to integrate Louisville, courted trouble and found it; John Beecher, the poet; Pat Watters, Atlanta journalist; Molly Dobbs, weary, tragically lovely, a survivor of early Southern labor battles; Margaret Long of the New South; me, shuffling in and out, with my metallic companion, which is behaving outrageously, though a slap, now and then, does wonders.

Rachel and Sara are resting, after their ordeal at the city jail. Each is a wisp of a girl. "At first," says Rachel, speaking ever so softly (I turn the volume way up), "the matrons were upset and nervous. We were on a hunger strike. They didn't know what to do with us. We calmed them down. We had discussions with them.

They were motherly. What did my parents think? I said my parents told me to do what I think is right. The matrons were astonished. They never saw anyone who believed in anything so strongly. They always believed civil rights people were wild and beatnik and communist. When we arrived, they were openly hostile. When we left, they were openly sympathetic. They kept telling us how we had improved, how much nicer we were now. They told us something of their own lives. I really think . . ." She pauses.

"Think what?"

Even more softly, almost a whisper: "I really think we may have opened them to thoughts they hadn't had before."

Sara picks up the story. "We shared the cell with two juvenile delinquent girls. They were in for staying out all night. They had been arrested repeatedly. They were more at home in jail than at home. They were poor whites. When we told them what we were in for, they became terribly frightened of us."

I laugh. "Of you?"

"Oh yes. Demonstrators, to them . . . They were afraid of each other. Afraid the other girl would disapprove. They became more friendly when they discovered it was an effort to be hostile. If they were nice, it was easier. They gave me a blanket."

Rachel interjects. "We weren't hostile. A lot of young civil rights people come in angry. It dawned on everyone that there is no need to be hostile to these people. I think . . ."

"Yes?"

"I think we learned something, too."

The pretty young neighbor is helping Virginia prepare whatever there is to eat.

"When I was a child, it was no big thing playing with Negro children. I didn't think they were so terrible or smelled bad. They smelled no worse than I did. When I hear something terribly stupid or cruel, I can't let it go by. I get angry very easily. I've learned to control my temper: if it gets too boisterous, I walk out.

"With older people, it's less discussed. Young people can get mad at each other and make up. Older people can't. I think younger people want to talk about it. Nobody has ever told me to shut up. I think they're questioning themselves. I really feel their consciences are bothering them. They always want to argue with me. When I've got them stuck, they can't concede, though they haven't a leg to stand on. They get that funny look on their face."

"What kind of funny look?"

"Astonishment. They will make a joke, if they don't get angry.

"I'm proud of being a Southerner. When you're proud of something, you examine it more carefully. Like a new dress or something. If I like it, I'll lay it on the bed and look at it awhile."

"What do you think will happen after all this . . . ?"

"It will be business as usual, but there will be a difference. A sense of loss."

"Loss of what?"

"When I was a little girl, I thought the South was charming and the Negro people so picturesque. So did most Southerners. Even though this lovely life was at the expense of a whole race. They will miss it, but that's how it's going to be.

"I would have marched today, but I don't want my husband to be disinherited by his family. He depends on them financially. He's studying to be a composer. My husband's parents are not barbaric. But—anybody who doesn't agree with them is a communist."

"How do they get along with your parents."

"They have never met."

John Beecher is in and out of the house; he's on the track of stories, covering the event for the *San Francisco Chronicle*. He is of Abolitionist ancestry, a great-grandnephew of Henry Ward Beecher and Harriet Beecher Stowe.

"I attended the Virginia Military Institute. That's where Stonewall Jackson went. There I became acquainted with the brutal system of hazing. I was conscious of the brutishness that was so much part of the South. After one year and eight days there, I was expelled for refusing to be a stool pigeon in a hazing case. I was taken out of my room in the middle of the night before a student court. There were no charges against me because I never hazed. The court consisted of boys who had beaten me the year before. I refused to recognize this mockery, so they kicked me out.

"I went to work in the mills. I preferred it to VMI, where the scions of the aristocracy trained for distinguished careers. I always had considerable contempt for Southern pretensions of culture.

"The men at the mills were decent, except on the subject of race. They became irrational. Outside the mill, there were shacks and cribs, where Negro prostitutes holed up at twenty-five cents a throw. When I was fifteen, the men were after me to go over the fence with them. You're not a man unless you were kicked by a mule or slept with a Negro woman. They said it more bluntly than that.

"There was a tremendous emphasis on sex. The Southern boy was knowing at an early age. I remember, at the age of five, seeing white grammar school boys assault Negro girls in the woods as they came home from school. It was considered quite a triumph. There was an emphasis on physical sports, too, especially involving bodily contact. I was brought up to fight every day. There was a pecking order in the neighborhood to test your manhood each day. I know it's easy to oversimplify, but there was a worship of force and violence.

"I don't think the majority of Southern whites are racist in depth. If the law were seriously enforced, they would accept it. The person himself would agree at once, were it not for the fear of what the other would say."

The phone rings persistently at the Durrs. Each time Virginia picks it up, there are some brief words followed by a click. I shall have to ask her about that. At the moment, she is too busy ministering to her guests. As some depart, others come in. Grand Central Station.

We have been seated around the parlor, watching Martin Luther King on television. He ends his talk. Molly Dobbs is particularly moved by one phrase: "Instead of food on the table, the poor white has been fed Jim Crow." That's her people, poor whites. She has come from the hilly, piney woods. "After the Civil War," she says, "the small farmers were pushed up there, where the soil is poor. They never owned slaves. The landed gentry stayed in the black belt."

She speaks with tenderness of her mother and father. "As a poor white, I have what some people think is a childlike faith in the deep yearnings of white people who have no leadership and no education. I'd never like to have the word 'redneck' ever used.

"I believe I have very intelligent parents, poor cotton farmers. There's a whole group, even uneducated farm people, who teach their children not to use dirty words about Negro people. You'll find a great many people in the piney woods recruited by the Klan. But there is another heritage. Being a prejudiced person was considered being an ignorant person. And they valued education. They are like people in Mexico. If this person can draw or write or play an instrument, he has stature.

"My childhood impressions are very vivid. Yearning for a textbook in high school. I begged for one. Had one with missing pages. So happy to have it. When I graduated with honors, they were amazed. When I wanted to go to college, my father said sure. Others were puzzled. It disturbed the professor of psychology at Birmingham Southern who said children of farmers and workers have lower IQs than children of professionals. He thought I was a freak, I suppose. That year, the Eskimos had the lowest IQ.

"I don't like meeting a person who can't read or write. It's painful. I almost became an intellectual snob. My salvation was, I cared deeply for people who were hurt. I can't stand human behavior less than what it can be. It hurts me. When I was fourteen, I was organizing in town and teaching old people how to do the ABCs. An old man said, 'It would be nice to be able to write my name before I die.'

"The Baptist Church frightened me when I was a child. So much fear in it, so much hate. I had to live almost alone in the woods, growing up. Read everything I could get my hands on. The Bible, two or three times. It's amazing how many classics are stuck away, even in the most primitive schools. And poetry, it has a way of molding people.

"There's a terrible loneliness. I think if people had time to talk, as we do now, relaxed, they'd be delighted to express themselves. I know a farm woman who writes her letters to me, and it's like poetry. She doesn't know it's poetry. Gray's 'Elegy' made a radical out of me. Who knows whose gifts are buried? That poem hit me so hard. George Wallace is making a great mistake in allowing poetry in schools.

"I saw some people today in work clothes, miserable, completely rejected. They are the forgotten people. So callously used by Wallace, by the Klan. Today . . . I never thought it was true. I had to see it to believe it. Like the white guy and the old black woman. It'll take a little time. There's been great tension. It'll take time like the first pain of shock."

"Labor pains . . . ?" I mumble.

"Very much like a girl who's having her first baby. She knows her life has been altered. Now it's out in the open. People will begin to talk with people sooner than we think." A long pause. Softly, "I hope."

George Wallace's face is on the TV screen. He is talking of outside agitators, who have come into Montgomery on this day to stir things up. He mentions Carl Braden, among others. Carl is seated on the floor, near the davenport. I hold up my whiskey glass and salute him. He smiles and nods. It is not the first time he has been so honored.

Myles Horton smiles wistfully. Highlander Folk School, of which he is founder, had among its participants Martin Luther King and Rosa Parks. On more than one occasion Wallace has paid acrid tribute to him. Myles remembers earlier marches of this sort, with no more than a Gideon's Army taking part. "We knew one another by name, by face. Old friends, old struggles. Today, there were so many thousands, I hardly knew anybody out there. They were from all over. It was great." Poignance and a quiet joy.

Uh oh, there goes that phone again. I watch Virginia as she lifts the receiver. Perhaps it's a friend calling. No, the conversation, if any, is too abrupt. She holds the receiver in her hand, glances at it, and lets it drop onto the hook. She moves toward a guest.

It's getting dark outside. The gathering is gradually breaking up. E. D. Nixon's rolling bass is heard. He remembers when he called on Cliff Durr to get Mrs. Parks out of jail. It was December 1, 1955. This is sort of a tenth anniversary. He was president of the city's branch of the NAACP. Rosa Parks was his secretary. His was the first private home that was bombed. "I was always able to have a few white people on my side. When there was a case in court, I'd call Mrs. Durr and she'd get some other white women and they'd sit in court, in the first row. Judge would go easier."

Perhaps it's something about the oncoming darkness. He recalls an experience in the thirties. "I got a call about a sheriff who beat a woman to death. I got a telephone call about two o'clock in the morning from a white man: 'I don't like what happened. I can't tell you on the phone. Come see me.'

"It was pouring rain. You might think I was crazy, but I drove forty miles out there. My wife says if headaches cost a dollar, I'd go to the drugstore and buy me a dozen headaches. I walked on the front porch. Knocked on the door. Would I get a shotgun blast? I hear a man's voice, 'Is that you, Nixon?' He opened the door and told me what had happened. But he wouldn't sign anything. I don't blame him. If he did, they would have done something to him.

"The grand jury met. Same man called and said, 'You ought to have her sons there. They saw it.' I got ahold of the dean at Miles College: 'Put them boys on the train. I'll get your money for you.' I met the train. I said to the clerk, 'I want these boys to testify before the grand jury.' She almost fell dead. 'The sheriff issues subpoenas,' she said. He's the man who done the killin'.

"I walked into his office. A short, fat fellow with hobnailed boots, two pistols, handcuffs, bullets around his belt, blackjack in back pants pocket, shirt all open. I said, 'You Sheriff White?' He said, 'I'm Sheriff White.' I said, 'My name is E. D. Nixon. I represent the NAACP.' You oughta seen him when I said that. 'I'm here to ask you to subpoena these boys. They got a grand jury at three o'clock about the killin' of their mother.' He looked at me. He didn't know what to say.

"He pulled out a pencil. He licked it. He took him so long to trace out the boys' names. I said, 'You know the state pays eight cents a mile for travel. Both these boys are entitled to transportation.' He said, 'It's a hundred miles from Birmingham!' I said, 'That's correct. And thirteen from Montgomery to where the case is, and three miles from the college to the station. So you got 116 miles.' He said, 'Yeah, that's right.'

"He started figurin' on a piece of paper. I could see he didn't know what he was doin'. So I figured it out ahead of time. I wrote the figure and I said, 'I believe when you get through figurin' yours up, this'll tally.' He grabbed my sheet and said, 'Yeah, that's right, that's right.' He wrote a voucher. I got the money.

"Of course he was acquitted. The woman died 'from causes unknown.' But he couldn't believe his eyes. He couldn't believe a Negro had the courage to challenge him. I had nothing on me. If I had a pocket knife, and had been arrested, that's all they needed."*

It was E. D. Nixon who issued the call to all black preachers of the city as the bus boycott got under way. It was he who suggested the young pastor, Martin Luther King, Jr., as head of the Montgomery Improvement Association. The rest is history . . . and today . . .

Our hostess is tired, I know, though she tries not to show it. It has been an exhilarating two days. And something else, too. "Five vicious calls today," she says. It's not quite matter-of-fact, nor does it sound astonishing.

"Why?" somebody asks.

"Because I've got you in the house. They're like rattlesnakes. Anonymous letters. Children get kidded for having nigger lovers as parents." She's not talking about herself and Cliff now; they've been through this too long. Threats, idle or real, are not on her mind. It's a historic moment and she sees a lesson.

"The issue is people or money. I reckon I sound like an old New

* Studs Terkel, *Hard Times* (New York: Pantheon Books, 1970).

Dealer and that's what I am. I do wish that all those lovely people who came down here today and who are leaving today would go back home and fight it out on their home grounds. We're here and we, who love the South, can't leave it. We can set the pattern down here that can be a lesson for the rest of the world. The South can be a new Jerusalem."

Cliff is reflective. During all the day's exhilaration, he has been listening quietly; occasionally, talking quietly. He sees this as more than a "Southern problem." He sees parallels. "The pattern of human behavior is pretty much the same." He remembers his tenure in Washington. He saw how McCarthy took over. How the Dies Committee was laughed at, at first. How fear took over. The silence of people "who didn't want to get their immaculate linen splattered with mud." How they justified muteness: "We don't like excess, but he's alerting us to danger."

"Here it isn't really prejudice. It's conformity. There was moderate Southern reaction, in many circles, to the 1954 Supreme Court decision. Had Eisenhower gone on TV and made an appeal, he'd have given decent people down here courage to speak out. He did nothing. The White Citizens' Councils moved into the vacuum. The hoodlums beat tribal tom-toms. In a year, the leaders came to make the same noises. While slogans were shouted by demagogues, the good people talked about grandchildren, fishing, and football.

"Civil rights is an unfortunate term. Civil liberties is the issue. In Washington, if you shouted 'Red,' the other had to prove he was a good American. 'Nigger lover' is the trigger word here. The Southern tradition is invoked as if there were only one. We had antislavery societies here more than anywhere else. After the Civil War, the Yanceys took over. William Yancey was a counterpart of George Wallace. Came the fear of being labeled.

"When you have a sense of being attacked from the outside, you point to the wrongs in the North. What right have hypocritical Yankees to lecture us? There's a basis for this, but I think the South should set its own standards.

"My feelings today are mixed. I hate to see pressure, though it is essential. We should have done it ourselves. I have the same feeling about our visitors. They will go back home, but will they shut their eyes to problems there?"

There are about five or six of us left. It's later than we had thought. The phone rings. Someone on the other end says a woman has been shot on her way back to Selma. There has been scattered shooting at cars of civil rights workers along the road. National Guard protection had ceased at four in the afternoon.

An angry John Beecher is on the phone. The FBI is reticent; information is grudgingly offered. Beecher is pulling teeth. "You have her name, don't you?" His ancestral Abolitionist blood is boiling. "Spell it, please. L-I-U-Z-Z-O. From Detroit, you say?" There is silence in the parlor.

The good-byes are murmured. Myles Horton says something to E. D. Nixon, as all of us are leaving. "You've had that call before, many times, I suppose." Nixon nods. We shuffle out into the dark. Out among the magnolias.

Friday morning, Six-thirty. I'm in a cab, heading for the airport. On my lap, the *Montgomery Advertiser*. The headline is about a civil rights worker who was killed last night. Her picture is on the front page. Viola Liuzzo. I remember her. She's that ebullient young woman who greeted us at the airport about forty hours ago. Oh yeah.

The cabbie is a good-looking blond kid in his early twenties. His charcoal-gray straw hat is perched, comically, on top of his head. He is easy of manner and exudes an open, good nature. Every once in a while, he squints at the rear-view mirror. We're the only car on the road; he can't be concerned with traffic. I catch his eye; he's studying me.

"Too bad about that woman," he drawls. A slow, easy drawl.

"Yeah," I mumble.

"Most people come down here is out of place."

"How's that?"

"Even though it may be a nationwide thing, most people has got the wrong impression of the whole thing."

I don't have to say anything. He's dying to let it out. My raised eyebrow is enough.

"Martin Luther King is the worst kind of nigger and that's the kind of nigger that causes trouble. All he does is stirring up these people and causes trouble among our niggers. He's just doin' it to make money and he's makin' money off the local niggers." A note of hurt in his voice. "He's talkin' about God sendin' him here to Alabama. We know the Bible says the devil comes as an angel of light. If King claims to be the big preacher as he does and leads marches on towns, that's not the kind of religion the Bible teaches. Around here, we know most niggers is peaceful. We know that King comes down here to make money. These niggers down here are uneducated. They don't know everything that's goin' on."

I lay back against the leather and shut my eyes. I've had little sleep and could use some shut-eye. I think of a 104-year-old black preacher, puffing away at a fifteen-cent cigar. "Man ain't nothin' but an animal. After all, he's just the highest type of animal . . ." Fool that I am, I blurt out a word, a trigger word. Like a wayward husband, mumbling a strange love's name in his sleep. I, eyes closed, mutter, "Wallace."

It delights and saddens the youngblood. "People down here have more respect for George Wallace than any governor I ever known." His voice takes on a singsong quality, much like a young mother's lullaby, though, unfortunately, it affords me no comfort. "They know that if any governor comes out of office a broke man, it'll be Governor Wallace. He's spent every penny he's got. He's dedicated his whole life to the benefit of the people of Alabama and that includes niggers same as whites. He's proved this over and over again. Governor Wallace has done it. All King does is talk. After this is over, we're gonna have the same thing."

"Will your life be different?"

"Naw, sir."

For the first time I notice his freckles. He has clear blue eyes. And a face of innocence.

We reach the terminal.

4

Big Bill

> This train is bound for glory, this train
> This train is bound for glory, this train
> This train is bound for glory
> Nobody ride it but the righteous and the holy
> This train is bound for glory
> Now this train.

What would Big Bill Broonzy have thought of Freedom Summer, sit-ins, the March on Washington, Selma to Montgomery . . . ? Often, he comes to mind.

Big Bill died at five-thirty A.M. It was a rainy, stormy morning, as though to signify a big man passing through. August 15, 1958. He was on his way to a Chicago hospital. He was somewhere between sixty-one and sixty-four years old. Did he have a birth certificate? In Scott, Mississippi, a baby as black as William Lee Conley Broonzy may not have made a howling appearance on the county rolls. His twin sister says he was sixty-one. Let it go at that.

It is 1947. Or is it '48? Four of us are in a jalopy, bump-bump-bumping through a quiet Indiana town, or so it seems. Lafayette, here we come. We're on our way to Purdue University. We've been on the road ten days, give or take a day. We've been offering concerts at colleges in the Midwest. "I Come for To Sing" we call our program.

Big Bill sings country blues, many of his own, others of his friends'. Win Stracke sings frontier songs. Larry Lane offers Elizabethan ballads. I am the narrator, and piece them together, after a fashion. In any event, at this moment we are tired, hungry, and thirsty.

We pull up near a tavern. It's a workingmen's haven. Through the window, we see craggy faces, lumberjacket shirts, blue denim, and a young, pudgy, laughing bartender. A spirit of bonhomie pervades. It reflects the energy of a John Steuart Curry. It is pleasing, especially to Win and me. How often have we performed for laboring men such as these; at union meetings, rallies, soup kitchens, and on the picket line. We envision a shot, a few beers, and a liver sausage sandwich or two.

"Uh oh," says Bill. "They won't serve me. You guys go in. Bring me a ham sandwich. I got some whiskey here." He smacks his pocket.

Damn. Win and I are indignant. Bill had cast no more than a casual, almost imperceptible glance that way. How does he know? How dare he jump to such conclusions? These are, after all, hardworking guys, decent men. He smiles. Aw, come on Bill, fer Chrissake! Let's take a vote, somebody says. Bill is outpolled, three to one. Larry Lane, gentle Larry, says, "Really, Bill . . ." The minority of one sighs, as though he's gone this route before. "Okay," he says, "you win."

As we enter, all conversation ceases. Did somebody, the Great Engineer, press the STOP button? We stroll toward the bar. You can cut the silence with a knife, a sharp knife. It is *High Noon*. Wow, it's a long walk. Did it seem that long to Gary Cooper?

Shot and a beer is the order for four. Say, that liver sausage looks awfully good. The man behind the bar is genial enough. Politely, he murmurs, "I can serve three of you gentlemen."

> I was in a place one night
> They was all havin' fun
> They was all buyin' beer and wine
> But they would not sell me none. . . .

Win's lyric bass, *furioso*, is heard by all assembled. Aside from Bill, he's the biggest man in the place. The richness of his tone is, in this instance, unappreciated. I am muttering something, impotently and absurdly. Larry looks sad. The bartender is sorry, too, he says, though he's smiling as he says it. The profane gibberish the three of us mumble is of small matter. We are licked, as we slink out, X-rayed as we are by the hooded eyes of good, solid workingmen. One man is laughing softly. It is Bill. We are losers, the three of us without and the clods within. Only Bill is the winner, a laughing winner.

> You know I can't lose
> Baby, I can't lose
> Not with this moppin' broom I use. . . .

Lafayette, here we go. We are driving around and around and around. Nobody says much of anything. Bill chuckles to himself; his own private joke. He doesn't rub it in; that's not his way. He merely knows what he knows and now he knows that we know. He passes the bottle around. Never has a green whiskey gone down so quickly, though harshly.

"There's a place," he says. He points toward a fancy-looking tea room. Is the man crazy? We have just been given the boot by the lower class; this is definitely upper class; in any event, genteel middle. Oh well, what can we lose? Perhaps the man knows something.

Two little old Edith Wharton ladies welcome us. It isn't liver sausage, but it'll do. Lead, kindly light. As I remember, the sun slants its way through lace curtains, casting a filigreed shadow on the floor; the appointments are neat but not gaudy; and the ladyfinger'd treats are sustaining enough. An endearing moment.

(As I attend to this memoir, Win Stracke reminds me that our two hostesses had ushered us perkily and politely into the kitchen rather than the dining room. How dare he throw such a curve at me? It's *my* memory. And didn't Ivy Compton-Burnett speak of life as no more than a mounting block for art? Unfortunately—or is it fortunately?—I had, at the time, neither a Uher nor a Sony as a corroborating companion. Were I a betting man, though, I'd bet on Win. Damn it.)

How *does* Bill know such things? What makes him a student of social behavior? He's no sociologist. Where did he get his degree? He's no expert in urban studies.

> I was born in Mississippi
> Arkansas is where I'm from. . . .

"Man I worked for in Arkansas, all his kids went to college. Come home doctors, lawyers, girl a schoolteacher. I wished I could go to college some day. Well, I did. I went to college in Ames." True. At Iowa State, not long after our concert there, he landed a job as campus janitor.

It's Big Bill's razor-whet lovely sense of irony that's enabled him to get from here to there and back. Cheated, euchred, gypped, triple-crossed, he invariably comes up with an ace.

On a visit to his "mama" (born in slavery, died in 1957 at the age of 102), he drives his big secondhand Buick into a filling station. It's just outside Little Rock. Long, long before Carol Channing's little girl from Little Rock and certainly long before Orval Faubus lived in the mansion. (Ironically, young Orval may have been, at the time, attending Commonwealth College in Mena, Arkansas; a cooperative, radical school.) A colored man is driving what appears to be a luxury auto. Nasty Charlie, at the gas pump, is about to get especially so.

"Whose car is this, boy?"

"Man I work for, my boss," says Bill, as a matter of course. Of course.

Bill is speaking the truth, *his* truth. Always, he has been his own boss. Always, he has worked for himself, even when he worked for others. Not at the age of eight, perhaps. That's when he started in as a plow hand, under the tutelage of his father, a Mississippi cotton farmer. From then on, though, he was on his own. Gandy dancer, porter, short order cook, molder, preacher, piano mover. Mover and shaker.

I notice this about Bill. No matter how humiliating the circumstance, he never allows himself to be humiliated. Nor does he ever get belligerent. Oh, I've seen him sore. Oh yeah. He has a way, out of necessity, of making adjustments.

"My mama always said when you got your hand in the lion's mouth, don't do nothin' till you get it out."

Is it 1956? We're performing at a folk club in Chicago. Bill is singing "Plow Hand Blues." It is an astonishing moment, as he evokes a portrait of a Delta life in all its tragic breadth. It is his *cante jondo*, his deep song. Some flamenco artist, somewhere, may be as soaring, though I'll have to hear it to believe it. I've heard Bill sing this scores of time, but tonight it is different. He has never sounded this way. I am floored.

> I wouldn't tell a mule to get up
> No, if he sit down in my lap
> I wouldn't tell a mule to get up
> No, if he sit down in my lap
> Now I declare I'm through with plowin'
> Ooohhh, Lord, that's what killed my old grandpap.

Now the guitar cries out. It is only Bill's guitar that stings in this manner. There is a moment in Satyajit Ray's film *Pather Panchali*: the little girl dies, the mother screams; we hear, not her voice, but the wild sitar of Ravi Shankar. Only that instant, to me, equals Bill's.

I hear a scraping of chairs. Insolently loud. Four young hipsters, heavy-lidded, two white, two black, are standing up. Once again, they scrape their chairs. They shuffle out slowly, deliberately so. One of them makes a joke; the others laugh. Cool, man.

Later, at the bar, seated next to Bill, I am raging. Bill is amused. On other occasions, as M.C., I have easily, casually quieted drunks and other disturbers of the peace. Tonight, at that moment, I was stunned, and, as in a bad dream, stared at the young barbarians. Bill pats me on the shoulder. He finds me very funny. He buys me a drink.

"Place I work for in Buffalo, man pays me off first night, first set." Bill is talking as though nothing unusual had happened tonight. "He says they don't like what you singin'. Who wants to hear that old-time stuff? Horse and buggy. Nobody's gonna pay to hear that these days."

"Listen . . ." I say to Bill, "I don't give a damn about that bastard in Buffalo. What happened here tonight . . ."

"*You* listen," says Bill. "I'm talkin' 'bout a mule dyin' on me. What do these kids know 'bout a mule? They never seen a mule. How do you expect somebody to feel 'bout somethin' he don't know? When I was in Europe, all those places, Milano, London, Hamburg, I seen cities bombed out. People tellin' me about bombin's. What do I know about a bomb? The only bomb I ever did see was in the pictures. People scared, cryin', losin' their homes. What do I know 'bout that. I never had no bomb fall on me. Same thing with these kids. They never had no mule die on 'em. They don't even know what the hell I'm talkin' 'bout."

That Bill. Not that he didn't have a frailty or two or three. Sometimes, he'd get us in one hell of a jam. There was that night at the Blue Note. It was a jazz club, the best in Chicago. Frank Holzfeind, who ran it, took a fancy to "I Come for To Sing." He especially admired Bill. We worked the place on Mondays. Usually, it is dark that night, as Duke or Count or Benny or Fatha Hines rested. We drew fairly good crowds, although I'm certain Frank didn't make a nickel on us. We lasted more than a year of Mondays.

This night, the place is, for some inexplicable reason, jammed. Duke is in the house, too. He digs Big Bill. It is nine o'clock. Where is Bill? We're due to go on—now. I call the Broonzy home. His wife Rose answers.

"He's on his way . . ." she says.

"Good," I say, giving Frank the a-okay sign.

". . . to England," says Rose.

So that's why Bill, just the other day, had given me the phone numbers of Memphis Minnie, Tampa Red, and Roosevelt Sykes. During his sabbatical, one or the other of them shouted the blues at the Blue Note. Why didn't he tell us about England, damn it? It comes to me after a cooling off. God, after years and years and years on the razor's edge, of close shaves with The Man, avoidance of head-to-head had become a habit he couldn't break. No matter. On this night, I am furious. Yet why, throughout the two performances, are we laughing? Is it because I recognize myself in Bill's cop-out? Haven't I, all my life, avoided scenes?

> My suitcase packed, my trunk's already gone
> Now you know about that, baby
> Big Bill won't be here long. . . .

No scenes, no recriminations. Especially with women. As for his feelings toward them, consider Leporello's *Madamina*. Yet there is one difference: the blues singer is far more gentle than the Spanish Don. Big Bill's women have all been warmhearted. Some less than others. Some more so.

> Willie Mae, don't you hear me callin' you
> If I don't get my Willie Mae
> I declare there ain't no other woman will do.

Fond memories. Sly ones. All become a piece of Broonzy poetry. Consider his way with the pretenders. Often, he comments on caste, especially among his own people.

> She said her mother was a Creole
> And an Indian was her dad.

The black-skinned singer remembers being denied admission to the church of which his light-skinned grandmother was a member. Here, Bill touches on a universal ethnic truth. How often the nose of the German Jew is out of joint when he encounters the Polish Jew. With what hauteur the blond Florentine passes by the swarthy Calabrese. And in what tone of voice does the "lace curtain" Irish refer to the "turkey"?

Big Bill has lost track of the exact number of blues he's written;

some 360, give or take a half-dozen. So many he had handed to others. "Why not? If it suits 'em better'n me, why shouldn't they have it? Don't do any good layin' aroun' here. It's all wrote."

And he insists on keeping green the memory and song of his friends no longer here. "Leroy Carr, he's gone. Big Maceo, he's gone. Jim Jackson, Richard M. Jones, ol' Lead, they're gone. If I don't sing their blues, who will? Maybe the blues'll die some day. But I'll have to die first."

It is early in 1958. Bill is seated all by himself in an enormous room. It is his last session. His voice may not be what it was, but it is strong enough. His breathing is labored, but when he sings, he calls upon some reservoir yet untapped. Listen: he wants to sing *all* the blues of *all* his friends. And he wants to say something about each. It may take two days, it may take three days . . .

Three of us are in the control room. The engineer Bill Randle, the Cleveland disk jockey who is bearing the expense, and I. We say nothing. More than a window glass is between the singer and us. We are strangers, friendly strangers, but strangers nonetheless. Big Bill is crossing that lonesome valley and he's crossing it by himself.

He is miles away, dirt roads and turnpikes of miles away. And how many, many years away? But it is *now* that counts. He is wasting no time.

"Machine goin'?"

I nod. The impersonal spool of tape is revolving. He murmurs into the mike: "I'm gonna sing some blues of other guys. Friends of mine. They're all gone. That's why I'm gonna sing 'em."

Leroy Carr. A faint smile plays around his mouth. "Once I remember me an' some other guys, we went over to his house an' woked him up in the middle of the night, got him outa bed an' made him sing this blues."

> In the evenin', in the evenin'
> Mama, when the sun go down. . . .

How many times have I heard him sing this one. There is that one Sunday afternoon; this I remember above all others. It is a memorial for Jimmy Yancey, who has just died. Mama Yancey is in the audience, rocking, keening, moaning softly, "Sing it, baby, sing it." Eyes closed, head toward the heavens, Bill is shouting for the widow. For all widows. Even the cool dead-eyed young men and their cool dead-eyed girls who patronize this pseudo-Bohemian tavern stop their play-acting at the bar. Even they are astonished.

> Yes, it's so lonesome, it's so lonesome
> I declare, when the one you love is not aroun'
> When the sun go down.

This night at the studio, Bill is singing for keeps. The vibrating "yeah-ay-ay-ay-ay oooh-oooh-oooh" is more than just a lamentation for a woman gone off. It is for life itself.

> So good-bye, old sweethearts and pals
> Yes, I declare I'm goin' away
> I may be back to see you again, little girl
> Some old rainy day. . . .

As he finishes, he says to the mike, "He's gone." A pause.

Richard M. Jones. "He's the man who wrote this next song." Bill tells about a girl, Georgia White. It was her big hit. "Good-lookin', friendly, all the fellas liked her. Her husband watched her every move. He was her valet, he dressed her, he looked after her every need."

> I'm troubled in mind, baby, I'm so blue
> But I won't be blue always
> You know the sun, sun gonna shine
> In my back door someday.

As he finishes this one, he says to the mike, "He's gone."

Leadbelly. "He was foreman, what we call straw boss of the work gang. 'At's how he got his name Leadbelly. Him an' Sleepy John Estes. He'd sit under the tree while the other guys did the work. His hips was gettin' full of lead."

> Take this hammer, take it to the captain
> Tell 'im I'm gone, tell 'im I'm gone. . . .

It isn't sung Leadbelly's way. Bill is singing it his way. A different tempo, a different feel. Yet, it's a work song, all right. Both men did more than their share of it. I'm thinking of Leadbelly, as Bill remembers him.

Leadbelly is driving the car. Duke of Iron, the Calypso singer, and I are in the back seat. We have come from a concert in Urbana,

TALKING TO MYSELF

at the University of Illinois. Pete Seeger, Brownie McGhee, and Betty Sanders are in the other car. Leadbelly is driving pretty fast, too fast. He has the unfortunate tendency of looking backwards as he talks. Stupidly, I ask him about an early experience. He delights in telling the story, as he gestures with one hand. The other is lightly on the wheel. *He is looking directly at us.* We're hitting about eighty miles an hour. Duke and I are terrified. We cling to one another. In his precise West Indian dialect, Duke pleads, "Oh, please, Huddie Ledbetter, please do not look at us." I'm too scared to say anything. Is that a Mack truck coming our way? We are zigzagging on either side of the white line. Leadbelly is driving the car as though it were a tractor. He is in high good humor. How we reach Chicago in one piece is something I have not yet quite figured out. Leadbelly enjoyed the trip.

> If he asks you was I laughin'
> Tell 'im I was cryin'. . . .

Song ended, the murmur: "He's gone."

Time out. Time out for all of us.

It is Saturday. Bill is going under the knife the following Monday. He has a feeling; he can't be kidded. It isn't the illness that worries him so much. It's the knife. Will they go at his throat? No, the doctors have told him. It's the lung. But the knife . . .

One day, in explaining how he writes a blues, he chose the knife as the subject. "How many things can you do with a knife? You can cut fish, you can cut your toenails. I seen guys shave with it, you can eat beans with it, you can kill a man. There. You name five things you can do with a knife, you got five verses. You got yourself a blues."

He is staring silently at the mike. Where is he? On a Mississippi field, helping his tenant-farmer father, pushing a single sweep at the age of eight and quickly graduating to the double shovel? Or is he in Arkansas, just outside Little Rock, where a young, strong way-better-than-six-foot plow hand is turning up the loam? London? Paris? Amsterdam? Marseilles? Where an American singer of the raw blues is shouting out his life?

Senegal? Bill's visit to West Africa was an overwhelming experience. Always, he talked of it. "I look at these people an' I felt I must have been there before, my people I mean. All my family is

tall. I looked at these seven-footers, I felt like a midget. I run into
a family called Broonzie. They spelt it 'ie' instead of 'y,' but it was
the same name. Yeah, I think my ancestors came from there."

Senegal. How could Bill recount any experience without humor?
He remembers a night in Dakar. "In this club, I see this beautiful
girl. I'm goin' over to her, but a man says no, no, she belongs to
somebody else. He points to a Senegalese. That don't bother me. I
had a few drinks. Just then, somebody comes in askin' for help. His
car is stuck in a hole outside. This Senegalese, he stands up . . ."

Bill pauses in the telling. His eyes go up, up, up in his head. His
head goes up, up, up. I see the Senegalese, too. He is at least fifteen
feet tall. Bill casually continues, "The guy goes outside an' all by
hisself he lifts the whole back of that car an' sets it on the road."
Bill pauses. I see the guy, too. He's Jean Valjean.

"Well, what happened?" I ask Bill. He has given no indication
of continuing the story.

"Whatcha mean what happened?" My question appears to have
bewildered Bill.

"What about the girl?"

"What girl?" asks Bill innocently.

Bill's fingers play lightly over the guitar. Slowly, easily, the memories, the songs, flow. Men named See See Rider and Stonewall
Jackson. Women named Alberta and Crow Jane. Negro reels from
slavery days. "My uncle wasn't freed till he was twenty." He smiles
as he remembers family disputes, sinful songs his uncle sang to his
mother's disapproval. "She run him outa the house." Spirituals. "The
blues can't die because it's a natural steal from the spiritual. I sung
spirituals before I sung the blues."

> Ananias, Ananias, tell me what kind of man Jesus is
> Spoke to the wind, wind stopped still
> Spoke to the sea, sea got ca'm
> Spoke to the sick, sick got well
> Spoke to the dead, dead did rise
> . . . Tell me what kind of man Jesus is.

"Younger people say you're cryin' when you sing like that. Who
wants to cry? Back in them days, people had nothin' else to do but
cry. Today, they do nothin' but talk."

Softly, he goes into "Swing Low, Sweet Chariot." I have never,
ever heard it, really, till now. It is not the way I heard it in school.

Not the way the Fisk Jubilee Singers did it. Not the way Paul
Robeson or Marian Anderson did it. Nor was it Mahalia's way. It
was Bill's way. A man was calling out . . .

> I-i-i-i look to Jordan, now what did I see
> Comin' fer to carry me home
> A-a-a-a-a band of angels, comin' to me
> Comin' fer to carry me home
> I-i-i-i-f you get there before I do
> Ple-e-e-ease tell them all that I'm comin' too
> Comin' fer to carry me home.

"Home" sounding ever so soft after the imploring call. Journey's
end.

We know this is the last one. Everybody can tell. It's the way Bill
looks at his guitar. Now he looks at us. An intimation of a smile.
How I know that smile. I glare at the revolving reel.

Bill is retuning his guitar. This one calls for extra-special tuning.
"You guys can go for a drink while I'm doin' this." We do so. Now
he's ready.

We hear a guitar, but it's like no guitar we've ever heard. It's a
human voice, not one but a whole ramshackle town. Now Bill is
talking as the guitar moans. A simple narrative of a terrible flood,
people losing homes, crops, everything. And Joe Turner comes
along, he's two men—a white and a black—and he helps out. "And
they would start cryin' an' singin' this song." And now that chord—
whang!—only it isn't that—it's crying, everybody's crying—a cry of
salvation.

Big Bill packs up and goes home.

5

Northern Lights

It is midnight as the plane lands. The Northern Lights, green and yellow, are dancing all over the sky. My brother danced that way at Dreamland.

We have come to Kiruna. It is five hundred miles to the north of Stockholm. We're in the Arctic Circle. Here is one of the largest iron mines in the world. Here, three years ago, slightly more, in December 1969, was a wildcat strike against the company, state-owned. It was Sweden's most astonishing and celebrated strike in forty years.

Karen Lindholm is our driver. Her husband is a city fireman. They have two small children. Her father worked in the Kiruna mines. "He died of heart trouble. I think it was from too much hard work . . ."

Down in the Kiruna mine, a young man is drilling at rock and gravel. The light is dim. It is noisy. He is wearing huge earmuffs. I've stuffed lamb's wool in my ears. He is twenty-six. He came from a small town near Kiruna, and has been on this job six years. Yes, he took part in the strike. Too low wages. He puts in eight hours a day, five days a week. He has a small boy. No, he wouldn't mind his son being a miner.

A young Finn, excited by the presence of visitors, is grinning as he sits high on the truck. He is driving it around and around and around. He is a wild and carefree cowboy. He is eighteen. It is his

first real job. He is elated. Especially at a time when jobs are not
to be had for the asking. Where he came from, everybody is very,
very poor. Had he ever heard of the strike? No. All he knows is: he
has a *job*. He's happy. He spins the truck around with a daredevil's
verve . . .

An old union man tells of the grievances that led to the strike.
The miners hadn't received a raise in ten years. Prices had gone up.
Taxes were heavy. People to the south were much better paid. Piece-
work was wearing them out. They wanted a monthly wage. Condi-
tions were bad, especially the air. It was a redress of these grievances
they sought. Further, the strike would acquaint the rest of the
country with their circumstances. What did Stockholm know of
Kiruna? The strike lasted seven weeks. It was won. It has become
something of a Swedish saga.

We are 540 meters down into the bowels of the earth. It is not
too deep, as mines go. Still, it is the largest underground mine in
the world. I am wearing boots, a raincoat, and a rainhat. In the
changing room I see my reflection. I am the Uneeda Biscuit Boy.

In 1921 I am the Uneeda Biscuit Boy as I go down under
Niagara Falls. My mother wants me to see it. She'll not go down
with me. It's a gyp, but she thinks I ought to have the experience.
At the seedy Buffalo hotel, she had words with the clerk. We were
gypped, she says. At Niagara Falls, we are riding around in a cab.
She and the driver have words. He's overcharging us, she says.
Naturally. I am sinking deep into the leather. He suggests we take
a sightseeing bus. He'd be glad to let us off. I put my two cents in;
oil on troubled waters. She gently pushes me back into the leather.
"Drive on, robber," she says. It's all right, under the Falls. Nothing
astonishing.

In 1962 I am the Uneeda Biscuit Boy. I am five thousand feet
down in the Vlakfontein gold mine. It's not very far from Johannesburg. The lift is very fast. Everything is efficient here. No more than
three minutes ago, I was above ground with Mr. Buchanan, the
safety director. He was explaining how young men can do very well
working in this South African mine.

They start on livable salaries. They are trained for three years.
After that time, they can become shift bosses, mine overseers, and,
eventually, managers. The rental of their homes is nominal. Look

at their gardens. They have barbecues, tennis courts, and bowling on the green. At the club, which they can join, all the drinks are very fine and very cheap. Buses pick up their children and take them to any school they desire.

I am impressed.

"You're talking about whites?"

"Yes, of course."

A small black man, wizened, age indeterminate, is called over.

"Boy" Mr. Buchanan's voice is sharp, precise, authoritative.

"Yes, baas."

"How long have you been here?"

"Since 1937, baas."

"Why do you come back to the mines?" Mr. Buchanan's tone is kindly, fatherly.

"Whooo-aaa—I'm comin' from Naga . . ." He doesn't appear to get the drift.

Mr. Buchanan's voice is no-nonsense now. His questions shoot out in machine-gun tempo. "Why do you work in the mines? Is it good to you? Does it treat you well?"

"Yes, baas."

"You're very satisfied with the mines?"

"Yes, baas."

"You hear that?" Mr. Buchanan addresses me. I heard it.

"Come on, let's 'ave a look." We march to the compound, where three thousand "boys" are quartered.

The compound is circular, surrounded by high walls.

"Why is it shaped this way?" asks Jack Wallace.

"You can have a good vantage point at all times," says the manager of the compound.

"Why is that necessary?" asks Jack. He sounds even more the *naïf* than I.

"It's just that you can see everything for every situation," explains the manager. "Everything's within striking distance."

There are twenty to a room; ten double-deckers. A stove is in the middle. "Once a week, they can get raw meat, which they can cook 'ere."

"What are they eating now?" asks Jack. He's something of a gourmet.

"Offal with curry and porridge," says the manager. He addresses a "boy," who has his mouth full.

"You like it? Very satisfyin', right?"

The "boy" nods vigorously.

We file into the huge kitchen. The blacks watch us without expression. The mess hall manager says, " 'Ere's the bread. It's lovely stuff. Some of the finest you can get." I taste it. *Chacun à son goût.* "Kaffir beer. Two percent alcohol. If you drink a bottle of this a day, you'll have no more stomach ache, I promise. Taste it, if it suits you. It's an acquired taste." He's right. It is an acquired taste.

They have been recruited from Portuguese East Africa, Rhodesia, "German West," Angola, as well as the kraals of South Africa. There is a wild pluralism of different languages and dialects. "We keep all the tribes separated, so there will be no fights," says another who has the mellifluous voice of Alec Guinness. Is that why? I don't ask it, I'm just wondering.

There is a common patois, spoken in the mines. Everybody is taught it. Kitchen Kaffir. The South African Broadcasting Company does not allow the word "Kaffir" to be used on any of its channels. It is derogatory to black people, Carl Douglas Fuchs, the chief, had told me. Mr. Fuchs made it clear that the government is very conscientious in its efforts to avoid any offense to blacks.

Black miners are engaged by the NRC, Native Recruiting Corps. It has agents in the kraals and depots in the cities. "They flock to these jobs," says Mr. Buchanan. Do I detect a hurt in his voice? "They are not as pushed around as outside people think they are. You've seen no boy abused, 'ave you? The atmosphere is contentment. It doesn't cost 'em a penny when they come 'ere. When they leave, they can sit around home for a six-month 'oliday and come back. Believe me, very few Europeans in Africa can do that." I believe him.

"They come back time after time. If they weren't contented, they wouldn't come back."

"How long is a contract?" asks Jack.

"It may be from four months upwards. When a boy signs a contract, he's got to fulfill it."

We're heading toward the mouth of the mine. My tape is almost running out. Should I change reels now? No, I can just get one more question in.

"Suppose one of them runs off before the contract ends?"

"He's classed as a deserter," snaps Mr. Buchanan. "Come on, let's 'ave a look." I guess he's tired of the conversation. I change reels. We enter the lift.

There is drilling; rock breaking; the stope, a horizontal shaft, where the miner works in a crouch. A red band on the wrist indicates a "first-rate boy." He can do any work. A green band is for the one not as strong. See, they *are* considerate. A young white guy, the shift boss, is urging the men on in kitchen Kaffir. He's quite authoritative for one so young.

We're in the smelting department. A fiery furnace. A huge vat. Molten gold, the color of the hot sun. It is all ablaze. We are overwhelmed. There is a gold bar on the table. Nobody says anything. We are in a Presence. Softly, a murmur is heard. "Nine hundred troy ounces. Twenty-eight thousand dollars." I move toward it. I try to lift it. It doesn't budge.

"So this is what's it's all about," I say.

There is light laughter.

A voice says, "What 'appens, you people just lock it up eventually at Fort Knox."

Much laughter.

A young Finn, ruggedly handsome, is seated behind the desk. He is a top union officer, highly respected by everybody in the community. He had been one of the leaders, one of the heroes, of the strike. A firebrand. He comes from a long tradition of radical Finns. He's the one I've been looking for, I'm sure. During a long stream of conversations with labor officials who had weathered all the troubles, I was missing something. The *feel*. What was it really like? As I press the ON lever, I'm like a gold prospector who sees the glint in the dust. I'm excited.

We are talking for what seems a good hour. The spent cassette tells me that. I am vaguely unhappy. Something is not happening. I know that in his recollections he is trying his damnedest, but nothing is coming forth that I can put my hands on. I hear the words—"struggle," "workers," "bosses," "solidarity"—yet I feel no spark.

On the way to the airport, bound once again for Stockholm, I'm restless, disappointed. I discovered much, except that which I most sought. I found out little about the people who had taken part in what appeared to be a memorable event—a strike against the state.

Karen Lindholm is driving. The Sony is ON. A matter of habit. Karen is describing the landscape, I'm half-listening: I'm dead tired. Perhaps it's something in her voice . . .

I remember her saying something two days ago. Something about her father dying of heart trouble. She thought it was overwork. Perhaps . . .

"Do you remember the strike, Karen?"

"Oh yes." She is speaking even more softly than usual. Her eyes are luminous.

"What do you remember?"

"It was very cold, in the middle of winter. They were walking in the darkness. Nobody said a word. There was no sound. I could hear nothing more than the feet in the snow. They were marching like soldiers. They had tears in their eyes. I can still see that picture."

She pauses. She makes a sharp turn in the road. I hold tight my tape recorder. I glare at the cassette. It's revolving.

"They were fighting for something which we all knew—they must be right. That's what we felt."

"Was it a sudden event?" I hardly hear myself.

"I think it's something that had been in the mind for years. I remember when I was a small girl, we went out. It was the part of town where mostly the engineers lived. We went down there one day to pick blueberries, some children. And a lady came out and said, 'You have no business here. It's for engineers' children. Go back . . .'"

Another turn in the road. The airport is in sight. The tape is almost running out. I sneak a glance at her. Her eyes are glistening.

"The difference between the people on the top and the workers. The strike-workers realized they were somebody. Some workers read books. I don't think a great many, because of the language. Many are Finnish. And the hard work."

"Did your father read?"

"My father read quite a bit. From eleven years old on. When he started working in the forest and for the railroads. He was always interested in the workers' programs. Every day he talked of the mines. He told me about it. I was nearly twenty when I first went down to the mine. I saw how hard it was. He was building a railroad in the mine when he became ill . . . He died some years before the strike. Oh, he'd have liked that strike. When I saw those people outside, I thought of my father. I could nearly see him walking with a flag, his paper in his hand . . ."

The tape runs out. It's all right. Oh yeah, it's all right.

In a restaurant in Stockholm, on the day before my return to Chicago, I run into Karl Selander. He is in his middle sixties, lean, a touch weary; he is dressed neatly enough; his eyes twinkle. He and his missus are seated at a table, adjacent to that of me and my missus. He addresses me: "Excuse me, I have seen you on telewision yesterday." I have never seen him before. Yet he's familiar. God damn it, haven't I met him before?

Funny how it happened. On my penultimate day in Sweden, I see a play by Ionesco. It is *Macbett*. In the small auditorium of the Swedish National Theatre, I see a magnificent comic production. Though I know not a word of Swedish outside of *tack så mycket*, thank you very much, I dig this piece of theater. Harriet Andersson, one of Bergman's most ill-starred, put-upon, destroyed women, is wildly nutty and hilarious as a lecherous Lady Macbett. It's about the absurdity and clownishness of men in power.

During the second act intermission, I am approached in the lobby by someone from Swedish television. Nixon has this day fired Archibald Cox. Would I participate in a discussion on the air. Holy Christ. When?

Now. The program goes on in half an hour.

What about the last act of *Macbett?*

Well, you know he gets killed. How about it?

Okay.

Karl Selander leans over toward our table and says he liked what I said on television last night. One thing leads to another, you know? He's a retired welder, got sick on the job, his lungs. Oh yes, he is enjoying life. He has a nice pension. "My father met Mark Twain. You like Mark Twain?"

"Oh yeah."

"He was a pilot."

"Uh huh."

"My father also."

Wait a minute, wait a minute. Our plane leaves in a few hours. Where's the damn Sony? Oh, it's upstairs at the Diplomat. I look toward my wife. She looks toward the heavens. Do I hear a sigh?

"Yoseph Conrad, you like him?" Karl Selander looks at me. Has he found a kindred spirit?

I'm weak on Conrad.

"Too bad," he says. "I like Yoseph Conrad."

I shove my wristwatch three inches from my face. Hell, we've got lots of time. Would Mr. and Mrs. Selander honor us by having coffee and cognac at the hotel? It's just around the corner. I have this little machine, you see . . . ?

At the hotel we have some cognac and test the Sony. On occasion, during exhilarated moments, I have forgotten to press the ON lever. I lost Michael Redgrave that way. To test his voice, Karl sings:

> How dry I am, how dry I am
> Only God knows how dry I am . . .

"A friend of mine learned me this song in 1932. He came from Bridgeport, Connekticut. He was workless, he go back to Sweden.

"When I was a young man, we were very interested in politics. In the street, when we meet, we was speaking politics every night. We had meetings at four o'clock in the morning we finished. More than now. Too bad. They are more interested in cars, the vacation house. They playing bridge and talking about ice hockey and football. In my factory, where I work before I get sick, only five percent read political news in the paper. Too bad.

"I don't think I'm better than the others. I have only six years in school. But have plenty of books at my home. I have a bicycle. I live near the forest. We have elks, we have deer, we have foxes. I have a cat; he is fourteen years. I have a good wife. I have two daughters, academic. I have grandchildren. We have a yolly time together. You come back to Sweden and see me in my home. I have a wonderful view of Stockholm."

He studies me. "You are tired. I go now. When you come back . . ."

"No, no, no, no," I say. "Maybe you are tired?"

He laughs delightedly. "No, no. I have the high time of my life. I don't believe in God or destiny. I am agnostic. But after I meet you, I thank God I meet you." We laugh. The cognac is indubitably working. Aahhh, let's have another snifter. He proposes a toast in Swedish.

"I bought an antiquated book," he continues. He mentions the writer's name. I can't make it out. "She was friend of Bellman. You know him?"

This guy I know. He was the Robert Burns of Sweden. The Bard. Aksel Schiøtz, the Danish singer, had been one of my guests. He had recorded some of Bellman's lovely works. Karl is so happy that I know. He sings a snatch of one of Bellman's songs. "She write a diary. I have read it two times before.

"At last I'm going to write my life's history for my grandchildren to read. I have told my grandchildren about my life. Now I try to do my best to write to express my experience. I have no ambition to be Vilhelm Moberg." He laughs. "I just want my grandchildren to read it when I'm died." Softly, "Too bad I haven't any writer line to my father. Too bad."

Time out. We chat of this, that, and the other. He looks at the Sony. I press the ON lever.

"You know what I would like to do if I wasn't sick? Be a welder and go to Vietnam and work there. I'm good welder."

There is a long pause. I'm studying the cassette. It's moving.

He resumes. "I was in Mexico in 1968. In Oaxaca. I read much about history of art in Oaxaca. I save money. I stop smoking in 1956. I save all my cigarette money and I pay a ticket by Air France by Paris, Boston, Mexico City. And I pay for extra journey to Oaxaca to study Azteca and Maya culture."

Apropos of nothing, he says, "Excuse my English, not very good." Oh boy. I protest. We're slightly smashed now. He sings "How Dry I Am" in an operatic fashion. We laugh. He sings a little nonsense song in Swedish. "I sing it for my grandchildren. I made it myself in a fantasy." He sings an old radical workers' song in Swedish. I hear the word *arbeta*.

"You like Einstein?" he asks.

"Sure."

"He says art is more than the scientific . . . You like Voltaire?"

I like Voltaire.

"Voltaire says a blind man can't see but the lame can show him the way. You like Gibbon?"

I like Gibbon, too.

"I love Gibbon," he says. "I have Gibbon at home."

"Plutarch? You like him?"

"I like you," I say.

"Immanuel Kant," he says. He pauses. A long silence. I am trying to stay awake. The cognac. He is wide awake. "Yeah?" I mumble.

"Immanuel Kant, he said feeling is stronger than . . ." Again, Karl Selander pauses. He shuts his eyes, as though trying to remember something. He opens them again. Another thought?

"Hitler said to people in the thirties, they kill but they don't run on the grass. They was educated to keep off the grass. You can't go on the grass, but you can shoot him." He addresses me. "That's the situation in the world today, isn't it?"

We say good-bye four times. In Swedish and in English. At the

door he looks once again at the Sony. I stumble back and press the
ON lever.

"I like music," he says. "You listen to Palestrina, organ, that's
heaven. Oh, music . . . Mahalia Yackson. You know her?"

Yeah. What? I look up at him. I'm wide awake now. "How do you
know about Mahalia Jackson?" I ask.

"I heard her on Swedish radio. A man, he talk about religion.
When she sings gospels, that's better than when the priest is speaking.
Now she's die."

"You like her, huh?"

"Oh, I like her very much. I like it when the bells are ringing, not
when the priest is speaking."

God damn it, I knew he looked familiar. Of course. I know
who Karl Selander is. He's McPherson, passing me a little nickel blue
book. He's Sprague, slipping a buck in the flowered hat of Lucy
Parsons. He's Bob Warner, the lover man. He's One-Arm Cholly,
waving his stub. He's Civilization, scribbling letters to the world.
He's my brother Ben, dancing on a dime. He's the whole damn,
dream-possessed bunch, ringing bells . . .

I am in my mother's hotel. I am standing outside the door.

Afterword

The early eighties.

My red muffler is whipped across the shoulder of my black rain-coat, which I've slung around myself; my instant cape. I am Lau-trec's Aristide Bruant. I am slouched on the side seat in the rear of a Chicago bus.

Across the aisle, loud and clear, are a couple of Stanley Kowal-ski's nephews. Their nubile companions, giggling for reasons that may be Classified, are in tight-fitting jeans and making the most of it. The air is celebratory.

I hear excited references to Kansas and Chicago.

"Stockyards, eh?" I interject. Just to get the ball rolling for better or for worse.

"Whaaa—?" declares one of the nephews.

"Kansas City and Chicago had two of the biggest. Sandburg, re-member? 'Hog Butcher for the World.' No more, I'm afraid. Gone to the feed lots."

"*Kansas* an' Chicago," corrects the acned wonder. "Dey're rock bands. Kansas City's a *city*. Kansas is rock."

It doesn't take a house to fall on me. The Aragon Ballroom is two stops ahead. Dark most of the time, it comes bleakly alive when the rockers, not quite Rolling Stones or The Who, come to town. The marquee is looming larger. Despite a light bulb or two out here and there, I make out tonight's attractions. I make out Kansas. I make out Chicago.

Fifty years ago, at this palace of dreams, my brother, Ben, a dancing fool, danced into a dancing lady who became his wife. He was Vernon Castle to her Irene. All the bulbs on the marquee were working then: Wayne King, The Waltz King. Or was it Isham Jones? Oh, the Aragon . . . In a little Spanish town 'twas on a night like this.

"Whatever happened to Bob Dylan?" I've always believed you'll never know unless you ask.

"Bob who?" inquires a Jodie Foster look-alike. She has a heart-shaped face and a maroon headband. She stares intently at my red muffler.

"Dylan. Bob Dylan." Realizing there may be a problem in communication, I raise my voice. Hopefully, some pimply blade to the front of the bus will know. No soap. Perhaps nobody heard; there is a mass disembarkation. Already, outside the Aragon are straggled lines of blades, their ad hoc roommates, and a few bloods and foxes. Patiently waiting. Your huddled masses yearning to breathe free.

"Never heard of 'im," says Jodie, friendly enough. "Sorry." She and her companions brush past a slouched and astonished Bruant.

"Kansas City's a *city*," nephew calls out from the center doorstep. Do I detect a touch of hurt in his voice? "Kansas." He points toward the marquee. Exeunt.

There is nothing to be sorry about, I want to tell her. God knows, it's not her fault. She is the ultimate consumer. Yesterday's goods were good yesterday. This is today. Yesterday is Olden Tymes. Yesterday's Tet offensive is as prehistoric as the Battle of Marathon. And yesterday's adenoidal idol of her young aunt is today's Bob Who. Which is as it should be for the ultimate consumer.

There is no more need for her to be sorry than for the students at Wabash College. In Crawfordsville, Indiana, where the main street bears the name of its most celebrated son, General Lew Wallace, who gave us *Ben Hur*, I appear as a one-night lecturer. It is an assemblage of young men. (It has not turned coeducational.) Clean-cut, sweet-faced, attentive, courteous.

They laugh at all my jokes. They roundly applaud all my sallies at entrenched corporate power. They are especially responsive as I lace into public servants who behave as private servants. They cheer as I have a high old time with the tent-house Toby in the White House. I feel great.

At the reception that follows, some of the faculty members feel great, too. "These are very conservative kids from very conservative families. You really got to them." The euphoric moment is just that, a moment. As the boys come by, offering congratulations along with a fresh can of Miller's Light, they let me know that Ronnie is their man. And their dads' and their moms'.

"Why did you applaud me so hard when I rapped him?" I thought I had cited chapter and verse.

"You're a terrific entertainer. You're fun."

I've had more than enough of Miller's. I definitely need something stronger.

For the record, two or three boys linger.

"How come we never heard this stuff before?"

"Didn't your folks ever tell you about the thirties? The Depression?"

"Only that things were tough."

"What about your history books?"

"Only that things were tough."

"World War Two?"

"Oh, sure. We beat the Germans. The Japanese, too. Right?"

"We?"

"The United States."

In any event, history is about yesterday. Today is what it's all about.

A woman, elderly yet with the air of a sad young girl, delicately boned, genteel, comes over. She softly kisses me on the cheek. "It has been so long since I've heard this sort of talk." She's a townswoman. Her family were among Crawfordsville's early settlers. She was a Vassar girl long, long, long ago. "It's so lonely these days."

It's so lonely these days. That's what Jessie Binford said some years before. Jane Addams' old friend and colleague. She had returned to Marshalltown, Iowa, at the age of ninety. Her father had been one of the town's founders. "Take a town like this. Nobody seems to care about the things we feel are wrong. They're putting lots of money into schools, especially gymnasiums.

"The commonest thing I hear in a town like this is fear of the unknown. They've got just that one word. Communism. They don't even know what it means. Fear, fear, fear. They know something's wrong, but they're scared to death. I think they'd even accept the Bomb. They say: There's nothing we can do about it, so why worry? I ask too many questions.

"We began pretty well here in America, didn't we? When you think of all the promise in this country . . . I don't see how you could have found much greater promise. Or a greater beginning. Nothing stays the same, I know. We should have the intelligence and the courage to see the many changes that come into the world and will always come. But what are the intrinsic values we should not give up? That's the great challenge that faces us."

These days, most of my fellow passengers on the airliner are young men bearing attaché cases. And several young women bearing identical attaché cases. These are no-nonsense young people, undoubtedly Business Administration majors. They immediately, on being seated, flip out pocket calculators. Neat tablets of paper, yellow and white, lined and unlined, appear. They are unaware of others on the plane.

Among the others are flight attendants. One is holding forth a tray of food. The earnest young men working on his calculator pays no attention. The flight attendant is inordinately patient.

"Would you care for lunch?" she asks.

He doesn't look up. She tries it once more for size. A touch louder. He says nothing to her. He indicates with a slight movement of the head. She puts down the tray. He hasn't seen her at all.

They are known to flight attendants as "the baby executives." Of all the passengers served, I'm told, these new people are the most disturbing. "They're really scary," an attendant tells me. I'm scared, too. I see stone-cold Keir Dullea in the film *2001*. Or for that matter, HAL, the computer. And we're only in the early eighties.

Whatever happened to the Humanities majors? I don't see *them* on airliners. A few years ago, John Fielding, out of Texas, reflected on the day he was denied tenure at a state university. He had met all the requisites, but it was a buyers' market in the Humanities. The university had the pick of the Ivy League crop. Bye-bye, Professor Fielding.

"There are a whole lot of us over thirty: artists, failed historians, philosophers, mathematicians, overqualified and underemployed. Unemployed humanists. What's gonna happen ten years from now, when they start turning gray? What's gonna happen when bitterness sets in? They'll be unemployed, but will they be humanists?"

At the Atlanta airport, I walk from the gate toward the escalator. It takes me down to the train that will carry me and my fellow passengers toward one or another of four concourses. It is a smooth ride. There is silence, though the car is crowded. The silence is broken by a voice. It calls out the stops. The voice is flat, robotic. I know it was a baritone once. I *know* it was a man's voice. Yet it is *deliberately* something else. It is not a robot imitating a human. It is a human imitating a robot.

Sharing my side seat is a weary Hispanic mother. Her baby, all swaddled, is plopped between us. At one of the stops, a couple hurries on, squeezing through as the doors are closing. The voice lets us know that the train was delayed by the wayward two. It is not a scolding tone. It is dynamically identical to its other sounds. Nobody laughs. I am astonished.

I address the baby beside me: "What is your opinion of all this? Are the zombies taking over? Do you think our species will become extinct?" (I subscribe to Moms Mabley's theory. She had recounted her advice to John Foster Dulles. "Dulles ast me, 'How do you hip a chile, Moms?' I said, 'Dulles, you cain't hip a chile. A baby ain't got no mind but he's got a brain. He's already hip.'") My voice carries. The acoustics of the car are great. There is no response from any of the others. Not even a passing glance at a loud, nutty old clown. The baby looks up at me and grins the biggest grin since FDR. Moms was right. There is hope after all.

Three Illinois Center, Chicago.

The radio station from which I have been broadcasting, Mondays through Fridays, for the past thirty curious years, recently moved into this building.

Each day, I walk from the bus, cross Michigan Boulevard, and enter the funhouse. Immediately, I shuffle, skulk, limp (simulated), galumph (you don't stroll) through subterranean caverns of hair stylists, video game parlors, fast-food emporiums, adult-food shops (X-rated?) and places with charming French names. I whistle "East St. Louis Toodle-oo" or "Für Elise" or "Sweet Adeline." At times I howl "Amazing Grace." I even mumble in tongues. Anything to make the dark journey go faster.

Sometimes, in the manner of an old-time train caller, I holler "Zombie Canyon!" The echo carries. The acoustics are great here, too. Naturally, I expect a startled or, at least, an irritated response. Nothing. One time, I was John McCormack singing out "Let us wander, oh my darlin', down Lobotomy Lane" to the tune of "Mother Machree." Nothing. Another time I did Conrad Veidt as Cesare, the somnambulist, in *The Cabinet of Doctor Caligari*. I held forth my hand, brushing it softly against the wall, and slowly, slowly, stalked *misterioso*. Nothing.

One day, I may wear Marcel Marceau whiteface. The hallmark of the classic clown. I doubt whether it will have any effect, but I am determined, heigh-ho, the wind and the rain, to play out the Fool until—until what? Armageddon?

Having thunk the unthinkable, I have spoken the unspeakable. So has the late George Kistiakowsky, Oppenheimer's Los Alamos colleague. I heard him shortly before he died, addressing a gathering of young scientists. He was in his eighties and had terminal cancer. "I may be the only one in this room who will die in bed."

The White House Toby, on a number of occasions, has spoken the unspeakable, too. Unlike Kisty, fools like myself, and millions of other nervous Nellies, this one shows no fear. On more frequent occasions, he grins winningly. Alfred E. Neumann has nothing on him. And he doesn't even wear whiteface. Attention, though, is solemnly paid him by solemn commentators and solemn columnists and absorbed by solemn millions. "The President announced today . . . "

When the late mayor of Chicago died, a figure of unprecedented clout, proper obeisance was paid. His legacy was a city more segregated than any other, aside from Johannesburg. It is conceivable that Richard J. Daley might have been a different mayor—and ours a different city—had sycophancy among so many of our Respectables not become the order of the day. It is upon this we should reflect rather than on the nature of the man who died.

I know not what course others may take, but as for me, give me Catatonia or give me Charlie Chaplin. At the moment, a great many of us live in our fifty-first state, Catatonia. It is far more populous than California, New York, Pennsylvania, Ohio, Illinois, and Michigan put together. Include Texas, of course. Since I choose to live outside that state, I wear the Fool's motley. It makes things easier.

Fortunately, the neighborhood where I live suits me fine. It has halfway houses, nursing homes, and all of the United Nations' anonymous representatives; as well as Appalachians, Ozarkians, and Native Americans. And bag ladies, of course. Unfortunately, poverty is its lot; though there is spirit enough here for fifty neighborhoods. At times, the dispiritedness of dreadful circumstance overwhelms. It appears to crush. Yet there is a throb of life here, hardly found elsewhere. It is called Uptown.

A few months ago, I had trouble with the corner newspaper vending machine. I had dropped my quarter in for the morning Chicago *Sun-Times*. (This was before its takeover by the Australian troglodyte, Rupert Murdoch, and the departure of my favorite columnist, Mike Royko. I have since switched to the *Tribune*, a matter that would hardly lay the ghost of Colonel McCormick.)

It was the fifth quarter within a month I had lost to this mechanized predator. I kicked it. Hard. Again and again, I rammed my foot against it. I shook it as a maddened father shakes a recalcitrant child. I cursed it aloud. I was inventing a wholly new vocabulary of expletives. I was W. C. Fields in lethal combat with the picket fence. I was losing the battle. I was about to surrender. Furious. Impotent. That's when she came along.

I had seen this bag lady several times before. She was hard to miss. Ageless, she tipped the scales at hardly more than a hundred pounds. She usually bore two huge paper bags that probably outweighed her. She wore two coats, whether it was ten below or ninety above. She belonged.

As I gave the damnable monster one last whack, bruising my hand badly (I still bear a nasty scar), she joined me. She took over. She banged it with her elbow, with her shoulder, with her knee, with the exhilarating fury of her whole being. Once, twice, three times. It was three, the magic number. There was a rattling as from a dying dragon. The quarters flew out, overflowing the slot. A Las Vegas jackpot. I plucked out five quarters. She scooped up the rest. She went her way. I went mine. Not a word was exchanged between us. Not even a glance. Yet we were kindred spirits. My kind of town, Uptown is.

Our Fifth Avenue, our Champs-Elysées, our Nevsky Prospekt is Argyle Street. Sunday-Morning-Coming-Down Boulevard. Walk the strip between Sheridan and Kenmore, especially on Sunday, and you'll get the idea. A mother lode for Diane Arbus, were Diane Arbus still around catching our strangeness. It is our street, not "theirs." It may be a Luna Park or Riverview funny-house mirror, but it's *our* mirror. If you have any doubt, ask the Fool.

See. See how that raggedy kid, a small, delighted Latino, call him Tico, see how he runs, darts, leaps with such agility between the U-Haul and the '67 Chevy. Hear. Hear the Paducah beauty, twenty-three going on fifty, calling out to nobody in particular. Observe. Observe the inscrutable Oriental (why is he so wistful?) peering through the window of his Ma-and-Pa grocery while Mama-san busies herself at the counter. The American Dream. Seoul was never like this. Listen. Listen to the two black dandies say something funny to the lean brown girl embracing the lamppost. She can't stop laughing. *Funneee!*

Look. Look at these three others making it down the street the hard way. The girl (can she be more than eighteen?), Himalayan, bearing mountains of flesh, waddles on. Her face, lifted upright by mounds of chins, is a baby doll's, a *Playboy* Playmate's. She is laughing, too. Indeed, she is radiant. The companion, strutting at her left, a chocolate cadaver, Wilt the Stilt in height, is gesticulating excitedly. Dig. Dig, he's making a joke. The third of these merry-makers is twisting, twitching, and Morris-dancing along, though laboriously. He is palsied, cerebrally so. The hollow sounds erupting tell us that he is enjoying the joke, too. Immensely. Oh, I love you, Junie Moon, thinks the Fool.

Stumbling out of Foremost Liquors, a fifth of J & B in a brown paper bag, the Fool shuffles into *the* tavern. There are other such oases in these parts, any number of such places for people to get in out of the rain, especially when there is no rain at all. But this one has something going for it. Something *spess-ial,* the Welsh would say. Something edgy. Call it *je ne sais quoi.* The Fool has multiple choices, but he knows—don't ask him how he knows—that this is his dear-hearts-and-gentle-people place. *Entrez-vous.*

Take This Job and Shove It. Loud and clear out of the jukebox. It's Johnny Paycheck's way of saying hello. Again and again and again. The barmaid is Ollie, hard-pretty; a miracle out of Scriptures had she been soft-pretty after so many hard days' nights. Bad teeth. She's been shoving quarters into the machine, quarters left as a tip after each drink by the sloshed Fool. Paycheck's her boy, again and again and again. Does the Fool sense that it's her way of saying shove it?

The Fool, who lives in a house on a tree-lined street—close by, yet five planets away—is on his fourth boilermaker. It does seem silly, what with a good enough fifth of J & B in a brown paper bag at his elbow. His neighbor, slouched low on the adjacent stool, a weary black, age indeterminate, has a brown paper bag at his elbow, too. A quart of muscatel. You pays your money and takes your choice.

"She likes that song," the Fool, who catches on quick, mumbles at his musky friend. The other shakes his head, looks at the wine while it's red, and chuckles softly as though it's a private joke between himself and his brown paper bag. He's the only black in the place. The others are Kentucky, Tennessee, West Virginia people. Bad teeth. They're busy with one another talking Appalachian talk. A randy joke or two. A job lost, another found and lost. Tomorrow, Monday Morning Coming Up, a day at the day-labor exchange. A woman who has run off, a man wearing horns. Harsh laughter. Then soft: home. Home, that's what they're talking about most. Where they were, not where they are. They don't know where the hell they're at. Neither does the Fool, who is entering a mellow twilight zone. His neighbor may know, but he ain't talking; that's between himself and his brown paper bag.

Ollie has other fish to fry. At the street end of the bar, she nudges a seated skeleton. Something is passed about Kentucky. There is a short laugh. What the Fool hears isn't that funny, but what the hell, he joins in, too.

Ollie freshens his beer.

"Kentucky, eh?" He squints at her. He can do little else; his eyelids weigh heavily.

" 'At's me all over," she says.

"Ever been to Whitesburg?"

The Fool had been there a few months before, looking in at Tom Gish. Tom runs the *Mountain Eagle,* a local newspaper. He had returned to his hometown, realizing the journalist's dream of being a small-town editor. Among his own people. They kicked the bejeepers out of him, his own people did. Tom had written something about strip mining laying waste the land. Tom is still bleeding. Whitesburg.

"Sure I been to Whitesburg," says Ollie. "My brother's a jailer. 'At's how I kept *outa* jail."

The Fool laughs appreciatively. He shoves two more quarters at her.

"Put 'em in the box," she says. He stumbles off the stool and does as requested. Anything to win Ollie's approval. After all, her brother's a keeper.

He points at his shot glass. Ollie pours something into it. He tugs at his trousers pocket, hears the sound of ripping cloth, and comes up with three badly wrinkled bills. He slaps them on the counter.

"May I buy you one?" he says to his neighbor.

The musky man looks at the Fool, smiles, nods. "Gotcha covered."

Ollie pours out some red wine.

"How about you? Would you care for one?"

"Why not?" says Ollie, as she goes for the white.

"Miners are havin' a rough time," he says out of the blue. It's not really out of the blue, the strike's been going on for some time and the TV is full of it, telling the story in a half-assed way.

"They never had it so good," says Ollie.

The Fool shuts his eyes tight. His head is throbbing, intimations of a hangover bearing down. It is slowly dawning on him that Ollie's a fink. He's a Wells-Grand romantic, dreaming of Aunt Molly Jackson, a refrain of "Which Side Are You On?" fiddling around in his head and somehow can't see the hard-working Cumberland barmaid as the mine operators' darling. Yet Ollie is indubitably a fink. And down at the other end of the bar, are they all finks, too? The whole world looks finky when you're out of love. His neighbor stares into his muscatel. He shoulda stood in bed, the Fool.

"ERA women is pigs!" It is a loud *pronunciamento* from the shadowy end of the bar. He had been aware of vague mumblings in that precinct, but hadn't noticed the patrons there. A couple of couples had been occupying space and, after a fashion, spooning. "A man, if he's half a man, wears the pants in the family an' any woman who thinks different's a pig an' oughta be horsewhipped."

The Fool shields his eyes as he searches out the voice, a no-fooling-around contralto. She is an extra-large blonde, bearing a striking resemblance to Miss Piggy. Her consort is a sad, silent horse.

"Why do you say that?" The Fool, indubitably a fool, doesn't really know when to quit. His voice is low, mellow, as though hawking Gallo wines on TV. He has assumed his sincere, persuasive tone.

" 'Cause 'at's what they are—pigs—an' oughta be horsewhipped."

"Why do you say that?" He is Mastroianni now, the smiling, silly Marcello of *La Dolce Vita*'s last reel.

" 'Cause they're pigs an' oughta be horsewhipped."

This is getting nowhere. He slides off the stool and moves toward the shadows.

"*You're* a woman," he says.

"*All* woman." It's more of a challenge than a declaration.

"Well, then," says the Fool, smashed out of his skull, "don't you like yourself?"

"Hey." The other woman, larger than our Phyllis Schlafly and even more blond, disengages herself from a bespectacled daddy, whose eyes are out of focus. "That's my stepdaughter. Watch your language."

"Oh," he says, sinking deeper into the slough, "we're merely having a discussion."

He fumbles out another quarter, finds his way to the jukebox, and presses down on B-7. Twice. He needs Johnny Paycheck. Back at the old stand, he finds Ollie waiting for him. She is not smiling.

"Sir."

"Yes, ma'am."

"This is a family bar."

"Oh, I know."

"We can't have that."

"We were just having a friendly discussion."

"Sir, this is a family bar."

"May I have another beer, please."

Ollie flips open a Meister Brau and carefully pours it into his glass.

When I wipe off my clown make-up, I have been inclined lately to look at the world through the glass darkly. I am finding the human comedy less and less comedic. Though I am unaccustomed to this bleak vision, it comes upon me with more frequency each passing year.

My friend James Cameron has been saying in recent months what I find difficult to put into words. They stick in my throat. Cameron, the nonpareil of British journalists, whose compassionate eye and understanding heart have made his dispatches from worlds far away and next door among the most eloquent and revealing of our epoch, writes:

> I am now quite reconciled to total pessimism about the destiny of the human race. I specifically and quite calmly give it a very few more years. The selfish aspect of this is that where not long ago I cared very bitterly about this, I no longer do. The only impulse that

drives me to the daily newspapers now is the simple and ignoble one of curiosity.

At the same time, I no longer argue the propriety of anyone's logic. All sides now have made so many errors so often that they are now wholly engaged in the occupation of trying to prove that at least one of their past misjudgments was sound. . . .

Most of us continue to survive, as we say, by the indulgence of our creditors and the generosity of our friends. I have had a multitude of both. May it continue—not necessarily long, but for a while. Hope subsides, but curiosity remains.

Yet Jessie De La Cruz, out of the fields of the American Southwest, who has lived lives rather than a life, says stubbornly: "With us, there is a saying: *La esperanza muere al último*. Hope dies last."

I find myself caught between the two. I am Beckett's two tramps waiting for Godot. Yet I am also the blind Pozzo, who on being asked, "Where to?" replies, "On."

Oh sure, there's Ollie and the acned wonders and the college boys and HALs in three-piece suits. There are also the young at Rocky Flats and a young Jessie Binford somewhere. And an old Vassar girl and an abruptly aware young flight attendant. And Aunt Molly's niece. And there's Joe Begley, the most obstinate of all. Joe, at the general store in the Kentucky ghost town, says his piece. "You don't give up, because a handful of people can win in this country. A handful of people in the beginnin' saved this country. They did the fightin' while three quarters of the people, by God, watched it. To the last goddam flicker of my life, I'm gonna be challengin' all the way."

And there's Bonnie.

The Fool, so occupied with Ollie at the "family bar," paid scant notice to the gaunt, big-boned woman, nursing a beer. She had bad teeth, too. And a baby in her lap, who occasionally had a nip of the malt. And a cigarette between her fingers. She had been for several minutes watching the trembly old man at the wall telephone. He was having a Godawful time trying to make connections with a daughter in West Virginia.

Bonnie was obviously a regular. Stein of beer in one hand, baby against her shoulder, cigarette dangling from lower lip, she eased her way laboriously off the stool, toward the old man.

The Fool had paused on his way out, near the two. From their talk in rich Appalachian dialect, he sensed they were strangers to one another. She took the receiver from the old man's hand and performed the most remarkable balancing act the Fool had ever seen. It was even greater than one he saw years ago at the Palace: the Levantine Wonders.

Bonnie, with some of the old man's coins in her right hand, beer in her left, receiver squeezed against that shoulder, burping the baby contentedly set at the other shoulder, was carefully enunciating into the mouthpiece. The West Virginia phone number came over slow, loud, and clear. Phenomenal.

As she deposited the last of the old man's coins, there was a pause. What? It took another quarter. The old man held out his hands helplessly. She glanced toward the bar. She had a few coins there. "Just a minute, operator. Hold your horses." At that moment, the Fool, fumbling in his pockets, God, came up with a quarter he didn't know he had. He held it out toward her. Bonnie took it, dropped it in the box. A glance at the Fool, eyes blinking once. A pause. Bonnie's mouth almost devouring the mouthpiece: "Is this Erymadean Hitchcock?" A pause. "Just a minute." The old man took over. Bonnie eased her way back to the stool, all her baggage intact. The Fool made for the door.

How come he had hardly noticed Bonnie, while all the time occupying himself with Ollie? It wasn't a question of the generous-hearted *or* the mean-spirited. There's more than enough of both to go around. Perhaps he should have paid more attention to something Dorothy Day said some time ago: "I'm looking toward a world in which it would be easier for people to behave well."

The Fool gets a grip on his brown paper bag and slowly, carefully, as though walking a tightrope, moves toward the door.

On the Magnificent Mile, on Argyle, somewhere between Kenmore and Sheridan, invigorated by the Sunday air, he finds himself galumphing alongside Junie Moon and her two companions. Junie, all four hundred pounds of her girlishness, is laughing, still laughing. Wilt the Stilt is gesticulating excitedly. Their buddy, twisting, twitching, and Morris-dancing along, is letting go with a hollow noise, clearly enjoying the joke. The Fool, his brown paper bag clasped to his pouch like a kangaroo's baby, is smiling. Now they are four.

Fools of the world, unite. You have nothing to lose.

The Ultimate Fantasy: My First Inaugural Address

On November 4, 1984, running as an Independent candidate, I was overwhelmingly elected Forty-first President of The United States. The world, as well as this country, was astonished and exhilarated.

My friends, I am calling upon your intelligence. Never in any epoch of human history has our intelligence been a more necessary weapon in our arsenal for survival than it is today. Never has it been so assaulted as during our past Administration. For that matter, it has been seldom called upon by any Administration since the end of World War Two.

I shall not at any time during this brief talk use the words Family, Flag, God, or Country. Nor shall I use the phrase Standing Tall. I am your President, not your Phys Ed instructor. I assume, without self-righteously proclaiming it, that you believe in the faith and in those ideas that evoke the spirit of free thoughtful beings in a free, thoughtful society.

In my travels across the land, I have run into thousands of you, in all manner of circumstance. In those casual and sometimes astonishing encounters, I have discovered something I had already known in my gut: each of you is endowed with a native intelligence, not yet fully tapped. On the contrary, conditioned as you have been by Official Banality—and, all too often, Official Venality—your intelligence, your naturally endowed intelligence, has been unnaturally shoved into cold storage.

Thus we find ourselves in a humiliating bind, unworthy of us. Though we regard ourselves as free, we are in thralldom. We are in a strange kind of bondage. I am, therefore, as my first act in office, issuing a second Emancipation Proclamation.

As a President, some hundred and twenty years ago, said: *We must disenthrall ourselves from the tired dogmas of the past*. A past that in our case came into being at the end of World War Two. We must disenthrall ourselves from the Russian Syndrome.

Archibald MacLeish pointed this out in 1949 in a singularly prescient essay:

> Never in the history of the world was one people as completely dominated, intellectually and morally, by another as the people of the United States by the people of Russia from 1946 to 1949. American foreign policy was the mirror image of Russian foreign policy: whatever the Russians did, we did in reverse. American domestic politics were conducted under a kind of Russian upside-down veto: no man could be elected to public office unless he was on record as detesting the Russians, and no proposal could be enacted, from a peace plan at one end to a military budget at the other, unless it could be demonstrated that the Russians did not like it. American political controversy was controversy sung to the Russian tune.

What Archibald MacLeish said then is emphatically true now.

What about the Russians? That is precisely why I have called upon George Kennan to become our Secretary of State. He probably knows more about the Russians than any living American. He knows of their shadowy side, of their fears, their depredations, yes, their paranoia, as well as of their sufferings and hopes. Just as they are our mirror image, we are theirs. Mr. Kennan understands this and warns us that in dehumanizing them, we are dehumanizing ourselves.

In George Kennan, the Secretary of State will reflect a touch of class, instead of the vulgarism that has so long been the embarrassing hallmark of that office. We, as an intelligent society, deserve no less.

It is time we heard our best voices. If we are to survive, if this planet is to make it through the night, we have no other choice.

George Kistiakosky, who had worked with J. Robert Oppenheimer in Los Alamos, and who, too, was an adviser to President Eisenhower, addressed an assemblage of young scientists in Chicago shortly before he died. He was in his eighties and had terminal cancer. Listen carefully to what he said: "I may be the only one in this room who will die in bed."

Albert Einstein, whose genius was ultimately responsible for the atom bomb—talk about irony—warned all the peoples of the world—yes, that includes us—of "the unprecedented disaster which they are absolutely certain to bring on themselves unless there is a fundamental change in their attitudes toward one another. The unleashed atom has changed everything except our way of thinking, and thus we drift toward unparalleled catastrophe."

We have made a quantum leap scientifically: unless we make a quantum leap socially and politically, we have had it as a species. Remember, the dinosaurs were powerful, but because they could not adjust to the changing nature of the earth, they disappeared. We are powerful, and unless we adjust to the changing nature of our earth, we, too, shall disappear. Since we humans are alleged to be the highest form of animal life because of our intelligence, I am calling on precisely that attribute: your intelligence and mine. And, of course, of the Russians as well.

The twentieth-century scientist was updating the reflections of the nineteenth-century President: *We must disenthrall ourselves. . . .* In short, we must think anew.

It is the most daring challenge we have ever faced.

Thomas J. Watson, chairman emeritus of IBM, adds his voice. "This is a critical moment for American democracy. Americans in great number are listening to their own common sense. They are beginning to see through the smoke screens created by the misuse of technical expertise. . . . They are on the verge of recapturing their destiny from exploitive manipulation. They had better hurry."

That is why our new Secretary of State has proposed an immediate across-the-board fifty percent reduction in the nuclear arsenals of both superpowers at once, *without further wrangling among the experts.* The fifty percent left on each side would still be far more than enough to devastate the adversary. The extras are a tribute to lunacy, let alone an outrageous waste of your tax money.

The scientist, the industrialist, and the statesman, all three appeal to our life-wish rather than to our death-wish. I do, too.

We are all painfully aware of the alarming rate of suicide among our young people these days. I submit it has to do with their fear of nuclear holocaust. Though they seldom talk about it, a profound fatalism possesses them. It is so overwhelming, you can taste it. A young girl I met recently told me quite casually: "I worry about my little niece. She's only three and so lively and beautiful. I'd like to see her live out her life. I don't worry about myself so much. After all, I've lived seventeen years."

It is understandable. The young—and that goes for the rest of us, too—have only a dim sense of the present, let alone of the future. It is because we have no sense of the past. We have lost our sense of history.

We know that George Washington was the Father of Our Country. But do we know what he said in his Farewell Address of 1796? "The nation which indulges toward another an habitual hatred is in some degree a slave. It is a slave to its animosity, which is sufficient to lead it astray from its duty and interest."

Another President's reflection of a more recent past is also too little remembered. President Dwight D. Eisenhower said in 1959: "Every gun that is made, every warship launched, every rocket fired, signifies in the final sense a theft from those who are hungry and are not fed, those who are cold and are not clothed. This world in arms is not spending money alone. It is spending the sweat of its laborers, the genius of its scientists, the hopes of its children."

The Pentagon has planned to build 226 MX missiles at a cost of 110 million dollars each. Somewhat more than 20 trillion dollars. For each missile that is canceled, poverty in 101,000 female-headed households could be eliminated for a year. If the whole program were canceled, poverty could be eliminated for all the children in the United States twice over. If Congress, taking leave of its senses, were to pass this measure, I shall, of course, veto it *in toto*. I'd rather feed a hungry child than overstuff a Pentagon welfare bum any day.

With the specter of unemployment haunting our land more than at any time since the Great Depression, we must find jobs for the jobless. The greater the Pentagon budget, the *fewer* jobs there are. Things are not what they were in the forties, when the war helped end the Depression. Pentagon money today goes primarily into highly sophisticated weaponry and highly skilled workers, relatively few in number. For each billion dollars spent on the military, ten thousand *fewer* jobs are created than were that same billion spent on non-military needs. Once used, the weapon goes bang. It is kaput. Useless. A school lasts. A hospital lasts. A child-care center lasts. A library lasts. A park lasts. There we have it. More people at work on something life-giving than on something death-dealing. As intelligent people, can there be any question which we prefer?

What about the Russians?

Senator Fulbright recalls a conversation between President Eisenhower and Nikita Khrushchev in 1959. Each spoke of the tough time he was having with the hardliners in his country. I have a strong suspicion that the hardliners of both societies have a great need for one another. After all, where would one be without the other? Parkinson's Law may be at work here. Counterfeit jobs.

A journalist friend of mine remembers a cocktail party in Vienna. A CIA man recognized a KGB man. They greeted one another as old acquaintances. Of course. Their style may differ, but in substance, one is the mirror image of the other. The cloth of ours is of a neater cut and theirs more slovenly, but they sing the same song: "Embraceable You."

Our goal—and, I assume, that of thoughtful Russians, if they mirror us as they appear to do in every other respect—is to put these bozos out of work. Let them find honest jobs.

As Eisenhower said: "I think the people want peace so much that one of these days governments had better get out of their way and let them have it."

May I add a personal note here? Mine will not be an Imperial Presidency. I see no need for you to rise as a matter of ritual whenever I enter a room. I am your servant; you are not mine. For journalists to do so, en masse, as we've so often seen on TV, is not especially reflective of a free, thoughtful, democratic society.

I should like to see the spirit of the town meeting born again. Whether it be in the neighborhood of a large city, in a small-town church, in a schoolhouse, in a living room, in a tavern, for that matter, I urge you to meet with your fellow citizens and openly discuss, argue, debate any matter you feel is meaningful, whether it be local, national, or international. Once you do that, your juices will start to flow. You will feel that you really count. This Administration will remain open to all ideas, not merely those of the experts. Their batting average hasn't been *that* good. I have faith in your intelligence and awareness. I have faith in the genius of the American people, once they disenthrall themselves from preconceived notions.

I feel confident in this faith, having met so many of you. I remember a woman who came to Chicago from the Appalachians of Kentucky. Peggy Terry had barely gone through fifth grade in school. Yet she became the eloquent voice of her community. "I think of all the races of people," she said, "and I want to be friends with them. I wish they'd hurry up with Esperanto so I could learn it and we could talk with each other. The reason I have so much hope, I know darn well if I could start out being the ignoramus I was, not knowing anything, anybody can do the same thing. It's no big secret. It's just something that has to touch you and suddenly you realize what a big world there is. And what a small one it is. You just want to know about everything. I believe everybody is capable of the same thing." I believe it, too.

The road ahead is tough, but it will not be nearly as tough if we call upon our intelligence as this woman has.

Nancy Jefferson, a black woman of my acquaintance, remembers life on a small Tennessee farm. "Down in the country, we used to have to ring the bell if there was trouble or we'd ring it for dinner. You used to pull this rope. Sometimes if it was especially cold, you'd keep pullin' and keep pullin' the bell. You'd think you'd never hear a sound. Maybe by the time your hands got raw almost, you'd hear a little tinklin' of the bell. That's the way I visualize the community. We all keep pullin' at the rope and our hands are gettin' raw, but you do hear a little tinklin'. We gotta do it. We must do it. We have no choice. We gotta keep pullin' and I believe the bell will ring." I believe it, too.

Peggy Terry, Nancy Jefferson, and Albert Einstein shared the same vision. There is, of course, a caveat. We must, as the old school teacher used to say, put on our thinking caps. We must always challenge the doctrine of the announced idea. Especially if it no longer works.

Four hundred years ago, Galileo challenged the doctrine of the announced idea. On seeing the heavens through his telescope, he discovered that Copernicus was right. The earth was not the center of the universe, but merely one part of a greater whole. A respected part, but no more than a part.

And what is the discovery of our age? It is the discovery that no one race, no one people, no one land—no matter how glorious its beginning, no matter how affluent its society—is the center of the earth. Rather, all races, all lands, all societies are individual centers, all respected parts of a greater whole—the Earth. Just as the Earth is part of this one same universe with millions of other planets, so are we but one part of this Earth with billions of other humans. The arrogance of power is as obsolete as the Neanderthal. It is only humanity that is contemporary.

Yet, we of this favored land do have a power: a power to point the way toward the vision of Albert Einstein. Not the one he feared, but the one he hoped for. If we do so, we shall win the profound admiration and affection of the world. A world made safe and sane.

I look to you and your concerted intelligence for guidance. We can, as Martin Luther King expressed it, live together as men or die together as fools. The choice is ours. I have faith we will choose wisely and that we, and the others on this planet, will prevail.

Born in 1912, Studs Terkel grew up in Chicago, and graduated from the University of Chicago in 1932 and from the Chicago Law School in 1934. He has acted in radio soap operas, has been a disk jockey, a sports commentator, a TV m.c., and has traveled all over the world doing on-the-spot interviews. Currently, he has a daily radio program on WFMT Chicago which is carried on other stations throughout the country.

His previous books, *Division Street: America*, *Hard Times*, *Working*, and *American Dreams: Lost and Found*, have received international acclaim and were all best sellers in the United States. His most recent book is *"The Good War": An Oral History of World War Two*.